The Cambridge Companion to

BENJAMIN BRITTEN

EDITED BY
Mervyn Cooke
Lecturer in Music, University of Nottingham

CAMBRIDGE
UNIVERSITY PRESS

PUBLISHED BY THE PRESS SYNDICATE OF THE UNIVERSITY OF CAMBRIDGE
The Pitt Building, Trumpington Street, Cambridge CB2 1RP, United Kingdom

CAMBRIDGE UNIVERSITY PRESS
The Edinburgh Building, Cambridge CB2 2RU, United Kingdom http://www.cup.cam.ac.uk
40 West 20th Street, New York, NY 10011–4211, USA http://www.cup.org
10 Stamford Road, Oakleigh, Melbourne 3166, Australia

First published 1999

. Printed in the United Kingdom at the University Press, Cambridge

Typeset in Adobe Minion 10.75/14 pt, in QuarkXpress™ [SE]

A catalogue record for this book is available from the British Library

Library of Congress cataloguing in publication data
The Cambridge companion to Benjamin Britten / edited by Mervyn Cooke.
   p.   cm. – (Cambridge companions to music)
Includes bibliographical references and index.
ISBN 0 521 57384 X (hardback) ISBN 0 521 57476 5 (paperback)
1. Britten, Benjamin.   I. Cooke, Mervyn, Dr. II. Series.
ML650.C3   1998

786.2–dc21   97–41860   CIP   MN

ISBN 0 521 57384 X hardback
ISBN 0 521 57476 5 paperback

08169   27ᵗʰ Oct
2017

1 0 AUG 1999

1 2 DEC 2017

0 6 FEB 2001

1 2 MAR 2001

0 4 JAN 2002

- 6 APR 2002

2 5 MAR 2006

2 5 SEP 2006

WITHDRAWN

789 BRIT   MERVYN COOKE (ED)
THE CAMBRIDGE COMPANION TO BENJAMIN
BRITTEN

Cambridge Companions to Music

The Cambridge Companion to Bach
Edited by John Butt
0 521 45350 X (hardback)
0 521 58780 8 (paperback)

The Cambridge Companion to Berg
Edited by Anthony Pople
0 521 56374 7 (hardback)
0 521 56489 1 (paperback)

The Cambridge Companion to Brahms
Edited by Michael Musgrave
0 521 48129 5 (hardback)
0 521 48581 9 (paperback)

The Cambridge Companion to Chopin
Edited by Jim Samson
0 521 47752 2 (paperback)

The Cambridge Companion to Handel
Edited by Donald Burrows
0 521 45425 5 (hardback)
0 521 45613 4 (paperback)

The Cambridge Companion to Schubert
Edited by Christopher Gibbs
0 521 48229 1 (hardback)
0 521 48424 3 (paperback)

The Cambridge Companion to Brass Instruments
Edited by Trevor Herbert and John Wallace
0 521 56243 7 (hardback)
0 521 56522 7 (paperback)

The Cambridge Companion to the Cello
Edited by Robin Stowell
0 521 62101 1 (hardback)
0 521 62928 4 (paperback)

The Cambridge Companion to the Clarinet
Edited by Colin Lawson
0 521 47066 8 (hardback)
0 521 47668 2 (paperback)

The Cambridge Companion to the Organ
Edited by Nicholas Thistlethwaite and Geoffrey Webber
0 521 57309 2 (hardback)
0 521 57584 2 (paperback)

The Cambridge Companion to the Piano
Edited by David Rowland
0 521 47470 1 (hardback)
0 521 47986 X (paperback)

The Cambridge Companion to the Recorder
Edited by John Mansfield Thomson
0 521 35269 X (hardback)
0 521 35816 7 (paperback)

The Cambridge Companion to the Saxophone
Edited by Richard Ingham
0 521 59348 4 (hardback)
0 521 59666 1 (paperback)

The Cambridge Companion to the Violin
Edited by Robin Stowell
0 521 39923 8 (paperback)

Contents

Plates

Contributors

Stephen Arthur Allen is currently completing his D.Phil. thesis on 'Benjamin Britten and Christianity' at Somerville College, Oxford. He has given papers on Britten's music at Oxford and Aldeburgh, and as part of a session on music and religious belief at the 1997 international conference of the American Musicological Society. In 1996 he conducted the Sydney Symphony Orchestra at the Sydney Opera House in the première of *Wurrekker*, a work for piano and orchestra which he co-composed with Frederick Scott.

Arved Ashby is Assistant Professor of Musicology at the Ohio State University. He completed his Ph.D. at Yale University, and has since pursued interests ranging from Mahler to Robert Ashley, with particular emphasis on modernist aesthetics and the relationship between Schoenberg and Berg. He is currently preparing a study of the relations between concert music and film, writing a book on Berg's early twelve-tone aesthetic and editing a re-evaluation of modernist music.

Mervyn Cooke was Director of Music at Fitzwilliam College, Cambridge, before his appointment as Lecturer in Music at the University of Nottingham in 1993. His publications include studies of Britten's *Billy Budd* and *War Requiem* (Cambridge University Press, 1993 and 1996), a monograph on *Britten and the Far East* (The Boydell Press, 1998) and two volumes on jazz (Thames & Hudson, 1997 and 1998). He is co-editor (with Donald Mitchell and Philip Reed) of the forthcoming third volume of Britten's letters to be published by Faber & Faber. His compositions have been broadcast on BBC Radio 3 and Radio France and performed at London's South Bank, and he is also active as a pianist.

Clifford Hindley studied Classics and Philosophy at Oxford, and Theology at Cambridge. Starting with New Testament scholarship (on which he published several articles), in mid-career he moved to the Civil Service and maintained a strong interest in music as an amateur pianist and choral singer. Following retirement, he has made a study of same-sex relationships in Britten's operas, with articles appearing in *Music & Letters*, *Musical Quarterly*, *Cambridge Opera Journal* and *History Workshop Journal*; he has also published articles on Greek homosexuality.

Paul Kildea was educated at the Universities of Melbourne and Oxford, where he worked closely with Malcolm Gillies and Cyril Ehrlich. He has broadcast on BBC Radio 3 and contributed articles and reviews to various journals. He is currently editing Britten's collected writings for Oxford University Press, who are also due to publish his doctoral thesis on the social and economic history of Britten's music; future projects include a volume on *Owen Wingrave*. He has conducted performances of many Britten works, including the *War Requiem*, and in 1997 he made his Opera Australia début with Janáček's *The Cunning Little Vixen*.

Judith LeGrove read Music at Jesus College, Cambridge, where she wrote a dissertation on Britten's *The Burning Fiery Furnace*. She is currently Cataloguing Manager at the Britten–Pears Library, Aldeburgh, and contributes to the Aldeburgh Festival programme books, as well as assisting in the preparation of Britten's juvenilia for performance and publication.

Antonia Malloy-Chirgwin read Music at the University of Oxford and completed a Master's degree at the University of Surrey, where she researched the creation of the libretto to Britten's *Owen Wingrave*. Since then, she has worked extensively on *Gloriana*, with particular reference to the circumstances of the opera's genesis; her account of the work's critical reception was published in Paul Banks (ed.), *Britten's 'Gloriana': Essays and Sources* (The Boydell Press, 1993). Her other interests include music theatre and the history of orchestration.

Christopher Mark lectures at the University of Surrey. He graduated from the University of Southampton, where he subsequently pursued doctoral research into Britten's music under Peter Evans. A revised version of his thesis, *Early Benjamin Britten: A Study of Stylistic and Technical Evolution*, was published by Garland in 1995. He has also published articles on Tippett, Bartók and Roger Smalley, and is currently writing a book on Smalley for Harwood Academic Press's 'Contemporary Music Studies' series.

Donald Mitchell was Britten's publisher from 1965 onwards, and has long been internationally recognized as the leading authority on the work of both Britten and Mahler. His edition (with Philip Reed) of the first two volumes of Britten's letters won a Royal Philharmonic Society Award in 1992; his other studies of the composer include *Benjamin Britten: Pictures from a Life* (with John Evans; Faber & Faber, 1978), *Britten and Auden in the Thirties* (Faber & Faber, 1981) and the Cambridge Opera Handbook on *Death in Venice* (1987). Several groundbreaking articles on Britten have been reprinted as part of an anthology of his writings, *Cradles of the New* (Faber & Faber, 1995).

Philip Reed completed his doctoral dissertation on Britten's music for film, theatre and radio, and went on to become Staff Musicologist at the Britten–Pears Library; he is currently Head of Publications at English National Opera. He co-edited (with Donald Mitchell) the first two volumes of Britten's correspondence, and his many other publications include an edition of Peter Pears's travel diaries, the Festschrift *On Mahler and Britten* for Dr Mitchell's 70th birthday, and detailed source studies of *Billy Budd*, *Gloriana*, *Peter Grimes* and the *War Requiem*.

Eric Roseberry read Music at Durham University with Arthur Hutchings and A. E. F. Dickinson. He subsequently worked as a BBC producer with Hans Keller and later as a music lecturer at Sussex University with Donald Mitchell. He is now a freelance musician and writer specializing in the music of Britten and Shostakovich. His Ph.D. thesis on the latter was published in 1989, and his recent work includes an essay 'Shostakovich and his late-period recognition of Britten' in Cambridge University Press's *Shostakovich Studies* (1995), edited by David Fanning.

Philip Rupprecht is Assistant Professor of Music at Brooklyn College and the Graduate Center, City University of New York. He read music at Selwyn College, Cambridge, and went on to receive the Ph.D. in Music Theory at Yale University in 1993. Currently a Wolfe Fellow in the Humanities, he is writing an analytical study of Britten's works for Cambridge University Press's 'Music in the Twentieth Century' series.

Arnold Whittall is Professor Emeritus of Music Theory and Analysis at King's College, London. His many writings have given particular emphasis to opera from Wagner onwards, and to twentieth-century British music. His book *The Music of Britten and Tippett: Studies in Themes and Techniques* (Cambridge University Press) was first published in 1982, and his articles on Britten have dealt with such topics as the harmonic character of the *War Requiem*, the relationship between text, drama and music in *Billy Budd*, and the significance of certain genres (e.g. pastoral and hymnody) for the composer.

Ralph Woodward was Organ Scholar and Acting Sub-Organist at Durham Cathedral before winning an Organ Scholarship at Queens' College, Cambridge. He conducted the Queens' Chapel Choir's first two CDs, and his edition of Stanford's *Queens' Service* has been published by Stainer & Bell. He now combines freelance conducting and teaching with his duties as Assistant Organist at St Catharine's College, Cambridge; recent conducting engagements have taken him to the Battersea Opera Festival, Sunderland Empire Theatre and the Northumbrian Recorder and Viol School.

Acknowledgements

The editor and contributors extend grateful thanks to the staff at the Britten–Pears Library, Aldeburgh, for their customary helpfulness and efficiency throughout work on the project, and to Britten's publishers (Boosey & Hawkes, Faber Music and Oxford University Press) for their assistance on various matters, and for their kind permission to reproduce music examples from those of Britten's works in which they hold the copyright. Copyright © Faber Music Ltd, London and reproduced by kind permission of the publishers: music examples 1.6, 1.7, 8.6, 8.7, 8.8, 8.9, 8.10, 8.11, 8.12, 9.6, 13.3, 13.4, 13.5. Extract from *Wozzeck* (example 12.2b) copyright 1926 by Universal Edition A.G., Vienna; copyright renewed 1954 by Helene Berg; reproduced by permission of Alfred A. Kalmus Ltd. Reproduced by permission of Boosey and Hawkes: music examples 4.1, 4.2, 4.3, 5.1, 5.2, 5.3, 5.4, 5.6, 5.7, 5.8, 5.9, 5.10, 6.1b, 6.2b, 7.1, 7.4, 7.7, 7.8, 8.1, 8.2, 8.3, 8.4, 8.5, 9.2, 9.3, 9.4, 11.1, 11.2, 11.3, 11.4, 12.2a, 13.1, 13.2, 14.2, 14.3, 14.4, 14.5, 15.1, 15.3, 15.4, 16.1, 16.2, 16.3, 16.4.

All illustrations appear by courtesy of the Britten–Pears Library, where special thanks are due to Kieron Cooke and Jenny Doctor. All quotations from Britten's correspondence and diaries, and extracts from manuscript facsimiles, are © The Trustees of the Britten–Pears Foundation and appear by permission; these may not be further reproduced without the written permission of the Trustees. Quotations from the Diaries of Imogen Holst are © The Estate of Imogen Holst and are quoted by permission of the Holst Foundation; quotations from William Plomer's correspondence and libretto drafts appear by kind permission of Sir Rupert Hart-Davis. Chapter 7, which is a condensed version of an article first published in 1993 ('Britten and Shakespeare: Dramatic and Musical Cohesion in *A Midsummer Night's Dream*', *Music & Letters* 74/2, pp. 246–68), appears by permission of Oxford University Press.

The editor owes a special debt of gratitude to Vicki Cooper at Cambridge University Press for her constant enthusiasm, patience and accessibility in overseeing the book from inception to completion, and to Alan Finch, Kathryn Bailey and Caroline Murray. Thanks are also due to Andrew Comben and Cyril Ehrlich for their generous and insightful suggestions regarding Chapter 2, and to Eileen Bell (Britten Estate) and Jenny Doctor (Britten–Pears Library) for their skilful editorial assistance with Chapter 10, in connection with which Charles L. Mandelstam (the Britten Estate's attorney in New York) made a valiant attempt to break through the barrier of concealment.

Abbreviations

AW*BT* Arnold Whittall, *The Music of Britten and Tippett: Studies in Themes and Techniques* (Cambridge University Press, 1982; second edition 1990)

BB*AA* Benjamin Britten, *On Receiving the First Aspen Award* (London: Faber & Faber, 1964, reprinted Faber Music, 1978)

BB*PG* Paul Banks (ed.), *The Making of 'Peter Grimes'*, 1: *Facsimile of Benjamin Britten's Composition Draft*, 2: *Notes and Commentaries* (Woodbridge: The Boydell Press, 1996).

BSB John Evans, Philip Reed and Paul Wilson, *A Britten Source Book* (Aldeburgh: The Britten Estate, 1987).

CM*EB* Christopher Mark, *Early Benjamin Britten: A Study of Stylistic and Technical Evolution* (New York and London: Garland, 1995).

CP*BC* Christopher Palmer (ed.), *The Britten Companion* (London: Faber & Faber, 1984)

DH*OB* David Herbert (ed.), *The Operas of Benjamin Britten* (London: Hamish Hamilton, 1979; reprinted, The Herbert Press, 1989)

DM*BA* Donald Mitchell, *Britten and Auden in the Thirties: The Year 1936* (London: Faber & Faber, 1981)

DM*CN* Donald Mitchell, *Cradles of the New: Writings on Music 1951–1991*, selected by Christopher Palmer, edited by Mervyn Cooke (London: Faber & Faber, 1995)

DM*DV* Donald Mitchell (ed.), *Benjamin Britten: Death in Venice* (Cambridge University Press, 1987)

DMHK Donald Mitchell and Hans Keller (eds.), *Benjamin Britten: A Commentary on His Works From a Group of Specialists* (London: Rockliff, 1952)

DMJE Donald Mitchell and John Evans, *Pictures from a Life: Benjamin Britten 1913–1976* (London: Faber & Faber, 1978)

DMPR Donald Mitchell and Philip Reed (eds.), *Letters from a Life: The Selected Letters and Diaries of Benjamin Britten 1913–1976*, volume 1: 1923–39; volume 2: 1939–45 (London: Faber & Faber, 1991)

EWW*B* Eric Walter White, *Benjamin Britten: His Life and Operas* (London: Faber & Faber, 1970; second edition, revised by John Evans, 1983)

HC*BB* Humphrey Carpenter, *Benjamin Britten: A Biography* (London: Faber & Faber, 1992)

MC*BE* Mervyn Cooke, *Britten and the Far East*, Aldeburgh Studies in Music No. 4 (Woodbridge: The Boydell Press, 1998)

MCPR Mervyn Cooke and Philip Reed, *Benjamin Britten: Billy Budd* (Cambridge University Press, 1993)

MC*WR* Mervyn Cooke, *Benjamin Britten: War Requiem* (Cambridge University Press, 1996)

MKB   Michael Kennedy, *Britten*, Master Musicians (London: Dent, 1981; revised edition 1993)

MSBC Murray Schafer, *British Composers in Interview* (London: Faber & Faber, 1963)

PBBG Paul Banks (ed.), *Britten's 'Gloriana': Essays and Sources*, Aldeburgh Studies in Music No. 1 (Woodbridge: The Boydell Press, 1993)

PBPG Philip Brett (ed.), *Benjamin Britten: Peter Grimes* (Cambridge University Press, 1983)

PEMB Peter Evans, *The Music of Benjamin Britten* (London: Dent, 1979; second edition, Oxford University Press, 1990)

PHTS Patricia Howard (ed.), *Benjamin Britten: The Turn of the Screw* (Cambridge University Press, 1985)

PRMB Philip Reed (ed.), *On Mahler and Britten: Essays in Honour of Donald Mitchell on his 70th Birthday*, Aldeburgh Studies in Music No. 3 (Woodbridge: The Boydell Press, 1995)

PRPP Philip Reed (ed.), *The Travel Diaries of Peter Pears, 1936–1978*, Aldeburgh Studies in Music No. 2 (Woodbridge: The Boydell Press, 1995)

RDWB Ronald Duncan, *Working with Britten: A Personal Memoir* (Bideford: The Rebel Press, 1981)

Chronology

(Dates in parentheses refer to first performances, unless otherwise specified.)

YEAR	BIOGRAPHY AND WORKS	OTHER COMPOSERS
1913	Born, Lowestoft UK (22 November)	Schoenberg, *Gurrelieder* (23 February)
		Debussy, *Jeux* (15 May)
		Stravinsky, *Le sacre du printemps* (29 May)
1919	Begins piano lessons and starts composing	Strauss, *Die Frau ohne Schatten* (10 October)
		Elgar, Cello Concerto (27 October)
1923	Begins viola lessons	Sibelius, Symphony No. 6 (19 February)
		Walton, *Façade* (12 June)
		Stravinsky, *Les noces* (13 June)
		Milhaud, *La création du monde* (25 October)
1927	Studies composition with Frank Bridge	Berg, *Lyric Suite* (8 January)
		Krenek, *Jonny spielt auf* (10 February)
		Stravinsky, *Oedipus Rex* (30 May)
		Weill, *Mahagonny* (17 July)
1928	Composes *Quatre chansons françaises* between leaving South Lodge prep school and entering Gresham's School, Holt	Lambert, *The Rio Grande* (27 February)
		Weill, *Die Dreigroschenoper* (3 August)
		Schoenberg, Variations for Orchestra (2 December)
		Gershwin, *An American in Paris* (13 December)
1929	Composes *A Wealden Trio* and *The Birds*	Beecham's Delius Festival, London
1930	Performs his *Bagatelle* at Gresham's (1 March); composes *A Hymn to the Virgin* in school sick-bay; leaves school and takes up a scholarship at Royal College of Music (22 September)	Shostakovich, *The Nose* (12 January)
		Schoenberg, *Von heute auf morgen* (1 February)
		Berg, *Der Wein* (4 June)
		Stravinsky, *Symphony of Psalms* (13 December)
1931	Wins Farrar Prize at RCM (July); composes String Quartet in D and *Thy King's Birthday*	Copland, Variations for Piano (4 January)
		Walton, *Belshazzar's Feast* (10 October)
		Stravinsky, Violin Concerto (23 October)
1932	Wins Cobbett Prize with Phantasy, string quintet (22 July); *Three Two-Part Songs* (12 December)	Ravel, two Piano Concerti (5 and 14 January)
		Poulenc, Concerto for Two Pianos (5 September)
		Prokofiev, Piano Concerto No. 5 (31 October)
1933	*Sinfonietta* (31 January); wins second Farrar Prize at RCM (July); Phantasy, oboe quartet (6 August); *Three Divertimenti* (11 December); awarded ARCM (13 December) and leaves RCM	Varèse, *Ionisation* (6 March)
		Szymanowski, Violin Concerto No. 2 (6 October)
		Shostakovich, Piano Concerto No. 1 (15 October)

1934 *A Boy Was Born* (23 February); *Simple Symphony* (6 March); attends ISCM in Florence (April); *Holiday Diary* (30 November)

Shostakovich, *Lady Macbeth of Mtsensk* (22 January)
Rachmaninov, *Paganini Rhapsody* (7 November)

1935 Film scores for GPO Film Unit (from May onwards), including *The King's Stamp*, *Coal Face* and *Night Mail*; begins collaboration with W. H. Auden; *Te Deum in C* (13 November); incidental music to Shakespeare's *Timon of Athens* (19 November) and Slater's *Easter 1916* (4 December)

Bartók, String Quartet No. 5 (8 April)
Vaughan Williams, Symphony No. 4 (10 April)
Gershwin, *Porgy and Bess* (30 September)
Walton, Symphony No. 1 (6 November)

1936 Signed up by Boosey & Hawkes (January); Suite for violin and piano (6 March); *Russian Funeral* (8 March); *Two Lullabies* (19 March); attends ISCM in Barcelona (April); *Our Hunting Fathers* (25 September); *Temporal Variations* (15 December); vocal settings of Auden's poetry; film score to Rotha's *Peace of Britain* and feature film *Love from a Stranger*; incidental music to Slater's *Stay Down Miner* (10 May) and Aeschylus/MacNeice's *The Agamemnon* (1 November); arranges Rossini as *Soirées musicales*

Berg, Violin Concerto (19 April; attended by Britten)
Prokofiev, *Peter and the Wolf* (2 May)
Vaughan Williams, *Five Tudor Portraits* (25 September, in same programme as Britten's *Our Hunting Fathers*)

1937 *Reveille* (12 April); friendship with Peter Pears (spring); *Variations on a Theme of Frank Bridge* (27 August); radio cantata *The Company of Heaven* (BBC, 29 September); *On This Island* (19 November); incidental music to Auden/Isherwood's *The Ascent of F6* (26 February), Slater's *Pageant of Empire* (28 February), Bridson's *King Arthur* (BBC, 23 April) and MacNeice's *Out of the Picture* (5 December)

Bartók, *Music for Strings, Percussion and Celeste* (21 January)
Copland, *The Second Hurricane* (21 April)
Berg, *Lulu* (2 June)
Bliss, *Checkmate* (15 June)
Shostakovich, Symphony No. 5 (21 November)

1938 Meets Copland at ISCM in London (June); radio cantata *The World of the Spirit* (BBC, 5 June); Piano Concerto (18 August); film score to *Advance Democracy*; incidental music to Slater's *Spain* (22 June), Auden/Isherwood's *On the Frontier* (14 November) and Catto's *They Walk Alone* (21 November)

Bartók, Sonata for Two Pianos and Percussion (16 January)
Stravinsky, *Dumbarton Oaks* (8 May)
Hindemith, *Mathis der Maler* (28 May)
Barber, *Adagio* (5 November)

1939 *Ballad of Heroes* (5 April); incidental music to Priestley's *Johnson over Jordan* (22 February); sails to Canada with Pears (29 April); moves to New York with Pears (27 June); music for White/Helweg's *The Sword in the Stone* (BBC, June–July); *Young Apollo* (27 August)

Harris, Symphony No. 3 (24 February)
Prokofiev, *Alexander Nevsky* (17 May)
Cage, *Imaginary Landscape No. 1* (9 December)

1940 *Les illuminations* (30 January); Violin Concerto (28 March); radio music to Auden's *The Dark Valley* (CBS, 2 June); *Canadian Carnival* (6 June)

Dallapiccola, *Volo di notte* (18 May)
Stravinsky, Symphony in C (7 November)
Schoenberg, Violin Concerto (6 December)

1941	*Introduction and Rondo alla Burlesca* (5 January); *Sinfonia da Requiem* (29 March); radio music to Lawrence/Auden/Stern's *The Rocking-Horse Winner* (6 April); operetta *Paul Bunyan* (New York, 5 May); String Quartet No. 1 (21 September); *Scottish Ballad* (28 November); *Mazurka Elegiaca* (9 December); arranges Rossini as *Matinées musicales*	Messiaen, *Quatuor pour la Fin du Temps* (15 January) Schuman, Symphony No. 3 (17 October)
1942	Koussevitzky Foundation commissions *Peter Grimes* (January); *Diversions* (16 January); sails to UK with Pears (16 March); *Seven Sonnets of Michelangelo* (23 September); *Hymn to St Cecilia* (22 November); *A Ceremony of Carols* (5 December); radio music includes Sayers's *The Man Born to be King* (summer) and joint US/UK documentaries	Shostakovich, Symphony No. 7 (1 March) Martin, *Le vin herbé* (26 March) Strauss, *Capriccio* (28 October)
1943	Prelude and Fugue for 18-part strings (23 June); *Rejoice in the Lamb* (21 September); *Serenade* (15 October); radio score for Sackville-West's *The Rescue* (25–6 November); first volume of folksong arrangements published	Webern, Variations for Orchestra (3 March) Copland, *Fanfare for the Common Man* (12 March) Messiaen, *Visions de l'Amen* (10 May)
1944	Visits Eichstätt POW camp and performs *The Ballad of Little Musgrave and Lady Barnard* (February); two Auden settings for *A Poet's Christmas* (BBC, 24 December)	Tippett, *A Child of Our Time* (19 March) Bartók, Concerto for Orchestra (1 December)
1945	*Festival Te Deum* (24 April); *Peter Grimes* (Sadler's Wells, 7 June); visits German concentration camps with Menuhin (July); incidental music to Duncan's *This Way to the Tomb* (11 October); String Quartet No. 2 (21 November); *The Holy Sonnets of John Donne* (22 November); film score to *The Instruments of the Orchestra* (29 November)	Prokofiev, Symphony No. 5 (13 January) Shostakovich, Symphony No. 9 (3 November) Martinů, Symphony No. 4 (30 November)
1946	Radio music for MacNeice's *The Dark Tower* (BBC, 21 January); revised version of Piano Concerto (2 July); *The Rape of Lucretia* (Glyndebourne, 12 July); incidental music to Cocteau/Duncan's *The Eagle Has Two Heads* (4 September) and Webster/Auden's *The Duchess of Malfi* (20 September); *Prelude and Fugue on a Theme of Vittoria* (21 September); *Occasional Overture* (29 September); *The Young Person's Guide to the Orchestra* (15 October); founds English Opera Group (autumn); second volume of folksong arrangements published; begins series of Purcell realizations	Stravinsky, *Symphony in Three Movements* (24 January) Prokofiev, *War and Peace* (12 June) Copland, Symphony No. 3 (18 October)

1947	Moves to Aldeburgh, Suffolk; *Albert Herring* (Glyndebourne, 20 June); *Canticle I: My Beloved is Mine* (1 November); Christmas music for *Men of Goodwill* (BBC, 25 December); third volume of folksong arrangements published	Weill, *Street Scene* (9 January) Menotti, *The Telephone* (18 February) Schoenberg, String Trio (1 May)
1948	*A Charm of Lullabies* (3 January); *The Beggar's Opera* (24 May); *Saint Nicolas* opens first Aldeburgh Festival (5 June)	Lutoslawski, Symphony No. 1 (1 April) Henze, Symphony No. 1 (25 August)
1949	*Let's Make An Opera* (Aldeburgh, 14 June); *Spring Symphony* (9 July); *A Wedding Anthem: Amo Ergo Sum* (29 September); incidental music to Duncan's *Stratton* (31 October)	Bernstein, Symphony No. 2 (8 April) Messiaen, *Turangalîla-symphonie* (2 December) Dallapiccola, *Il prigioniero* (4 December)
1950	*Lachrymae* (20 June)	Schaeffer/Henry, *Musique concrète* (18 March)
1951	Realization of Purcell's *Dido and Aeneas* (1 May); *Five Flower Songs* (24 May); *Six Metamorphoses after Ovid* (14 June); *Billy Budd* (Royal Opera, 1 December)	Gerhard, *The Duenna* (27 June) Stravinsky, *The Rake's Progress* (11 September)
1952	*Canticle II: Abraham and Isaac* (21 January)	Cage, *4'33"* (29 August)
1953	Companion of Honour (1 June); *Gloriana* (Royal Opera, 8 June); *Winter Words* (8 October)	Stockhausen, *Kontra-Punkte* (26 May) Shostakovich, Symphony No. 10 (17 December)
1954	Incidental music to Roussin's *Am Stram Gram* (4 March); *The Turn of the Screw* (La Fenice, 14 September)	Stravinsky, Septet (23 January) Varèse, *Déserts* (2 December)
1955	*Canticle III: Still Falls the Rain* (28 January); contributes two songs to Duncan's *The Punch Revue* (28 September); embarks on five-month world tour with Pears (31 October)	Tippett, *The Midsummer Marriage* (27 January) Boulez, *Le marteau sans maître* (18 June)
1956	Visits Indonesia (January), Japan (February) and India (March) as part of world tour	Barraqué, *Séquence* (10 March) Nono, *Il canto sospeso* (24 October)
1957	*The Prince of the Pagodas* (Royal Ballet, 1 January); moves to The Red House, Aldeburgh (November)	Stravinsky, *Agon* (17 June) Hindemith, *Die Harmonie der Welt* (11 August)
1958	*Songs from the Chinese* (17 June); *Noye's Fludde* (Orford, 18 June); *Sechs Hölderlin-Fragmente* (14 November)	Tippett, Symphony No. 2 (5 February) Boulez, *Doubles* (16 March) Cage, Piano Concerto (15 May)
1959	*Nocturne* (30 January); *Fanfare for St Edmundsbury* (June); *Missa Brevis* (22 July)	Stockhausen, *Gruppen* (24 March) Dutilleux, Symphony No. 2 (9 December)
1960	*A Midsummer Night's Dream* (Aldeburgh, 11 June); *Cantata Academica* (1 July); friendship with Rostropovich and Shostakovich (September); *Fanfare for SS Oriana* (3 November); revised version of *Billy Budd* (BBC radio, 13 November); fourth volume of folksong arrangements published	Boulez, *Pli selon pli* (13 June) Ligeti, *Apparitions* (19 June) Messiaen, *Chronochromie* (16 October) Mahler (arr. Deryck Cooke), Symphony No. 10 (19 December)

1961	Cello Sonata (7 July); *Jubilate Deo* (8 October); fifth and sixth volumes of folksong arrangements published	Lutoslawski, *Jeux vénitiens* (24 April) Penderecki, *Threnody for the Victims of Hiroshima* (31 May)
1962	*War Requiem* (30 May)	Tippett, *King Priam* (29 May)
1963	Visits USSR (March); *A Hymn of St Columba* (2 June); *Psalm 150* (24 June); *Cantata Misericordium* (1 September); composes *Night Piece* for Leeds Piano Competition	Henze, Symphony No. 5 (16 May) Tippett, Concerto for Orchestra (28 August; dedicated to Britten)
1964	*Cello Symphony* (12 March); *Curlew River* (Orford, 12 June); *Nocturnal after John Dowland* (12 June); composes cadenzas to Haydn's Cello Concerto in C (18 June); Aspen Award (31 July)	Stravinsky, *Abraham and Isaac* (23 August) Messiaen, *Couleurs de la cité céleste* (17 October) Cowell, Concerto for Koto (18 December)
1965	Visits India (February); Order of Merit (23 March); *Gemini Variations* (19 June); *Songs and Proverbs of William Blake* (24 June); Cello Suite No. 1 (27 June); *Voices for Today* (24 October); *The Poet's Echo* (2 December)	Stravinsky, *Huxley Variations* (17 April) Boulez, *Eclat* (26 March)
1966	*The Burning Fiery Furnace* (Orford, 9 June); composes cadenzas to Mozart's Piano Concerto K482 (July); visit to USSR to spend Christmas with Shostakovich	Tippett, *The Vision of Saint Augustine* (19 January) Xenakis, *Terretektorh* (3 April) Stravinsky, *Requiem Canticles* (8 October)
1967	*Hankin Booby* (1 March); *The Building of the House* (opening of Snape Maltings concert hall, 2 June); *The Golden Vanity* (3 June); realization of Purcell's *The Fairy Queen* (25 June)	Ligeti, Cello Concerto (19 April) Copland, *Inscape* (13 September) Stockhausen, *Hymnen* (29 November)
1968	*The Prodigal Son* (Orford, 10 June); Cello Suite No. 2 (17 June)	Birtwistle, *Punch and Judy* (Aldeburgh, 8 June) Berio, *Sinfonia* (10 October)
1969	*Children's Crusade* (19 May); Snape Maltings concert hall burns down (7 June); arrangements of J. S. Bach's *Geistliche Lieder* (18 June); Suite for Harp (24 June)	Maxwell Davies, *8 Songs for a Mad King* (22 April) Shostakovich, Symphony No. 14 (29 September; dedicated to Britten)
1970	Concert tour of Australasia (spring); re-opening of Snape Maltings (7 June)	Carter, Concerto for Orchestra (5 February) Tippett, *Songs for Dov* (12 October) Lutoslawski, Cello Concerto (14 October)
1971	*Who Are These Children?* (4 May); *Owen Wingrave* (BBC TV, 16 May); *Canticle IV: Journey of the Magi* (26 June)	Bernstein, *Mass* (8 September) Ligeti, *Melodien* (10 December)
1972	At work on *Death in Venice*	Tippett, Symphony No. 3 (22 June) Maxwell Davies, *Taverner* (12 July) Crumb, *Vox Balaenae* (10 October)
1973	Heart surgery (8 May); *Death in Venice* (Snape, 16 June)	Maderna, *Satyricon* (16 March)

1974   Revises *Paul Bunyan* (summer); Cello Suite No. 3   Glass, *Music in 12 Parts* (1 June)
       (21 December)   Tavener, *Ultimos Ritos* (23 June)

1975   *Canticle V: The Death of Saint Narcissus* (15   Boulez, *Rituel* (2 April)
       January); revises String Quartet in D (7 June;   Berio, *Chemins IV* (17 October)
       composed in 1931); *Suite on English Folk Tunes*
       (13 June); *Sacred and Profane* (14 September)

1976   *Paul Bunyan*, revised version (BBC radio,   Stockhausen, *Sirius* (18 July)
       1 February); *A Birthday Hansel* (19 March); Life   Glass, *Einstein on the Beach* (25 July)
       Peerage (12 June); *Phaedra* (16 June); composes
       Welcome Ode (August) and *Praise We Great Men*
       (unfinished); arranges folksongs with harp
       accompaniment (summer); dies on 4 December,
       aged 63; String Quartet No. 3 given posthumous
       first performance on 19 December

Introduction

MERVYN COOKE

Not long ago I attended a formal dinner at a college belonging to one of Britain's most ancient and prestigious universities, and was introduced to the institution's head of house as someone engaged in researching the music of Benjamin Britten. 'Really?' came the Master's reply. 'There's not much point to the Aldeburgh Festival now that Britten and Pears are both dead, is there?' Before I could respond, the Master had moved swiftly down the line, presumably to impart another morsel of wisdom in whatever subject-area was appropriate to the next guest. After dinner, I sat next to the wife of a senior fellow and was introduced in a similar manner. 'Well,' she said as she sipped her coffee thoughtfully, 'I'm afraid I find Britten's music just too *aggressively* homosexual, don't you?' This time I managed to issue a sophisticated rejoinder (the single word 'Why?', if I remember rightly), upon which she rapidly changed the subject.

The persistence of such bigoted views on Britain's most internationally successful and respected twentieth-century composer seems scarcely credible as the century draws to a close, and it remains an uncomfortable fact that – in his native country, at least – a small but vociferous body of commentators still seeks to denigrate Britten's self-evidently significant artistic achievements. Britten was himself no stranger to such negativity, and the seeds of an incipient critical malaise were sown as early as the 1930s when he was making a name for himself as a precocious newcomer armed with a formidable compositional technique embodying a resourcefulness and flexibility never before encountered in British music. From the influences of French impressionism and the Second Viennese School evident in the *Quatre chansons françaises* (written in the summer of 1928 at the age of fourteen, and discussed by Christopher Mark in Chapter 1) to the emulations of Mahler, Stravinsky, Schoenberg, Shostakovich and Prokofiev in works dating from his time as a composition scholar at the Royal College of Music (1930–3), the range of music absorbed by Britten was phenomenally broad. During his working apprenticeship as a composer for the GPO Film Unit (1936–8) – a famous product of which is examined by Philip Reed in Chapter 3 – and as the creator of incidental music for stage projects mounted by the Group Theatre and Left Theatre in the same period, Britten's ability to assimilate any musical idiom required of him grew still more pronounced. His stylistic boundaries broadened to the extent of absorbing jazz elements, either reproduced in straight pastiche (as in his music to a west-end production of J. B. Priestley's *Johnson over Jordan* in 1939) or more subtly disguised (witness his brilliantly inventive score to the Auden–Isherwood collaboration *The Ascent of F6* in 1937).

Such astonishing technical facility was not destined to endear Britten to the infamously insular critics of inter-war Britain, all the more so because he had resolutely rejected the idiom of earlier Establishment composers such as Vaughan Williams by responding to almost exclusively Continental influences. Compositional 'cleverness' was itself looked upon with suspicion in those years, and Peter Evans has justifiably criticized Vaughan Williams's music for its 'disdain for technical finesse approaching irresponsibility'.[1] Vaughan Williams is reputed to have referred to the young Britten's music as 'very clever but beastly' during his time as a student at the Royal College, lamenting the fact that an English public schoolboy of his age should be writing 'this kind of music'.[2] For his part, Britten felt Vaughan Williams's music to be blighted by 'technical incompetence', and declared (with the benefit of several decades of hindsight) that his own attempt 'to develop a consciously controlled professional technique . . . was a struggle away from everything Vaughan Williams seemed to stand for'.[3] Britten's *Variations on a Theme of Frank Bridge* (1937), perhaps the finest outcome of the young composer's prodigious eclecticism, were hailed at the time of their première merely for their 'virtuosity', 'brilliant ingenuity' and 'strikingly original effects'.[4] His Piano Concerto, dating from the following year, provoked this schoolmasterly outburst from the same distinguished reviewer:

> This is not a stylish work. Mr Britten's cleverness, of which he has frequently been told, has got the better of him and led him into all sorts of errors, the worst of which are errors of taste. How did he come to write the tune of the last movement? Now and then real music crops up . . . but on the whole Mr Britten is exploiting a brilliant facility that ought to be kept in subservience.[5]

Years later, Britten's virtuosic early instrumental scores would be more warmly appreciated for their wit, ingenuity and vivid characterization (aspects explored by Eric Roseberry in Chapter 12), and seen as laying the firm yet flexible stylistic foundations on which the composer's later work would build. His output of instrumental music came to include several substantial 'symphonic' scores and a small body of impressive chamber music (examined by Arved Ashby and Philip Rupprecht in Chapters 11 and 13 respectively), putting paid to wearily repetitive allegations that Britten's success was restricted to text-based projects such as opera and vocal music (the latter surveyed by Ralph Woodward in Chapter 14).

During Britten's sojourn in the USA in the Second World War, attempts to tarnish his reputation took a more sinister and personal turn. A notorious example was a statement by George Baker of the Royal Philharmonic Society in a letter published by the *Sunday Times* on 15 June 1941:

> In your last issue, Mr Ernest Newman, under the heading 'Thoroughbreds', said he had 'been fighting single-handed the "battle of Britten"'.
>
> There are a number of musicians in this country who are well content to let Mr Newman have this dubious honour. The young gentleman on whose behalf he fights, Mr Benjamin Britten, was born in 1913. He is in America. He may have had perfectly good reasons for going there, and may decide to return to his native land some time or other. In the meantime I would like to remind Mr Newman that most of our musical 'thoroughbreds' are stabled in or near London and are directing all their endeavours towards winning the City and Suburban and the Victory Stakes, two classic events that form part of a programme called the Battle of Britain; a programme in which Mr Britten has no part.

It was, of course, the spectacularly triumphant staging of *Peter Grimes* in 1945 that secured Britten's international reputation soon after his home-coming – although that success, too, was tainted by open resentment against the three-man team of conscientious objectors (Britten, Peter Pears and Eric Crozier) responsible for mounting the opera's first produc-tion. Britten's pacifism was nevertheless to prove a deep and lifelong commitment which, as Donald Mitchell reveals in Chapter 10, by no means bore artistic fruit merely in those scores where the preoccupation is most obvious.

In the immediately post-war years, Britten's creativity and sense of cultural responsibility both seemed unstoppable as he produced a steady stream of universally acclaimed stage works and pursued his firm commitment to touring them to venues well outside the privileged milieu of central London. The evolution of the versatile medium of chamber opera, charted by Arnold Whittall in Chapter 5, was but the first of many compositional developments rooted in considerations of practicality and accessibility. The success of the Aldeburgh Festival, founded in 1948 and discussed by Judith LeGrove in Chapter 17, furthered the sense that here was a musician devoted to the wider community, his compositional gifts backed up by phenomenal talents as a performer which made him the envy of many a less-gifted composer. The warmly complimentary tone generally adopted by Britten's reviewers began to change around 1951, however, when the composer's former champion, the influential Ernest Newman, dismissed *Billy Budd* in print as a 'painful disappointment'.[6] The tone of other reviews of this Festival of Britain opera was unusually

carping. One writer shed intriguing light on the widespread shift in critical stance by commenting that 'one always resents having it dinned into
one's ears that a new work is a masterpiece before it has been performed;
and Benjamin Britten's "Billy Budd" was trumpeted into the arena by such
a deafening roar of advance publicity that many of us entered Covent
Garden . . . with a mean, sneaking hope that we might be able to flesh our
fangs in it'.[7] The débâcle surrounding the notorious gala première of
Britten's Coronation opera, *Gloriana*, brought this resentment swiftly to a
head in 1953 in circumstances re-assessed by Antonia Malloy-Chirgwin
in Chapter 6.

Ernest Newman's short-sighted response to *Billy Budd* had been
promptly rebuffed by Donald Mitchell, who had by the early 1950s begun
to make a name for himself as an outspoken champion of Britten's music
in the pages of his journal *Music Survey*.[8] Mitchell's editorial work with
Hans Keller led naturally enough to their decision to collaborate on a
volume of essays written by a long list of distinguished contributors and
entitled *Benjamin Britten: A Commentary on His Works From a Group of
Specialists* (DMHK), which appeared in 1952. The composer declared
himself to be delighted with 'the seriousness of it, the thoroughness of its
planning & editing, its excellent get-up, & the admirable quality of a good
deal of the contents'.[9] Less pleased were the representatives of the growing
anti-Britten lobby, startled as they were at the audacity of issuing a
detailed – and positive – study of a composer still only thirty-nine years of
age. Peter Tranchell spoke for them in a brutal review entitled 'Britten and
Brittenites', which took several of the symposium's contributors to task
for their modish use of 'musicological jargon', the author barely dis-
guising his resentment that here was a book daring to consider a living
composer 'great' in spite of his objection that 'the serious appraisal of a
creative artist's work must be left to posterity'.[10] Tranchell concluded by
extending 'to the subject of this hero-worship my condolences that the
book should not have been better written and that he should have been
the victim of so inopportune an outburst of noble intentions'.

It would have taken considerably more than a few griping critics to
check Britten's continuing meteoric career, however, and the international success of major scores such as *The Turn of the Screw* (1954) and the
War Requiem (1962) easily compensated for the temporary set-backs of
Gloriana (1953) and *The Prince of the Pagodas* (1957), neither of which
was initially well received – although posterity has since accorded both
works a more serious and balanced appraisal. Britten's stylistic horizons
continued to broaden in the 1950s with his investigations of dode-
caphony and Far Eastern cultures (his creative encounter with the latter is
outlined in Chapter 9), both of which encouraged him to strive for ever

greater economy and clarity in his music. The emotional impact of the *War Requiem* on the popular imagination, even more spectacular than that of *Peter Grimes* before it, kept him firmly in the limelight in the 1960s, and the work's stature was deemed by some to be sufficiently daunting as to make criticism 'impertinent'.[11] Needless to say, reaction against this view soon set in, fuelled by discomfort that *The Times* could loudly proclaim the work to be a masterpiece well before a note of the score had been heard in public.

Britten's respectability in musicological circles, initiated by the Mitchell–Keller symposium, began to grow steadily with the appearance of a number of analytical articles on his music in the 1960s. Several perceptive essays by Peter Evans would later form the basis for his detailed book on Britten's musical language (PE*MB*), first published in 1979 and followed three years later by Arnold Whittall's comparative account of the music of Britten and Tippett (AW*BT*). Whittall noted the significance of Evans's monumental tome as the first substantial study of any twentieth-century British composer 'to emphasize technical matters in a systematic manner'.[12] Both books remain the first resort for any would-be student of Britten's music, and have enabled a younger generation of Britten analysts to embark on more elaborate dissections of the composer's works with the confidence born of belonging to a well-established musicological tradition.

A handful of less technical accounts of Britten's life and work had already appeared during the last decade and a half of the composer's lifetime (including two books largely devoted to his operas, published in quick succession by Patricia Howard and Eric Walter White in 1969–70),[13] and Britten's death in 1976 at the age of sixty-three was quickly and inevitably followed by a rash of personal tributes. The first important step in objectively chronicling the composer's life and career in some detail came two years later with Donald Mitchell's and John Evans's vivid pictorial account (DMJE). Then, in 1981, Michael Kennedy's informative and concise biography (MK*B*) elevated the composer to the hallowed status of 'Master Musician'. In the same year, Mitchell began his concerted attempt to illuminate the socially, politically and artistically fascinating years of Britten's first creative period with his book *Britten and Auden in the Thirties* (DM*BA*), a topic reconsidered here by Paul Kildea in Chapter 2. Mitchell's work on Britten's early period culminated in 1991 with the appearance of an encyclopaedic two-volume edition of the composer's correspondence up to 1945, co-edited with Philip Reed (DMPR) – a mine of information on everything from the critical reaction to premières of Britten's works, to intriguing trivia such as the composer's preferred brand of toothpaste. The third volume of Britten's letters is currently in preparation, and the project is likely to extend to at least two further volumes thereafter.

The surge of interest in Britten studies in the 1980s would scarcely have been possible without the formidable research resources offered to scholars by the Britten–Pears Library, established at Britten's home at The Red House, Aldeburgh, at the start of the decade. Philip Brett's study of *Peter Grimes* (PBPG), published in 1983, showed how valuable Britten's libretto drafts and composition sketches could be in shedding light on the composer's working methods and extra-musical preoccupations, and his book became a model for later monographs on Britten's major works. Many of the essays in the present volume are indebted to the source materials at Aldeburgh for their insights.

Brett's more recent publications have continued to illuminate the creative results of Britten's homosexuality, a topic discussed with increasing frankness since the composer's death (though not always with equal relevance to his art). Clifford Hindley, whose work is represented in Chapter 8, has provided many perceptive and thought-provoking interpretations of Britten's operas from this perspective. Humphrey Carpenter's controversial biography of the composer (HCBB), published in 1992, set out to provide a warts-and-all account of Britten's private life and offers the most comprehensive account of the composer's character yet to be made available. The motivation behind Carpenter's close questioning of several men who were taken under Britten's avuncular wing in their youth is transparent enough, although none confessed to any physical dimension to the relationship. (Britten's complex attitude towards childhood and all that it symbolizes, which bore fruit not only in music specifically conceived for children to play but also in various stage and vocal works, is considered afresh by Stephen Arthur Allen in Chapter 15.) Carpenter's otherwise scrupulously well-sourced book unfortunately bases many of its assumptions concerning the tensions in Britten's psyche upon sexual incidents for which only the flimsiest of evidence survives: an alleged proclivity for little boys on the part of Britten's father, and Eric Crozier's recollection that Britten confessed to having been 'raped' while at school. The author's preoccupation with the latter trouvé inevitably colours his interpretations of the operas: thus the Novice's flogging in *Billy Budd*, of which the victim sings 'The shame'll never pass', is directly linked to Britten's putative 'rape', which took place 'possibly while undergoing a flogging'; the opera as a whole is reduced to an allegory of life in a brutal prep-school.[14] (It might strike the sceptical observer as somewhat odd, however, to find a composer allegedly so traumatized by sexual violation in his youth making a musical in-joke concerning rape in his comic opera *Albert Herring*, where he quotes from the earlier *Rape of Lucretia*: see

p. 103.) Carpenter's attempt to view all Britten's stage works as fundamentally autobiographical leads him up some amusing garden paths. The
spoken dialogue at the end of *Grimes* exists, we are told, because 'Britten
has perhaps identified so closely with Grimes that he cannot portray his
death musically. Death means for Grimes what it would mean for Britten,
the end of all music.' This theme is resumed in the discussion of *Owen
Wingrave*, which again contains speech at 'one of those moments in
Britten's operas that are too intense for singing' (!): Kate's challenge to
Owen to sleep in the haunted room is read 'as if Auden had suddenly
returned and had again thrown down his 1942 gauntlet' – a reference to
Auden's famous letter to Britten in which he advised him 'to suffer, and
make others suffer' if he were to develop to his 'full stature'.[15]

Consideration of the tensions and frustrations in Britten's personal
life may well lend added insight into the preoccupations that coloured his
stage and vocal works, but the ongoing fascination with the composer's
sexuality seems in danger both of lending too one-sided a slant to interpretations of his operas (the universal appeal of which continues to be
vividly demonstrated by numerous high-profile stagings across the
globe) and distracting attention from his purely musical achievements.
Much of the attractiveness of Britten's art lies in the scope if offers for
interpretation on numerous levels, whether arising from the designedly
ambiguous dramatic suggestions of his operas, or through a refined
musical language that somehow manages to speak directly to the wider
public while keeping even the most rigorously systematic musical analysts
in employment for the foreseeable future. In that 'somehow' lies the
simultaneous freshness and intellectual appeal of a style that, in Robin
Holloway's words, 'has the power to connect the avant-garde with the lost
paradise of tonality; it conserves and renovates in the boldest and simplest manner; it shows how old usages can be refreshed and remade, and
how the new can be saved from mere rootlessness, etiolation, lack of con-
nexion and communication'.[16]

Posterity, on the whole, continues to serve Britten well. Interest in the
composer's work has never been so widespread, and the quantity and
range of postgraduate dissertations devoted to his music on both sides of
the Atlantic is formidable. The richness and suggestiveness of Britten's
operatic language, in particular, ensure that no commentator can ever
hope to have the final interpretative word, and a vast amount of primary
source material relating to the composer has yet to be studied in the detail
it deserves. The present volume presents a varied collection of essays on a
wide range of topics central to Britten's career, some written by those who
knew the composer personally and were at the cutting edge of Britten
research at its inception, others the work of those who were much too

young to have formed a critical response to his music while he was still alive. One thing all the contributors share is their keen awareness of the rare ability of Britten's music to speak forcibly to a wide audience, even to those listeners whose lack of confidence in musical technicalities might influence them to fight shy of a contemporary idiom. This unusually wide appeal is reflected in the dauntingly extensive catalogue of recordings of Britten's music currently available, perhaps a more potent reflection of an undiminished appreciation of the composer's art two decades after his death than any amount of academic argument advanced in its favour. No one can today claim that Britten's music is not destined to outlive the memory of Pears's interpretations, as once was predicted by the more vociferous of the composer's detractors, or that Aldeburgh and its associated activities have not comfortably outlived the artists who nurtured them half a century ago.

PART ONE

Apprenticeship

1 Juvenilia (1922–1932)

CHRISTOPHER MARK

It is clear from the assuredness of his Op. 1, the *Sinfonietta*, that Britten was already a composer of some experience when he started work on the piece in June 1932 at the age of eighteen.[1] He himself hinted at the extent of that experience in interviews and articles published in the early and mid-1960s,[2] while evidence of it began to emerge in the late 1960s and early 1970s when he released reworked versions of a few childhood pieces: the *Five Walztes* [*sic*] for piano, originally written between 1923 and 1925 (published in 1970); *Tit for Tat*, a collection of songs written between 1928 and 1931 (1968); and a String Quartet in D major written in 1931 (1975). Because of the reworkings, however, the published versions of these pieces are not reliable as indicators of Britten's early achievement.[3] It was only after his death and the establishment in 1980 of the archive in the Britten–Pears Library in Aldeburgh, when access to unrevised material became possible, that a critical portrait of his juvenilia could begin to be constructed.

By 1987 most of the music composed before the *Sinfonietta* had been listed in *A Britten Source Book* (*BSB*), and a few key childhood works had been performed, recorded and published under the auspices of the Britten Estate.[4] Until much more recently, though, the only juvenilia available for study were these works and those donated to the British Library in lieu of death duties, so that commentaries on Britten's early progress have of necessity been circumspect.[5] Now that the entire corpus of extant juvenilia can be surveyed, it is clear that nothing short of an extended study will do it justice. What is offered here is a brief overview, with some more detailed observations on particularly significant pieces.[6]

It is well known that one of the major influences on Britten's compositional development was Frank Bridge, whom Britten first met in the autumn of 1927 and with whom he studied from January 1928. Bridge was initially reluctant to see him because he was 'always being asked to interview young people who were supposed to show musical promise, which they rarely had', but he was persuaded by Audrey Alston, Britten's viola teacher, to do so.[7] Clearly, he was impressed; and not least, one may surmise, by the sheer volume of music Britten had composed. The major items are listed chronologically in Table 1.1, although those dating from

1925 and 1926 were not all completed. For instance, the Octett of June 1925 has a substantial first movement, but the 'Presto' second movement peters out after a few bars, and no other movement was attempted. Other incomplete pieces include the Mass in E minor, abandoned in the middle of the Credo, and the second movement of the untitled orchestral piece, both also composed in 1925. However, the vast majority of pieces were completed, and this determination to see a project to its conclusion, plus the business-like presentation of his scores (the Symphony in D minor, for example, is provided with rehearsal numbers even though the possibility of a performance must have seemed unlikely), must also have convinced Bridge about Britten's seriousness. Most impressive of all, however, would have been the steady improvement of skills and the expansion of creative vision between 1925 and the middle of 1927, a period that, for reasons that will become clear, I shall divide into two: 1925 to mid-1926, and mid-1926 to late 1927.

In an earlier study of the juvenilia I observed that, on the basis of the pre-Bridge music I had been able to see, 'Britten's initial musical environ-ment was all too representative of the conservativeness and provinciality of English music-making'.[8] Examination of the complete corpus confirms that up to around April 1926 the underlying style is essentially classical and early romantic, with little sign of any influence more modern than Brahms, let alone any knowledge of contemporary developments. It is often not possible to determine specific stylistic models, still less model compositions, though Mozart, Beethoven, Schubert, Chopin, Schumann and Brahms all suggest themselves at various points.

Mozart's influence is most obvious in the Violin Sonata in D major (April 1925), especially at the end of the first movement,[9] but it is also present in the soprano aria 'Gratias agimus tibi' from the Mass in E minor (March–April 1925), not least in the wide vocal range (from b to a^2). At least one harmonic event in this aria, the bald shift from B minor to D major in bar 3, is more suggestive of Schubert, however, and it is he who is the guiding spirit behind *The Elected Knight*, a grand setting (multi-sec-tioned, along the lines of 'Viola' or 'Sehnsucht') of Henry Longfellow's narrative poem completed in June 1925. Another Schubertian third-shift, from B♭ to G♭, appears in the first of the Ten Walztes (1922–5).[10] Surprisingly, perhaps, there is little sign of Chopin in these pieces. However, the Polish composer clearly lies behind the second of the Two Fantasies 'Op. 17' (June 1925) as well as the Masurka [*sic*] in F♯ minor 'Op. 43a' (18 April 1926) and parts of the Fantasie in E♭ 'Op. 29' (10–24 December 1925) – principally in terms of texture, though the harmon-ically oblique opening of the first of these works suggests his influence too. Ex. 1.1 shows another oblique opening, the piano introduction to

Table 1.1: Chronology of Selected Juvenilia

1922–3	'Beware!' (voice and piano)
1922–5	Ten Walztes [*sic*]
?1924	'The March of the Gods into Paridise [*sic*]' (piano duet)
1925	Andante in F major (violin and piano)
	Fantasia (piano)
March–April	Mass in E minor (soloists, chorus and orchestra)
April	Sonata in D major (violin and piano)
June	*The Elected Knight* (voice and piano)
	Octett in D major (2 violins, 2 violas, 2 celli, 2 doublebasses)
	Two Fantasies, Op. 17 (piano)
28 July – 3 August	Piano Sonata (Grand) No. 3 in B♭, Op. 5
August–September	4 Scherzos (piano)
	Untitled orchestral piece in two movements
14 November	Rondo Capriccio in B minor, Op. 28 No. 1 (piano)
December	3 Fantasies (piano)
?1925/6	Allegro Appassionata in G minor (piano)
	Allegro ma non troppo in D major (violin and piano)
1926	
4 January	Suite No. 5 in E major, Op. 30 No. 2 (piano)
5–10 January	3 Toccatas (piano)
10–12 January	4 Etudes Symphoniques (piano)
7 April	Trio in Fantastic Form (violin, viola and piano)
17 April	Sonata in A (cello and piano)
18 April	Masurka [*sic*] in F♯ minor, Op. 43a (piano)
29 April	Overture No. 1 in C, Op. 44 (orchestra; version 2)
1–29 June	Ouverture (orchestra; under pseudonym 'Never Unprepared')
5 September	Suite fantastique for large orchestra and piano obbligato (second movement dated 21 April 1926)
26 September	Poème No. 1 in D (orchestra)
24 December	Poème No. 2 in B minor (small orchestra)
29 December – 3 January	Poème No. 3 in E (orchestra)
1927	
17 January – 28 February	Symphony in D minor (large orchestra)
12–14 February	Poème No. 4 in B♭ (small orchestra)
14–19 February	Poème No. 5 in F♯ minor (orchestra)
March–May	String Quartet in G
June–July	String Quartet in A minor
29 July – 2 August	*The Pale Stars are Gone* (chorus, piano and strings)
22 August – 5 September	*Chaos and Cosmos*, symphonic poem for large orchestra
27 September	Sonata No. 10 in B♭ (piano)
October–February	Sonata No. 11 in B (piano)
1928	
25 January	*Dans les bois* (orchestra)
6 March	*Humoreske* (orchestra)
11 April	String Quartet in F
16 April	Menuetto in A minor (piano)
16–23 April	Elegy (strings)
13 June	'Silver' (voice and piano)
13 June – 31 August	*Quatre chansons françaises* (soprano and orchestra)
31 December – 25 February	'Tit for Tat' (voice and piano)
1929	
1 January – 7 February	'A Song of Enchantment' (voice and piano)
7 January – 24 April	*The Quartette* (SATB soloists)
13 January – 25 October	*Elizabeth Variations* (piano)
26 January – 8 March	*Miniature Suite* (string quartet)
28 January – 21 March	Rhapsody (string quartet)
30 March – 22 April	Rhapsody (violin, viola and piano)

Table 1.1: (*cont.*)

30 March – 15 January	Bagatelle (violin, viola and piano)
June	'The Birds' (version 1)
21–31 October	*Introduction and Allegro* (viola and strings)
17 November – 24 December	2 Pieces (violin, viola and piano)
1930	
3 January – 17 April	*Quartettino*
11 April – 1 June	Piece (violin and piano)
9 July	*A Hymn to the Virgin* (double chorus)
1 August	Piece for viola solo [Elegy]
7 August	Movement for wind sextet (flute, oboe, clarinet, bass clarinet, horn and bassoon)
27 August	Sketch No. 1, 'D. Layton' (strings)
10 September	Sketch No. 2, 'E.B.B.' (viola and strings)
16 September – 27 December	3 Pieces (piano)
23 December – 17 January	'Vigil' (voice and piano)
1931	
February – 26 March	*Thy King's Birthday* (soprano, contralto and mixed chorus)
1 April – 6 May	*12 Variations on a Theme* (piano)
8 May – 2 June	String Quartet in D major
8–24 June	3 Small Songs (soprano and chamber orchestra)
12–28 August	*Plymouth Town* (ballet; orchestra)
26 December	*Psalm 150: 'Praise ye the Lord'* (chorus and orchestra)
1932	
19 January	*Psalm 130: 'Out of the Deep'* (chorus and orchestra)
25 January – 11 February	Phantasy in F minor (string quintet)
9 March – 4 May	Concerto in B minor (violin, viola and orchestra)
20 May	*Introduction and Allegro* (violin, cello and piano)
June	*Ballet on a Basque Scenario* (orchestra; incomplete)

the Andante in F major (1925); but here the homophonic texture and melodic cast suggest Schumann as a more likely model. As we might expect from the title, some of the strongest traces of that composer can be found in the Four Etudes Symphoniques (10–12 January 1926), particularly in No. 2 in A♭ minor, which seems to have been conceived as a study in hemiola.[11] Meanwhile Brahms is a more shadowy presence, hinted at by details such as the I–vii$^{\varnothing 7}$/V–V progression in B♭ over a V pedal in bars 25–6 of Waltz No. 8 of the Ten Walztes, and the weighty homophonic texture of the opening of the Rondo Capriccio in B minor 'Op. 28 No. 1' (1925).

The strongest influence up to the middle of 1926, however, was Beethoven. Later diary entries show the extent of Britten's admiration for him. On 13 November 1928 he declared Beethoven to be 'first . . . in my list of Composers . . . and I think will always be', while on 24 June 1929, after hearing Kreisler's recording of the Violin Concerto, he enthused, 'Oh! Beethoven, thou art immortal; has anything ever been written like the pathos of the 1st & 2nd movements, and the joy of the last?'[12] By the time he started to study with Bridge, Britten had acquired more miniature

Example 1.1

scores by Beethoven than by any other composer, including Symphonies Nos. 1 to 6 (the 'Eroica' was the first score he bought), the second volume of an edition of the string quartets, the Violin Concerto, and Piano Concerto No. 4.[13] One of Britten's most overt compositional references to Beethoven at this time is the protracted cadencing at the end of the first movement of the Octett in D (1925), which imitates the rhetoric of the final pages of Beethoven's Fifth and Eighth Symphonies. The Fantasie in E♭ 'Op. 29' ends in a similar fashion. The key of this is, of course, Beethoven's heroic key, and several traits associated with Beethoven in that vein are apparent. They include the highly dramatic appearance in the first part of the ternary form of the flattened seventh degree (D♭), which is protracted as a pedal before forming the root of a diminished-seventh chord that resolves to F minor; the use of the dotted rhythmic motif shown in Ex. 1.2 (subsequently, *a* is isolated for reiteration by itself); and the protracted use of syncopation in the coda. Further Beethovenian influence at this time can be seen in the orchestration of both the untitled orchestral piece (1925) and the huge (84-page) Overture No. 1 in C 'Op. 44' (29 April 1926); in the harmonic breadth of the fourth of the 4 Scherzos (August 1925–January 1926) – see Plate 1 after the second-time bar – and in the cadential 'winding-down' that occurs at the end of the *Trio in Fantastic Form* (7 April 1926).

Of greater interest than these various influences *per se*, however, is the use to which Britten puts them, though it would be perverse to attach too much importance at this stage in his development to formal and syn-tactical niceties: in numerous contexts the composer evidently delights in expressive details and grand gestures for their own sake, and it could be argued that such involvement in 'the moment' is a more important attrib-ute for a beginning composer. Perhaps it is not surprising that the compositional situations in which the details most often don't 'add up' are developmental and transitional ones: statements are generally more con-trolled. The Trio in Waltz No. 5 (bars 25–72 of the whole) demonstrates this.[14] This Waltz forms the first of the published *Five Walztes*, but the original Trio was severely pruned in 1970: only bars 25–40 – simple vari-ants of the initial four-bar phrase – remain, with very few alterations. The

Example 1.2

Plate 1 No. 4 of Four Scherzos (1925–6), autograph manuscript

Example 1.3

Example 1.4

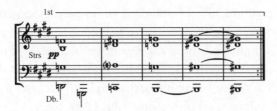

remainder of the original Trio was obviously seen as casting too much caution to the wind (it is clearly intended as intensificatory, with its sudden shift from 'maestoso' to 'vivace' in bar 29, its fractured harmonic progressions, and its left-hand crescendoing tremolos leading to grandiloquent V/V–V cadences). Endings of sections are sometimes the cue for harmonic 'purple passages', such as bars 23–31 of the Prelude of the Mass in E minor (Ex. 1.3) and the first-time bars of the first movement ('Presto con molto fuoco') of the untitled orchestral piece (Ex. 1.4). In general, though, even if the content is sometimes wayward, Britten had a reasonably secure grasp of form and long-term timing. Sometimes he followed conventional formal models, but he was equally happy to depart from them, as in the second movement of the Beethovenian Sonata in A for cello and piano (17 April 1926), which, after starting out as an Andante, turns into a scherzo.

Some of Britten's most expressive and polished music of this time comes from the setting of texts. A very early example is 'Beware' (1922–3), its simple but telling expression deriving from the contrast between chromaticism and diatonicism learnt from the lieder Britten heard and sometimes accompanied during musical evenings in the Britten household.[15] Another example is the ending of *The Elected Knight*. Marked 'lento pathetico', the sorrowful mood (occasioned by the opposing knights' slaughtering of each other) is distilled traditionally enough through chains of 7–6 suspensions; what is interesting in view of later operatic subject-matter is the appeal of a narrative with death as the final outcome.

The spring and summer of 1926 saw the beginnings of an updating of Britten's range of stylistic reference. He remarked in a letter to his mother dated 28 August that he had been to a concert at the Queen's Hall in London which 'was all modern music, and I have taken a great like to modern <u>Orchestral</u> music'.[16] The works included Ernest Schelling's *Suite fantastique* for piano and orchestra (1905), which he seems to have thought rather shallow, Delius's *Life's Dance* (1901; revised 1912), and three movements from Holst's *The Planets* (1914–16): 'Mars' (which he especially liked), 'Venus' and 'Mercury'. In fact, his fondness for orchestral music had already shown itself a few months earlier, when work on the Overture No. 1 initiated a one-and-a-half year period dominated by orchestral composition. By the standard of some of the surrounding pieces this overture, which exists in two versions, is disappointing: the material is undistinguished, the harmonic moves bald, and the orchestration clumsy. Neither have the stylistic horizons widened at this stage. They begin to do so, however, in his next completed orchestral piece, the Ouverture in B♭ minor (completed on 29 June) by 'Never Unprepared', the identifying motto Britten employed when he submitted the work to the BBC's 1926 Autumn Musical Festival Prize Competition.[17] The work is considerably more impressive than the earlier overture, not least in its orchestration. The wind and brass choirs are better voiced, for example, and the string writing is much more imaginative. The tonal moves within the otherwise standard nineteenth-century sonata-form design are also more adventurous. But perhaps the most remarkable feature of the music is its breadth, suggesting the example of Bruckner, or possibly, given the frequent use of measured tremolos, Sibelius.

More indicative of future directions, however, is the French influence in the *Suite fantastique* 'pour grand orchestra e con movemento quattro con pianoforte obbligato'. This, Britten's grandest conception to that date, was eventually completed on 5 September in time for his parents' silver-wedding anniversary, though the second movement ('Rondeau') was finished on 21 April before he began the Overture No. 1 in C. Cast in A minor, the work has as its first movement a reworking of the Trio from the second of the Ten Walztes.[18] Meanwhile 'Rondeau' displays here and there a genuine relish in orchestral sound for perhaps the first time in Britten's work, particularly in the solo passages for bassoon and trumpets and in the use of percussion (the latter evokes the Iberian music of Debussy and Ravel). The most striking orchestration in the work occurs in the huge (102-bar) cadenza of the fourth movement, entitled 'Fantasie-

Example 1.5

Concerto', where, during the last fifteen bars, the piano soloist is accompanied by six timpani (three players). This is clearly modelled on the slow movement of Berlioz's *Symphonie fantastique*, though Britten's use of the word 'fantastique' in his own title seems more likely to have been prompted by the Schelling work mentioned above (perhaps Britten's work was written as a criticism of the latter). In general the movement reverts to a more Romantic style, suggesting at times background models of Schumann and Grieg (the main key is again A minor). After the cadenza, however, a folk-like tune (Ex. 1.5) is introduced and played in various environments and guises, so that the work concludes with an English ambience.

At the end of September 1926 Britten embarked on the first of a series of works entitled 'Poème', completing the first on the 26th. Poème No. 1 is less resourceful orchestrally than *Suite fantastique*, but the series in general shows an increasingly imaginative and accomplished orchestral technique. In opening obliquely, Poème No. 1 also demonstrates increasing harmonic adventurousness. Poème No. 4 in B♭ (12–14 February 1927) continues Britten's exploration of oblique openings, with the B♭ triad outlined by the harp being blurred by conflicting pitches, including an E♮ and a G in the upper strings' melodic line, and a G♭ and a C in the viola. Principal harmonic shifts again include movement by major third (B♭–G♭–B♭ in bars 5–6). This is essentially a romantic legacy, but the blurred opening may suggest the influence of impressionism (Debussy – or perhaps, as a result of the concert mentioned in his letter of 28 August, Delius), and some aspects of the orchestration (frequent use of descending string tremolos, string divisi and harp arpeggios supporting woodwind solos) reinforce this. Debussyan method, if not Debussyan sound, also seems to lie behind the passage which begins as shown in Plate 2, where transpositions of a simple two-bar melody articulate a 'non-functional' harmonic succession.

The importance in Britten's mind of the Symphony in D minor (17 January – 28 February 1927) can be gauged by his subsequent arrangement of the work for two pianos, in which form it was no doubt

Plate 2 Poème No. 4 in B♭ (1927), autograph manuscript

performed in the Britten household. The forces required are very large, including triple woodwind plus oboe d'amore (which has a solo at the beginning of the third of the four movements, 'Andante'), eight horns, and percussion. The key is that of both Britten's mature symphonic instrumental works, *Sinfonia da Requiem* (1940) and the Symphony for Cello and Orchestra (1963); further premonitions of the *Sinfonia* include the major-minor (F♯/F♮) equivocations and D/B♭ juxtapositions in the

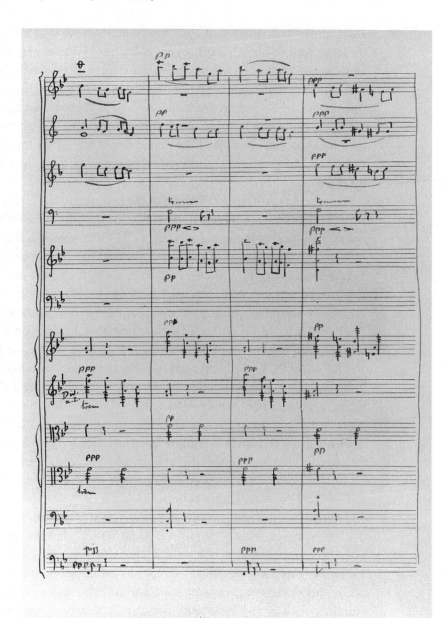

Plate 2 (*cont.*)

coda of the first movement, and the use of the major mode for the very
substantial Finale ('Allegro con brio'). Much of the work stems from the
Austro-German late-romantic tradition in expressive tone and gesture.
Britten had developed a significant interest in Wagner: he bought the
miniature score of *Siegfried Idyll* sometime between August and
November 1926 (and apparently often played it on the piano),[19] and
when he acquired the 'Prelude and Transfiguration' from *Tristan und*

Isolde in the first quarter of 1927 his Wagner scores totalled eight, just under a third of his miniature-score collection. Wagner may lie behind some of the chromatic counterpoint for strings in the first movement. Some moments, though, are post-Wagnerian; indeed a few, especially the opening of the Scherzo reproduced in Plate 3, suggest a composer who was to have a much more lasting influence: Mahler (though there is no documentary evidence that Britten had heard any of his music by this time, and Mahler is not an influence that looms large in the rest of the juvenilia).

It is the Austro-German flavour of the Symphony in D minor rather than the (less sustained) French stylistic leanings of the Poèmes that dominates the music of the remainder of 1927. (An exception is the modally inflected first movement of the String Quartet in A minor of June–July 1927.) Thus in the first movement ('Presto con molto expressione; ma non troppo agitato') of the String Quartet in G (March–May 1927) the essentially Germanic notion of opening obliquity already essayed in Poèmes Nos. 2 and 4 is expanded to the extent that no clear tonal centre is sighted until page 3, where G emerges as V of C in preparation for the second subject. The opening texture is Britten's most chromatic to this point in his output, and is notable for being integrated by a rhythmic figure, ♩♪♪♩♩, rather than a melodic shape. But perhaps the most interesting feature is the departure from the sonata-form archetype in the recapitulation: the latter is compressed and considerably varied, and is followed by an 'Allegro' coda which winds down to produce what seems to be Britten's first 'dissolving' ending, prefiguring those of the Phantasy Quintet and Phantasy Quartet (both 1932).[20]

Obliquity is put to highly atmospheric use at the beginnings of both *The Pale Stars are Gone* (29 July – 2 August 1927) and the 'symphonic poem for large orchestra', *Chaos and Cosmos* (22 August – 5 September 1927). *The Pale Stars*, for chorus, piano, and strings, sets part of the fourth act of Shelley's *Prometheus Unbound*, and contains some striking word-painting, such as the long-held, not-quite-resolving, gently dissonant chords underpinning 'winds that die on the bosom of their own harmony'. It also contains more diatonic, more 'English' sections (for instance the setting of 'The voice of the Spirits of Air and Earth'), an apparent retrogression in style in comparison with the Quartet in G that, as we shall see, is not unique in the juvenilia. *Chaos and Cosmos*, too, has passages that can be identified as English: the E-based folky viola tune that begins the second section ('Andante con molto moto e con molto expressione'), for instance, and the rhapsodic style in which it is extended. This is the more stable 'Cosmos' section; 'Chaos' ('Allegro moderato') is centred on an ambiguous half-diminished seventh (F♯–A–C–E), and it is

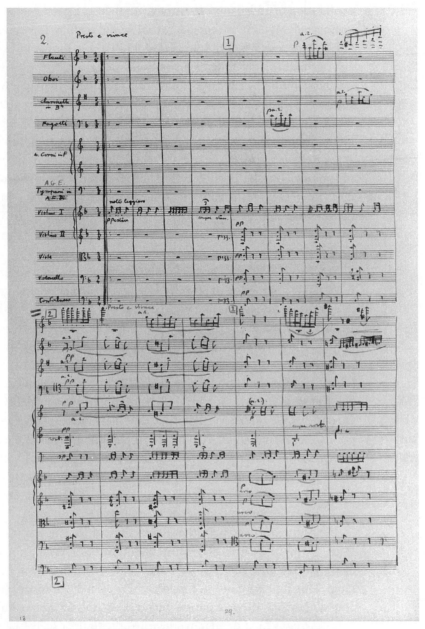

Plate 3 Scherzo from Symphony in D minor (1927), autograph manuscript

only at the end of this opening section that stable tonal orientation emerges (through V of E). The work is resolved in favour of 'Cosmos' when 'Chaos' string figures return within secure E major harmony.

The last substantial piece Britten completed before meeting Bridge on 27 October 1927 was the Sonata No. 10 in B♭ for piano (27 September 1927). This is characterized once again by opening obliquity and by the exploration of added-note harmony, but there is a good deal which seems unfinished. Much more consideration would seem to have gone into the first two movements of the Sonata No. 11 in B, also for piano, although the last of the three movements again looks rather rushed. This sonata was started at about the time of Britten's first meeting with Bridge but was not completed until sometime during the month after his first actual lesson, which took place over the period 11–13 January 1928.[21] The first movement, closer to C at the opening than the titular B major that emerges only at the close, is a sardonic march for which Prokofiev seems the most plausible model. But the 'Presto' section of the second movement contains the most interesting feature: the first instance in Britten of the influence of the metrical innovations associated with Stravinsky, with frequent changes of time signature and the overlaying of 2/4 and 3/4 in different hands.

It seems likely that Sonata No. 11 was discussed at the January lesson. It would be fascinating to know in exactly what terms. Britten referred to the nature of his lessons in a very general way in several sources, emphasizing Bridge's concern with professionalism and the importance of technique.[22] However, there is little detailed evidence of Bridge's response to specific contexts: there are only a few annotations on Britten's work (chiefly concerning alternative part-writing or harmonies, as in the Quartet in F (1928), Menuetto in A minor for piano (1928), and 'The Quartette' (1929) for SATB soloists), and these make relatively superficial points. It is impossible, therefore, to be definite about the part Bridge played in the major developments in Britten's style and technique. It seems likely that, rather than signalling specific directions, Bridge's principal role was to refine and coax, and at times (whether intentionally or not) to provide a position against which Britten could rebel.

It is, though, safe to infer that Bridge encouraged his pupil's interest in some of the more radical Continental figures, especially since Bridge's own style had undergone profound changes through his contact with the same. This influence did not emerge immediately, however. In *Dans les bois* (25 January 1928), a nature-picture probably stimulated by Bridge's *Enter Spring* (which Britten had heard at the time of their first meeting), the chief influence, not surprisingly, is turn-of-the-century French rather than contemporaneous Austro-German; and French, specifically Debussyan, influences also surface in *Humoreske* (6 March 1928), though they are less to the fore.[23] Meanwhile the String Quartet in F (11 April 1928) is conventional to a degree that suggests it might have been set as an exercise, though paradoxically it contains a quintessential Britten sonority – the syncopated major second, A/G, played by the second violin throughout the second movement. Elegy (16–23 April 1928), too, is an essentially diatonic work spiced with added-note chords, modal variants and fairly standard chromaticisms. Its fantasy-type form is rather diffuse, but the material is more economical, generated in the main from a small number of simple, concise thematic ideas.

Paralleling Britten's activity in the sphere of instrumental music was a passion for song-writing. As he himself wrote:

> between 1922 and 1930 when I was a schoolboy, I must have written well over fifty songs – most of them straight off without much thought; others were written and re-written many times in a determined if often unsuccessful effort to 'get them right'. The choice of poets was nothing if not catholic. There are more than thirty of them, ranging from the Bible to Kipling, from Shakespeare to an obscure magazine poet 'Chanticleer'; there were many settings of Shelley and Burns and Tennyson, of a poem by a schoolmaster friend, songs to texts by Hood, Longfellow, 'Anon', and several French poets, and one to the composer's own words ('one day when I went home, I sore a boat on the sands').[24]

Most of the songs are accompanied by piano. But the most celebrated and the most impressive of the songs completed before Britten entered the Royal College of Music were written for soprano and orchestra: the *Quatre chansons françaises* (13 June – 31 August 1928).

Given that the texts are French ('Les nuits de juin' and 'L'enfance' by Victor Hugo, 'Sagesse' and 'Chanson d'automne' by Paul Verlaine),[25] and given the French sonorities and procedures of some earlier orchestral scores, it is not surprising to find the influence of Ravel and Debussy; more surprising, perhaps, is what amounts to a reworking of the closing bars of Wagner's *Tristan und Isolde* at the end of the work, though Britten's interest in Wagner's music has been noted above. The correspondences are too close to be coincidental: both works end in the same key, enharmonically (B major in Wagner, C♭ major in Britten); the final cadences are very similar (both plagal variants); the spacing of the string parts is almost identical save for an extra E♭ in Britten; the last chord is stated three times by both composers; and the soprano ends on the same note. Even more intriguing is the apparent influence of Berg: the chord construction in bars 6–8 of the same song (Ex. 1.6) suggests the Viennese composer with its mixture of half-diminished chords (x), chords of fourths or fifths (y), and chords of fourth or fifth plus tritone (z).

The most remarkable idea in *Quatre chansons françaises* occurs in 'L'enfance'. A child sings outside the house where his mother lies dying, unaware of her condition: his innocence is symbolized by the flute's nursery tune, with which the movement begins.[26] The betrayal of that innocence is symbolised by the tune being at odds with the harmonic plane of the rest of the orchestra, both at the opening (bars 1–8) and

Example 1.6

during the setting of the poignant lines 'Et la mère, à côté de ce pauvre doux être / Qui chantait tout le jour, toussait toute la nuit' (bars 33–40: see Ex. 1.7).[27] The latter presents one of the most Brittenesque passages in the work both technically and, as Evans points out, in terms of its psychological acuity.[28]

It is clear from recent biographical research that Britten had a particularly intense relationship with his mother, and that he found separation from her painful when he moved to Gresham's School in September 1928; soon after he arrived he wrote to her saying 'I have had some horrible dreams lately about people being ill and dying.'[29] The possibility of impending separation influencing (consciously or subconsciously) the choice of 'L'enfance' as a text is intriguing, all the more so when the dedication of the songs – to his parents on their twenty-seventh wedding anniversary – is taken into consideration. Certainly leaving home was a major event, and even if Britten did not feel that this definitively marked the end of his childhood, it can be argued that the *Quatre chansons françaises* was his last childhood piece: although it is very far from the case that spontaneity is absent from the music he wrote between Autumn 1928 and the composition of the *Sinfonietta* in summer 1932, there is a distinct sense of composition being work rather than uninhibited play. It is at least worth asking the question whether Britten's obsession with lost innocence in his mature vocal works resulted in part from the imposition of

Example 1.7

adult, professional compositional responsibilities so early in life – however willing Britten might have been to adopt them.

The most obvious sign of the new seriousness is the amount of revising that Britten now undertook. Most of the major pieces of 1929 and the first half of 1930 were revised, or drafted in two or three versions. The *Elizabeth Variations* (13 January – 25 October 1929) appear to have been composed in a single day, but the work was later slightly revised and substantially extended by the addition of a sixth variation, a fughetta. The Rhapsodies for quartet (28 January – 21 March 1929) and violin, viola, and piano (30 March – 22 April 1929) exist in three and two versions respectively, while the Bagatelle (30 March 1929 – 15 January 1930) and 'The Birds' (first version, June 1930) have several preliminary drafts. The *Quartettino* (3 January – 17 April 1930), too, required a considerable amount of sketching.

The result of all this endeavour was a substantial gain in technique, the speed of which may be gauged by comparing the *Quatre chansons françaises* with the Rhapsody for quartet. Although these works were completed only just over six months apart, the definitive version of the Rhapsody displays a much surer touch in the unfolding of events as well as a marked advance in the art of transition. It is also a good deal more focused than the string Elegy completed eleven months earlier. The Rhapsody adapts sonata form in two ways. First, the sonata-form action is enclosed within an 'Andante' frame employing first-subject material. Second, sonata expectations are manipulated in the service of a refined and extended version of what was already for Britten a well-established harmonic archetype: the gradual emergence or clarification of the tonic.

No fewer than four other works from 1929 – three of them written for violin, viola and piano – end, like the Rhapsody, on C: the more diatonic *Elizabeth Variations*; the Rhapsody, in which C maintains a rather stronger profile than in the Rhapsody for quartet; the Two Pieces (17 November – 24 December 1929), in which the final accented unison C emerges rather less persuasively from more consistently non-tonal textures; and the Bagatelle, which partly reworks material from the Rhapsody for trio. Together with the Rhapsody for quartet and the *Introduction and Allegro* for viola and strings (21–31 October 1929), these works edge into increasingly chromatic territory, employing a style that owes much to late Bridge. The chromaticism peaks in the *Quartettino*; but before turning to that work a little more should be said of the *Elizabeth Variations* and another work with a diatonic basis, the *Miniature Suite* (26 January – 8 March), both of which introduce approaches of signal importance in Britten's development.

Indeed, in being based on a pitch-motto, C–E–B (the initials of Britten's sister, Charlotte Elizabeth (Beth) Britten), the *Elizabeth Variations* initiate an embryonic form of the intensive thematic working that was to characterize many of Britten's mature works; moreover, the notion of a 'fundamental shape', developed further almost immediately in the Two Pieces and *Quartettino*, plays an important role in such major works as *Our Hunting Fathers* (1936), *Peter Grimes* (1945), *The Turn of the Screw* (1954) and *Death in Venice* (1972). The *Miniature Suite*, too, has links with *The Turn of the Screw* in that, like the 'Screw' theme (see p. 106, Ex. 5.6), the main theme of the first movement ('Novelette') is built from a chain of disjunct fourths – A–D–B–E–C–F♯–D–G – though here the territory is diatonic rather than chromatic. Meanwhile the characteristic basis of the suite foreshadows much of Britten's instrumental music of the mid-1930s.

Mention of 'fundamental shapes' and intensive motivic working may bring to mind Schoenberg's concept of the *Grundgestalt* and the thematicism that informs so much of his music. It so happens that Britten was listening to and thinking about Schoenberg with considerable interest in late 1929 and early 1930 during the composition of the Two Pieces and the *Quartettino*. On 20 November he wrote in his diary that he was 'thinking much about modernism in art. Debating whether Impressionism, Expressionism, Classicism etc. are right. I have half-decided on Schönberg. I adore Picasso's pictures.'[30] A few months later, on 7 April 1930, he listened to a 'marvellous Schönberg concert' on the radio, including the Chamber Symphony, Op. 9 (in the arrangement by Webern), the

Suite for piano, Op. 25, and *Pierrot lunaire*, Op. 21; 14 April saw him buying a copy of the Six Little Pieces, Op. 19, and writing that he was 'getting very fond of Schönberg, especially with study'.[31] The Two Pieces are not actually called 'Zwei Stücke', but there is no doubting Schoenberg's background presence, even if Britten is not prepared to move away from tonal moorings to anywhere near the same degree. The beginning of the second piece even has a textural similarity with the opening of *Pierrot lunaire*, though it was apparently four months later that he heard Schoenberg's piece for the first time.

The Two Pieces are built on a motto of disjunct thirds, shown in Ex. 1.8 as Britten notated it. The lack of clef suggests that specific intervallic content is not so significant as contour, though thirds remain referential even if no single motive-form does. The same is the case in the *Quartettino*, the motto of which is shown in Ex. 1.9 along with some of the more important transformations. This is Britten's most ambitious work in the period between the *Quatre chansons françaises* and his entering the Royal College of Music in September 1930. Remarkably, there is no evidence of Bridge's involvement, though his Third Quartet (1926) must have been an important exemplar, not just of concentrated motivic techniques, but also of how to create a sense of motion in highly chromatic, non-functional textures: the controlling semitonal descent from A to E in the cello across the first 18 bars of the third movement has precedents (if not its actual source) in Bridge's Quartet (see for example Figs. 9ff. and 24ff. in the first movement of the Third Quartet). Another link between the *Quartettino* and the Two Pieces is the ending on a single accented pitch-class – this time C♯. As in the earlier work, such an emphasis cannot be regarded as a genuine tonal outcome, but it seems more appropriate here because C♯ is consistently stressed throughout the work.[32] If the trajectory of the piece cannot be said to involve the emergence or clarification of a tonic as in the Rhapsody for quartet, the overall formal gesture is very much related: the first movement does not attain closure, and while the second does, a sense of unfinished business persists until the clinching rhetorical gestures of the final page.

After completing a movement for wind sextet (7 August 1930) – for which a companion movement was begun but not completed – his next project, a series of three character sketches, was again for strings. Only two Sketches were completed: No. 1, subtitled 'D. Layton' (27 August 1930), and No. 2, 'E.B.B.' (10 September 1930); these pieces were performed under the title *Two Portraits* in 1996. No. 1 is a portrait of David Layton, a friend at Gresham's whom Britten was to describe in 1936 as 'my good looking, aristocratic, acme of ideal manhood, friend David Layton'.[33] No. 2, for viola solo and strings, is a rather melancholy self-portrait. Both

Example 1.8

Example 1.9

show something of a retreat from the chromaticism of the preceding instrumental works, No. 1 continuing Britten's predilection for ending with the C major triad, No. 2 beginning and ending in E Dorian. Neither Sketch was written up into a fair copy, suggesting that Britten was perhaps not entirely happy with them. Certainly they have problematic aspects: No. 1 has a tendency towards long-windedness due to thematic over-extension (the remorseless patterning of bars 3–7 is the first example of this), while the tune-and-accompaniment texture of No. 2 exposes the uncertainty of Britten's harmonic thinking at this time. But both have effective and memorable endings, especially No. 1, where – after a climax and aftermath at bars 250–66 of much greater harmonic clarity – violin I, violin II and viola soloists play the opening material in imitation over a sustained C major triad. Once again Bridge is the clearest stylistic reference: his fingerprints include the overlaid triads in bars 2–3 and 30–2; the semitonal voice-leading in the bass in bars 25–7, 30–2, 48–50, etc.; and the use of bass pedals as stabilizing devices at bars 56–62 (the tritonal approach here, D♭ moving to G at bar 56, is also reminiscent of Bridge) and 163–70 (both these pedals are on G and point to the eventual C outcome).

Twelve days after completing Sketch No. 2 Britten entered the Royal College of Music. John Ireland became his official teacher, initially setting him pastiche exercises such as the Mass in Palestrinian style that Britten worked on between October 1930 and January 1931.[34] However, Bridge remained his most trusted source of compositional advice, as Britten himself noted: 'I studied at the RCM from 1930–1933 but my musical education was perhaps more outside the college than in it. Although my teacher for composition was John Ireland, I saw Frank Bridge almost daily and I showed him every "major" work.'[35] In fact, it could be argued that the greatest educational opportunity afforded by the College came from its location: living in London allowed Britten access to performances of works that proved instrumental in helping him define his own territory.[36] The earliest of these performances – it took place on the day after he arrived at the College – was of Mahler's Fourth Symphony. Britten was equivocal about the impact of the work as a whole, writing in his diary that it was 'Much too long, but beautiful in [?] parts'.[37] We do not know which parts appealed most; if they were the luminous diatonic passages of the final movement they may well have contributed towards Britten's heavy investment in diatonicism in the first major work he completed at the RCM, the Christmas suite *Thy King's Birthday* (February – 26 March 1931; published by Faber Music in 1994 as *Christ's Nativity*). Another reason for Britten's apparent retreat from more radical territory might have been his need to distance himself from Bridge's influence; or it may reflect his exploration of aspects of Ireland's style, most obvious in the Three Pieces for piano (16 September – 27 December 1930) – three character sketches titled 'John', 'Daphne' and 'Michael' along the lines of the Sketches for strings. The most straightforward explanation is the work's relationship to the conservative English choral tradition: the original version of *A Hymn to the Virgin* (9 July 1930) had already taken what seems like a retrogressive step.[38] Or Britten might simply have been able to see greater potential for structural control and depth, and hence expressive power, in a fundamental diatonicism.

Thy King's Birthday inevitably invites parallels with *A Boy Was Born* (November 1932 and May 1933). Cast in five movements,[39] the earlier work seems to have been conceived on a larger scale than that disclosed by the finished product – several other settings were begun but not completed – so that *A Boy Was Born* may be seen as the successful second attempt at the realization of an ambitious idea. As it is, *Thy King's Birthday* is loosely structured in comparison with its successor: although there are thematic relationships between some of the movements, there is nothing like the motivic saturation of *A Boy Was Born*, or its rigorous large-scale control of harmonic areas. The looseness of structure in the earlier work was conveyed in Britten's diary entry for 30 March 1931: 'Write some more var. [the Twelve Variations for piano] in morning & stick my "Thy King's Birthday" together'.[40] Meanwhile the textural resourcefulness of *A Boy Was Born* is adumbrated in passages of 'Christ's Nativity' and 'Preparations', though the second part of 'New Prince, New Pomp' (from bar 20) has perhaps rather too much of the classroom about it (Britten had completed his Palestrinian Mass a few weeks earlier). The composer revived 'New Prince, New Pomp' for performance at the 1955 Aldeburgh Festival, but it is the other number heard (in a revised version) during his lifetime – 'Sweet was the Song', first performed at the 1966 Festival – that seems the most fully achieved and, through its simplicity, warm sonorities, and ambivalent modality, most indicative of the Britten to come.

Although Britten continued to write vocal music during his time at the RCM – the *Three Small Songs* (8–24 June 1931) and two Psalm settings, No. 150 (26 December 1931) and No. 130 (19 January 1932), are the most substantial examples – it was in instrumental music that the most important gains in technique were made. His first major instrumental score of the College years, the String Quartet in D (8 May – 2 June 1931) – the first pre-*Sinfonietta* instrumental score to see the light of day, when Britten revised it in 1975 after his heart operation – reworks the overall shape of the *Quartettino* and continues the composer's interest in thematic integration, though this time with a greater fund of motives (four basic shapes), allowing a greater variety of melodic invention. The opening unison seven-bar statement is drawn from the D major collection, reinforcing Britten's commitment to diatonicism. The final is ambiguous, and Britten seeks to brace the span of the work with a quest for a clearly defined tonal centre: as in the *Quartettino*, the first movement does not achieve closure, and the opening material returns at the end of the final movement (bars 272ff.) before matters are concluded with a D-based chord. This fundamental goal often seems to sink below the horizon, however, largely because of the diffusing effect of the clotted added-note harmony redolent of some of the senior figures associated with the RCM at that time.

A significant step towards a more focused style was taken in Britten's first stage work, the ballet *Plymouth Town* (composed 12–28 August 1931; the full score was completed on 22 November), written to a scenario by Violet Alford and based on the folksong 'A-Roving'.[41] The simple plot presages Britten's typical operatic subject-matter: an innocent sailor is led astray by the lure of drink and sex, and returns to his ship a wiser man, in Prodigal Son fashion. Musically, the textures are leaner and the writing generally more economical. Britten's celebrated gift for sharp character-ization is already apparent in the luminous 'Good Girl' music, while the passage depicting the errant sailor's lonely misery contains, in the high-lighted flattening of E to E♭, a highly Brittenesque gesture. Also prescient is a moment of drama in the 'Bad' Farandole when, after the crowd begins to fight amongst itself, the trumpets of the Marine Patrol are heard off stage,[42] subsequently taking over proceedings by developing their music into a march: the layering involved here anticipates that of Act II scene 1 of *Peter Grimes*. While modality is frequently less ambiguous than in stretches of *Thy King's Birthday* and the String Quartet in D major (the opening, for instance, is solidly B♭ Mixolydian), the role of movement away from referential collections (often involving the careful balancing of sharpwards and flatwards excursions) is rather more sharply defined. A new feature is the mirror harmony of the 'Good Advice' motif, presaging the string harmony at Fig. 11^{-2} in the slow movement of the *Sinfonietta*. Meanwhile, the use of pedals to build up tension over quite long spans is reminiscent of Walton, though Britten was yet to hear his Viola Concerto and *Belshazzar's Feast*.[43]

An important consequence of Britten's composing a dance work was that it concentrated his mind on rhythm: it is noticeable that, in compari-son with the String Quartet in D, the opening of the Phantasy in F minor (25 January – 11 February 1932) – the first major instrumental piece com-posed after the ballet – is far more propulsive rhythmically, even if later profiles are not quite so taut. The way in which the opening cello line builds through 'evolutionary variation' provides a foretaste of another process used to more powerful effect in later works, as does the semitonal friction introduced in bar 5 and subsequently amplified into a conflict between modes based on G and A♭ between Fig. 9^{+3} and Fig. 12 (though here the harmonic energy released is not harnessed to long-term struc-tural ends). A general intention to pursue a greater degree of focus is also apparent in the pared-down 'slow movement' textures, and in Britten's treatment of the fantasy form: the work was written as an entry for the Cobbett Chamber Music Prize, but the composer departed from the customary loosely organized assemblage in favour of a scheme developed in the nineteenth century and used most notably in the early twentieth century by Schoenberg in his First String Quartet, Op. 7, and First Chamber Symphony, Op. 9 – the integration, in one continuous span, of music of first-movement, scherzo, and slow-movement character. Once more the chief agent of integration is thematic variation and transformation, effected with perhaps even greater virtuosity than in the *Quartettino* and the String Quartet in D.[44] Again there is no underpinning tonal structure as such: the ambiguity of the dissolving ending (F minor/C minor) is a local phenomenon.

The Phantasy Quintet received its first performance on 22 July 1932 as the Cobbett Prize winner, and the String Quartet in D was tried out by the Stratton Quartet on 16 March 1932, but Britten did not hear many performances of his work at this stage (*Plymouth Town* was submitted to the Camargo Society but not taken up).[45] Perhaps the poor prospects for performance discouraged him from scoring the Concerto in B minor for violin and viola (9 March – 4 May 1932) – it exists only in sketch form, with detailed annotations as to instrumentation – though his diary entries might suggest he did not take the project further because he was so dissatisfied with his efforts: on 21 March he wrote of having written 'a fatuous slow movement for my concerto', and on the 29th he noted he had composed 'more of last mov. of Concerto in morning – I shall tear *that* up soon'.[46] But in many ways this is the finest version before the *Sinfonietta* of the three-movement archetype introduced by the *Quartettino*. Particularly noteworthy is the motivic integration of horizontal and vertical material (Schoenberg's 'unity of musical space'), as in the opening stretch reproduced in Ex. 1.10: the framework of fourths underpinning the horn's fanfare grows out of the underlying chord of fifths.

The distance from here to a work deserving the official status of Op. 1 is not great. The gap was bridged by the *Introduction and Allegro* (20 May 1932) and the incomplete ballet on a Basque scenario (June 1932). Both works consolidate or refine aspects of technique that contribute vitally to the dynamism of the *Sinfonietta*, especially movement through the circle of fifths by collection, which is more extensive than before (this plays a central role in the first and last movements of Op. 1),[47] and evolutionary variation (which makes a considerable advance in the *Introduction and Allegro*); the more propulsive rhythmic style of *Plymouth Town* and the Concerto is also consolidated. The area still requiring the most substantial work was the management of slow-movement textures: even after taking into account the need for greater expansiveness in a piece for two soloists, the Concerto has a good degree of rhapsodic indulgence in the middle movement (it may have been this that led to Britten's despairing

Example 1.10

comment quoted above), and the *Introduction and Allegro*, abetted by the fantasy format, hardly represents an advance. Indeed, the gains in slow-movement conception in Op. 1 are hard-won, and in his Op. 2, the *Phantasy Quartet* (1932) – his final exercise in fantasy form – Britten still finds it difficult to dispel the rhapsodizing tendency. The problem was one of identity: while his technique was already approaching that of a virtuoso, it would be a number of years before certain questions of style would be fully resolved.

2 Britten, Auden and 'otherness'

PAUL KILDEA

I marvel what kin thou and thy daughters are: they'll have me whipp'd for speaking true, thou'lt have me whipp'd for lying; and sometimes I am whipp'd for holding my peace. I had rather be any kind o'thing than a fool ... *King Lear*, Act I scene 4

In late September 1938 – in the aftermath of the Anschluss and the German invasion of Austria, and in the fool's-gold glow of the Munich conference – *The Times* published a delightfully pompous editorial:

> At moments like this it is especially fitting that we should pay homage to poets – not for their own sakes (they are sufficiently blessed in 'their magic robes, their burning crown'), but for the sake of that clearer vision which their eyes, superimposed on our own failing sight, can restore to us.[1]

Less than two years later, with W. H. Auden and Christopher Isherwood discovering a brave new American way of life, an epigram was printed in the *Spectator* (its author rumoured to be the Dean of St Paul's):

> 'This Europe stinks', you cried – swift to desert
> Your stricken country in her distress.
> You may not care, but still I will assert
> Since you have left us, here the stink is less.[2]

This short journey from the public's conscience to its whipping boy of course reflects the change in Britain's and Auden's domestic circumstances; yet it also delineates a *public* conception of the poet's role in society. This was a relatively new phenomenon – one shaped on the Somme and at Ypres but ultimately refined in the politically turbulent 1930s. Moreover, this public delineation of role came from both sides of the political debate: *The Times* was the Establishment newspaper, while the *Spectator* – not yet the right-wing zoo it would delight in being fifty years later – published many young and left-wing intellectuals of the day. Yet it is a mistake to specify a collective artistic identity in this decade, no matter how neat the parameters of Depression and War. Artistic frictions and factions existed then as they do now. There were, however, numerous circumstances which drew together artists in the 1930s, and which fostered the contemporary and retrospective tendency to classify a 1930s collective identity. As society looked more to artists for intellectual leadership, many responded, and in doing so defined themselves a social role. Vanity and self-importance were often the motivation; naivety and a sense of righteousness more often so. For many artists the events of the decade had a lasting effect on their work; for others, the overtly political nature of their art appeared dated once the war was over and the battle mistakenly assumed to have been won.

Auden and Britten created their own artistic identity in the 1930s, one which is often cited as the template of 1930s collectivism. Yet this is too pat and simple a description of two artists whose minds and work were changing and developing continuously throughout the decade – notwithstanding their appointment (particularly Auden's) as guardian or commander of the period's new, and supposedly constant, aesthetic. Yet the decade was anything but constant; both Britten and Auden, for example, arrived in the 1930s with hefty baggage, jettisoning some but collecting more before their symbolic (and actual) departure ten years later. Their intellectual development and expression was the result of several influences: upbringing and schooling; the political climate in England between the wars; changing concepts of class; debates about the function of the artist. Moreover, their friendship and artistic collaborations in the 1930s had long-term intellectual repercussions that shaped and drove their post-war work. And although it has become popular (and accurate) to describe Britten's post-war dramatic music in language of the 1930s – the individual, the crowd, the masses[3] – to locate these themes solely within the confines of his homosexuality is to rob each work of its vibrant intellectual origins, which are located firmly in the 1920s and 1930s.

By his own reckoning, W. H. Auden was 'mentally precocious, physically backward, short-sighted, a rabbit at all games, very untidy and grubby, a nail-biter, a physical coward, dishonest, sentimental, with no community sense whatever, in fact a typical little highbrow and difficult child'.[4] He grew up in a middle-class professional family with a doctor for a father and a university-educated mother. 'There was a rain-gauge on the lawn and a family dog. There were family prayers before breakfast, bicycle-rides to collect fossils or rub church-brasses, reading aloud in the evenings. We kept pretty much to ourselves. Mother was often ill.'[5] Auden read widely from his father's eclectic library – not the stockpile of a 'literary man nor of a narrow specialist, but a heterogeneous collection of books on many subjects'.[6] Instead of novels, texts on medicine, archaeology and the classics reigned. Auden's education, at Gresham's School in Holt (1920–5), included few of the Victorian excesses of other public schools. He recalled instead an often liberal education philosophy, where athletics was treated 'as something to be enjoyed and not made a fetish of', and where every kind of hobby was encouraged.[7]

Benjamin Britten experienced a similar upbringing and identical schooling – attending Gresham's from 1928 to 1930 – and he littered his recollection of this period with icons of middle-class adolescence:

> I had started playing the piano and wrote elaborate tone poems lasting about twenty seconds, inspired by terrific events in my home life such as the departure of my father for London, the appearance in my life of a new girl friend or even a wreck at sea ... At school I somehow managed to be able to fit in a great deal of composing with the extremely full life that every schoolboy leads. (I don't think my school work suffered nor my games, which I was passionately keen on.)[8]

Like Auden, Britten's reading was catholic; unlike Auden, however, the young composer's taste was exclusively literary, heavily dependent upon nineteenth-century (romantic) masterpieces. Such taste in literature was by no means unusual for someone of his background; school and home would have supplied such texts – and resonances with the subject-matter – with abandon. His library was supplemented with books of films or plays he had recently seen; word and image were married young in Britten's mind, an important factor in his development as an opera composer. A sample year of Britten's reading is detailed in Table 2.1. The collection, from 1933 (two years before Britten and Auden first met), is representative of this period in its predominantly conservative, non-political nature.

This careful, conservative taste in literature is reflected in the songs and choruses Britten set before 1932, the year of his Opus 1. Quite apart from the many instrumental and orchestral works, Britten's juvenilia include seventy-odd fragments or completed vocal works with identifiable authors – five of which are settings of biblical texts. Authors include Henry Constable, Walter de la Mare, John Fletcher, John Gay, Victor Hugo, John Keats, Rudyard Kipling, Henry Wadsworth Longfellow, Charles Sackville, Sir Walter Scott, Shakespeare, Shelley, Tennyson and Wordsworth.[9] On the whole, the poems demonstrate gentle respect of metre and rhyme, no doubt making them attractive to a young composer still developing ideas of form and genre. Although Britten's juvenilia include settings of a few texts by contemporary authors, they are neither political in conception nor modernist in demeanour; post-war political upheaval, economic and social restructuring, and startling new trends in English literature had not yet touched the composer.

Of the seventy-odd texts, fourteen are by Walter de la Mare. Although contemporary – he was born in 1873 and died in 1956 – de la Mare's poetry continued the vibrant pastoralist tradition of the nineteenth century. It

Table 2.1 Benjamin Britten: fiction read, 1933

Date	Author	Title
6/7 January	Henry James	*The Turn of the Screw*
23 January	Katherine Mansfield	Unspecified
18 February	John Galsworthy	*The Forsyte Saga*
18–21 February		*Man of Property*
5/6 March	Axel Munthe	*The Story of San Michele*
31 March	Erich Kästner	*Emil and the Detectives*
9 April	George Bernard Shaw	*Black Girl in Search for her God*
11 April	John Galsworthy	*White Monkey*
23 May	Charlotte Brontë	*Jane Eyre*
4 June	Anatole France	*The Blue Tree on the Wall*
1/8 August	Emily Brontë	*Wuthering Heights*
10 August	George Eliot	*Scenes from Clerical Life*
7 September	J. B. Priestley	*The Good Companions*
11 October	H. G. Wells	*The Bulpington of Blub*
29 October		Unspecified ghost stories
12 November	W. M. Thackeray	*A Tragic Tale*
19/20 November	H. G. Wells	*Joan and Peter*
22 November	Lewis Carroll	*Alice through the Looking-Glass*
2 December	Jules Renard	*Poil de Carotte*
25 December	Lewis Carroll	Unspecified

was a genre which fascinated Britten; many of his other early settings explore pastoral themes. One of the de la Mare poems – 'Silver' – is the perfect embodiment of this tradition, with its silver moon, fruit, trees, thatch, paws, feathers, claws, eyes, reeds and stream; nature assembled in one versatile, shimmering, mysterious hue. Britten's setting of this poem dates from 1928 – the year in which he entered Gresham's and began composition lessons with Frank Bridge. It is intensely chromatic and self-consciously impressionistic (his first Ravel miniature scores date from this year, and he had heard Bridge's *The Sea* the previous year, a work which had made a tremendous impression on him).[10] Yet for all its Continental harmonic aspirations there is, at least in the text, something reassuringly English. As Arnold Whittall argues, the pastoral genre emphasises the serene, Arcadian aspects of rural life. Nature is idealized and commonly invoked in a nostalgic, reverential manner.[11] And although this was by no means an exclusively English phenomenon, its adoption by those keen to forge an English identity in music in the face of German cultural domination made the two nearly synonymous. Britten's use of this theme was no childhood folly: his much later *Spring Symphony*, *Serenade* and *Nocturne* all celebrate pastoral poetry and images. But, as Whittall argues, these last two works play on the generic associations of the pastoral, perhaps in an attempt to wrest it back from a possessive Vaughan Williams.

Before 1932, then, a poem's words, structure and sound were perhaps more important to Britten than its ideas. His settings were 'functionless' –

aesthetic tributes to literary heroes, journeys through rural England, signposts in his developing craft as a composer. He had good instinct for words and phrases, while his choice of text reflected his middle-class upbringing, a Romantic view of nature, and his conception of what poetry was 'about'. Auden, too, considered home-life to be an important literary and artistic influence, later citing the intractable opinions and prejudices stemming entirely from his upbringing: knowledge was something to be sought for its own sake; life was ruled by mysterious forces; strangers and cheery gangs were disliked and best avoided, while businessmen and all who worked for profit rather than salary were contemptible.[12]

Although this eclectic list (including the unformulated reference to socialism) is more sophisticated than anything Britten would have penned at the time, there was still another bond between the young Britten and Auden. Their parents, as middle-class professionals, belonged to a Conservative-dominated culture – one designed and nurtured in southern England. The Tory Party remained in power in Britain – either in its own right or as the dominant force in a coalition – for all but three of the inter-war years.[13] It was in this political culture that Britten and Auden were born and bred; apart from the brief and unsuccessful Labour governments in 1923 and at the height of the Depression, they would have known no other. Moreover, this was no party of toothless tigers: in the inter-war years it had a large majority.[14] The Conservatives were born to rule, a catch-cry which either fuelled or explained the pervading air of political arrogance and superiority.

An understanding of the social make-up of the elected and the electors is vital if Auden's and Britten's response to the status quo in the 1930s is to make sense. In the 1930s the majority of elected Members of Parliament were educated at public school and university – in 1935, 81 percent and 57 percent respectively.[15] Moreover, almost half the members of inter-war Conservative Cabinets were aristocrats, with land, money and a way of life to protect. Understandably, the social and educational pedigree of successive Tory governments had a huge impact on life in Britain. As the historian Ross McKibbin has established, the whole rationale of the Conservatives between the wars – and the reason behind their electoral dominance – was the party's attitude towards the 'haves' and the 'have-nots':

> From the first half of 1920 onwards . . . Britain lived under a 'deflationary'
> regime which put the safety of the financial institutions ahead of the
> interests of manufacturing industry, which did not seek large-scale
> unemployment but was happy to live with it as part of a long-term
> 'adjustment', which pursued persistently deflationary budgets, determined

a fixed exchange rate that, when abandoned in 1931, more or less everyone said was indefensible, and, though it was not seen as such, *plainly put the anxieties of one social class over those of all the others.*[16]

As a result, stereotypes about working-class behaviour abounded, carefully differentiated from the habits and beliefs of the middle classes; 'class wisdoms became conventional wisdom and common sense was validated by class-pride'.[17] There were hefty economic arguments buttressing these conventional wisdoms. Entrenched middle-class fear of inflation – with the example of Germany's crippling hyper-inflation firmly in mind – gave the Tories a stick with which to beat believers and non-believers alike. Economic and social orthodoxies marched together hand in hand; then – as now – economic rationalism governed social conscience and, to a degree, behaviour. The intellectual and artistic repercussions of this union were never more obvious than in the new system of censorship. With apparently little effort, the government designed a structure which promoted institutionalized interference in art and free speech – sacred tenets of the Left.

With these carefully propagated, real or imagined, national or international threats to a new and comfortable way of life, to vote Conservative became the 'natural' thing for the middle classes to do; frighteningly, as McKibbin notes, those who did not were considered deviant. More significantly, perhaps, in a period when the Labour Party championed the rights and interests of the workers, many of its supporters were more interested in distancing themselves self-consciously from the status quo, expressing or reinforcing their 'otherness' through the ballot box. Labour ideology and bright-eyed idealism were sometimes a mere by-product.

There was something in this restructured, interventionist social system which was uncomfortably close to that experienced by both Auden and Britten at Gresham's. Indeed, their reaction to conservative English society was partly driven by a retrospective intellectual rebellion against their schooling. Although Gresham's had been academically advanced, it had also been socially repressive. Its code of honour – that students should not swear, smoke or do anything indecent, and should report on others if they so behaved – played on the boys' sense of loyalty and community. 'By appealing to it', Auden later noted, 'you can do almost anything you choose, you can suppress the expression of all those emotions, particularly the sexual, which are still undeveloped.' Moreover, like a modern dictator

you can defeat almost any opposition from other parts of the psyche, but if you do, if you deny these other emotions their expression and development, however silly or shocking they may seem to you, they will not only never grow up, but they will go backward, for human nature cannot stay still; they will, like all things that are shut up, go bad on you . . . The best reason I have for opposing Fascism is that at school I lived in a Fascist state.[18]

Although Auden was referring to Fascism in literal rather than colloquial terms, there was enough in England's increasingly conservative and uniform social climate for him to oppose – partly because of his developing political consciousness, and partly because of the similarities between *verkrampte* English society and the school he had left and now opposed. Moreover, Auden continued to think of school as a metaphor for socially repressive systems ('Politically a private school is an absolute dictatorship where the assistant staff play, as it were, Goering Roehm Goebbels Himmler to a headmaster Hitler'[19]) and transferred his schoolboy intellectual dissension into obvious protest. During the General Strike of 1926, when many of his Oxford contemporaries went to London to assist the government by driving buses or policing streets, Auden supported the strikers – in this instance not through an understanding of the arguments at stake, but 'out of sheer contrariness'.[20]

Britten's and Auden's rebellion against this familiar, adolescent social system was fuelled by their homosexuality. Before the decriminalization of homosexuality in Britain in 1967, gay men and lesbians trod the path of the non-Conservative voter between the wars: both stood outside the prevailing social conception of natural behaviour. The 'otherness' of a non-Conservative homosexual in the 1930s was complete. Jean Genet described part of this social conflict when he noted that a homosexual was a man 'who by his nature is out of step with the world, who refuses to enter into the system that organises the entire world. The homosexual rejects that, denies that, shatters that whether he wants to or not . . . to live with surprises, changes, to accept risks, to be exposed to insult . . .'[21] The language here is vitally important: systems, organization, rejection, denial, risks are primarily political not sexual terms. Homosexuality was a sociopolitical – not just personal – issue. Paradoxically, Genet's view was expressed outside the gay world as well. In the aftermath of legalization the Earl of Arran told his fellow peers that 'no amount of legislation will prevent homosexuals from being the subject of dislike and derision, or at best of pity. *We shall always, I fear, resent the odd man out.*'[22]

Auden and Britten dealt with their sexuality at different rates, and with varying degrees of gusto. At school Auden combined sexual priggishness with extreme repression, and drew deeply on his Anglo-Catholic background to lecture others on the dangers of masturbation. These dangers were certainly implicit in the school's code of honour, but there were wider social resonances – in Baden-Powell's army of sexually controlled boy scouts, and in the physical culture movement, for example.[23] This extension of the school code on yet another level – so that middle-class English society exhibited all the irritating, priggish characteristics of a minor public school – made it quite natural for Auden to debunk his once-held beliefs on human sexuality – and not merely out of contrariness. Helped by the sexually liberating environment of Oxford – which displayed the amorous characteristics of many an older public school – Auden embarked upon a number of affairs and exploits. He was helped in this by his newly liberated politics: as his colleague Louis MacNeice wrote at the time, comradeship was the 'communist substitute for bourgeois romance; in its extreme form . . . it leads to an idealization of homosexuality'.[24]

Britten was less quick to rid himself of Gresham's morality. His conflict with his own sexuality lasted for most of the 1930s. Auden had known him for less than two years when he penned this prescient observation of the composer's character:

> Underneath the abject willow,
>   Lover, sulk no more;
> Act from thought should quickly follow:
>   What is thinking for?
> Your unique and moping station
>   Proves you cold;
>   Stand up and fold
> Your map of desolation.[25]

Despite such implorations, Britten was slow to act on his sexual feelings (indeed in his setting of the poem Britten rebukes Auden's patronizing tone with a mocking accompaniment); without doubt he was not helped by his post-Gresham's education – certainly not in the way that Auden had been. The Royal College of Music, which Britten attended from 1930 to 1933, was as conservative as Oxford was liberal. Without the great University's quaint customs, dining clubs, intellectual pretences, union debates (the scandalous 1933 resolution 'That this House will in no circumstances fight for its King and Country', for example) and, most importantly, its geographic and demographic separation from Society Proper, the RCM stultified the young Britten – musically and personally. Its ambition for its students was far narrower than Oxford's: mere competence on a musical instrument was often and depressingly the *ne plus ultra*. Its anti-intellectual outlook ensured that the influence of Britten's schooling and home-life lasted well into the 1930s, unchallenged by anything other than his own doubts.

The traditions, hierarchies, prudery and language of Britten's schooling continued to hold sway over the composer for most of the 1930s. It is no coincidence that as late as 1937 – before he had rid himself of his Gresham's-formed opposition to sexual 'deviance' and had begun his first successful homosexual relationship – he described a meeting with William Walton in public-school vernacular: 'He is charming, but I feel always the school relationship with him – he is so obviously the head-prefect of English music, whereas I'm the promising young new boy. Soon of course he'll leave & return as a member of the staff.' Britten duly appointed Vaughan Williams headmaster and hastily made Elgar a member of the governing board.[26] Donald Mitchell has written of Britten's fascination with the innocence of his school days and of the tendency of Auden and his fellow writers to draw on the schoolroom as a literary source.[27] ('The saga-world is a schoolboy world, with its feuds, its practical jokes, its dark threats conveyed in puns and riddles and understatements', insisted Isherwood when describing Auden's early poetry.[28]) Mitchell has also written on Britten's language and his habit, in the 1930s, of using schoolboy slang (a characteristic of many artists and writers in the 1930s): things were often 'beastly nice', 'simply topping', and 'absolutely ripping'.[29] Each of Mitchell's points is certainly true, but more intriguing is the inherent contradiction between this cosy view of the schoolroom as haven – a tabernacle in which the myths, memories and sexual potential of preparatory and public school are jealously guarded and perpetuated – and the more severe reading of the classroom as a metaphor specifically for fascism or generally for an insidious social conformity.[30] The contradiction between these two views was never entirely resolved by either Auden or Britten, since the language of the schoolroom seduced and charmed its users (and its initiated readers) because of its *public* homosexual sub-texts and metaphors (as opposed to Forster's explicit, yet unpublished, private short stories or his novel *Maurice*). As Valentine Cunningham argues, 'Spender's attitude to the Spanish Civil War soldiery – like Owen's towards the youthful combatants of the First World War – is deeply mixed up in homosexual affections';[31] adolescent schoolroom imagery is his vehicle of expression. In his poem 'Ultima Ratio Regum', a boy lies dying under the olive tree, who was, in Spender's reality, 'a better target for a kiss'. It was Britten's reality too: soon after the outbreak of war, Britten wrote of his devastation at 'the fascists lining up all the little Popular Front boys against a wall & putting the machine guns on them. Imagine English boys of 14 even knowing what Popular Front means – much less dying for it.'[32] The fact that, at this stage of the war, such stories were unconfirmed and unlikely further emphasises Britten's easy identification with the symbology of the schoolboy. Moreover, the easy use of social and political vernaculars is of the utmost significance when analysing the later Britten–Auden collaborations.

For all their coy, homoerotic deference to the myth and associations of the Great English Public School, and their use of it in their work, first Auden and then Britten nevertheless developed a genuine interest in British and European politics in the late 1920s to mid-1930s. Some form of apostasy – some reaction to this stable upbringing, with its dominance of conservative economic and social values and its repressive moral code – was perhaps inevitable, but not necessarily political. Auden's first revolution, for example, was purportedly literary:

AUDEN: I have torn up all my poems.
COGHILL [Auden's Oxford Tutor]: Indeed! Why?
AUDEN: Because they were no good. Based on Wordsworth. No good nowadays.
COGHILL: Oh ...?
AUDEN: You ought to read Eliot. I've been reading Eliot. I now see the way I want to
    write. I've written two new poems this week. Listen![33]

The antithetical role-models are rather telling – Wordsworth reinforcing pastoral imagery to which even the adolescent Auden succumbed, Eliot being one of the true modernists in early twentieth-century English poetry. Yet new (political) ideas accompanied this new role-model: a refreshing rebuttal to the idea that the young Auden was a mythical figure – Athene, perhaps, who sprang, fully grown, from the brain of Zeus – born to take on the Messianic role he was assigned in the 1930s. A wonderfully evocative poem from September 1932 begins:

> I have a handsome profile
> I've been to a great public school
> I've a little money invested
> Then why do I feel such a fool
> As if I owned a world that has had its day?[34]

The iconography is clear: public school, investments, and even the handsome (well-groomed) profile are straight from upper-middle-class parlance – originally his own. Each trinket is debunked by the end of this first stanza, for such classic middle-class icons have no place in a culture struggling to survive. This decay and anticipated annihilation of civilization was a common enough theme in the 1920s, yet Auden's conversion to the cause was relatively late. Once undertaken, however, his poetry, reviews and prose developed the tenets of socialism.

Britten, too, underwent a literary rebellion, guided by Auden's watchful (if dogmatic) eye. Much later, in a BBC interview with the Earl of Harewood, he acknowledged his literary debt to Auden. 'I had always read poetry', he said, 'but the person, I think, who developed my love was the poet, Auden, whom I met, I think, in . . . [my] late 'teens.' The influence was not only literary, as Britten conceded ('I was very much influenced by Auden, not only in poetry but in life too; *and politics, of course, came very strongly into our lives in the late Thirties*'), although literature was perhaps its genesis:

> He showed me many things. I remember, for instance, he it was who introduced me to the works of Rimbaud, who was only a name to me then . . . [he] showed me the different periods in verse. I remember he showed me Chaucer for the first time. I'd always imagined that was a kind of foreign language, but as he read it, which was very well, I understood almost immediately what it meant, and I find now that it isn't so difficult to read – one must just have confidence and read ahead and then the meaning comes very strongly, very easily.[35]

The confidence to read and understand poetry outside the pastoral constraints of his upbringing was indeed an important gift; thereafter, Britten's literary taste became more sophisticated. This change in taste is illustrated by the fact that none of the poems Britten set as a youth appears in Auden's 1950 Viking Penguin anthology of romantic poets, yet many of those set by the mature composer are included.

As he conceded to the Earl of Harewood, Britten's growing literary sophistication was not concerned solely with style, since by 1935 Auden's politics and his literature were intertwined. Art was part of political discourse, and left-wing political ideology was the chosen weapon since it bucked against the pervasive uniformity of conservative middle-class values ('As if I owned a world that has had its day'). Defining and disputing ideologies of class was part of the politics of the left; giving the working class – the masses – a voice was an important element in this debate. But, as with homosexuality, class war would have been attractive to Auden regardless of its political associations as yet another tool with which to attack the well-defined buttresses of the status quo.

Rebellion against this status quo was not without ideological conflicts, two of which were serious. First, how were artists and composers to redress the biased, middle-class nature of high art in a way which appealed to and was understood by the working classes, but which still respected the generic expectations of the art form? And, second, how were artists to act as court poet – with or without magic robes and burning crowns – to a society and class they despised?

The origins of this first conflict, as far as they concern Britten and Auden, are easy to trace. Auden's 'contrariness' at school had set him apart from his peers and had developed in him a distaste for crowds. Yet by the time composer and poet met, Auden was aligning himself with the 'others' – paradoxically, in the 1930s Britain described above, these 'others' were in part working-class crowds, the masses. His 1935 collection of poems, *The Poet's Tongue*, contains much poetry of the people; as Samuel Hynes notes, Auden drew upon traditional popular forms such as the ballad, the riddle and the music-hall song, genres which previously played little part in high-art poetry.[36] Similarly, his libretto for Britten's first opera, *Paul Bunyan*, is a celebration of popular literary genres (see below). Yet the paradox remained; regardless of his ideological convictions, Auden maintained an *aesthetic* dislike of the masses:

> A digit of the crowd, would like to know
> Them better whom the shops and trams are full of,
> The little men and their mothers, not plain but
> Dreadfully ugly.[37]

Their men, their mothers and even their recreation were somehow ugly. Despite describing cinema as the 'art of the masses', Auden nonetheless directed scorn at the medium when it so suited. The Chorus in *The Dog Beneath the Skin* – Auden's and Isherwood's biting, satirical play – derided

> cinemas blazing with bulbs: bowers of bliss
> Where thousands are holding hands: they gape at the tropical vegetation,
> at the Ionic pillars and the organ solo[38]

– sounding uncomfortably close to Evelyn Waugh in his right-wing reactionary, nonetheless amusing, travelogue mode.

Paradox aside, there were practical difficulties for the middle-class artist wanting to write for or about the lower classes. D. L. LeMahieu collected a number of contemporary responses to this problem in his excellent book *A Culture for Democracy*. One account, written by Storm Jameson for *Fact*, outlines the writer's predicament: 'He discovers that he does not even know what the wife of a man earning two pounds a week wears, where she buys her food, what her kitchen looks like to her when she comes into it at six or seven in the morning.'[39] Often the response was to idealize or romanticize the working class. As John Carey states, the 'demand among intellectuals for a cosmetic version of the masses, which prompted the quest for peasants and primitives in pastoral settings, also sanctioned political rewritings of the masses, whether as stalwart workers or as the downtrodden and the oppressed'.[40]

Coal Face, the first of the Britten and Auden GPO film collaborations, offers precisely this most Romantic view of the proletariat.[41] Its intentions cannot be doubted, its pitch is clear (was there anything more working-class than a coal miner?) and its message is housed in the most

democratic of genres – film. Yet Auden's contribution clearly demonstrates the conflict in middle-class depictions of the lower classes:

> O lurcher-loving collier, black as night,
> Follow your love across the smokeless hill;
> Your lamp is out and all the cages still;
> Course for her heart and do not miss,
> For Sunday soon is past and, Kate, fly not so fast,
> For Monday comes when none may kiss:
> Be marble to his soot, and to his black be white.[42]

Neither language nor metre is simple. There are classical allusions to
Shakespeare's Petruchio[43] and Cleopatra, and the middle-class perspective of authorship is strong. It is the view of an educated, literary,
middle-class anthropologist – certainly not the perspective of the miner
himself. And although the coal miner effortlessly represented 'otherness'
– he is the complete antithesis of the educated middle classes – Auden's
(and to a lesser extent Britten's) attempts at ingratiating himself with this
potent symbol were self-conscious. Stephen Spender, a friend of Auden's,
would have concurred on principle: 'The attitude of the bourgeois communist or socialist to his proletarian ally is *inevitably* self-conscious.'[44]
Another contemporary writer and colleague, Christopher Isherwood, cir-
cumvented this difficulty by writing about his self-consciousness. In his
autobiographical *Mr Norris Changes Trains* (1935), the narrator attends a
Communist Party meeting:

> They were listening to their own collective voice. At intervals they applauded
> it, with sudden, spontaneous violence. Their passion, their strength of
> purpose elated me. *I stood outside it. One day, perhaps, I should be with it, but
> never of it.* At present I just sat there, a half-hearted renegade from my own
> class . . .[45]

This was, however, a moderately unusual literary device: inclusion, not
exclusion, was sought. Much of what was written by left-wing writers,
noted J. M. Hay in 1935, was unintelligible jargon to the working class.
'The proletarianization of our language is an imperative task of crafts-
manship and should result in the enrichment of written English', he
noted, in fetching jargon of his own.[46] Or, as the equally left-wing but
rather more literary Randall Swingler stated: 'We also want poetry that
can be cried in the streets, from platforms, in theatres; that will be sung in
concert-halls and in pubs and in market-places, in the country and the
town. Poetry to bind many together in a deeper sense of community.'[47] In
the renowned epilogue to the documentary film *Night Mail*, Auden and
Britten did just this. Auden used many (sometimes tenuous) rhymes and
kept the language and imagery simple. It is not the voice of the working

class, but neither has it the romantic visage of *Coal Face*. If anything, the author's voice is anonymous, while the rhythm of the poem ('This is the night mail crossing the border, / Bringing the cheque and the postal order') – particularly as it is highlighted in Britten's accompaniment – reflects that of the mail train, a clever marriage of form and subject.

Britten eradicated traces of middle-class authorship more easily than Auden, but not consistently. The trick was to avoid sounding as self-conscious as Auden and many of his contemporaries, but at the same time use a (musical) language readily understood by the intended audience. He did this by playing on the common associations of sounds and sonorities. As Mitchell has noted, Britten's work with the GPO Film Unit showed him to be an excellent mimic. Using an often odd assortment of instruments, he would weave mimicry, pastiche and parody into his film scores, confident that the associations of each were clear.[48] He introduced 'working-class vernacular' in other pieces such as *Russian Funeral* (which draws on a famous Russian proletarian funeral song) and the *Pacifist March*. Mitchell has said that no irony was intended in this military march for peace,[49] and here he touches on the chief problem Britten encountered in his works for 'others'. Pastiche, parody and, naturally, emulation exist because of readily defined connotations (as Mitchell notes, the *Pacifist March* is based on European proletarian marching songs). For them to work, their incorporation into a piece must be unambiguous. Unlike Britten's *Russian Funeral* and his later manipulation of genre associations (the pastoral, for example), the semiotics of the *Pacifist March* are in conflict with its purpose; there remains something unsettling about a quasi-militant call for pacifism.[50] When the semiotics of genre did not conflict with a work's 'function' or intention, however, the piece succeeded. The *Cabaret Songs* (1937), *On This Island* (1937), *Advance Democracy* (1938) and *Canadian Carnival* (1939) are examples of a successful marriage of association and purpose. 'Otherness' is depicted – whether it be the seedy cabaret rooms of Hitler's Berlin, or a gilded music room in Handel's England. In each case either the aims of each piece are modest, or the formal cohesion so tight that the inherent contradiction of the *Pacifist March* does not exist. Moreover, Auden's contribution to the *Cabaret Songs* and *On This Island* demonstrates a cohesive collaboration between composer and poet: his often unwieldy poems – both pre- and post-dating these works – were here replaced with words which deferred to defined musical genres. Auden's influence on Britten was now reciprocated.

Paul Bunyan, Britten's and Auden's folk opera of 1941, is full of pastiche, parody, emulation and – in a few cases – anticipation of later popular music.[51] The intention of each reference to other genres or styles is clear, yet the wide range of sources gives the opera an episodic and eclectic quality which undermines any real, cohesive voice of authorship.[52] Much later Auden blamed himself for this: 'I knew nothing whatever about opera or what is required of a librettist', he wrote on the composer's fiftieth birthday. 'In consequence, some very lovely music of Britten's went down the drain, and I must now belatedly make apologies to my old friend . . .'[53] And although initial critical response did single out the opera's unsingular literary make-up, Britten did not escape unscathed:

> In the plot, as in the score, is a little of everything, a little of symbolism and uplift, a bit of socialism and of modern satire, and gags and jokes of a Hollywood sort, or of rather cheap musical comedy . . . As for the sources of Mr. Britten's style, they are numerous and extremely eclectic. They range everywhere from Prokofieff to Mascagni, from Rimsky-Korsakoff to Gilbert and Sullivan.[54]

There would be little point in quoting Olin Downes were it not for his often perceptive ear – one which, in this instance, quickly identified the different styles, genres and debts in *Paul Bunyan*.[55] Irrespective of its critical merits, however, *Bunyan* tells us much about the nature of the mature Britten–Auden collaboration, notwithstanding Auden's self-deprecating and only partly accurate assessment of their working relationship; and it clearly indicates the response of each artist to his environment – in this case, post-Depression America on the eve of yet another world war. The nature of Britten's and Auden's relationship in this, the last of their formal collaborations (Britten later set Auden's *Hymn to St Cecilia*, but did so without direct intervention from the poet), hints at unfulfilled promise. For although Auden's shopping list of styles and forms is varied, what is most striking about the completed opera is how each isolated lyric – whether ballad, blues, baroque parable or Broadway chorus – is matched so completely by Britten's music. Both author and composer were singularly aware of the semiotics of each genre, and each remained totally attuned to the requirements and expectations of his partner. But an opera cannot be considered on each individual merit, and for all this promise, Britten was slowly becoming aware that Auden's large-scale dramaturgical discipline was not all it should be – a realization confirmed when the first draft of a proposed oratorio, *For the Time Being* (1944), arrived in the composer's hands. This was Auden at his most unwieldy – page upon page of dense text and barely perceptible dramatic structure or momentum. Britten set two excerpts, including one wonderful carol ('O lift your little pinkie and touch the winter sky'), but had learnt enough from the dramatic failure of *Bunyan* to leave the rest untouched. Besides which, Britten's early work on

Peter Grimes (with Peter Pears and then Montagu Slater) was showing him how a collaboration between author and composer *could* work, and the complete success of his second opera confirmed a pattern of collaboration rarely altered in the remainder of his dramatic output.

Britten's and Auden's artistic response to their new life in America is also a significant indicator of the way each man worked. On the simplest level, the selection of the mythical Paul Bunyan – father of the nation – as the subject of their first opera was an attempt to display their neo-American credentials; a fast-assembled American vernacular furthered their cause. Beyond this, however, the story is much more interesting, linking Britten's and Auden's pre-war British socialist ambitions with domicile in their newly adopted country. As Mitchell notes, *Bunyan*'s genesis was partly in the specific philosophy and policies of Roosevelt's America – his New Deal, with its Federal Theatre and its Works Progress Administration.[56] This was – writ large – America's GPO Film Unit: an officially sanctioned social conscience which, by its very structure (giving work to unemployed actors, writers and musicians), injected socialist ideas into mass entertainment.

The second of the ideological conflicts encountered by Auden and Britten in the 1930s – how they were to be court poet to a society they disliked – was as complicated as their first. It was hard for an artist to dissent when society demanded that he or she fulfil the role of sage. Yet dissent there was, much of it unpalatable to the ruling classes. The Poet as Fool was the Establishment's compromise; since, like Lear's Fool, he could be whipped for telling the truth *or* for lying, society was left as the arbiter of Truth. Although many artists took their role more seriously than this, they were often unsure of how to counter society's censorial eye. As Auden wrote to Isherwood in the mid-1930s:

> So in this hour of crisis and dismay,
> What better than your strict and adult pen
> Can warn us from the colours and the consolations,
> The showy arid works, reveal
> The squalid shadow of academy and garden,
> Make action urgent and its nature clear?
> Who give us nearer insight to resist
> The expanding fear, the savaging disaster?[57]

The writer of *The Times* leader in September 1938 quoted at the beginning of this chapter may not have shared Auden's literary gifts, but his hope that the poets would use their clearer vision to restore society's failing sight is identical to this rallying call – in this instance a plea to Isherwood, with his 'strict and adult pen'. Despite this similarity of outlook, when

Auden, Isherwood and Britten left England to settle in the United States, Establishment society showed exactly how much of an arbiter it could be. The *Spectator* ('Since you have left us, here the stink is less') was not the only voice of dissent. Questions were asked in parliament; newspapers and journals of every persuasion entered the fray; and even Evelyn Waugh, one of the decade's great Fools, mercilessly satirised the writers in his wartime novel, *Put Out More Flags*.[58]

But the conflict was present before the war. Britten's *Our Hunting Fathers* (1936) and *Ballad of Heroes* (1939) are both actual or tacit collaborations with Auden, and are both implicitly critical of English society. To Mitchell, the (international) political symbolism of *Our Hunting Fathers* is clear; yet the piece also attacked 'those members of English society for whom "the hunt" represented a way of life, an inviolable tradition'.[59] Attack the actions of the ruling class and you attack its values – values which Britten thought corrupt. *Ballad of Heroes* displayed its left-wing pedigree in its dedication to Montagu and Enid Slater, in the occasion of its première at a Festival of 'Music for the People', and in its genesis – as a tribute to those of the British Battalion of the International Brigade who had died in Spain. Those who stood at doors, 'wiping hands on aprons', shrugging shoulders while men went to fight a war of principle, are the work's targets:

> To you we speak, you numberless Englishmen,
> To remind you of the greatness still among you
> Created by these men who go from your towns
> To fight for peace, for liberty, and for you.[60]

This was dangerous territory for a pacifist – especially one who would have the same charge directed at him only months later. The Auden poem at the centre of the piece ('It's farewell to the drawing-room's civilized cry, / The professor's sensible whereto and why') is full of references to middle-class complacency in the face of evil. Britten set it as a *danse macabre*, reinforcing the point.

Quite apart from the critical response to these two works – whether it be favourable, puzzled, dismissive or ignorant – the ideological dichotomy they represented would have been difficult to sustain over a long period. Although it was possible for artists to stand on the outside throwing stones in, it was impossible to ignore the fact that, to the naked eye, they looked little different from the people they were stoning; few managed to cover their tracks. Moreover, as Margaret Thatcher proved in the 1980s in her battle with the BBC, artists had to be wary of biting the (Conservative) hand which fed them. Both Auden and Britten eventually came to this realization. According to Edward Mendelson, Auden was, at

first, quite happy to be 'Court Poet of the Left'; but, as Humphrey
Carpenter notes, by 1938 the role had become intolerable 'simply because
he did not have the political beliefs to sustain it'.[61] Although he never
became entirely apolitical, Spain, China, and his own society's political
and intellectual appeasement had taken their toll. America presented him
with a new palette, one untarnished by the old-world corruption of
Europe. His assaults remained breathtakingly sharp ('Patriots? Little
boys, / obsessed by Bigness, / Big Pricks, Big Money, Big Bangs'[62]) yet his
right to comment on England's 'others' was rescinded by his residency in
America. His observations became, once again, a little too self-conscious.
He remained fond of Britten, but contact between the two men was
minimal after the war; their friendship, with all its emotional and artistic
lessons, belonged most naturally to the 1930s.

Despite the appearance of belonging to Establishment society –
awards, royal patronage, fiftieth-birthday tributes, eventual admittance
into the House of Lords – Britten retained much of the sense of 'otherness'
that he had developed with Auden in the 1930s. It was demonstrated more
in his work than his lifestyle – a paradox which many have criticized. Yet
the 1930s were years of artistic paradox, and the lessons of this decade
were nothing if not clear. By returning to England in wartime, to face a
Conscientious Objectors' Tribunal, Britten unequivocally rejoined the
society he had rebelled against for much of the 1930s. There was an
important role in society for the artist. 'Otherness' remained a theme of so
much of his work, but it was presented in a gentler, less polemical manner.
Although in his later interview with Harewood Britten carefully distanced
himself from Auden and the period itself,[63] the two men had formed some
of their most basic artistic philosophies together. And although it was
Auden the Fool who wrote 'September 1939', the poem is remarkably
close to Britten's post-war artistic creed:

> All I have is a voice
> To undo the folded lie,
> The romantic lie in the brain
> Of the sensual man-in-the-street
> And the lie of Authority
> Whose buildings grope the sky:
> There is no such thing as the State
> And no one exists alone;
> Hunger allows no choice
> To the citizen or the police;
> We must love one another or die.[64]

3 Britten in the cinema: *Coal Face*

PHILIP REED

During the 1930s under the visionary leadership of John Grierson, the film units of two government agencies, the Empire Marketing Board (EMB) and the General Post Office (GPO), produced documentary films of interest and quality – and occasionally of innovation. While the EMB's earliest films had been 'silents', the acquisition of sound-recording equipment by the GPO Film Unit led to some deliberate experimentation in the sound film, and striking results were achieved. *Pett and Pott* and *The Song of Ceylon*, both with music by Walter Leigh, are possibly the most fascinating examples of the GPO Film Unit's earliest consciously experimental sound films and evidently provided useful role-models for the youthful Britten when he arrived as a new member of Grierson's team in May 1935.

Although Britten was first engaged to write a through-composed twenty-minute score for *The King's Stamp*, a documentary tracing the history and production of postage stamps, he was soon seconded to a more challenging and controversial project: a social documentary examining the conditions prevailing at the time in the mining industry. While *The King's Stamp* possessed some experimental qualities, it can hardly be claimed they extend to its soundtrack or musical score – whatever their respective merits overall.[1] Britten's next film score, however, shows a remarkable grasp of many experimental techniques; having demonstrated to his colleagues at the Unit what he could achieve in conventional circumstances, Britten was now chosen for *Coal Face*, from the outset a highly experimental production.

The composer's diary for 24 May 1935 recounts a significant event in relation to the nature of the *Coal Face* score:

> Go to Soho Square GPO Film offices at 10.30 to see some of the GPO Films with Cavalcanti. A very lovely one on 'Ceylon' with good musical effects –
> tho' not perfect – some of the music not particularly int[eresting]. A lovely
> little comedy by C[avalcanti]. 'Mr Pett & Mr Pott' work of genius – which the
> charming English Distributors won't buy! it being too silly! Also the famous
> 'Weather Forecast'.[2]

The following day Britten had further discussions with Alberto Cavalcanti and viewed more films including the 'charming and lovely' *Spring on the Farm*.[3] It is clear that Cavalcanti was demonstrating possibilities for film music to Britten, as a prelude to employing him on his own avant-garde project. The experimental values in circulation at the GPO Film Unit are crucial to our forming a complete understanding of the achievement of *Coal Face*. Never again was Britten to be quite so overtly modernistic in his film work, although certain later scores approach its level of attainment. While *Coal Face* was an exceptional artistic event – if for no other reason than it marked the first occasion that Britten set a text by W. H. Auden – it must, for all its innovations, be considered as a link in the chain of GPO Films principally concerned with the development of sound techniques. Britten advanced his own skills by observing Leigh's and Cavalcanti's earlier example.

The subject-matter of *Coal Face* – an impressionistic study of the mining world – is in fact unconnected with the visual topics of Post Office documentaries; nor was it produced under the auspices of an outside sponsor. Why, then, was a government-department film team making a documentary wholly unconnected with their normal professional brief? Part of the answer lies in the fact that from the outset *Coal Face* was considered an experimental production. The visual material was compiled from existing footage, including some discarded material shot by the distinguished director Robert Flaherty originally for the EMB Film Unit (the predecessor of the GPO Film Unit); while Cavalcanti indicated that Harry Watt (later to be responsible for *Night Mail* (1936) and *The Saving of Bill Blewitt* (1937), both with incidental music by Britten), Humphrey Jennings and Basil Wright also filmed miscellaneous sequences. Another member of the Unit, Stuart Legg, recalled the following concerning the film's genesis:

> [Grierson] gave me a lot of material to cut which had been shot in coal
> mines. He asked me to make it into a two-reeler. And this was the beginning
> of *Coal Face*, because when it was cut, I somehow managed to make it look
> like a film. And then somebody had the idea of carrying much further . . .
> and putting this whole interwoven soundtrack into it with Britten.
> Cavalcanti was in it by that time.[4]

In recent years, the finished appearance of the film has come to be considered the responsibility of Cavalcanti, in spite of numerous prints of the film displaying misleading credits – Britten's and Auden's names only, or simply those of Cavalcanti and Grierson. The latter recalled that Cavalcanti requested his name be deliberately omitted from any of the Unit's experimental productions – e.g. *Coal Face* and *Night Mail* – lest it jeopardize his employment prospects in the British feature-film industry.[5] Cavalcanti's close involvement in the project is not surprising, for he had been specifically engaged by Grierson to teach and experiment with sound techniques, and it was his interest in music that brought Britten into Grierson's fold. *The King's Stamp* presented the composer with a *fait accompli*; in *Coal Face*, however, Cavalcanti took the opportunity to involve the musician from the earliest moment the soundtrack was discussed, and at all levels of possible collaboration. He accorded the composer the same respect as any other member of the production team.

An equally important reason for making this film, despite its Post Office origins, was the political significance of the subject in question. Coal-mining was an industry in which five employees were killed every day in the course of their work (a statistic underlined in the film) and where the pits were still privately owned and (mis-)managed in contrast to the post-war national organization. From the outset the film intended to focus on society's prevalent attitude to miners, and emphasize their poor working conditions and the extent to which their lives were dominated by their employment. In so doing, *Coal Face* joined a succession of similar protesting politicized art works which sought to place the plight of the miners in the 1930s before the general public. Other examples include Montagu Slater's *Stay Down Miner*, for which Britten composed incidental music;[6] a play entitled *In Memoriam* by H. Cooper examining mining conditions in the Durham coalfield, which was submitted to the Left Theatre's 1935 play competition;[7] and a BBC Features Department production entitled *Coal* (1938), also devoted to the Durham miners.

The collective responsibility taken for the visual material was similarly adopted for the tightly constructed script of *Coal Face*. Britten's diaries afford us the opportunity to trace the daily development of the project and, with the surviving textual and musical sources held by the composer's archive, allow us to scrutinize the composer's immersion in all aspects of the film.

Following an interview with Cavalcanti on 27 May, Britten was evidently contracted to compose music for several films, most notably *Coal Face*. (The other projects included *C.T.O. – The Story of the Central Telegraph Office*, *Telegrams* and *The Tocher*.[8]) Work began on the script of *Coal Face* – at this stage provisionally entitled 'Miners' – two days later; Britten wrote in his diary for 29 May: 'Odd jobs at Films before a committee meeting on script of film on Mining in aft.' The next two days were similarly spent in this collective attempt to create a suitable text, and Britten indicates, apart from himself, the involvement of Cavalcanti, Legg, the artist William Coldstream (then working at the Unit) and Ralph Bond. As might be expected from the number of personnel engaged, progress was painfully slow. The composer wrote on 3 June:

> Go off to Soho Square at 10.30 [...] Spend morning & aft. at Soho & then to
> Blackheath 4.0–6.30 working at libretto of Mining film, with various people,
> & getting the full attention of none – hopeless job.

For several days Britten and Coldstream were sent out to undertake research for the film at various libraries, newspaper offices (the *Daily Herald*) and bookshops, in a bid to locate appropriate words. On 6 June their quest for authentic material led them to interview a Welsh miner. The script progressed more quickly under the triumvirate of Britten, Cavalcanti and Coldstream, and by 12 June, when Britten obtained a further (unidentified) book on mining, a prototype format and text were determined.

The literary sketches for *Coal Face* are unique in Britten's film oeuvre: they provide documentary evidence to substantiate the chronology unfolded above, indicating how intimately Britten influenced the shape and content of the script. The documents divide into two principal categories: typed material (*TSS I–III*) and seven handwritten sheets either pre- or post-dating the corresponding typescript versions. Probably the earliest surviving item is the draft scenario, *TS I* (Plate 4), which delineates a basic outline of the principal sections of the film; film-footage and corresponding durations have been subsequently added by Britten in pencil. The typescript has also been annotated by Britten to introduce three new subdivisions in section 2 and one additional item in section 4. The whole document is entitled 'Underground' – the film's first working title – in an unidentified hand in pencil.[9] The numeration of the sections used in this scenario appears in both subsequent typescripts (*TS II* and *TS III*), though it was eventually abandoned by Britten in his full score.

TS II forms the second page of a draft (page 1 is missing), comprising commentary material for sections 3(b), 4(a), 4(b) and 5 of *TS I*. Section 5 has been expanded to include two additional subdivisions: coal as an exportable commodity, and as a fuel for industry. (See also white notepapers *Wia–iiia* below for Britten's handwritten drafts of the same material.)

TS III (Plate 5) – entitled 'Miners', a later working title closer to the 'mining film' which appears in Britten's diary entries – represents an important stage, i.e. the closest that is known to the final version of the text set by Britten in his full score. It contains full details of the commentary, verbal descriptions of the music (including sung texts where applicable) and the accompanying visual material; a column has been reserved for the film-footage but remains unused (although there is a calculation in Britten's hand at the top of the first page). There are, however, several crucial items missing, including the male chorus chants (full score, Sequence VI/*TS III*, II(f); full score, Sequence IX/*TS III*, II(a)–(c));

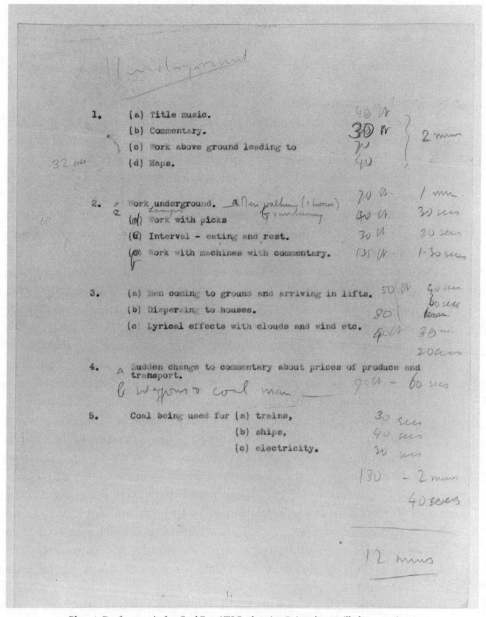

Plate 4 Draft scenario for *Coal Face* (*TS I*), showing Britten's pencilled annotations

however, it is just possible to decipher the words 'Scientific definition' in the music column at II(a) of this typescript. Most notably absent is the famous Auden lyric 'O lurcher-loving collier, black as night', although the heavy pencil blocks and lines around the sections presumably denote an absent text. Furthermore, it is clear from the typescript that the team of writers recognized that something was required even when the actual text had yet to be written: 'Chant gathering speed with women's voices calling. / Introduction of children's voices / Rising to lyrical climax.'

The assortment of pencil annotations and deletions suggests that *TS III* represents a working copy. The *verso* of page 1 included Britten's hand-written drafts for full score, Sequence VII/ *TS III*, II(e) – originally missing from the typescript and included at a later stage – which is concerned with the miners' resting and eating, and a list of possible first names for the miners' wives to call out (see *TS III*, III(b) – 'with women's voices calling'/full score, Sequence IX).

One miscellaneous (though significant) typed item is the final page of an alphabetical glossary of various specialist mining occupations; the previous page(s) is now missing. This fragment corresponds to the chanted list of miners' occupations used by Britten in Sequence IV (*TS III*, II(a)), and was probably assembled by Britten and Coldstream after one of their research forays. Charles Osborne has suggested that Auden compiled this list, but since it is merely alphabetical in structure its compilation would hardly have required a poet's literary skills.[10] Moreover, its presence in *TS III* and the conspicuous absence of the authentic Auden text further suggests it is not the poet's work.

The seven handwritten sheets divide neatly into two sets: those written on white notepaper (*Wi–iii*) and those written on blue notepaper (*Bi–iv*). They are all chiefly in Britten's hand and give a partial indication of the composer's involvement in the creation of the draft text for musical setting.

The three white notepapers (*Wi–iii*) contain two distinct elements. The *recto* pages form a neat draft in Britten's hand of *TS II*; they are paginated 7–9, so presumably the missing pages 1–6 related to the missing typescript page from *TS II*. This draft was probably written out by Britten preparatory to typing. The *verso* sides of two sheets (*Wi–ii*) were used by Britten for transcriptions of poetical texts, including 'Leaner than fleshless misery' from Shelley's *Queen Mab*, 'Yet to be just to these poor men' by Pope, an extract from Keats's *Isabella* and 'In the depths of the deep' from Shelley's *Prometheus*. *Wii* has an unattributed text beginning 'And the vast engines labouring in the mine' written in an unidentified hand, possibly that of Coldstream; the first line of the same poem also appears in Britten's hand on the fourth sheet of the blue notepapers (*Biv*). Two final poetry transcriptions can be discovered among the blue note-papers (*Bii recto*): in Britten's hand 'Such are born and reared at the mine's mouth under impending rocks', identified by Britten as Wordsworth; and the line 'Coal-mines & all that is down there, the lamps in the darkness, echoes, songs, what vast native thoughts looking through smutched faces', not identified by Britten but in fact by Walt Whitman.

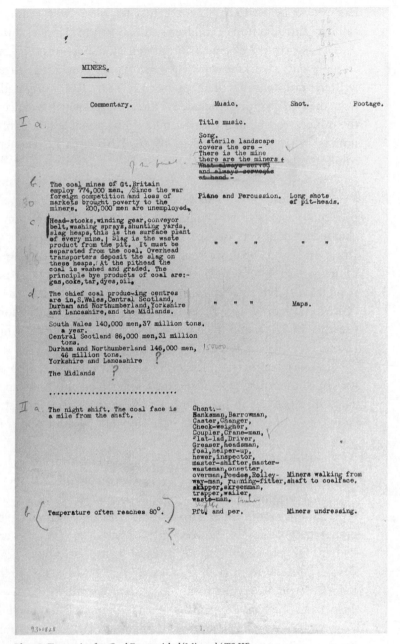

Plate 5 Typescript for *Coal Face* entitled 'Miners' (*TS III*)

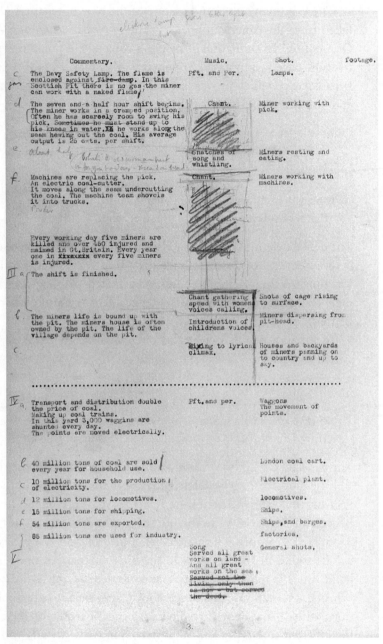

Plate 5 *(cont.)*

The Whitman text found on one of the blue notepapers (*Bii recto*) is taken from the American poet's *Leaves of Grass – Calamus*: 'A Song for Occupation'. Examination of Britten's copy of this poem reveals that the relevant page is annotated in pencil.[11] Also marked is the 'Song of the Broad-Axe',[12] which proves to be the source of the text for the title and end-title music drafts of *TS III*, I(a) and V:

> A sterile landscape covers the ore, there is as good as the best
>   for all the forbidding appearance,
> There is the mine, there are the miners,
> The forge-furnace is there, the melt is accomplis'd, the hammersmen are at
> hand with their tongs and hammers,
> What always served and always serves is at hand.

The pencil deletions on *TS III* indicate that the chosen texts were revised before being set by Britten. Evidently Coldstream's and Britten's search was not in vain. *Wii verso* comprises a sketch-plan for an unidentified male chorus sequence and the sentence, 'This is a stiff piece of coal', in Britten's hand.

Bi recto is not in Britten's hand and provides a 'Scientific definition' of coal missing from *TS III*, II(d). It reads:

>   understood
> By coal is ~~comprehended~~ all the fossil fuels contained in the earth's crust.
> Being an amorphous substance of variable composition, it cannot be as
> strictly defined as can a crystallized or definite mineral. Thus is:–

The passage was almost certainly transcribed from a reference book, possibly by Coldstream. The deleted lines, with the exception of the substitution of 'understood', correspond to the first part of the text used by Britten for Sequence VI in the full score. The second part of the text for Sequence VI comprises a chanted list of the different categories of coal. It can be found in two versions in the blue notepapers, both in Britten's hand: on *Bii recto*, where it is surrounded by the Wordsworth and Whitman quotations mentioned above, and the entire textual compilation entitled 'IId. Chant' (presumably the whole sequence of Wordsworth, the different coal-types and Whitman comprised an early version of the missing text); and on *Biii recto* where they are simply listed.

In the spring of 1935 Auden wrote to Basil Wright, who was working at the GPO Film Unit and whom he had first met at Oxford in 1927, asking if there might be an opportunity of some suitable employment at the Unit. He was immediately offered a full-time post from September that year, but in the meantime was invited to write material for two films, *Coal Face* and *Night Mail.* Wright has recalled Grierson's enthusiasm to enlist Auden on the staff,[13] and Grierson himself had already recognized the tremendous possibilities of poetry in the sound-film.[14] Auden for his part was keen to leave school teaching and was interested in the work of the Unit.

The extent and chronology of Auden's contribution to *Coal Face* is not altogether clear. The authorship of the seven-line lyric 'O lurcher-loving collier, black as night' is universally acknowledged; it was published and reprinted in Auden's lifetime, and appeared as the first of 'Three Fragments for Films' in *The English Auden* (p. 290), where Edward Mendelson dates it to June 1935. (For further discussion of this lyric, see pp. 47–9 above.) We have previously noted how Coldstream and Britten – and presumably Cavalcanti – felt the need for poetry to provide a fitting lyrical climax to the film; they had not found much success with their own efforts, as is perhaps suggested by the intermediate script. It would be perfectly natural to turn to Auden, an established poet, to fill the gaps; but to establish the form Auden's involvement took, and at what juncture it occurred, we must turn to Britten's diary entries and the genesis of the musical composition of *Coal Face* for circumstantial evidence.

Britten's first attempt at composing some of the music for the score took place on 6 June, probably before *TS III* had been settled: 'Spend morning sketching music for "Mining" film'. Further composing did not occur until 13–15 June, and this was not without difficulties; by the 15th enough had been achieved for the music to be copied, though Britten was not specific about which sequences were transcribed. However, on 18 June Britten held a chorus rehearsal:

> Straight back to Poland St. Rehearsing Rooms where for 4 hours (about 6–10) I struggle to make 18 members of the Covent Garden chorus fall in with my ideas – with some success in end. Everyone's very pleased with the stuff & I must say it comes off.

On the 19th the recording session took place:

> In aft. prepare matters; then percussion, piano (Howard Ferguson) & two extra perc from Blackheath Conservatoire (to play chains, rewinders, sandpaper, whistles, carts, water, etc.) arr. at 4.0; choir at 5.30 & 6.30; then with commentator – we rehearse time & again & gradually record, finishing with men at 12.0, & with commentator at 12.30. Return (like the rest of the crowd) by taxi at 1.30 with Cavalcanti & Grierson – absolutely dead.

Two points should be noted. First, throughout Britten's diary entries concerning the film there is no mention of Auden or his provision of a text of any kind; secondly, there was apparently no subsequent recording session for *Coal Face* after 19 June – all the music (including the choruses) was recorded on that single occasion. It appears that by 19 June 'O lurcher-loving collier, black as night' had been written, set by Britten and recorded by the Unit; Auden had fulfilled a specific role assigned to him by those already working more closely on the script (Cavalcanti, Coldstream and Britten). Whether Auden worked without personal contact with the Unit other than by letter or telephone is not clear; but we know that the first recorded meeting between Britten and the poet took place on 5 July 1935, i.e. after *Coal Face* had been completed. Britten recorded in his diary for that date:

> Have a quick haircut before Basil Wright calls for me in his car at 10.0 &
> takes me down to Colwall (near Malvern). Very lovely journey via
> Maidenhead, Oxford, Tewkesbury. Arr. 1.45 – lunch at Park Hotel where we
> put up. We come here to talk over matters for films with Wystan Auden (who
> is a master at the Downs School here – incidentally Bobby [Britten's elder
> brother, Robert] was a master at the Elms, another school in Colwall). Auden
> is the most amazing man, a very brilliant & attractive personality – he was at
> Fairfield, Gresham's but before my time. Work with him in aft. & then tea in
> Malvern. After that, watch the boys have a rag – and then eat at the Park.
> After that we have a drinking party with most of the Downs Masters (about
> 7) – but very boring.

Although Britten does not identify the film projects which he, Auden and Wright discussed during this visit (Britten and Wright remained at Colwall until 8 July), Humphrey Carpenter cites a letter by Auden probably dating from July 1935, in which Auden recounts composing verses 'for a film about the Night Mail to Scotland'.[15] That Wright (who scripted *Night Mail*) rather than Coldstream or Cavalcanti (who were involved in *Coal Face*) accompanied Britten points to early preparations for what was originally known as the 'Travelling Post Office' film. It has been suggested by Charles Osborne that Auden contributed to other parts of the *Coal Face* text: the list of specialist mining occupations; the mining disaster reports ('Fire followed explosions; five hundred men trapped half a mile underground'); and the chant text leading into 'O lurcher-loving collier' ('How much did we hew? how much fined for dirt?').[16] This additional level of involvement is less clear-cut, for if we examine *TS III* the passages cited by Osborne (with the exception of the list of mining occupations) are indicated by the word 'Chant' (see *TS III*, II(f) and III (a)). However, the absence of any exact text is hardly conclusive evidence of Auden's authorship; equally, it does not deny the possibility of his writing these texts. While the mining disaster reports were possibly researched by Britten and Coldstream from newspaper accounts (perhaps while they were at the offices of the *Daily Herald*), the chant as the miners return to

the surface may possibly be Auden's work. There is, however, no documentary evidence to support either argument. Auden's own recollections
of his collaboration on this film, while characteristically vague, seem
definitive:

> In the summer of 1935 Mr John Grierson ... asked me to write a chorus for
> the conclusion of a GPO Documentary film called *Coal Face*. All I now
> remember about this film was that it seemed to have been shot in total
> darkness, and a factual statement in the commentary – the miner works in a
> cramped position. My chorus, he told me, would be set by a brilliant young
> composer he had hired to work for him, called Benjamin Britten.[17]

One final observation concerning the script may account for the
authorship of those male chorus chants. Montagu Slater, poet, playwright
and librettist of *Peter Grimes*, has been cited by his widow, Enid, as being
involved with the GPO Film Unit and with *Coal Face* in particular, a
suggestion which Rachael Low corroborates. Moreover, Mrs Slater claims
that Slater and Britten met for the first time while working on *Coal Face*.
We can find, however, no further evidence to suggest that Slater was
involved in this film project. Rachael Low is evasive about her source for
including Slater's name in the list of credits for the *Coal Face* entry in her
filmography, and the present author has never seen Slater's name appear
on the title credits of prints of *Coal Face*; like Auden, neither is he mentioned in Britten's diary entries concerning this film. This does not necessarily preclude the possibility that Slater was consulted or contributed in
the same way as Auden, i.e. apparently at a distance, for Slater possessed
enviable knowledge of mining conditions[18] and, earlier in 1935, had gathered material in South Wales for a reportage account of the miners' sit-in
strikes.[19]

Auden's lyric provided the opportunity to make a specific effect in the
film. With the exception of the title and end-title music (see Plate 6 below)
it is the only sung (as opposed to chanted) chorus in the film; moreover,
its impact is heightened because it comprises the sole example of sung
part-writing in Britten's score, and thus contrasts sharply with the stark
octave sounds of the title and end-title music. Britten's striking setting for
women's voices (SSAA) – representing the miners' wives – marks out this
setting as the emotional peak of *Coal Face* (Ex. 3.1).

While *Coal Face* was intended to depict the conditions existing in the
mining industry, it equally identified the industry's importance to
national prosperity. This dichotomy is neatly balanced over the film's five
sections, in which the miner is depicted as both machine and human
being. These opposing elements are expressed by means of the interlocking parameters of the film: the visual material and the various

Example 3.1

subdivisions of the virtually continuous soundtrack. Britten's setting of 'O lurcher-loving collier' coincides with that moment in the structure at which the miner-as-machine/miner-as-human-being conflict is brought to its most extreme position (i.e. at the end of the third section). At this juncture he is now revealed as an ordinary man with wife and children; and, as such, unusual forces (within the prevailing stark sound of this score) were required. Britten explores the inherent contrast by means of a sophisticated hierarchy of sound-components, the interplay of which comprises the complete soundtrack. The technique is not dissimilar to that evolved by Walter Leigh for the soundtrack of *The Song of Ceylon*, where a comparably dichotomous relationship – between Western and Eastern cultures – was explored. Although Leigh's pioneering and penetrating analysis of his technical achievements in that film[20] had not yet been published when his younger colleague was composing *Coal Face*, experimentation was part of the GPO Film Unit's daily activities; we also have established that Cavalcanti had deliberately shown Britten some of their best experimental sound-films including *The Song of Ceylon*, and that Britten may possibly have had personal access to Leigh. These factors point to Britten's taking his cue from Leigh's special achievements in *The Song of Ceylon* as a basis for the organization of the soundtrack for *Coal Face*.

We can represent the range of Britten's approach to word-setting diagrammatically:

Prose			**Verse**
Miner as machine			Miner as human being
(Dark)			(Light)
(a) Commentary: unmetricated spoken text	(b) Commentary: metricated spoken text (one voice)	(c) Chant: metricated spoken text (chorus)	(d) Sung text

These categories may briefly be commented upon:

(a) *Commentary: unmetricated spoken text* is hardly ever used in *Coal Face*. The only substantial section begins 'The chief coal producing centres are in South Wales, Central Scotland . . .' Unlike in *The King's Stamp*, this straightforward method is not used here without some kind of background musical support, in this particular instance a repetition of the title music, Sequence I ('A sterile landscape covers the ore'), reproduced at an artificially subdued level. Even when that ceases Britten provides a short percussion *ad lib.* link to effect the changeover to the subsequent sequence, for the composer is at pains to provide a virtually continuous scored soundtrack in this film.

Within Britten's scheme the statistical nature of the text, accompanied by maps in the visuals, is used to represent an extreme position in the film: the miner regarded as merely a unit of productivity.

(b) *Commentary: metricated spoken text (one voice)*, and (c) *Chant: metricated spoken text (chorus)* are the most widely deployed methods of word-setting in *Coal Face*, whether the text be straightforward prose or a contrived attempt at verse. The commentator's voice is exclusively reserved for factual statement (see Ex. 3.2), where the metricated text imbues an appropriate air of formality matched by his own authoritative voice. The control exercised over the spoken text – as much as would be possible if it were sung – permits accurate alignment with any desired imagistic effects in the instrumental ensemble of percussion and piano. Furthermore, this precision could be most beneficial at the later, editing stage. Whereas the commentary clearly represents the miner-as-machine aspect of *Coal Face*, the spoken (chorus) chant, echoing similar devices employed in *Pett and Pott* and *The Song of Ceylon*, tends towards the humanity of the miner. The first chant, Sequence IV (an alphabetical recitation of the different mining jobs), reinforces this intention by

Example 3.2

coinciding with the first appearance of the miners on the screen, and sub-sequent references to mining disasters (in Sequence VIII) and the social life of the miner (in Sequence IX) confirm the meaning. For Sequences IV, VI, VII, VIII and IX, Britten has annotated his score with detailed indications in respect of the position of each chorus part in relation to the microphone; with the exception of Sequence VII, all the annotated sequences are examples of this chant technique. These markings represent a brave attempt to provide an additional layer of dynamic and spatial control which was probably influenced by Cavalcanti's experiments in sound recording. The intention suggests a dramatization of the text, enlivened by purely technical means. Ultimately the concept was doomed, if not to failure, then to a very limited success at the mercy of the poor quality of the recording equipment and the even greater inferiority of the reproduction facilities available in the cinemas of the period. Britten's diary for 18 June suggests that the idiom provided considerable difficulties for a chorus of experienced performers. These drawbacks serve to indicate the technically adventurous nature of this film. The often-cited reversed recording of a cymbal clash to represent a train passing through a tunnel is a clear development of Leigh's 'swinging microphone' technique in *The Song of Ceylon*, incidentally also involving cymbals. This stroke of recording inventiveness is the only sound in the entire film which is not (obviously) present in Britten's score, but was later edited into place. Ironically, in some prints of *Coal Face* the alignment of the imagistic device is miscalculated for the sound fails to coincide with the train.[21]

(d) *Sung text* represents the opposite extreme from the unmetricated spoken word, possessing both pitch and rhythm, and forms the apotheosis of the human element of the film. It is adopted on three occasions during *Coal Face*: the title music (Sequence I); a shortened version of the end-title music (Sequence XIII); and the Auden setting in Sequence IX.

The title music (Plate 6) immediately places the important contrast between man and machine by juxtaposing the lyrical, arching contours of the chorus (E minor tonality) with punctuating chords from the percussion and piano (ill-defined tonality). Particularly telling is the rising arpeggio to the word 'mine' and the more emphatic minor ninth to 'miners', further strengthened by the descending octave leap and move away from the prevalent harmonic foundation.

Sequence IX (Plate 7) develops a typical imagistic device employed throughout this score, and first heard in the title music (see Plate 6): rising scales usually beginning low in the register, and undoubtedly associated with the depth and darkness of the mines. Organic development of the motivic concept can be observed in Sequences II (see Ex. 3.2), V and XII (the shortened reprise of Sequence I). In Sequence IX this imagistic technique is developed more subtly, by evolving a fragmentary melodic contour in the very lowest regions of the piano keyboard coupled to the chanting male chorus. As it rises through the keyboard register, the contour becomes more continuous, the frequency of the chanted words from the male chorus intensifies, and the general dynamic level increases from *piano* to *forte*. The complexity of the sound image is intended to dramatize musically the visual images of the miners rising to the surface after their shift. We should further note the suspended cymbal representing the whirring sound of the colliery lift. The subject-matter of the text relates to the miners' sense of anticipation, readily conveyed by Britten's setting. As the whole short section reaches its peak – highest, loudest notes from the piano, and loudest and most intense chanted text – women's voices are introduced calling the names of their menfolk.

The naturally lyrical quality of the women's voices in 'O lurcher-loving collier' is emphasized by the style of the piano accompaniment employed. Whereas in *The King's Stamp* the role of the two pianos was largely confined to providing a traditional harmonic and melodic support (although when the pianos were used imagistically the results were most impressive), in *Coal Face*, where the composer's concept of the score as a whole was far more imagistically orientated, a greater part of the soundtrack's experimentation lies in the use of the piano as an extension of the resourceful percussion ensemble. Thus, when in *Coal Face* the piano-writing resorts to a more conventional type the impact is all the greater. In Sequence IX this quality is felt most strongly in the piano's arpeggio figuration (see bar 5 of the Auden setting) which relates to the rising triadic motif in Plate 6 (at 'There is the mine'), and by the complete absence of any percussive timbres.

In this sequence we should note the nature of Britten's word-setting, which adumbrates a favourite device of the mature composer: the overlapping of phrases of the text and the judicious repetition of certain

Plate 6 *Coal Face*, full score, Sequence I (title music), pp. 2–3

Plate 6 (*cont.*)

Plate 7 *Coal Face*, full score, Sequence IX, pp. 28–9

Plate 7 (*cont.*)

words for enhanced effect,[22] intended on this occasion to be further emphasized by the microphone markings indicated on the score. In the first part of Sequence IX such a manner of word-setting is employed, whereby a simple line of text, e.g. 'If all you soccer fans had by mistake any gumption you'd play northern union like sensible beggars', is split between all four parts of the chanting male chorus (see bars 18–23).

The persistent refrain 'We're going up' is notated in such a way as to suggest the visual images it accompanies, with stems rising on the stave and a crescendo each time it appears (see bars 12–15, for example). It also provides a vital factor in the sense of anticipation within the movement itself.

A similar practice of word-setting is adopted for the Auden text itself, where antiphonal effects between the divided vocal lines are emphasized by the slower tempo. Britten's setting alternates the first two pairs of lines of Auden's poem between the sopranos and altos, before moving to a richer two-part texture at 'For Sunday soon is past and, Kate, fly not so fast'; the repetition of 'Kate' for dramatic emphasis is characteristic of the mature composer. Equally typical is the approach to the final pair of lines ('For Monday comes when none may kiss: / Be marble to his soot, and to his black be white') where Britten splits the text between the sopranos ('For Monday . . .') and the altos ('Be marble . . .'); however, by overlapping phrases he is able to produce an unusual collusion of phrases (see bars 62–77).

In spite of its wide-ranging modulatory character – a consequence of the principal melodic idea – the Auden setting settles upon a conclusive E minor chord sounding in the highest register of the women's voices; Auden's matchless words succumb to wordless, siren-like sounds. The final tonality is important for it forms part of a loosely linked chain of identical tonalities (sometimes only suggested) across the span of the score, namely: Sequence I; the end of Sequence III (a prominent reminiscence of Sequence I); the final bars of Sequence V (itself presenting motivic elements properly belonging to the Auden lyric); and the first version of Sequence XII, the end-title music. In *Coal Face*, the conventional musical unity, through thematic, harmonic and tonal control, is not as obvious or rigorously schematic as in *The King's Stamp*; the experimental nature of the project apparently allowed timbral values to be more significant than motivic ones. However, the cited examples do present evidence of a deliberate motivic and conceptual association of which this pointing of a home tonality is another significant example, similar in function to that of C major in *The King's Stamp*. If E minor is to represent the tonality of the miners in *Coal Face*, then it will equally well serve as the ultimate tonal resting-point for their womenfolk, in spite of having been reached in the Auden setting by a circuitous route of shifting tonalities beginning in A.

Example 3.3

We have discussed at some length the nature of the methods of word-setting in this film score, but one final use of the singing voice requires our attention. Sequence VII employs wordless singing (humming) from tenor and bass soloists with the addition of a whistler to evoke the strange, brooding atmosphere of the mine at night (see Ex. 3.3: the second bar of the whistler's part of this extract is crossed through in the manuscript). It accompanies a brief exchange of dialogue between two miners as they eat and rest. The texture comprises a layered tripartite combination, each vocal element possessing its own character, metre and tonality (C, E♭ and E). There would appear to be no direct precedent for this hummed/whistled montage among the GPO Film Unit's previous documentaries, although the technique is obviously an extension of the kind of overlaid choral patterns advocated by Grierson in his article 'The G.P.O. Gets Sound'.[23] The inclusion of hummed pitches was hardly an orthodox musical procedure but we may be more surprised by the incorporation of whistling in the score.[24] The latter is a notoriously difficult skill to acquire, particularly when precision of pitch and rhythm is required by the elaborate effect envisaged here.

Sequences X and XIa represent a specific experiment in imagistic development in which an expanded percussion ensemble replaces conventional post-synchronized natural sound. Each successive visual image is represented by a highly imaginative percussion gesture: shunting coal waggons by side drum, chains, sandpaper and whistles (bars 1ff.); horse-drawn coal carts by two sizes of coconut shell (an obvious effect but with a less obvious rhythm) and the wheeling of a small cart on asbestos (bars 31ff.); the whirring of an electricity generator by the combination of a triangle, a suspended cymbal struck by a side-drum stick and trip gear (bars 48ff.); locomotives by the bass drum, small and large drills, sandpaper and whistle (bars 61ff.); ships by a complex mixture of a cup in a bucket of water (both emptying and filling), a rewinder, cymbals, bass drum, notched wood with wooden sticks, and a cardboard cylinder to act as a hooter (bars 85ff.); and the industrial consumption of coal (scenes of factories) by a sheet of metal struck by a wooden mallet, a gong, chains and a whistle (bars 115ff.).

This sequence was composed last of all, on 17 June, and formed the outcome of close discussion with Cavalcanti. As Britten's diary reveals, the composer himself was fully aware of the innovative nature of the sequence:

> Spend day at studio experimenting & talking over details, & measuring feet
> of film for Coal-face, with Coldstream. Back here by dinner & then work till
> 12.30 [a.m.] at some more music for the film – it is entirely experimental
> stuff – written for blocks of wood, chains, rewinders, cups of water etc. etc.

There can be no doubt that the enlarged percussion group, resourcefully combining conventional instruments with household objects, was a development of Walter Leigh's instrumentation of the title music for *Six-Thirty Collection* (GPO Film Unit, 1933), which was scored for a rewinder, a pair of typewriters, an empty beer bottle (blown to mimic a ship's siren), a projector, two pieces of sandpaper, and the studio bell, with the addition of cymbals, triangle and trumpet.[25] In Britten's hands, however, the concept is developed to such a degree as to employ no fewer than twenty-two 'instruments', including 'sheet of metal & wooden mallet', 'small cart on sandy asbestos' and 'cup in bucket of water', deployed in four groups. It is extraordinary that in *Coal Face* every single noise heard on the sound-track – while apparently 'natural' in origin – is, in fact, the product of Britten's detailed instrumentation, both in this sequence and earlier in the score. Britten was to return to this type of percussion scoring in *Night Mail* for the sequences depicting the locomotive pulling away from the station platform.

Throughout the present discussion we have suggested that Britten built upon his predecessors' achievements in creating such a formidably inter-esting score. The work of Leigh stands out as the prime example: films such as *Six-Thirty Collection*, *Pett and Pott* and *The Song of Ceylon* must be considered in relation to *Coal Face* and vice versa. From our present vantage point, we can recognize a typical trait of work in *Coal Face*: Britten's impressive ability to transcend his eclectic tastes by absorbing a wide variety of compositional approaches into a distinctive personal style.

Coal Face can also be recognized as a prime example of the collective creative act, in which director, producer, script-writers, cameramen, editor and musician all made meaningful and interrelated contributions to the overall concept. One of the most significant features was the extent of the composer's contribution, both to the scenario and the text. Unlike *The King's Stamp*, where Britten was presented with a *fait accompli,* in *Coal Face* he was fully involved in the project from an early stage. The group method of working was to form the basis for the most successful of his subsequent film scores and was to spread to his work in the theatre and the radio studio. Furthermore, it formed the successful pattern of his later working life in the opera house, and in his multifarious collaborations with solo instrumentalists and singers.

PART TWO

The operas

4 'He descended into Hell': Peter Grimes, Ellen Orford and salvation denied

STEPHEN ARTHUR ALLEN

In his introduction to the original production of *Peter Grimes* in 1945, Britten stated: 'I wanted to express my awareness of the perpetual struggle of men and women whose livelihood depends on the sea – difficult though it is to treat such a universal subject in theatrical form.'[1] Pears stated that 'Ben and I had imagined the sea as being in the orchestra so it was not necessary to see it on stage.'[2] If the 'sea' can be understood almost as another operatic character, it becomes so primarily through its symbolic representation of human emotions; it may be seen to have the potential for providing a commentary on the dramatic action, mediating between it and the audience. This function is clearly to be seen in the six orchestral interludes that punctuate the opera, two located in each of the three acts. It is essential to distinguish between Britten's specifically programmatic designation of four of these as 'Sea Interludes' ('Dawn', 'Sunday Morning', 'Moonlight' and 'Storm') for the purposes of creating a concert-hall orchestral suite, and their greater psychological and narrative import – undesignated beyond the generic title 'Interlude' – in the operatic context.[3]

Britten's 'sea' may, in fact, be read as a metaphor of Peter Grimes himself. A great deal of ink has been spilt in the fifty years since the opera's première by critics and scholars wrestling to understand the 'divided' character of Britten's Grimes.[4] The unresolved ambiguities of his character only begin to become explicable when he is understood as an incarnation of the dualism at the core of Britten's musical personality. As Hans Keller memorably put it: 'Peter Grimes is the living conflict. His pride, ambition, and urge for independence fight with his need for love; his self-love battles against his self-hate.'[5] This dualism is revealed on the one hand by the Peter Grimes (himself not without conflict) who is first encountered in the lyrical phrases and luminous string accompaniment as he mounts the dock to account for the mysterious death of his latest boy apprentice (William Spode) during the inquest – or covert trial – of the 84 Prologue. It is this Grimes who is the visionary singing of stars and galaxies in the somewhat incongruous setting of an English pub in Act I scene 2. It is he who sings of peace prior to the raging storm: of his tender – and genuine – love for the widowed schoolmistress Ellen Orford, whom Philip

Hope-Wallace contrasted with the incompleteness of Grimes's character as 'a wonderfully realised secondary figure in the opera'.[6] This is Britten's 'Apollonian' or 'Good' Grimes. Fighting with and ultimately overwhelming him is the aggressive Peter Grimes inherited from Crabbe's poem: it is he who churns up the orchestral music of Interlude II and strikes Ellen to the ground in Act II scene 1. It is he who cruelly manhandles his apprentice in the service of his selfish ambition during Act II scene 2 and collapses quite mad at the end of the opera. Whether his guilt is real or imagined, its power is ultimately strong enough to cause him to succumb to the Borough's judgement and commit suicide at sea. He is rooted in Crabbe's 'Dionysian' or 'Evil' Grimes. Such a struggle is universal to fallen man, accounting in part for the opera's continuing wide appeal in spite of the central characters' dramatic incongruities. What makes Grimes a genuine anti-hero is the ultimate failure of the potential 'Good' of his character to win out against the 'Evil'. This turns the opera into a kind of modern Faustian parable and directs the exclusive attention on Grimes towards other possibilities that could have led to Grimes's salvation should he have chosen to pursue them.

Through the character of Ellen Orford we discover a new perspective in the opera. Pears wrote in a letter to Britten dated 1 March 1944:

> The more I hear of [*Peter Grimes*], the more I feel that the queerness is unimportant & doesn't really exist in the music (or at any rate obtrude) so it mustn't do so in the words. P[eter]. G[rimes]. is an introspective, an artist, a neurotic, his real problem is expression, self-expression.[7]

The removal of any overtly homosexual theme from the work places a greater significance on the outcome of Grimes's relationship with Ellen Orford. Philip Brett's research on the opera's source material and sketches confirms this view of the finished libretto. Most interestingly, Brett has also been able to demonstrate that Britten's and Pears's concern to remove any suggestion of a motivation for Grimes rooted in sadism and homoeroticism (elements that the opera's librettist, Montagu Slater, wanted to retain) led to a shift of emotional focus from Grimes and the boy to the relationship between Grimes and Ellen, bolstering her significance considerably in the process.[8] It was not until these changes were effected that Britten began composition of the music.

In order to appreciate the importance of Ellen's perspective in the opera we will need, briefly, to look at the poem by George Crabbe on which the opera was based.[9] In the section 'Ellen Orford' from Crabbe's *The Borough*, Ellen is described as having lived a savage life in which an indestructible Christian faith shines through to the end. Britten marked out several lines from 'Ellen Orford' in his copy of the poem: 152–4,

198–9, 218–19 and 336–7.[10] In the course of Crabbe's text, Ellen encourages her husband's conversion to Christianity. However, he – like Grimes – rebels and commits suicide.[11] Notably, the closing words of the poem, and of her life, exemplify her spiritual essence: 'And as my Mind looks cheerful to my end, I love Mankind and call my God my Friend.'

In Crabbe, Grimes and Ellen never appear together. Slater admitted that he borrowed aspects from other poetic characters to inform the secondary and minor ones in the Borough of the opera.[12] But the operatic Ellen, while living in the Borough, is not of it: as a symbol of a real and living Christianity she stands apart, both from the Borough's values and from the impotent legalism of its religious adherents – typified by the Anglo-Catholic Rector (Horace Adams) and the Methodist lay-preaching fisherman (Robert Boles).[13] For the audience, then, Ellen provides a highly desirable third alternative to siding with either Grimes or the Borough, without having to abandon an appropriate pity for all three. Read in these terms, Ellen becomes the opera's fallible spiritual heroine. The implicit narrative she embodies, partially prefigured in the 'Elegy', 'Dirge' and, particularly, the 'Sonnet' settings in the *Serenade* (1943), is left open-ended in *Peter Grimes*. Immediately following the opera, the themes of sin, repentance and forgiveness were to re-emerge in Britten's song-cycle *The Holy Sonnets of John Donne* and the roles of the Christian chorus in *The Rape of Lucretia* (1946), written for the joint creators of the original Peter Grimes and Ellen Orford – Peter Pears and Joan Cross.

It may be too fanciful to speak of an opera called *Ellen Orford* within *Peter Grimes*, but who else seated on stage during the opening inquest hears Grimes's music as we do – the music Michael Kennedy associates with the 'haloes of sound' of the Evangelist in Bach's *St Matthew Passion*?[14] Surely not the Borough, which is characterized through music of bumbling neo-baroque badinage. Both Grimes and Ellen are almost 'drowned' by the buzz of Borough gossip in one of several short choruses that, interestingly, Stephen Walsh also associates with the Bach Passions.[15] These are accompanied by 'chattering' semiquaver figures in the woodwinds while the horn quartet fills out the voices, as 'Ellen Orford' is called out by the lawyer (and self-appointed judge) Swallow. The women of the Borough immediately react with gossip: 'O when you pray you shut your eyes And then can't tell the truth from lies', identifying – if resisting – Ellen's spiritual essence, which they cannot comprehend. She is an outsider, too.

Yet, as Pears commented, 'Ellen Orford loves [Grimes]. She would do anything for him and tries to keep him on the rails.'[16] As Ellen and Grimes are left on stage after the clearing of the court, her significance becomes evident in what Britten himself termed the 'love duet'.[17] The bitonality of

Example 4.1

their initial keys – Grimes in F minor and Ellen in E major (united enharmonically by the equivalence of A♭ and G♯ but otherwise remote) – is noticeably calmed when Grimes adopts Ellen's key for the final octave phrases (Ex. 4.1).[18] These phrases contain minor ninths, an interval that Peter recalls both prior to and (in orchestral terms) during Interludes II and VI. Throughout the opera, 'flat' music (i.e. music with flat key signatures or accidentals) tends to be associated with the Borough and its values.

Interlude I, which opens Act I, flows directly from this 'love duet': the orchestral music suggests that some kind of emotional dialogue between Ellen and Grimes is being introduced. The tonality (based on A, Britten's habitual symbol of purity) and sonority of the harp suggest that it could

Example 4.1 (*cont.*)

be a beautiful though sometimes strained (i.e. a 'normal') relationship. The initiative and outcome depend on Grimes and indeed the low brass chords already contain a harmonic form of what Peter Evans has labelled motif *x* – the motif that, in melodic form, will mark the doom of their relationship in Act II scene 1 (see Ex. 4.2). The brass also introduce what will here be termed an 'Ellen motif' (motif *e*; see Ex. 4.3 below) which evolves through Interludes II and III. Interlude I is the first of two (possibly three) 'Ellen Interludes' which open each act, the second being Interlude III which opens Act II (and the third Interlude V opening Act III). These are complemented by three mid-act 'Peter Interludes': Interlude II in Act I, Interlude IV (the passacaglia) in Act II, and Interlude VI in Act III.[19] The evidence for the status of Interlude V as an 'Ellen Interlude' is more tenuous: it is the interlude that seems to stand most independently of the opera, as if outside it. Edward Sackville-West noted that it had greater depth of feeling than the other five Interludes, and it may be felt that the preponderance of 'feminine' thirds in a stable rhythmic structure is of the same equilibrium as much of Ellen's music elsewhere in the opera. On a subjective level the music seems to have a feminine quality, and seems to evoke metaphysical sighing and crying. It

Example 4.2

gives the impression of being a narrative requiem. Such associations are, however, admittedly more oblique. Significantly, it is the music of Interlude I that concludes the opera: thus implicitly it is Ellen that bridges and 'narrates' the action of *Peter Grimes*. This technique was to be employed explicitly through the narrative frame provided by Captain Vere in Britten's second venture into grand opera, *Billy Budd* (1951).

The music of Interlude I continues as the curtain rises, accompanying the set-pieces of the first scene as we are introduced to members of the Borough and their foibles. These individual sketches are drawn against a broad hymn-like melody with a text taken virtually intact from Crabbe's poem. It is a hymn, not to God, but to the Borough characters themselves in relation to both Nature and, by implication, Grimes's nature. Sung by the fishermen and women, it bespeaks a far greater depth than the liturgical worship of Act II scene 1, and betrays the Borough's true spiritual centre of gravity.[20] This impression is reinforced by the powerful framing effect created by the recapitulation of the tune at the opera's conclusion as Grimes drowns out at sea.

The orchestral fabric is finally broken, significantly, by Grimes's rough first entry into the action at Fig. 20 – an off-stage cry for help in landing his boat, in E♭. Balstrode helps him as the storm approaches. The return of the Interlude music at Fig. 23 as Ned Keene, the Borough's apothecary and quack, announces that another boy apprentice has been secured for Grimes, suggests appropriately that Ellen has a hand in it. This impression is confirmed by her support for Keene against the carter Jim Hobson at Fig. 26 to a statement of the Interlude music on a chord based on D♭, adding a notable air of luminous suspense.[21] Though unusual, this is not sinister, as Swallow's verdict at the inquest was that Grimes should only get another boy apprentice on the condition that he also get 'A woman to help you look after him.' Pears commented: 'Ellen keeps a kindly eye on him, hoping secretly that her care for the boy will bring her nearer to Peter and that perhaps one day they will all three share a home.'[22] However, the Borough's indignant incredulity at her overt support for Grimes leads directly into Ellen's first major aria at Fig. 28:

> Let her among you without fault
> Cast the first stone
> And let the Pharisees and Sadducees
> Give way to none.
> But whosoever feels his pride
> Humbled so deep,
> There is no corner he can hide
> Even in sleep.
> Will have no trouble to find out
> How a poor teacher,
> Widowed and lonely, finds delight
> In shouldering care.

Britten sets the lines of this aria to music that evokes the world of oratorio – strong 'masculine' descending scales in F major for Ellen, emphasized by the lower register of the voice, and strong ascending D major scales in the orchestra. Almost all Ellen's music in the opera employs regular rhythms in a manner of word-setting encountered in Britten's earlier songs. Peter Evans cites Sonnet XXX from the *Seven Sonnets of Michelangelo* as an example of this style, in which the 'deliberately unnaturalistic delivery directs our attention beyond [the regular rhythm] to the expressive significance of each melodic interval. What in one sense can appear an understatement can therefore in another represent an emotional essence.'[23] Ellen's relatively stable 'emotional essence' is thus contrasted with the unstable rhythmic character of much of Grimes's and the Borough's music. This 'unnaturalistic delivery' may also direct our attention to her reflective, narrating position beyond the immediate world of the opera.[24]

Sackville-West noted that Ellen's aria has the effect of 'trouncing the villagers and taking responsibility on herself', subjecting her to complete vulnerability on Grimes's behalf as she 'lays down her life' for him.[25] Musically, the aria also completes our introduction to a sequence of tonal regions – E, A and D – that Brett associates with Grimes's 'fantasy world' and I associate with Ellen's narrative voice; these interpretations are not necessarily mutually exclusive, as long as it is qualified that Ellen's love for Peter is both real and genuine (i.e. they are 'fantasy' keys for Peter but 'real' keys for Ellen). Against the opera's primary A is pitted the Borough's primary E♭, establishing a tritonal (*diabolus in musica*) relationship indicative of Peter's Faustian progress.[26]

At Fig. 31 the storm music begins, and a fugal chorus is initiated by Balstrode at Fig. 32. Here the semitonal tension implicit in Grimes's 'The truth, the pity and the truth' (Ex. 4.1) begins to become more explicit, indicating the slowly gathering tragedy. This interval is retained by Britten for its traditional signification of 'sin' and heightened stress. It is thoroughly exploited during the storm music both of the next Interlude and the ensuing pub scene (Act I scene 2). Boles's shouts of 'God has his ways which are not ours, His hightide swallows up the shores. Repent! Repent! Repent!' during the storm chorus (Figs. 31–7) are, like many of his other statements, spiritual truths put into the mouth of a hypocrite.

The second half of scene 1 is dominated by Grimes and his altercations with Balstrode. This retired sea captain – who is not unsympathetic to Grimes – recognizes the value of this private moment in allowing Peter an opportunity 'To free confession: set a conscience free!' It is another key spiritual opportunity that Grimes refuses to take. Balstrode also identifies Ellen's genuine and unconditional love for Grimes in his statement: 'Man – go and ask her, Without your booty, She'll have you now.' But Grimes's nature is too proud (and masquerades as pity): as Pears stated, he 'longs to accept Ellen's love but refuses'.[27] His divided attitude towards Ellen is revealed in two passages immediately prior to and during Interlude II. The transformation of the tension/sin indicated by the minor ninth at Fig. 41 (a semitone displaced by an octave, quoted from their love duet) as he ruminates on the death of his former apprentice into a major ninth as he yearns to find peace with Ellen registers powerfully as his main psychological dilemma (i.e. the need for the semitone to release into the whole tone). The harmonic return of the minor ninth at the words 'With her the mood will stay' expounds the conflict of his social pride with his love for Ellen, which erupts in Interlude II. Whereas the music of the first half of the scene issues from Interlude I and Ellen, the music of this second half seems to be swept up by this powerful 'Peter Interlude'. At Fig. 54 we hear a new form of motif *e* that, as David Matthews has demonstrated, is directly associated with Ellen's opening melody of Act II (see Ex. 4.3). Now, however, it is compressed into semitonal patterns. It is as if Grimes is battling to hold on to Ellen against his compulsion to destroy her. Peace and the harbour that Ellen offers are recalled at Fig. 60 but the storm music confirms what we already fear as it swamps her out. The baptism that Grimes has elected is not one of the redemption of love, but of sleep, death and oblivion in 'Davy Jones's Locker'. Ellen's presence in the music – albeit in Grimes's mind – is as potent as it was in Interlude I. The schizophrenia revealed in the pub during his 'Great Bear and Pleiades' aria (Fig. 76) and his sociopathic disruption of the round song 'Old Joe has Gone Fishing' (Fig. 79) – another moment where the Borough attempts to 'drown' him out – can only arouse our frustrated compassion as we witness the unfolding of the inevitable when Grimes tugs the newly delivered apprentice, John, from Ellen's arms and out into the storm at the end

Example 4.3 Motif *e*

of the act. The storm music from Interlude II, that punctuates this scene in five broken outbursts as the pub door opens and closes, finally bursts forth unabated at the conclusion of the round, significantly with the entry of Ellen, the boy and the carrier.

The ascending motif introduced by the woodwind during Interlude III at the start of Act II is given pitch and textual closure by Ellen at Fig. 6^{+10}. This may be seen to be a second 'Ellen motif' (motif *e2*) which she sings again in the crucial (Phrygian) moment at the 'Adagio' before Fig. 26 (Act III scene 2) where it is heard simultaneously with Balstrode's singing of *x* (see Ex. 4.4). What is particularly fascinating about the relationship between these motifs is that Grimes's motif *x*, first announced fully by him later in Act II scene 1, is a free retrograde of motif *e2* (transposed in Ex. 4.4 to make the connection clearer), itself inverted in Ellen's 'We shall be there with him.' Flat notes are added to the opening woodwind figures of Interlude III to create a darker tension in an otherwise sunny scene, as do the B♭ and E♭ entries of the church bells – the English associations of which are offset by the same oriental resonances derived from McPhee's Balinese gong (see pp. 168–9) as the sonorous bass notes of Interlude I (see Ex. 4.2), which shares its key of A with Ellen's opening melody. The quasi-passacaglia nature of this Interlude (the 'ground' in the horns identified by Peter Evans) symmetrically balances the full-blown passacaglia (Interlude IV) at the conclusion of the scene. The thirds of this horn figure and the superimposed thirds of the string phrases at Fig. 3^{-10} emphasize the signification of this Interlude's femininity.[28]

As the Borough hypocrites worship, Ellen proceeds to sing of her compassion for children as she knits outside the church with John. The essential 'brightness' of her keys is contrasted with the 'flatness' of the liturgical commentaries Britten puts into the mouths of the off-stage congregation. This unseen service (consisting of hymn, responses, Gloria,

Example 4.4

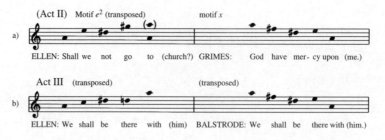

Benedicite and Creed) continues to interact with the drama of the foreground music as Ellen discovers John's bruise at Fig. 10, where she identifies what she at least feels to be Peter's betrayal ('the treason of the waves Glitters like love'). Britten here uses the key of B – the pitch that Mervyn Cooke has identified with the theme of mutiny (a form of treason) in *Billy Budd*.[29] There follows at Fig. 12 a strikingly unconventional setting of the Benedicite. David Matthews has suggested that it has something of a Balinese flavour about it.[30] The frenzied tempo and obsessive cultivation of the Phrygian (minor) second recall Interlude II and, surely enough, Grimes emerges in order to take the boy on his capitalistic enterprise. In his exchanges with Ellen, his Messianic delusions manifest themselves – it is *his* Sunday and Ellen is to believe in *him* – and as Ellen tries to show him that his desire for materialism and status are delusional she questions: 'What aim, what future, what peace will your hard profits buy?' It is Grimes, not Ellen, who is eaten by Borough values.

At the cathartic centre of the opera, after their altercations over a long dominant pedal F, Grimes strikes down the real Ellen (Fig. 17) while retaining a fantasy Ellen in his mind. Thus, as Pears put it, 'his pride, his ambition, his whole overwrought frustration, his inability to admit failure as possible, his feelings of betrayal, are all concentrated into a savage attack on his one true loving friend'.[31] Grimes crucially reverses Ellen's motif *e*2 to create the first undisguised statement of *x* as he concedes to the judgement and value system of the Borough in a Lydian B♭ with the defiant cry: 'And God have mercy upon me.' The Faustian resonances of this moment – hidden in the wordless liturgical creed played by the horns (i.e. 'And He [Christ] descended into Hell') – are veiled by Britten's deliberate manipulation of the text from Peter's original cry of 'To hell then . . .' (in the composition sketch) to 'So be it . . .'. This connection is, however, belatedly disclosed in Act III scene 2 at Peter's cry of 'To hell with all your mercy. To hell with all your revenge. And God have mercy upon you' (Fig. 50). This full revelation of motif *x*, latent from the music of Interlude I until this moment, is very significant. As Walsh puts

Example 4.5

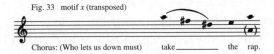

Fig. 33 motif *x* (transposed)

Chorus: (Who lets us down must) take_____ the rap.

it, 'from the moment that Grimes renounces salvation (in everything but his actual words) the theme [motif *x*] pursues him as relentlessly as ever the Furies pursued Orestes.'[32]

Grimes's reversal of Ellen's motif is gleefully and obsessively taken up by the Borough as they pour out of church to the memorably pithy fragment from Crabbe's poem – 'Grimes is at his exercise' – in a large ensemble that, incidentally, has a subtly American flavour to it (cf. 'The Christmas Party' in *Paul Bunyan*, Act III scene 2). Inevitably, a showdown between the Borough and Ellen now takes place. As she attempts an aria at Fig. 31 (in A minor), explaining to them her motives, they continually cut her off in a mounting ensemble of anger and evil suspicion until they slap her down too (metaphorically) to motif *x* at Fig. 33 (Ex. 4.5). Against their accusations she sings: 'O hard hearts, hard, hard hearts, pity those who try to bring a shadowed life into the sun.' The 'shadowed life' could apply both to Grimes and his boy apprentices, who (in Peter Porter's words) 'are attendant angels of his fallen state. His violence towards them might even be deemed no more than a Satanic desire to get them used to the notion of reigning in Hell rather than serving in Heaven.'[33]

The self-righteous, hypocritical mob, sanctified in its own mind by the religious ritual, roars off to confront Grimes at his hut, accompanied by Hobson's drum. This, like every other supposed 'confrontation' between Grimes and the Borough-as-protagonist, *never actually takes place* – interesting non-occurrences, given the customary reading of the opera as an individual against society! Ellen, on the other hand, is confronted directly by the Borough twice and by Grimes once: if *Peter Grimes* is, as Edmund Wilson observed in 1945, an opera about war, then perhaps it is Ellen who embodies Britten's pacifist convictions.

At the conclusion of this scene, Ellen is left on stage alone with Auntie and her two 'Nieces'. Her identification with blatant 'sinners' adds to the poignancy of this moment, and their quartet is justly celebrated.[34] It inhabits the sound-world of the 'Requiem aeternam' from the *Sinfonia da Requiem* – especially in details such as the seconds in the flutes. Peter Evans has linked the flutes' falling thirds to the thirds of Interlude I. Such connections, also illustrated in the build-up of thirds at Fig. 3[-10] in Interlude III (one thinks of the chains of thirds of the women's sewing aria in Act I scene 1 of *The Rape of Lucretia*) lend credibility to the suggestion that Britten confers a signification of the feminine upon this interval. The false relations created by the 'sighing' bass-line at Fig. 41 also recall those of the orientalized bass/bells of Interlude III. Arnold Whittall has commented that 'Britten's personal voice is perhaps at its clearest in such contexts, where economy of means is the dominant factor rather than in moments of high drama and elaborate ensemble.'[35]

Wilfrid Mellers claimed that in *Noye's Fludde* 'the passacaglia theme [of the storm episode] is also God's law which is beyond change'.[36] The passacaglia in Interlude IV is based on motif *x*, recalling Grimes's earlier plea 'And God have mercy upon me' but with an additional beat suggestive also of the motif's second text, 'Grimes is at his exercise.' We have heard this theme taken up obsessively in the second half of Act II scene 1 by the hypocritical Borough which identifies his rebellion with 'his exercise' and self-righteously rises up to execute judgement upon him on God's behalf – even though, in the very act of taking God's vengeance into their own hands, the Borough folk place themselves under that same judgement. Grimes is surely prophetic during his final moments in the opera when he cries out to them: 'And God have mercy upon you'. This same motif implies cries of 'God have mercy . . . God have mercy . . .' as it emerges out of the great climactic moment of Interlude VI at Fig. 47⁻⁶ in Act III. Evans links the significance of these statements with that of Berg's leitmotif 'Wir arme Leut' in the final interlude of *Wozzeck*.[37] If Grimes has unrepentantly rebelled against God's law – the law on which he swore in the inquest of the Prologue to the same dominant seventh, transposed, to which he dies in his final mad scena (Act III scene 2) – it is only logical that his guilty emotions expressed through his physical passions rage against it as they do in Interlude IV and the succeeding scene with the boy in his hut. Ironically, this tends to give a ring of truth to Boles's earlier prophecy: 'What [Grimes] fears is that the Lord follows with a flaming sword' (Act II, Fig. 19).

The orchestral variations of the passacaglia are given textual significance during Act II scene 2 when Grimes is with the boy in his hut.[38] Aggression towards the boy is contrasted with the tenderness of his (now fantastic) dreams of life with Ellen. The death of the boy as he slips down the cliff as they attempt to escape from the approaching mob, if not directly caused by Grimes, is at least caused by the consequence of his choices. Swallow's mock-baroque music as the men inspect Grimes's empty hut forms a mini-frame (with the Prologue music, from which Swallow quotes) to the first two acts, save for the disturbing celesta music as Balstrode ignores the retreating mob and follows Grimes down the cliff-face while the curtain falls.

Interlude V leads to Act III scene 1. What at first appear to be harmless

Example 4.6

(+ 8va)   Pe - ter   Grimes! . . .

Borough dances at the Moot Hall (a barn dance, waltz *alla Ländler*, horn-pipe and galop), transmogrify via the clarinet theme during the waltz (Fig. 13) into the blood-lust cry of the final mob-hunt for Grimes (Fig. 41).[39] Evans has ingeniously shown how the great choral shouts after Fig. 43 are rooted in motif x – God's immanent judgement suggested once again (Ex. 4.6).[40] It is during this scene that we discover the full conse-quences of the interference in events by that 'respectable lady', Mrs Sedley. It is also the scene in which we hear Ellen in an aria that is the most overtly detached from the dramatic action. It is virtually impossible to under-stand the full significance of this moment, as many commentators under-standably fail to do, without setting it into the perspective of Ellen that has been the central thrust of this present chapter. Her 'Embroidery Aria' (Figs. 23–5) is a critical and extensive lament on the theme of betrayal, signified principally by being in the same B (now minor) of her discovery of John's bruise in Act II scene 1. The music is ingeniously contrived by Britten to suggest the very act of embroidery with weaving and tugging of thread.[41] It is tempting to suggest that the events in the opera are being recalled by an older Ellen (perhaps married to Balstrode?), again antici-pating Vere's framing of the events in *Billy Budd*. B major is asserted as Ellen sings her variant of motif $e2$ and Balstrode simultaneously sings its inversion, motif x (see Ex. 4.4b).

Interlude VI is arguably the least known and most fascinating of the six. After a loud blast that disperses the mob, we hear three fatalistic Mahlerian strokes that anticipate in rhythm (if not in pitch) the three abrupt chords that conclude the opera. A nervous flute figure follows, obsessively quoting the 'I'll marry Ellen' motif. Then comes a condensed version of Grimes's vocal line 'And she will forget her school-house ways' (Act II, Fig. 61) in the lower register of the solo harp. Next we hear a con-densed version of the minor ninth from the love duet and the motif that summarizes both Grimes's recollection of the drowned apprentices and the salvation he forfeited with Ellen (Act I scene 1), heard on the three solo violins at Fig. 45. The repeated E♭ that follows on the oboe recalls 'The Great Bear' aria, while the repeated falling semiquavers at the end of a duet for clarinets (itself based on 'Wrong to try!' from Act II scene 2) again recall 'what harbour shelters peace?' After the huge Gershwinesque climax at Fig. 46, the woodwind repeat descending cries of the motif to 'God have mercy . . .'. Again the recollection of these motifs, bound together by a dominant seventh on D played by the horns, ensures the consistent presence of Ellen's voice in the Interludes. As the chorus intone their ghostly cries of 'Grimes, Peter Grimes' they suddenly flower into a sweet E♭ triad at Fig. 49[+5] which, according to Whittall, is 'out of character for the vengeful chorus, but . . . evokes the tenderness of Ellen, whom Grimes is remembering at this point'.[42] Britten's use of unadorned speech for Balstrode's final instructions to Grimes to sink himself with his boat and Ellen's naked exclamation 'No!' can be easily rationalized when heard in a reading from Ellen's perspective. The decorated E♭ of Grimes's final remembrance of 'Her breast is harbour too, Where night is turned to day' can no longer act as a potential dominant onto the A♭ stressed in the earlier love-duet music ('The truth . . . the pity and the truth'; see Ex. 4.1 above).[43] Thus it is bypassed as the music of Interlude I returns, and the cycle begins again – an eternal requiem to Peter Grimes held in Ellen's memory.

5 The chamber operas

ARNOLD WHITTALL

The success of *Peter Grimes* owes much to Britten's convincing use of substantial forces; his creation of appropriately powerful and imposing textures for the depiction of sea, storm and the social menace of a crowd bent on vengeance and retribution. *Grimes* is grand opera after the model of Verdi, Puccini, Berg and Gershwin, a genre which aimed to hold and persuade a substantial audience in a large theatre. Yet this was not how opera, music drama, had first been conceived, and by the middle of the twentieth century it seemed clear to many composers that the romantic and late-romantic eras had explored only one of the ways in which music and drama might interact.

Britten's interest in such precedents for a more intimate kind of music theatre as *Dido and Aeneas* and *The Beggar's Opera* would have been sharpened by his regard for twentieth-century compositions like Holst's *Sāvitri* (three singers, at most twelve players in the orchestra) and various works by Stravinsky (*Renard*, *The Soldier's Tale*) which turned their backs on opera as traditionally conceived. In a manifesto of 1946 Britten put the point with characteristic directness: 'I am keen to develop a new art-form (the chamber opera, or what you will) which will stand beside the grand opera as the quartet stands beside the orchestra. I hope to write many works for it.'[1] The impulse behind this 'new art-form' was nevertheless not purely aesthetic. Eric Crozier, who produced the première of *Peter Grimes*, has described how increasing frustrations and anxieties connected with that event led him to suggest 'that we should form a small company of gifted singers . . . with ourselves as artistic directors, no chorus, and the smallest group of instrumentalists that Ben would find acceptable'.[2] Crozier was well aware that this new kind of opera would need to be able to work in larger theatres as well as smaller spaces. After all, most performances of Britten's chamber operas actually take place in theatres large enough to stage his full-size operas as well, and the special intimacy of *The Rape of Lucretia* (first performed at Glyndebourne on 12 July 1946), *Albert Herring* (Glyndebourne, 20 June 1947) and *The Turn of the Screw* (La Fenice, Venice, 14 September 1954) might be felt to have an even greater impact when they are staged in less-than-intimate surroundings. Crozier himself had no doubt that, as far as *The Rape of Lucretia* was concerned, 'the quality and vitality of the voices with instruments were much better in large theatres than in small. There were no complaints of thinness or raggedness in texture.'[3]

It was Crozier who suggested André Obey's play *Le viol de Lucrèce* (1931) as a suitable text for Britten's first chamber opera, offering as it did a small-scale yet strongly dramatic narrative in which a virtuous, sensitive individual is traumatically violated and driven to self-destruction.[4] With its classical aura and use of narrators to provide a frame for the drama, Obey's dramatic conception could hardly have been more different from that found in *Grimes*. Yet Britten's acceptance of the Lucretia story is logical enough, given its direct association with his favoured theme of the conflict between the vulnerable and the vicious: and even the decision to write an opera set in classical times is less surprising when the work is viewed in the context of a precedent like the incidental music he had composed for Edward Sackville-West's radio play *The Rescue*, based on Homer's *Odyssey*, in 1943. The appeal of a classic topic could also be connected to Britten's increasing engagement with Purcell. In 1946 it was possible to sense a degree of kinship between the dramaturgy of *Dido and Aeneas* and that of verse-dramatists prominent at the time, like T. S. Eliot, Christopher Fry and Ronald Duncan. As Britten's manifesto suggests, a genre of chamber opera acknowledging such associations offered an attractive alternative to the more mainstream operatic heritage that underpins the vitality of *Grimes*. Yet what Britten and Duncan achieved in *Lucretia* was more than a scaled-down grand opera, aesthetically as well as commercially appropriate for the post-war Age of Austerity. The work gains strength and conviction both from its questioning of grand-operatic conventions, and also from its reassertion, in contemporary terms, of certain musical and dramatic values more evident in the works of Monteverdi and Purcell than of Wagner or Richard Strauss. Yet *The Rape of Lucretia* is not a wholehearted 'number opera' after baroque or classical models: rather, as *Grimes* had done, it subjects the nineteenth-century concept of through-composition to the constraints of persistent and resourceful allusions to earlier operatic genres: aria, recitative, ensemble.

Ronald Duncan's libretto for *The Rape of Lucretia* has consistently attracted criticism, and Peter Porter's characterization of its poetry as 'damply effulgent' is a representative judgement.[5] While Duncan stayed quite close to the Obey text as far as matters of plot are concerned, his style is very different, not least the Christian allusions which, as Eric Walter White observed, create a 'severely dogmatic tone' that is 'far removed from the pagan spirit of Shakespeare and Obey'.[6] Puritanical constraints on unfettered paganism were, nevertheless, part of the appeal for Britten, and the libretto conveys a strong sense of the tension between formality and deep feeling on which the drama depends, and on which the music is able to build. Alongside that tension Duncan established another, between the immediacy of dramatic events and the framing commentary, which proves to be the source of much of the opera's most engaging ambiguity, the interaction between past and present.

Although the score declares that the Male and Female Choruses 'do not take part in' the tragedy itself, they react, respond to and interpret it in ways which make them much more than disengaged observers. Unable to confine the action to a past which they recollect in tranquillity, they recreate the action in the present – standing in, as it were, for librettist and composer: and even if they know in advance what the outcome of the action will be, their foreknowledge intensifies rather than dilutes the impact of that outcome. The Choruses are the very model of detached scholars: they are shown 'reading from books', and the sheer plainness of some of the recitative through which they communicate risks excessive musical dryness. Yet they are also fully implicated in the terror and pity of an action which is actual, not recollected: enacted, not merely narrated. In this respect, the present tense of the text's first line – 'Rome is now ruled' – is decisive.

Much critical attention has been given to the Christian gloss of the opera's epilogue – added at Britten's request to ensure a sufficiently substantial closing episode.[7] But Christian – or post-pagan – perspectives are part of the Chorus material throughout: the text of the first scene observes that 'This Rome has still five hundred years to wait / Before Christ's birth and death', and promises that 'We'll view these human passions and these years / Through eyes which once have wept with Christ's own tears'. The Christian perspective here intensifies a 'then/now' dichotomy in which the 'then' is inevitably more vivid dramatically. A Christian gloss is therefore far from perfunctory, and its ideological 'otherness' is as explicit as that of church, congregation and vicar for Grimes in the earlier opera, though to very different effect. The clash of then and now, rapacious instinct and formalized virtue, in *Lucretia* is found at its fullest dramatic extent in the Act II Interlude, structured to suggest a set of chorale variations and with melodic material that obsessively restricts itself to a narrow compass (Ex. 5.1). Just as this uncomfortable passage can be associated with the aura of what Philip Brett has termed 'a religion which celebrates the victim, and therefore the very concept of victimisation',[8] so it also takes us to the heart of the opera's way of questioning musical conventions.

Many commentators prefer to concentrate on *Lucretia*'s resourceful references to conventions, especially to the various genres of the number opera. But these intersect with other genres, like march, chorale prelude or lullaby, that are not essentially operatic, and the relevance of which

Example 5.1

Choruses

f

Here in this scene you see vir - tue as -

sailed by sin with strength___ tri - umphing   etc.

may be cued by the text. For example, the line heard early in Act I scene 1, 'So, here, the grumbling Romans march from Rome', determines the basic character of the whole episode as a martial fantasia. Reiterated dissonances for the full ensemble contrast with the 'domestic' rectitude of the piano-accompanied recitative, but this contrast is not so complete as to exclude motivic interaction, and it eventually dissolves as the march music, associated with the restlessness and potentially uncontrolled aggressiveness of Tarquinius and his soldiers, leads into the hymn-like phrases in which the Choruses adopt an air of compassionate detachment from events which might otherwise seem all-too-vividly violent (Ex. 5.2). The text here is undeniably sententious. Yet the ponderous formality of the words is countered by elements of instability in the music – for example, alternations of major and minor inflections of the kind illustrated in Ex. 5.2 – that are among Britten's most familiar, and effective, stylistic attributes.

After the opening Chorus statements of Scene 1 an atmosphere of menace is created through the disconcerting interaction of nocturne and drinking-song, genres which could hardly be more different yet which are each destabilized by Britten's characteristically oblique use of tonal harmony. As the scene proceeds it becomes clear that all three men are weak in different ways: Tarquinius is lecherous, Junius is jealous, while Collatinus is the innocent idealist trusting in his wife Lucretia's virtue. The alternation of recitative and arietta here may not be generically ambiguous, but it is extremely flexible, enabling the action to flow along without obvious reliance on the more clear-cut divisions of baroque and classical precedent. At this stage of Scene 1 we also encounter one of the opera's fundamental topics, which Brett has defined as the 'ambiguous nature of beauty',[9] and which is, of course, inseparable from the ambiguous nature of virtue. The predominant factor, nevertheless, is the childish argument between Junius and Tarquinius, and the climax of the episode comes down to a schoolboy 'dare', as Tarquinius decides to 'prove Lucretia chaste'. The Interlude illustrating the ride to Rome is pure libido-music, yet Britten prefers the rhythmic and textural constraints of such time-

Example 5.2

honoured models as toccata or moto perpetuo to an expressionistic frag-
mentation as Tarquinius loses the last vestiges of self-discipline. The elements of vocal display in the Male Chorus's narration also offer an
unsettling formality to interact with the explosively direct emotions.

Scene 2 is a clear dramatic and musical complement to Scene 1. The
two flowing work-songs for the women – spinning and linen-folding –
stand in direct opposition to the men's drinking-song, and while, as in
Scene 1, song and recitative interact, the role of recitative to deepen
psychological perception is enhanced in Scene 2 by contrasting intrusions
which represent the approaching menace. The songs are sad as well as
serene, their subtle harmonic instabilities shaped around the key line
'death is woman's final lover'. The climax of the scene is the 'rape' of Scene
2's gentle music by Tarquinius's toccata as he arrives at Lucretia's house.
For its ambiguous epilogue, Act I then returns to a form of night music –
the 'goodnight' ensemble – which adumbrates a precarious synthesis of
formality and feeling in minuet-like phrases built from four-beat melodic
motifs that cut across the three-beat pulse (Ex. 5.3). As in Scene 1, there is
little serenity in this night-music, and the foundations have been laid for
even more intense explorations of comparable topics in Act II.

After an initial narrative which is considerably more turbulent than
that which began Act I, and in which the 'then' of the singers representing
the troubled Romans and the 'now' of the commentating Choruses
increasingly interact, Act II returns to night-music, in the Female
Chorus's lullaby-like description of Lucretia asleep. This time the contrast is provided first by the Male Chorus's speech-song description of
Tarquinius's approach, then by Tarquinius's own surprisingly tranquil
arietta. Only as he urges Lucretia to wake does his music make sinister
advances to the lullaby genre, and the violence of the rape itself is anticipated by the way the lullaby's music yields to that of Tarquinius's arietta.

The dialogue between Tarquinius and Lucretia is probably the score's
least inspired section: here, for the only time in the work, a sense of
formality in the exchanges seems counter-productive, depriving the very
different emotions of their necessary force. Even so, there is considerable

Example 5.3

Andante grazioso

pp   cresc.   mf

[Orchestra only]

dramatic power in the increasing stylization of what would otherwise be obscenely explicit, and the musical explosion of the 'Chorale-Prelude' Interlude, with its almost manic blend of outrage and compassion, is as powerful in its way as the Act I Interlude depicting Tarquinius's ride to Rome.

After a finely controlled scaling-down of pace and density, Act II scene 2 begins with the opera's most untroubled music, as Bianca and Lucia welcome the morning sunshine and sing their flower-arranging song. As song turns more towards arioso, so the mood darkens, and although the recitative exchanges between Lucretia and her attendants have some of the awkward rhetoric of the music prior to the rape – an even more explicitly Purcellian economy might have been welcome here – the return of song refocuses emotion to gripping effect. Lucretia's wreath-making establishes the aura of funeral march which will dominate the rest of the score, though never obtrusively. Its second stage is that of Lucretia's second entrance, 'dressed in purple mourning': what follows, of course, is not an expansive final aria but a flexibly structured dialogue between Collatinus and Lucretia, and only after Lucretia's death is a purely musical form allowed to dictate the dramatic structure. Of all the genres found in the opera, passacaglia is in one sense the most abstract, the most confined yet also the most cumulative. Just as the *Grimes* passacaglia grows from a lament for the dead apprentice into what seems like an outpouring of grief in face of all intolerance and human weakness, so the *Lucretia* passacaglia brings the philosophical and dramatic themes of the work into synthesis. The Epilogue can then allow the emotional intensity to dissipate to some degree, although the ending, returning to highly expressive alternations of major and minor inflections, is finely poised between acceptance and regret.

Taken literally, the terminology of Britten's 'manifesto' on chamber opera means that the difference between compositions for orchestra and string quartet is more one of scale than of formal principle. Just as sonata form is as viable a structure in a string quartet as it is in a symphony, so the essential forms found in the two types of opera need not be different. Nor need the 'essential forms' in a tragedy be different from those of comedy, and the most obvious contrasts between *The Rape of Lucretia* and *Albert Herring* are in matters of musical character, and in working out the consequences of a less stylized, more naturalistic type of music drama.

It may well be inevitable that passages of arioso and dialogue in twentieth-century opera will tend more towards the through-composed structuring associated primarily with Wagner – although, as many later nineteenth-century and early twentieth-century operas prove, such structuring need not bring with it anything remotely resembling a Wagnerian style. This will be particularly the case in less-than-tragic operas, and the most fundamental difference between *Herring* and *Lucretia* is that the tension between formality and feeling so crucial to the earlier work is transmuted into a form appropriate for comedy, to exploit a tension between the social pomposity of those in power and the child-like decency and innocence of those who are in varying ways subordinate and repressed.

When regarded in these terms, it is not surprising that *Herring* should seem, in Donald Mitchell's phrase, a 'serious comedy'.[10] Even as 'a parable of liberation'[11] its serious dimension cannot be denied. As Philip Brett argues,

> the power of this remarkable score stems ultimately from Britten's own ambivalence about a society which on the one hand he desperately wished to serve and on the other he profoundly mistrusted. Behind *Herring* lies all the tension of *Grimes*, but projected through comedy, and softened by one rather unexpected element – the genuine celebration of physicality and sensuousness in the music of Sid and Nancy.[12]

In this respect, at least, one could also claim that 'all the tension' of *Lucretia* also lies behind the comedy, since in *Lucretia* 'physicality and sensuousness' are not so much celebrated as projected – very graphically – as the agents of personal and social catastrophe, of 'liberation' as destruction. Brett's claim that, in writing *Herring*, 'the composer must have realised that liberation cannot be achieved without repossession of the body and of feeling; and, puritan though he was, he found a way of encapsulating that thought in music',[13] seems all the more true if the no less potent presentation of a very different, tragic view of physicality in *Lucretia* is recalled: and these are certainly not topics restricted to the world of chamber opera.

Like *Lucretia*, *Albert Herring* stems from a French source – a story by Guy de Maupassant.[14] The librettist, Eric Crozier, effected a fairly strong transformation of the original in transferring a rather dark tale into the very different environment of a Suffolk town in which it is appropriate to depict a 'rite of passage' as a reaffirmation of conventional social values: the time, after all, is 1900, not 1946. The musical genres employed in *Albert Herring* are those appropriate to the society depicted and to the comic, at times parodic, complexion of the drama. Dances, children's games (a marker here for the musical world of *The Turn of the Screw*), march, anthem, threnody, and various lyrical pieces often quite close to the world of light music are all to be found. The formal mix of closed numbers and more 'symphonic' arioso and recitative is familiar, yet the ways in which these diverse structures are characterized are more consistently assured than in *Lucretia*, perhaps because the dramatic context is less stylized, the subject-matter less intense. As one of the earliest commentators on the work, Erwin Stein, perceived, Britten's effectiveness as an opera composer stemmed from the way 'the forms were arranged for every detail to stand out with its right emphasis', and Stein noted that in *Herring* 'transitions and recitatives have become more integrated [than they are in *Lucretia*] though naturally the structure of the comic opera remains light and loose'. Acknowledging Britten's avoidance of 'post-Wagnerian quasi-symphonic forms', Stein remarked that 'the ancient tree of recitative yields uncommon fruits to Benjamin Britten'.[15] Norman Del Mar was another early admirer of recitatives which he also saw as an advance over those in *Lucretia*, 'not only in the complex interplay between a large number of participants, but also in the mastery with which the accompanying skeletal harmony is devised'.[16] Del Mar concluded that not only was Britten's melodic invention more 'spontaneous and inevitable'[17] than in the first chamber opera, but that there was also greater richness in the developmental treatment of the musical motifs themselves.

Britten evidently relished the opportunity for soloistic treatment of his instrumental ensemble, the chance to think in terms of individual details as well as broader effects. Yet, while *Albert Herring* is a chamber opera, it has a substantial cast of characters. Its ten principals are only two fewer than those needed for *Grimes*, and it is the main function of Act I scene 1 to introduce and characterize a large proportion of them. Since this scene does not include Albert himself, or the pair of young lovers Sid and Nancy, Britten's generic models are not lyric; rather he alludes to various types of dance – to tarantella and its close relative the jig, as well as the waltz. There are also references to Anglican chant and to fugue, which, in its neo-baroque manifestation, is a particularly easy target for pompous parody. Such unambiguous musical humour could invite superficiality, but Britten is careful never to allow any single allusion to outstay its welcome, and, while avoiding those 'post-Wagnerian quasi-symphonic forms', as Erwin Stein observed, his main concern is to build the relatively short single segments of characterization into large formal units, giving the scene as a whole an exhilarating sweep and momentum. Scene 2, in which the news of Albert's election as 'King of the May' (no suitable 'Queen' being available), balances Scene 1 in giving greater emphasis to lyrical music, though with the lightest of touches. Sid and Nancy are presented in an almost scherzo-like way, while the music for Albert's Mum, and the opening children's game, provide links to the dance-like rhythmic bounce of the first scene.

Act II scene 1 begins with anticipations of Scene 2's pastoral/nocturnal moods, the opening horn call promising a new world of sensuality and self-assertion. But the scene of Albert's 'coronation' is mainly occupied with further explorations of the kind of comic genres introduced in Act I scene 1. Here, as there, subtleties of technique underpin such broadly humorous effects as the reference to *Tristan* when Sid spikes Albert's lemonade with rum – a reference gleefully amplified when Albert drinks the potion – and it could be argued that the absence of a large orchestra, with the corresponding need to create atmosphere and character in delicate rather than bold fashion, helps to intensify the purely musical interest of the scene. It is in Scene 2 that Albert himself achieves maximum musical prominence, and his tendency towards more lyric forms and contemplative moods finds fulfilment. His long scena, with its clearly defined sections of action and reflection, involves a basic progression from timidity to confidence, and the music moves from its initial pastoral/nocturnal mode, through lyric forms which suggest cavatina or romanza, to the more dance-like determination which seem to bring Albert closer in character to his mother and the various civic worthies.

Just how stable this new-found determination on Albert's part will be is, naturally, a topic for Act III. First the music progresses from agitation to mourning (Albert missing, presumed dead) in a way that underpins a basic if ambiguous sense of irony, and Britten's determination to avoid solemnity is shown by his sly citation of Lucretia's motif when Superintendent Budd refers to 'a criminal case of rape'. The chaconne-like Threnody in which all the characters – Albert apart – reflect on matters of life and death is an imposing climax to the entire work (Ex. 5.4), and it also provides an effective foil to the opera's understated dénouement. On his return Albert proves – musically – that he will neither simply revert to his earlier timidity nor demonstrate a transformation of character that has no relevance within Loxford society. The music with which he asserts his new-found independence at first seems dangerously like that of his mother; soon, however, it moves closer in spirit if not in substance to that of Sid. Whether or not he might again become a 'wayfaring lad' in the future, Albert seems content for the

Example 5.4

All characters except Albert
Slow, sustained

In the midst of life is death, Death a - waits us one and all:

Death at - tends our smal - lest step, Si - lent, swift and mer - - - - ci - ful.

moment to exercise his maturity within a familiar society rather than beyond it.

However great the relief with which Britten moved from grand opera to chamber opera after *Grimes,* it was not the case that grand opera was forever proscribed. After *Albert Herring* his creative pendulum swung back in the direction of larger designs, first in the *Spring Symphony* (1949), and then in *Billy Budd* (1951) and *Gloriana* (1953). At the same time his commitment to the English Opera Group was kept alive in *The Little Sweep* (1949) and his versions of *The Beggar's Opera* (1948) and *Dido and Aeneas* (1951), and a return to chamber opera might have seemed even more attractive after the traumas connected with the first production of *Gloriana*.[18] Even though it appears that the commission from Venice for *The Turn of the Screw* specifically for the smaller forces of the English Opera Group was secured well before the *Gloriana* pre-mière,[19] it might be imagined that Britten would have been most reluc-tant to provide another work on the scale of the Coronation opera: and, indeed, he never composed exclusively for large-scale operatic forces again.

Britten's long-established familiarity with Henry James's short story about the corrupting of a young boy and girl by the unquiet spirits of a former valet and governess is well documented,[20] but this familiarity should not reduce appreciation of the audacity inherent in choosing the tale as an operatic subject. Not only does it challenge conventional moral-ity with a directness enhanced rather than diluted by James's literary style:

Example 5.5

it depends, as an opera, on the availability of a boy soprano able to sustain
a demanding solo role. By 1953 Britten had written extensively for children's choirs and had used boys and girls for relatively minor parts in
earlier operas, as well as for more central roles in a minor opera, *The Little
Sweep*. But the need for *The Turn of the Screw* to have a treble in a leading
role was both a challenge and a risk. In itself, it would have pointed the
composer in the direction of chamber opera, in order to reduce the likeli-
hood of relatively weak voices being drowned in instrumental sound. But
the nature of the tale itself, its claustrophobic atmosphere, its stifled
intensity and sense of confinement of just four living characters to the
doom-laden estate of Bly, make the idea of an operatic version involving
full orchestra and elaborate staging hard to imagine.

Less predictable, given the nature of Britten's preferred operatic structures up to this time, was the specially concentrated way in which he
responded to the title's image of turning and tightening. If he had wished
to make a strong point of devising a structure based on the interaction of
twelve-note thinking and tonality, Britten might have required of his
librettist an outline containing either six or twelve scenes per act, so that
the total would exhaust the twelve possible keynotes either once or twice.
Naturally enough, nothing so theory-led emerged, although there is a
degree of symmetry between the two acts: the eight scenes of each
prompting a basic sequence of keynotes in which the second octave
inverts the first, in a 'serial' relationship of I-11 to P-0: Act I's progression
from A to A♭ employs P-0 (that is, the basic eight-note row untransposed),
while Act II uses I-11 (the inversion of P-0 transposed up eleven semitones) to move back from A♭ to A in a different way (Ex. 5.5).

The quotation marks around 'serial' are necessary to underline the fact
that serialism in the orthodox sense has no role to play here. Had Britten
wanted to explore more thoroughgoing interactions between tonal and
twelve-note techniques he might have followed the example of Berg, who
had demonstrated (principally in the *Lyric Suite* and the Violin Concerto)
how such an interaction could work. But the highly ramified calculations
of a Berg – even when the result was intensely expressive, overtly emotional music – were foreign to Britten's way of working. Nor does it make
much sense to compare him to Stravinsky, who also began to work with
the interaction between serialism and tonality after Schoenberg's death in
1951, before committing himself to a comprehensive, and essentially

Example 5.6

Theme

atonal, twelve-note technique in *Threni* (1958). Britten never employed consistent successions of row-forms after the model of Schoenberg, Webern or Stravinsky, and his decision to base the orchestral interludes in *The Turn of the Screw* on a theme that used all twelve notes without losing sight of the basic tonality of A (Ex. 5.6) was surely more the result of its psychological appropriateness as an image of an obsessively intensifying control (Quint's hold on Miles) than of a decision to transform his compositional ethos from within. Britten's musical language was undoubtedly enriched and intensified by his willingness to use twelve-note successions melodically and even, as *The Turn of the Screw* demonstrates, to use twelve-note chords as embodiments of extreme horror; but the roots of that language remain fixed in tonality, and in the effects of the 'emancipation of the dissonance'[21] on basic triadic identities and progressions.

What the opera may owe to Berg is not its interaction between serial and tonal but a formal design, like that of *Wozzeck*, in which orchestral interludes are crucial to the character of the whole, bringing an element of abstract, even symphonic structuring to the work. Yet Berg's elaborate mapping of his operatic scenes onto a wide range of different musical forms involved the kind of intellectual plotting for which Britten had little inclination. The formal outline of *The Turn of the Screw* – a Prologue, then the theme, and fifteen instrumental variations, separating and preparing sixteen concisely organized operatic scenes – helps to ensure a steadily accumulating expressive intensity that is far from abstract, and by no means suffers from comparison with Berg's great drama of inexorable advance to catastrophe.

The Prologue, which begins the opera with a detached narration not

Example 5.7

too dissimilar in style to the opening of *The Rape of Lucretia*, was not part of the original plan, but added after Britten had composed the first three scenes and feared that the work might simply be too short.[22] As a result, the Prologue leads with particular subtlety into the opera's main action, by outlining the main elements of the (already composed) principal theme, and providing a vivid portrait of the Governess as someone both indecisive and impulsive. The first full statement of the orchestral theme on which the subsequent fifteen variations will be based, accumulating to a menacing twelve-note chord (see Ex. 5.6), is then presented as an extended, intensifying upbeat to the music of Scene 1 ('The Journey') with its firm tonal centre of A and its excited mood of anticipation. Formally speaking, Scene 1 can be regarded as a development of the Theme, a free recitative pinned down by the percussion ostinato, and flowering at its climax into a motif in the vocal line in which turning and twisting graphically represents the Governess's doubts and fears (Ex. 5.7).

Variation 1/Scene 2 ('The Welcome') follows the pattern of Theme/Scene 1 in the sense that the variation provides an intensifying upbeat to the scene itself, and prepares its predominant character and material: again, the scene is in some ways a development of the variation. But Scene 2 is also an excellent illustration of the fact that, while this opera is indeed concentrated and concise, the individual scenes can embrace strong contrasts of mood and generic prototype. The principal tone is that of the children's exuberant welcome for their new governess, the first use in the work of material which is inherently simple, yet can quickly darken and become more sinister.

With Variation 2/Scene 3 ('The Letter') Britten changes the pattern, and intensifies the integration. While the variation material now grows directly out of the previous scene, using the expansive idea associated with Bly, the scene gradually turns away from this, first to a development of the Governess's 'anxiety' motif as she reads the letter announcing that Miles has been expelled from his school, then to an ensemble built around the children's song 'Lavender's blue'. This ensemble is a particularly telling and beautiful example of Britten's ability to penetrate to the heart of a dramatic situation riven with ambivalence and tension by the use of simple yet subtly dissonant inflections of consonant source material; and it is the opposition of security and instability that comes to a head in

Example 5.8

Variation 3/Scene 4 ('The Tower'). The contrast is already implicit in the variation itself, between the broad, serene depiction of the surroundings at Bly and the fluttering, shuddering sounds of nature that presage the Governess's agitation after she has seen the apparition of Peter Quint for the first time. The music of the scene first extends and explores that of the variation, then changes for a second part which develops a new idea, deriving from the main theme's repeated fourths, and representing the Governess's agitation (Ex. 5.8).

The mood of sinister anxiety that ends Scene 4 is carried over into Variation 4/Scene 5 ('The Window'). The Variation introduces the harsh, march-like version of 'Tom, Tom the Piper's son' which shows the children's darker side for the first time. But this is only a prelude to the longest and most complex scene in the opera so far. The children's song is followed by an orchestral development of the agitated material from Scene 4, as the Governess again confronts Quint's ghost. Then, the main part of the scene takes the form of an extended dialogue between the Governess and Mrs Grose in which the story of the deaths of Quint and Miss Jessel is told, to a freely evolving musical structure based on the Governess's first motif of anxiety and indecision. The contrapuntal accumulations of this as Mrs Grose explains the manner of Quint's death are chilling, and help to ensure that the Governess's reaction – her determination to take full responsibility and protect the children without seeking any outside help – comes across as further evidence of her vulnerability.

Variation 5 presents a version of the first of Scene 6's two 'learning songs' for Miles. This scene ('The Lesson') offers a strong contrast between its two main components, the engaging 'grammar song', with its clear-cut tonal basis, and the wistful melancholy of 'Malo', with its riddle-like text matched with music that is both simple in motivic outline and ambiguous in tonal orientation, not least because the melody tends to fit dissonantly with its supporting triads (Ex. 5.9) – an effect which Britten will return to at the end of the opera. Variation 6 then exploits the flowing material that will feature in the early stages of Scene 7 ('The Lake'), and at first it seems as if this scene might provide a parallel to Scene 6, with two very different learning songs for Flora. The structure is more extended and diverse, however: not only is Flora's lullaby to her doll preceded by a dialogue between her and the Governess, but the appearance of Miss

Example 5.9

Jessel's ghost leads to an outburst for the Governess, developing her 'agitation' motif, that shifts the mood of the opera decisively. From now on there can be no false hopes that all will be well, at least until the reason for the ghosts' appearance has been confronted.

Variation 7/Scene 8 ('At Night') moves towards that confrontation by making clear that the hitherto silent ghosts are actively malevolent. The more self-consciously poetic text, and the more florid music, also mark a clear departure from a musical atmosphere determined by the children's songs and the Governess's insecurity. Both the eerie figuration and the full statement of the main ('Screw') theme in the variation (the first since the end of the Prologue) come to dominate the music of Scene 8, which is in three principal parts, the first haunted by recurrences of Quint's melismatic incantation, the second comprising exchanges between Quint and Miss Jessel, and the third a culminating ensemble which moves from a duet for the ghosts to a brief sextet as the other characters join in and the 'Screw' theme is heard again in the orchestra. The brief coda, as Miles sweetly confesses that he is 'bad', confirms that the scene's tonal centre, and the first act's overall goal, is A♭. It is from this centre that Act II starts out.

Variation 8/Scene 9[23] ('Colloquy and Soliloquy') parallels the final stages of Act I, but with important differences. The variation prepares the material of the first part of the scene in the usual way, and, as a dialogue for Quint and Miss Jessel, this grows dramatically out of the middle part of Scene 8. At its climax there is a recollection of the full statement of the 'Screw' theme that occurred near the end of Scene 8, which is enclosed, as the ghosts sing their culminating duet of menace and hatred, by reiteration of Yeats's line 'The ceremony of innocence is drowned'. This is set to a form of the Governess's motif of doubt and instability (Ex. 5.10; compare with Ex. 5.7), and a powerful dramatic and musical link is established between human frailty and supernatural malevolence. While it is easier in the story than in the opera to regard the ghosts as figments of the Governess's imagination, Britten underlines the complicity of ghosts and governess in driving Miles to his death.

In the second half of Scene 9 the ghosts' affirmations are immediately

Example 5.10

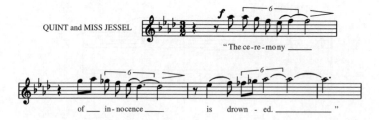

QUINT and MISS JESSEL

"The ce - re - mo ny _____

of ___ in - no - cence _____ is drown - ed. _____ "

followed by the Governess's admission of confusion and failure, a rapid, concentrated aria which keeps turning back, with the force of an obsession, to the same A♭/G♯ centre that has governed the ghosts' music. Variation 9/Scene 10 ('The Bells') is still more concentrated, after the pattern of the scenes involving the children in Act I. The variation music continues throughout the first part of the scene, in which Miles and Flora sing an increasingly sinister 'Benedicite'. The second of the scene's three main parts is also dominated by recurrences of the bell music as the Governess has her disturbing conversation with Miles. The final part, like that of the previous scene, is for the Governess alone: whereas Scene 9 ended with her expression of confusion, Scene 10 ends with her apparent admission of defeat, and her determination to leave Bly. It is this music of apparent decisiveness which carries over into Variation 10. Scene 11 ('Miss Jessel') then starts with new material; but it has the familiar two-stage structure, a song of lament for Miss Jessel, interspersed with the Governess's words of fear and outrage, then another *scena* for the Governess alone, which is itself in three parts: an introduction expressing her new determination to stay and ask for help, the orchestral representation of her writing a letter to the children's guardian, and the more tranquil sung version, an arch of melody which, in this context, seems almost – and ominously – serene.

Variation 11/Scene 12 ('The Bedroom') demonstrates the increasingly recapitulatory nature of the material, with Miles's 'Malo' song and Quint's melismata reappearing. The tighter turning of the screw may also be embodied in the way the entire scene continues the developmental process begun in the variation, with its eerie woodwind canons and sudden bursts of agitation. Separation of variation from scene is even less appropriate in Variation 12/Scene 13 ('Quint'), in which agitated rhythmic patterns interact with Quint's mixture of arioso and speech-song as he urges Miles to steal the Governess's letter to the children's guardian. So, too, with Variation 13/Scene 14 ('The Piano') the distorted classical style of Miles's initial 'variation' continues into the scene as the Governess and Mrs Grose sing his praises. Different piano music, also played by Miles, then accompanies Flora's cat's-cradle song, and continues as the Governess discovers that Flora has tricked Mrs Grose and run off. Variation 14 functions both as the musical climax of the previous scene, with its Tchaikovsky-like bravura, and as an introduction to Scene 15 ('Flora'). Like earlier scenes, this one moves from action involving several characters (the music focusing on Flora's childishly petulant denial that she can actually see Miss Jessel) to the Governess's solitary reflections on her predicament.

The final Variation (15) frames its inversionally related recitatives for piccolo and timpani with three differently spaced twelve-note chords which swell out from *ppp* to *fff*. After this uncompromising representation of a state of extreme crisis, Scene 16 ('Miles') is formed as a passacaglia introduced by dialogue in recitative between the Governess and Mrs Grose, its recurring motif the idea associated with Mrs Grose's recognition that Quint is a force for evil. Initially the passacaglia material itself might seem almost incongruous for such a climactic stage in the drama; since Britten is concerned to portray the boy's nonchalant manner, the music is marked 'smoothly and elegantly'. Quite quickly, of course, the smoothness is disturbed, the elegance ruffled, as Quint's A♭-based music clashes with the passacaglia's A major, and the final stage of the conflict (worked out by Britten in a revision to the original conclusion)[24] involves a bitonal confrontation between a recapitulation of Quint's 'On the paths, in the woods' and the Governess's insistent questioning, aimed to encourage Miles to exorcize Quint's influence by naming him. In one of Britten's most intense, characteristically ironic dénouements, a harmonic resolution – the assertion of A♮ as bass note and tonic, and the 'defeat' of Quint represented by the fact that his final melisma is now in A, not A♭ – is obliged to accommodate tragedy rather than triumph, and the inspired use of the 'Malo' song as the music fades away confirms this tragedy by contrasting the disorientated melody with the grimly decisive A major reiterations of the harmony.

More intensely than any of Britten's earlier operas, *The Turn of the Screw* exploits the way that dramatic situation and musical character cohere around the image of 'strangeness' – the presence of something irrational and threatening that disorientates and destabilizes. In *The Rape of Lucretia*, what destabilizes Lucretia herself is all too real, yet nothing in the drama discourages the attitude that her reaction is disproportionately extreme, her rejection of her husband's words of comfort almost more chilling than the fact of the rape itself. Lucretia has indeed been driven beyond reason. In *Albert Herring* Albert is 'destabilized', provoked into his gesture of escape, by observing the open sexuality of Sid and Nancy, and again his reaction may seem extreme, even if his sanguine attitude on his return to Loxford indicates that any 'extremeness' in his behaviour has been (comically?) temporary. It is hard to imagine anything temporary about the Governess's predicament at the end of *The Turn of the Screw*, or to feel that her reaction is disproportionate to the tragedy in which she has played such an active part. James, of course, does not tell us what the reaction of society is to these events, but we may judge that it will not be sympathetic, and nor would Britten have expected it to be.

Britten's three chamber operas offer very different perspectives on a common theme. In *The Rape of Lucretia* vulnerability is shown as an exemplary instance of moral rectitude and physical fidelity within a pervasively corrupt culture. *Albert Herring* then offers the other side of the coin, since Albert's vulnerability and innocence are set aside after a 'rite of passage' from which he emerges more self-assured and self-assertive than he was before, but ready to occupy a place within the society that had previously made life hard for him. *The Turn of the Screw* offers the bleakest picture of all, in that not only is the vulnerable, innocent child corrupted and then destroyed, but 'society', in the guise of well-meaning yet vulnerable adults, fails to offer the protection that is the child's right. In the intimate world of the chamber operas, there is a particular clarity and conviction to the musical presentation of these topics that ensures for all three works a high place in Britten's output as a whole.

6 *Gloriana*: Britten's 'slighted child'

ANTONIA MALLOY-CHIRGWIN

Gloriana was conceived during a skiing holiday Britten spent with Peter Pears and the Harewoods in March 1952. In his memoirs, the Earl of Harewood recalls an après-ski discussion of great national operas, amongst them Smetana's *The Bartered Bride*, Musorgsky's *Boris Godunov*, Wagner's *Die Meistersinger* and, above all, Verdi's *Aida*, which Britten cited as 'the perfect expression of every kind of nationalist feeling, national pride'.[1] When it was pointed out that no such work existed in the English repertory, the answer seemed obvious – he would have to write one. Given that Elizabeth II had just acceded to the throne, it was natural for a composer with Britten's innate sense of occasion (and practicality) to suggest that this opera should be part of the forthcoming Coronation celebrations. It was then almost inevitable that the subject should be the first Queen Elizabeth, although Henry VIII was considered, and rejected, before the decision was made. By the time the holiday was over, Britten had already chosen as his source Lytton Strachey's *Elizabeth and Essex: A Tragic History*,[2] which the Earl had recently read, and settled on his preferred librettist – William Plomer, with whom he was currently working on ideas for children's operas.[3] Within a few weeks, royal approval had been given to the scheme and funding had been promised – at that stage either directly from the Treasury or from Covent Garden – and things seemed set fair for another major triumph for Britten and for British opera. Few could have predicted the storm of critical abuse that would ensue.

Unfortunately, in the event all the seemingly auspicious circumstances surrounding *Gloriana*'s conception conspired to act against it. First and foremost, its association with the Coronation celebrations ensured maximum public exposure for both work and composer. This resulted in a wide variety of critical opinion, some of it from commentators who were unfamiliar with modern British opera, and some of whom had personal grudges against Britten. There was a certain feeling of unjust favouritism on the part of the Establishment in supporting a new opera when at least four important works – prize-winners in the 1951 Festival of Britain competition – remained unperformed, and a further three were then nearing completion and would ordinarily have been produced before any more recent newcomers were given an airing.[4] By the time of the première, further ill-will had been generated by the publication of an early assessment of Britten's work entitled *Benjamin Britten: A Commentary on His Works From a Group of Specialists* (DMHK), the consistently laudatory tone of which some sceptical commentators found inappropriate (see p. 4). The issue of *Gloriana*'s funding also proved to be contentious. In the wake of the war's end, the old Council for the Encouragement of Music and the Arts had become the Arts Council, a body empowered to give financial support to such initiatives as it deemed worthy. This was innocuous in itself, but the idea of a possible state control of the arts filled many with fear and dread, so that the Arts Council was viewed with some suspicion. The funding it provided for *Gloriana* (via Covent Garden) provoked much ill-will, not least because of the shameless extravagance it represented to a country not yet entirely free from the effects of wartime deprivation. It is one of the ironies of *Gloriana*'s history that, in spite of its promising beginning, it appears with hindsight that the opera was likely to be doomed from the start.

The tone of the first critical response was almost universally damning. General opinions ranged from the lukewarm ('It has some charm, but it's not great'[5]) to the downright condemnatory ('the opera was unworthy of the great occasion, uninspired, missing the main glories of the times, its music inharmonious and wearisome . . .'[6]). Nearly every aspect of the work came in for unfavourable comment. Britten and Plomer were blamed for their choice of subject, which many felt was completely unsuitable for the occasion, one writer even calling it 'an insult to our lovely pure young [Queen] Elizabeth'.[7] A major flaw was found in the structure of the work as a whole, some feeling that the authors had failed to integrate decorative and narrative elements: 'The weakness of *Gloriana* lies in its unhappy combination of pageantry and psychological drama.'[8] The opera's ending, in particular, was singled out as 'little short of disastrous',[9] and was dismissed as inappropriate and miscalculated. The music itself failed to satisfy on several counts: the score was described as 'suffer[ing] from under-nourishment'[10] and its contents were found to be 'thin-blooded, nervous, ungenerous'.[11] Finally, Britten was several times accused of pastiche in his musical allusions to Elizabethan forms and styles.[12]

Not all such criticism can be written off as the result of the unfavourable public circumstances of the opera's première. There were other factors operating that the opera's first audiences could not have known about – factors concerning Britten and Plomer, and their day-to-day work in the early stages of *Gloriana*'s evolution. Britten was always wary of talking about the intensely personal business of creation, and it is only now that materials such as his letters and working manuscripts are available for study that we are able to piece together the pre-publication history of his compositions. Perhaps *Gloriana*, more than any of his other operas, benefits from the study of such material, since in this case it provides not only a fascinating insight into Britten's intentions and the unique difficulties he faced in translating them into reality, but also a new perspective on the less satisfactory aspects of the results he achieved.

Before turning to the letters and manuscripts themselves, a few words are necessary about Britten's customary practices in preparing a new opera. Throughout his life he retained a preference for a structured approach to his creative work. The needs he discovered and methods he established early on changed little as he matured, so that the genesis of *Death in Venice* followed a broadly similar pattern to that of *Peter Grimes*, and most of the operas in between. A brief summary of these needs and methods will enable us to understand the process by which *Gloriana* was written, and to see how the unusual circumstances surrounding its birth may have affected the work as a whole.

A study of the genesis of Britten's other operas shows that his primary need was time – time for a subject to suggest itself, time for the first germ of an idea to mature, time to work on the libretto, and time to compose the music. The average time-span for work on a new musical drama was roughly two-and-a-half years, as in the case of *Grimes*,[13] although as many as eight years might elapse between Britten's first recognition of his potential source and its full operatic realization, as the history of *Curlew River* shows.[14] Next, he needed a congenial and available collaborator with whom to prepare the libretto. All Britten's librettists were his personal friends before they were invited to work with him, and ideally the two (or more) creators would live side-by-side until the composer had a text that he was happy to set. Ronald Duncan, for example, recalled that he and Britten undertook work on *The Rape of Lucretia* 'at the same desk',[15] and this must have been a factor in the unusual speed with which the opera was completed. Britten insisted on playing a full part in writing the libretti for his operas, and it could seriously hamper progress if he could not share his ideas freely with a co-operative collaborator.

The actual writing of the libretto usually fell into three distinct phases – the reduction of the source to an operatic scenario, the sketching of the text, and the finalizing of the libretto proper – and Britten habitually delayed composition until the second stage had produced at least one version of the libretto in typescript. Several versions of the libretto might be prepared before composition could begin, *Billy Budd* generating as many as four pre-composition texts.[16] The final version was often different again, since musical considerations usually necessitated many small revisions. Britten's collaborators soon discovered that, as one of them wryly put it, 'no libretto can really be complete until the composer has finished the score'.[17] Changes could be called for even after the work was first performed, although large-scale revisions at this stage were the exception rather than the rule.[18]

Once Britten began to compose, he followed a strict daily schedule and usually worked through the text from beginning to end. By the time he actually came to write the music he usually had a clear idea of the overall shape and details of the piece, which meant that he was able to work with what appeared to others as breathtaking speed – the whole of *A Midsummer Night's Dream*, for example, was composed in around nine months (see p. 129). Eric Crozier, who worked with the composer on *Albert Herring*, *The Little Sweep* and *Billy Budd*, recalled that Britten 'would sometimes say that he had done all the work on a piece and now it was only a question of "finding the right notes". But the way he said this made it plain that he regarded it as the most important stage and one not wholly under his control.'[19] When the composition sketch – always written in pencil, with an eraser close at hand – was finished, Britten turned to the orchestration, for which he followed the same pattern of working as when he composed. It became increasingly common practice to employ others at this point, although their contributions were limited to mechanical tasks such as preparing the manuscript paper for the composer's use by marking up staves and ruling bar-lines. The final stages of preparation involved more mundane jobs such as producing vocal scores and orchestral parts, with which again Britten often sought assistance.

When we examine the circumstances of *Gloriana*'s genesis, we realize at once that they permitted only the barest minimum of time for the work to mature. Conceived in March 1952, the entire opera had to be ready for rehearsals to begin a year later, and the première was firmly booked for June 1953. Although Britten's agent was willing to allow him to abandon all other plans for the period, he remained committed to running the Aldeburgh Festival in the summer of 1952, and this was followed by a lengthy European tour which kept him out of the country until the end of August. Time was now very short, and he could not afford any delay, since he was still nominally committed to providing a new opera for the Venice Biennale Festival in a year's time.[20]

If Britten was somewhat frustrated in his need for time, he must also have had difficulties with his librettist's lack of immediate availability. To begin with, Plomer was an established author and poet in his own right, and had obligations that he was either unable or unwilling to sacrifice for the sake of the new libretto.[21] In addition to this, he was periodically troubled by ill-health – not just his own, which resulted in hospitalization during a crucial stage of work on the libretto, but also that of his father. To make matters even more difficult, he had a lifelong dislike of the telephone, describing it as 'the nasty little black vulcanite public convenience',[22] and avoided using – and even owning – a phone whenever possible. This meant that joint work on the libretto was confined to a series of meetings, most of which took place at Aldeburgh and lasted several days, linked by an exchange of letters. From Britten's point of view this situation cannot have been ideal; he was under a great deal of pressure to get a very important and public work written quickly, and he was working with a librettist who was not always able to give the project his undivided attention.[23]

In spite of the obvious difficulties ahead, Britten began very enthusiastically. On 11 May 1952 he wrote to Plomer, telling him 'I long to start planning', and describing his vision for the opera: 'My feelings at the moment are that I want the opera to be crystal-clear, with lovely pageantry (however you spell it) but linked by a strong story about the Queen and Essex – strong and simple. A tall order, but I think we can do it!' These 'feelings' raise several issues that recur throughout *Gloriana's* evolution.

First, it is clear that the opera's characteristic combination of the spectacular and the dramatic was apparent to Britten from the very beginning. He did not underestimate the problems of integrating the two, although he felt confident that he and Plomer could solve them. Significantly, the spectacular was foremost in Britten's mind, with the story simply providing a framework for a series of attractive tableaux. He later explained that the decorative elements had a twofold importance, claiming that 'we consciously planned the work . . . to show off certain facets of English musical life, such as the remarkable ballet and choral singing . . . [and] if you want to give a just picture of the Elizabethan age you need to show the rich ceremonial aspects of life at that time'.[24] Given his lifelong concern for the nurture and development of the British musical identity – which resulted, perhaps most obviously, in the creation of the Aldeburgh Festival – it is not surprising that he took this very public opportunity to compliment and promote what he saw as traditional British areas of strength. Secondly, although the actual story was of lesser importance in Britten's eyes, he was aware that it must be sufficiently strong to hold the decorative scenes together. The first stage of preparing the work was to extract such a story from the chosen source – not an easy task, since Strachey's *Elizabeth and Essex* contains a multitude of incidents from the lives of the Queen and her courtiers, many of which are inseparable from the political history of their time. Initially Britten and Plomer were fascinated by the relationship of the ageing Elizabeth and her young favourite, and this shaped their selection of incidents from Strachey – the opera actually charts the decline, rather than the initial development of, this doomed entanglement. Although the story they eventually compiled had a tragic conclusion, this was in keeping with Britten's intention to provide a significant and lasting contribution to the repertory, as he put it, to give 'serious music . . . a place of importance such as it used to enjoy in the life of the community'.[25] The third and most important point to note from Britten's original vision for the opera is his concern for clarity and simplicity, which proved to be a guiding principle throughout the preparation of *Gloriana*. It governed every aspect of his work with Plomer, from the treatment of Strachey's source at the large-scale planning stage through the choice and combination of individual words to the writing of the music itself.

By early summer, this vision was beginning to assume a definite form and shape. Plomer met with Britten in Aldeburgh at the start of June, and it was presumably at this time that the two men undertook the main work of extracting the material of a 'strong story about the Queen and Essex' from their literary sources. Only one scenario survives complete, which is reproduced in Plate 8; this was based on an incomplete handwritten scenario written on the same headed notepaper. When Plate 8 is compared with its Strachian source, the full strength of Britten's commitment to simplicity becomes apparent. Plomer noted that 'in opera one must simplify everything down to the operatic scale; one can't permit complexities of character and history to get in the way of the musical flow';[26] in practice, this meant that much of the original novel had to be jettisoned, including almost all Strachey's fascinating account of Elizabethan politics. This left only a handful of incidents which Britten and Plomer then expanded into separate scenes in accordance with their own purposes. Not all scenes were inspired by Strachey: one of Plomer's first acts as librettist was to send Britten a copy of J. E. Neale's biography of Elizabeth I,[27] and this provided the inspiration for the Norwich Progress scene as well as some of the details of later episodes.

The scenario also shows how Britten and Plomer were beginning to work out the place of pageantry in the opera as a whole. At this stage two 'diversions' were envisaged, one the Norwich Progress at the start of Act II, and the other after Essex's return from Ireland midway through Act III. This second decorative episode eventually developed into a scene in its own right, featuring the narration of Essex's desperate deeds by a blind ballad-singer. Interestingly, it was originally conceived as part of the same 'diversionary' strand as the Norwich Progress, while the Ball at the end of Act II was not planned as a spectacular scene at this stage. Assuming that Britten continued to think of Act III scene 2 in this way, the ratio of decorative and narrative scenes in the finished work is actually three to five (rather than the usually cited two to six) – another indication of the importance assigned to 'lovely pageantry'.

Shortly after Britten had drawn up this scenario, Plomer made another visit to Aldeburgh, probably to start work on the libretto proper. It was now the second week of July, and Britten's imminent departure for the Continent demanded rapid progress. The two men must have covered considerable ground in the few days they had together; by the time Britten left for Europe on 14 July, Act I scene 1 had been written and revised, a draft of Act I scene 2 was either complete or nearing completion, and Act II scenes 2 and 3 had been planned in detail. On 24 July he wrote to Plomer, giving his considered responses to all this material.

One of the first comments Britten made in his letter concerned the literary style of Plomer's drafts of the first two scenes: 'I think that metre and Rhyme (especially the latter) make the <u>recitatives</u> very square, and unconversational', and suggested that 'we take out a word here and there to break them up'. When we turn to the early version of Act I scene 1, it is easy to understand his objections. For example, the Queen's reaction to Essex's and Mountjoy's justification for their quarrel reads:

> Halt! In Heaven's name be dumb!
> Each of you accusing each!
> E'en when alewives, fishwives wrangle
> They must make an end of speech.

She replies to Raleigh's comments a little later in the same vein:

> Raleigh, your wit flies free,
> We find your judgement mild.
> Approach my subjects both,
> I'll have you reconciled.

This is very much the voice of Plomer in his most popular poetic works,[28] but the writing is too regular, and the rhymes too contrived, to invite inspired musical setting. Plomer obviously accepted this, and removed his rhymes to produce more naturalistic lines:

> Halt! In Heaven's name be dumb!
> E'en when fishwives wrangle
> They must make an end of words …

> Raleigh, your wit flies free,
> We find your judgement mild.
> Approach my subjects both
> And hear my judgement now.

Plomer later summarized the techniques he had to adopt in writing the libretto, techniques tailored to Britten's specific requirements: 'In general,

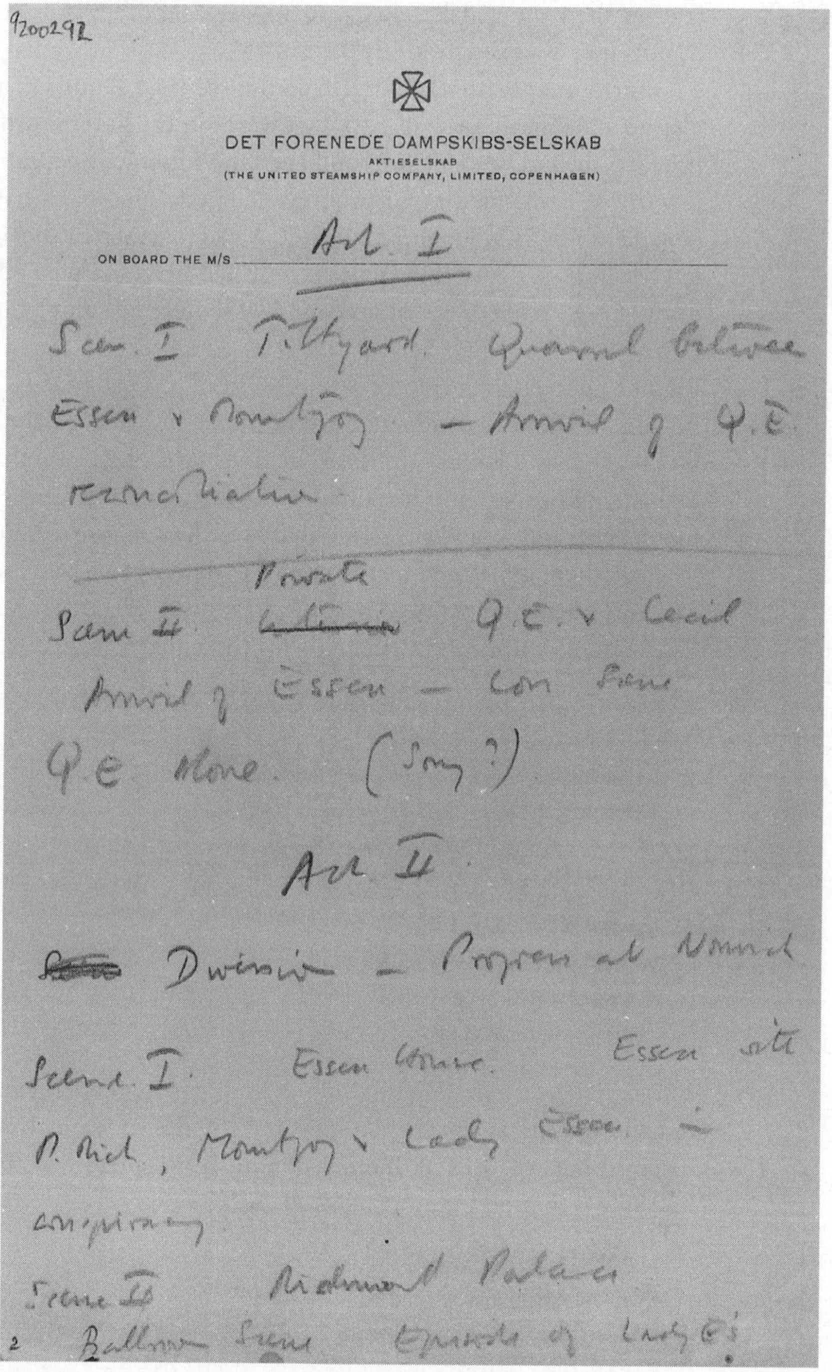

9200292

☒

DET FORENEDE DAMPSKIBS-SELSKAB
AKTIESELSKAB
(THE UNITED STEAMSHIP COMPANY, LIMITED, COPENHAGEN)

ON BOARD THE M/S _____ *Act. I* _____

Scen. I   Tiltyard.   Quarrel between
Essex & Mountjoy   — Arrival of Q.E.
reconciliation.

                    Private
Scene II.   ~~interview~~   Q.E. & Cecil
   Arrival of Essex   — love Scene
Q.E. alone.   (Song ?)

                    Act II.

~~Scene~~   Diversion — Progress at Norwich

Scene. I.   Essex House.   Essex with
P. Rich, Mountjoy & Lady Essex   —
conspiracy

Scene II.   Richmond Palace.
2   Ballroom Scene   Episode of Lady E's

Plate 8 First complete scenario for *Gloriana*, in Britten's hand

Plate 8 (*cont.*)

the lines have been kept short, often with only two or three stresses, and the language fairly direct and colloquial, in order to sustain a brisk dramatic interchange between the characters.'[29] His willingness to forgo his usual poetic style suggests that he shared Britten's commitment to simplicity and clarity.

When Britten returned to Aldeburgh at the end of August, Plomer visited him almost immediately, bringing the first versions of Act II scenes 2 and 3 for discussion. There was evidently some disagreement over their content which had to be resolved at this time. The original plan was that Act II scene 2, as well as demonstrating Mountjoy's relationship with Lady Rich and the conception of the Essex–Mountjoy–Rich plot to gain power, would also introduce Lady Essex in a sumptuous dress; this would later be stolen, and worn by the Queen to shame the Essexes in the following scene. Britten, however, was uneasy about this scheme, and in his letter of 24 July suggested that all references to the 'too fine dress' be dropped from Act II scene 2 and its appearances confined to the subsequent scene. Plomer remained loyal to their first plan, however, and went ahead with drafts of the two scenes, promising in a letter dated 2 August to 'explain why when we meet'. The explanation must have been made during Plomer's visit at the start of September, but he clearly failed to convince Britten: Plomer's original handwritten draft of Act II scene 2 shows all mentions of the dress deleted, and a second draft of Act II scene 3 survives which follows the alternative plan proposed by the composer in July. This new treatment of the dress episode was much more successful, and provided the basis for the final version of the scenes in question. Britten's vision had guided him correctly: the emergence of the rebel quartet in Act II scene 2 is strengthened by the removal of the non-immediate issue of Lady Essex's apparel, while the dramatic effects of Act II scene 3 (the visual impact of the dress as worn by Lady Essex at the start of the ball, and the humiliating use to which it is later put) are heightened by their compression into a single scene.

So far the genesis of *Gloriana* had followed the usual pattern for Britten's operas. However, from September 1952 onwards it deviated quite significantly. First, there appears to have been no distinct 'typescript' stage of work on the libretto preceding the start of the composition. Instead, the typescript was prepared one scene at a time, once the text of the scene in question was more or less finalized in draft. This meant that, rather than producing one complete typescript at a single sitting, Britten and Plomer built up a collection of individual scenes in typescript over a period of two or three months in late 1952. The first scene cannot have been typed up until the end of September (at the earliest), and as late as December Britten was still sending Plomer the first typed versions of sections of the last scene. The reason for this unusual practice was obviously lack of time, and this is reflected in the similarity of drafts of the later scenes with their typed counterparts – there was clearly no opportunity for long deliberation or extensive rewriting.

One of the consequences of this way of working was that the conclusion of the opera, which perhaps required more careful thought than any other part, had to be the most hastily written. Although Britten had outlined *Gloriana*'s ending in his letter of 24 July, work on the preceding scenes (during the summer and early autumn) and Plomer's illness (in November) had delayed the production of even a draft of Act III scene 3 until very late in the year. Plomer was at Aldeburgh – ostensibly to convalesce – from 7 to 9 December, and again over the Christmas period, and both draft and typescript were produced within the month. Britten confessed that this part of the opera gave them 'a great deal of trouble', and explained that 'we wanted to focus very much on the Queen in a different way from before and we wanted to do something quite fresh with the time element'; this was the reason for the much-criticized change from song to speech at this point: 'the absence of the singing voice would be more effective than the voice continuing to sing'.[30] The hurried circumstances in which it was first written perhaps account for the fact that it was the ending that received the major reworking when the opera was revised for the 1966 revival.[31]

The lack of a clearly defined 'typescript' stage also had an effect on Britten's compositional methods. It is a strikingly uncharacteristic feature of *Gloriana*'s genesis that Britten began setting the text before *any* of it existed in typescript and before the last few scenes had even been drafted. On 8 September he wrote to Eric Walter White to say '(hush!) I have already penned – no, pencilled – the first notes', and by the time of Plomer's next visit, at the end of the month, he had completed the Prelude. At one point, the composer actually 'overtook' Plomer, writing the music for Essex's response to his Irish commission in Act II scene 3 before Plomer had provided him with the text for it.[32]

Perhaps even more unusually, Britten did not follow his usual practice of composing through the opera from the first scene to the last in chronological order. He was forced to leave the Norwich Progress scene (Act II scene 1) until he had completed the other scenes because of uncertainties surrounding its performance. The difficulty lay with the management of the Royal Ballet, who were anxious to make a sizeable contribution to the Coronation festivities and did not initially relish sharing the stage with an opera. Resentment about being restricted to what Britten (somewhat disparagingly) described as 'two little ballets where they can hop around and make their little bows'[33] in the second act of *Gloriana* led to a disagreement over a suitable choreographer.[34] It was not until early 1953 that matters were finally resolved. Not surprisingly, Britten found himself unable to begin composing the main balletic scene until he knew what status it would have in the gala as a whole, and so the music of Act II scene 1 was not started until January 1953, by which time the rest of the composition sketch had been completed.

In writing the music itself, however, Britten followed his established practices. His haste to start composing may have been increased by a feeling that musical ideas, which had probably been brewing in his head through-out the summer, were ready to be committed to paper. This was not always a straightforward process, and the erasures and deletions in the composition draft of *Gloriana* reflect the difficulties Britten sometimes encountered: he later confessed 'I can quite often go to the paper perfectly clear what I'm going to do, and ... find that it doesn't work out like that ... Quite often ... when you put a thing down on paper it lacks a certain quality which it may have in your imagination, which is not quite so precise as the actual instruc-tions for the performers.'[35] The composition sketch of Act II scene 2 shows Britten dealing with this problem (see Ex. 6.1). He clearly approached the start of the Prelude with three main musical ideas in mind (Ex. 6.1a): quaver figures (marked x), flute tremolos (marked y) and celeste flourishes (marked z). At first he worked them in this order, but then decided to re-organize them (Ex. 6.1b). Now the unusual timbres of the flute tremolos and the celeste combined to open the piece, and were continued for an extra bar (to allow for an altered repetition in the minor) before the more mundane quavers appeared. This second, and final, version is far stronger and more effective, since it immediately suggests an evening atmosphere and the playing of the fountain featured in the love duet between Mountjoy and Lady Rich later in the scene.

Certain technical decisions had obviously been made before Britten committed the music to paper. Perhaps most importantly, he had rejected at a very early stage any idea of a direct imitation of Elizabethan styles. Imogen Holst related in her diary on 8 October: 'When I said he'd got the right Elizabethan flavour with contemporary materials he said I was to swear to tell him directly it began to turn into pastiche.' Britten certainly made recognizable use of Elizabethan dance forms and rhythms in the courtly dances of Act II scene 3, but retained his characteristic melodic and harmonic idiom throughout. Shortly before the opera's première, he told a reporter 'I have always been interested in the period, and have thought a great deal about it to try to get the atmosphere. But I have not "half-timbered" my music.'[36] Even in his setting of the second Lute Song in Act II scene 2, where he based his opening phrase on the first line of John Wilbye's madrigal 'Happy, O Happy He',[37] he remained true to his

Example 6.1 (a)

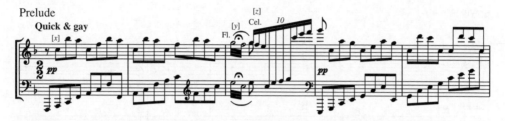

Example 6.1 (b)

own creative voice. A comparison of the original (Ex. 6.2a) with its treatment in *Gloriana* (Ex. 6.2b) shows immediately that Britten's 'borrowing'
was limited to the harmonic progression of the first phrase, and the subsequent development of the material was entirely his own. Given that the
text of the second Lute Song was not written by Plomer, but by the original Earl of Essex, this bow in the direction of the Elizabethans does not
seem out of place – especially since Britten was careful to match the mood
of the original Wilbye text.[38]

The opera's composition sketch was finished on 13 February 1953.
Typically, Britten began work on the orchestration immediately afterwards. Here again he was guided by decisions made at an earlier stage. His
main concern was for simplicity, partly as an outworking of his original
vision, and partly to ensure clear delivery of words by his singers. For the
most part he shunned full orchestral effects, preferring instead to depict
dramatic moments by careful combinations of a few instrumental
timbres at a time, as in the Essex/Mountjoy duel in Act I scene 1, which is
accompanied only by strings with the occasional horn interjection. The
rare occasions when he did make use of the entire orchestra were carefully
calculated, both musically and dramatically. One of the most striking uses
of tutti effects is found at the end of the Ball scene (Act II scene 3), where
the stage orchestra, which alone has provided the music for the on-stage
dances, is gradually overcome by the full pit orchestra's ominous commentary on the 'Victor of Cadiz' theme.[39]

Once the orchestration stage had been reached, Britten turned to

Example 6.2

a) Wilbye

b) Britten

Imogen Holst for help in preparing the manuscript full score. She had originally been employed the previous September to speed up the production of rehearsal material, and stayed on with Britten well beyond the completion of *Gloriana*, continuing with editorial duties and becoming increasingly involved with the running of the Aldeburgh Festival. As the founder member of Britten's 'support team' she became invaluable, not least because she demonstrated that it was possible to delegate some of the routine chores to others, thus freeing him to concentrate on the creative work of composition itself.[40]

Thanks to Imogen Holst, the full score of *Gloriana* was completed on 13 March 1953, a mere month after the composition sketch had been finished, and rehearsals for singers and instrumentalists were able to go ahead as planned. As usual, minor changes were introduced at this stage, but the most significant alterations did not take place until the 1966 production was being prepared, when the Epilogue in particular was strengthened by the removal of much inessential and potentially puzzling material (such as the introduction of the Queen's godson, Sir John Harrington, who originally made his first and only appearance in the opera's last minutes).[41] It had taken just over twelve months for *Gloriana* to evolve from a semi-serious suggestion to a large-scale opera – an achievement rarely equalled in Britten's creative life.

Example 6.2 (*cont.*)

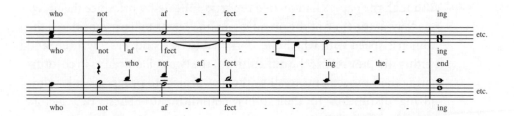

In an interview at the time of the 1966 production, Britten likened *Gloriana* to 'a slighted child'[42] – an apt simile in view of the way the work was almost universally misunderstood at the time of its première. Now that we have seen something of his intentions and methods in writing it, we can return to the first critics and, to some extent, redress the balance in its favour.

One of the most difficult aspects of the opera for the original audience was its subject-matter, but, as we have seen, Britten perceived the tragic story as essential to provide suitable weight for a piece worthy of the solemnity, as well as the glory, of the Coronation season. *Gloriana* was never conceived as a mere *pièce d'occasion*, much though the gala audience might have wished it had been. Another area of critical misunderstanding lay in the structure of the opera as a whole. Those who complained that the decorative and narrative strands hung rather loosely together had missed the whole point of Britten's carefully planned form: it is obvious from his first stated vision of the work that pageantry and drama constituted two quite distinct types of material which were never intended for close integration. The trouble he took over the decorative scenes reflects the important role he assigned to pageantry in the opera, not least because of the opportunity it provided for paying tribute to British musical tradition.[43]

Perhaps the most important factor ignored by *Gloriana*'s first judges was the pressure under which Britten was forced to work to ensure that the opera was ready in time for the Coronation celebrations in June 1953. Although the papers had carried reports of the new work since the previous May, at the time of the première no one seems to have considered the immense speed with which the work had to be – and was – written, and neither did they realize the difficulties of the two collaborators in co-ordinating their movements to allow the new project to progress while minimizing disruption to their other commitments. These two factors certainly affected Britten's creative processes, and parts of the opera suffered as a result. The ending, in particular, was a victim of the compression of his working methods, and the fact that it was successfully revised for the 1966 production demonstrates the benefits of a longer maturation period.

Criticisms of the music of *Gloriana* can similarly be traced to misunderstanding and ignorance. The style, which was felt by many at the time to be uncomfortably understated, now appears entirely consistent with Britten's emerging compositional principles. With hindsight, his frequent use of small groups within the orchestra (rather than tuttis), and his preference for transparent textures, can be seen as part of the creative development that led to the sparse and haunting sound-world of works such as the Church Parables in his later years. Ten years after *Gloriana*'s première, Britten defined his creative ethos as 'clarification', adding that 'my technique is to tear all the waste away; to achieve perfect clarity of expression is my aim',[44] and the music he composed for the opera reflects this growing concern for economy of means.[45] The score also reflects his stated aim to avoid the mock-Tudor, while suggesting something of the Elizabethan atmosphere by his re-interpretations of the forms and styles of the period.

Having examined both the public and private history of *Gloriana* we are in a position to consider the work from a fresh viewpoint, taking into account both the social factors affecting the opera's première and the personal factors affecting its genesis.[46] Since the 1963 concert performance (mounted at the Royal Festival Hall in honour of Britten's fiftieth birthday), and the 1966 production which followed, the work has enjoyed increasing recognition. As one commentator put it, 'to unite within a musically satisfying formal entity unrestrained public ceremonial and a nervous personal drama presents a composer with many especially difficult problems, but these Britten seems to have resolved with much more success than was originally granted him'.[47] Perhaps *Gloriana*'s early misfortunes can now be viewed from a more balanced perspective, and Britten's 'slighted child' fully welcomed into the operatic family.

7 Britten and Shakespeare: *A Midsummer Night's Dream*

MERVYN COOKE

Britten's *A Midsummer Night's Dream* is undoubtedly the most successful Shakespearean opera to employ Shakespeare's original text as the sole basis for its libretto. The choice of a pre-existing text was partly a pragmatic response to the composer's decision to write (at comparatively short notice) a full-scale opera to celebrate the opening of the newly refurbished Jubilee Hall at the Aldeburgh Festival in June 1960, and the opera's music was composed within the astonishingly short space of nine months. The task of adapting Shakespeare involved the judicious shortening of the play to around half its original length and presented the composer with a number of challenging dramatic problems. Britten stressed the importance of faithfulness to the original literary source in an interview published a few days before the opera's first performance on 11 June 1960.[1] Shakespeare's *Dream*, however, conveniently provided him with an unusual degree of narrative flexibility on account of its continuous action, reflected in the First Quarto edition of 1600 by the complete absence of act or scene divisions. The plot develops by juxtaposing self-contained groups of characters; and because both lovers and rustics are ignorant not only of each others' existence but also of the fairies' presence, certain aspects of dramatic sequence are rendered relatively unimportant.

Shakespeare's play is set within a symmetrical frame provided by static scenes at the Athenian court, with Theseus and Hippolyta removed from the action and unaffected by the magic of Oberon – although it is implied that their marriage cannot take place until the dispute between Oberon and Tytania is resolved. Theseus's judicial pronouncement on Hermia initiates many of the complications exacerbated by the supernatural powers at work in the wood, and his nuptials provide the ceremonial conclusion to which the activities of all the characters progress. In deciding to cut most of the play's exposition (Act I scene 1, lines 1–127),[2] Britten sacrificed one of Shakespeare's fundamental cohesive devices and thus inevitably lessened the dramatic justification for the closing scene at Theseus's court. The principal unifying element in Britten's opera becomes the magic wielded by Oberon, and this is strongly reflected in the music of Acts I and II, which both employ structural symmetry deriving from the activities of the supernatural characters. The loss of Shakespeare's expository scene allowed Britten to clarify the drama's time-scale by concentrating the action into one night (Acts I and II) and the following day (Act III), in contrast to Shakespeare's characteristically ambiguous double-time scheme.[3] The simple process of concentration involved merely the transposition of Lysander's and Hermia's first dialogue and the rustics' first rehearsal of 'Pyramus and Thisbe' to the woodland setting, the latter involving several minor textual alterations ('tomorrow night' becoming 'tonight', and 'here' replacing 'there').

The source materials employed in the compilation of the libretto, now preserved at the Britten–Pears Library, provide a fascinating testament to the rapidity with which the opera's highly disciplined structure took shape. Britten remarked that he and Pears 'worked with many texts, but principally from facsimiles of the First Folio and the First Quarto',[4] yet their copies of these facsimiles are unmarked and appear to have been little used. Of far greater interest are their annotated copies of the old Penguin edition,[5] on which the preliminary libretto drafts were clearly based. Both copies are heavily marked in their owners' hands, and the annotations are sufficiently divergent to indicate that the collaborators took an independent approach in the initial stages. In Britten's copy, a note on the flyleaf lists the dates of the earliest sources for the play, and against the printed list of *dramatis personae* he jotted down preliminary ideas for casting – including Hugues Cuenod and not Pears in the role of Flute (see Plate 9).[6] By each rustic's name, Britten noted his overriding characteristic: 'slow' (Snug), 'high' (Flute), 'old man' (Snout) and 'thin' (Starveling), in addition to drawing attention to the contrasting statures of Hermia and Helena. The annotations in Pears's copy are less extensive, but sometimes reflect notably different ideas, as in his plan to telescope the rustics' preliminary meeting and their subsequent rehearsal into a single composite scene. Pears's copy contains the first attempt at an operatic scenario on a blank page at the back which corresponds closely to the final version apart from the order of events at the end of Act I and start of Act III (see Plate 10). In spite of the smaller number of annotations in Pears's copy of the text, his influence on the shaping of the work was clearly considerable and Britten wrote to Ernst Roth at Boosey & Hawkes on 16 February 1960 to say: 'Since Peter really did the bulk of the work of adaptation, I think it is only right that he should have the usual librettists' percentage of the royalties.'

A typescript copy of Act I was prepared from the Penguin edition on the basis of Pears's scenario, and the annotations Britten subsequently added to this document first reveal his concern for structural cohesion: a single fabricated line is inserted ('Compelling thee to marry with

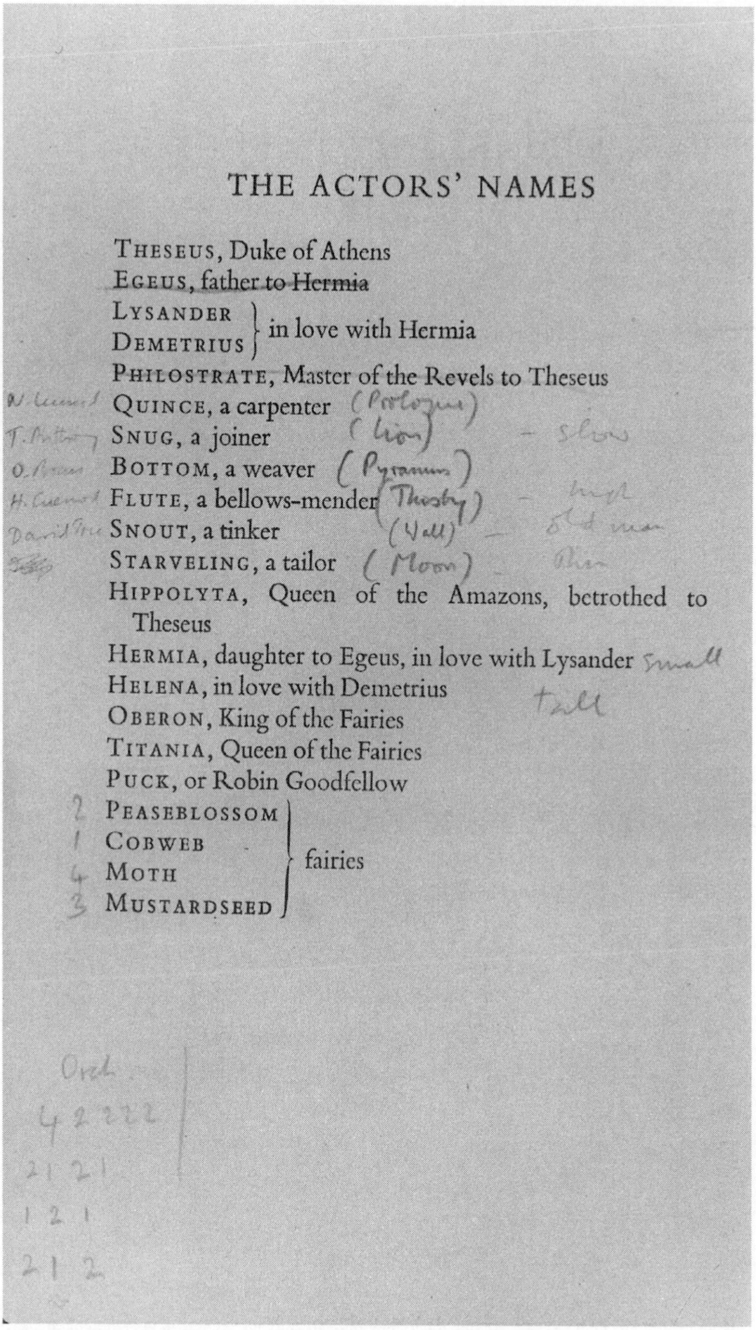

THE ACTORS' NAMES

THESEUS, Duke of Athens

EGEUS, father to Hermia

LYSANDER ⎫
DEMETRIUS ⎬ in love with Hermia

PHILOSTRATE, Master of the Revels to Theseus

QUINCE, a carpenter *(Prologue)*

SNUG, a joiner *(Lion)* — *slow*

BOTTOM, a weaver *(Pyramus)*

FLUTE, a bellows-mender *(Thisby)* — *high*

SNOUT, a tinker *(Wall)* — *old man*

STARVELING, a tailor *(Moon)* — *thin*

HIPPOLYTA, Queen of the Amazons, betrothed to Theseus

HERMIA, daughter to Egeus, in love with Lysander *small*

HELENA, in love with Demetrius *tall*

OBERON, King of the Fairies

TITANIA, Queen of the Fairies

PUCK, or Robin Goodfellow

PEASEBLOSSOM ⎫
COBWEB ⎪
MOTH ⎬ fairies
MUSTARDSEED ⎭

Plate 9 Britten's annotations to the *dramatis personae* in his copy of the Penguin edition of Shakespeare's *A Midsummer Night's Dream*

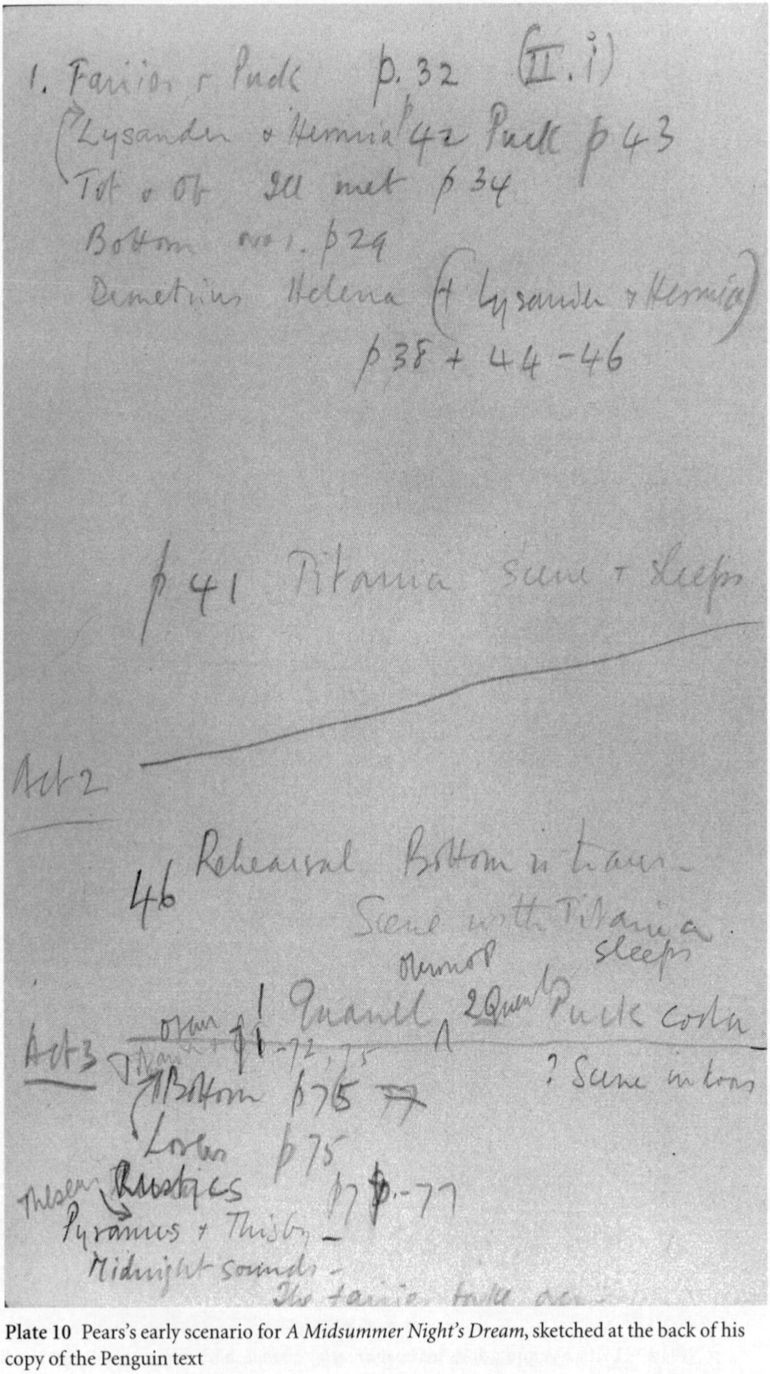

Plate 10 Pears's early scenario for *A Midsummer Night's Dream*, sketched at the back of his copy of the Penguin text

Table 7.1 Structure of Britten's Act I

Musical symmetry	Action	Dramatic symmetry	
Ritornello I			
Aria	Fairies (II.1.1–59)		
Duet	Oberon and Tytania (II.1.60–144)	Fairies	
Arioso	Oberon and Puck (II.1.146–85)		Oberon
Ritornello II			
Accomp. recit.	Lysander and Hermia I (I.1.128–76)	⎰ Lovers A	
Ritornello III			
Arioso	Oberon (II.1.180–87)		Oberon
Accomp. recit.	Demetrius and Helena I (II.1.188–244)	⎱ Lovers B	
Arioso	Oberon and Puck (II.1.247–64)		Oberon
Ritornello IV			

(Mirror) | Recit. | Rustics I (I.2.1–103) | Rustics (Mirror) |

Ritornello V			
Accomp. recit.	Lysander and Hermia II (II.2.34–62)	⎰ Lovers A	
(Spoken)	Puck (II.2.65–82)		Puck
Accomp. recit.	Demetrius and Helena II (II.2.83–153)	⎱ Lovers B	
Ritornello VI	Tytania (II.2.1–8)		
Aria	Fairies (II.2.9–25)	Fairies	
Arioso	Oberon (II.2.26–33)		Oberon
Ritornello VII			

Demetrius', an addition showing awareness of the dangers inherent in cutting Shakespeare's informative opening scene), and a symmetrical structure for the entire act is established. Plate 10 shows that Pears had placed the rustics between the first appearances of Lysander and Hermia and of Demetrius and Helena, retaining the play's sequence of events. Britten now chose to delay the rustics' entry and continue directly with the entrance of Demetrius and Helena, thus creating the strict symmetry illustrated in Table 7.1. On the same page of the typescript he inserted Oberon's lines 'Be it on Lion, Bear, or Wolf, or Bull, / On meddling monkey or busy Ape' (II.1.180–1) for a second time before Demetrius's entrance, an addition that not only frames the Lysander/Hermia scene but also illustrates Oberon's preoccupation with his spell and suggests that both lovers' scenes take place simultaneously.

Act II is also represented by a typescript used by Imogen Holst in the preparation of the performance materials, and proved to be far simpler in construction. The act consists of two large-scale set pieces forming the climax to Shakespeare's plot: the first portrays Tytania's doting on the transfigured Bottom, while the second develops the lovers' recriminations to such intensity that Puck is forced to intervene to avert disaster. These two extended episodes are united by Britten's use of recurrent 'sleep' music (see below), thus preserving something of the musical symmetry of Act I without emulating its dramatic symmetry.

No preliminary libretto draft survives for Act III, which was heavily corrected in the final typescript libretto alongside relatively clean copies of the updated texts for Acts I and II. Pressure of time undoubtedly meant that work on the text of Act III was fairly rushed, and this is corroborated by a number of inconsistencies in the published libretto of the final act. Act III follows the overall shape of Act II by falling into two large-scale composite scenes, here separated by an orchestral interlude, but the absence of a unifying musical scheme for the act as a whole allows the disparity between them to become acutely apparent. This incompatability is, on one level, effective in highlighting the stark contrast between the enchantment of the first two acts and the mundanity of Theseus's court. Peter Evans first demonstrated the subtlety of the transition between these scenes, which features the increasing proximity of Theseus's hunting horns, but pointed out that 'the listener-spectator is bound to feel a sense of disenchantment . . . in terms of the operatic experience he has to discover a place for two entirely unknown and inevitably stiff characters'.[7] This was the first and most obvious problem caused by the loss of Shakespeare's opening scene. Unlike the play, which sets out from normality and is developed in a forest symbolic of 'withdrawal from and return to the autonomous self'[8] before being concluded in the normality with which it began, Britten's version establishes the woodland setting as its norm – and the sudden intrusion of Athenian court life in the closing pages may seem an arbitrary conclusion.

The plot of Shakespeare's *A Midsummer Night's Dream* is so well known that minor inconsistencies in Britten's opera have passed unnoticed from a natural tendency for an audience to assume that events which have not in fact taken place on (or off) the stage have actually occurred. A close comparison of the libretto of Act III with the parallel passages of Shakespeare's play reveals that structural problems arose from the manner in which elements of three scenes were combined to form one composite operatic set-piece. The opening lines of the play were relocated to the beginning of the opera's palace scene, Britten being careful to alter Theseus's 'four happy days bring in / Another moon' and 'Four days will quickly steep themselves in night' (I.1.2–3, 7) to the single day required by his new time scheme. After the lovers have related their experiences, Britten alters Theseus's line 'Egeus, I will overbear your will' (IV.1.178) to 'Hermia, I will o'erbear your father's will', thereby providing a somewhat tardy explanation for 'the sharp Athenian law / (Compelling thee to marry with Demetrius)'. This is the first – indeed the only – oblique reference in the opera to the character of Egeus, who was excised in the interests of economy.

A curious dramatic loophole is created by Britten's alteration of the play's sequence of events in Act III – the very procedure which had made the first two acts such dramatically cogent units. The episode in which Theseus resolves the lovers' predicament is transferred from its original location in the wood (IV.1) to form part of Britten's composite palace scene. This transposition appears reasonable enough at first glance, but several significant dramatic details are overlooked as a result. In Shakespeare's sequence of events, Theseus discovers the lovers asleep in the wood, acts as an arbitrator in Egeus's dispute, and finally declares: 'in the temple, by and by, with us, / These couples shall eternally be knit' (IV.1.179–80). It is clear from Snug's comment in the play's subsequent scene that the weddings take place on the way to the palace: 'Masters, the Duke is coming from the temple, and there is two or three lords and ladies more married' (IV.2.15–16). The company then proceeds to the post-nuptial celebrations at Theseus's court. Britten retains only the lovers' awe-inspired comments from the first scene (IV.1.186–93/197–8), and, since the issue has yet to be discussed with Theseus, Snug's observation is modified by omitting its reference to marriage. The opera's palace scene opens with the lines adapted from Act I scene 1 and continues with the entrance of the lovers and Theseus's arbitration. It may therefore be seen that the retention of lines IV.1.179–80 (quoted above) at this point under-mines the plot: Snug has informed us that the Duke has already been to the temple (in Britten's version, for no apparent reason), and, since there is no conceivable moment between Theseus's declaration and the end of the opera in which the lovers may legally be united, it can only be assumed that they go to bed unmarried and the fairies conclude the work by bless-ing pleasures which are, in fact, illicit. In his copy of the Penguin text, Britten marked the interlude following Act IV scene 2 as 'Transformation scene to *Temple*' (my italics) rather than to the palace – a confusion retained in the typescript libretto – which seems to indicate an uncharacteristic miscomprehension on the composer's part at this point in the plot.

Striking evidence that Britten and Pears were very much aware of the problems inherent in cutting the play's opening scene – and took steps to rectify them – survives in a draft for a Prologue to the opera written at Britten's request by Myfanwy Piper in December 1959 when he was at work on the music of Act II.[9] This was essentially a summary of Theseus's proclamation, derived from Shakespeare's opening scene and designed to be announced by two heralds before the opera's action began.[10] Britten had drafted a handwritten synopsis of the Prologue's content which was typed at the head of the final libretto typescript:

Act One

Prologue, by a Herald (possibly two Heralds) announcing:
(a) Theseus's wedding with Hippolyta
(b) Hermia compelled by her father's ruling to marry Demetrius or
      otherwise to enter Nunnery

(not yet written)

Four bars of music labelled 'Prologue' to be found on a discarded page of the opera's composition sketch show how seriously Britten was contemplating this projected addition to the opera.[11]

Few audiences armed with a little foreknowledge of Shakespeare's play are likely to notice the uncharacteristic slips described above, and they are not sufficiently serious to detract from the impressive musico-dramatic cogency of the opera as a whole. The constituent groups of Shakespeare's kaleidoscopic drama are principally characterized by familiar contrasts in orchestration, which need not concern us here.[12] Of more importance to the structure of Act I is the manner in which the musical forms employed by each group of characters contribute to the overall symmetrical effect (see Table 7.1), and the success with which the ritornello sections linking each episode not only bind together the disparate events but also introduce musical techniques later to be of importance in Acts II and III. With the notable exception of the rustics' presentation of 'Pyramus and Thisbe', the only characters given music approximating to the closed forms of pre-Wagnerian opera are supernatural. Although this scheme was no doubt partly suggested by the frequency with which Shakespeare's fairies speak in strophic verse, it fulfils an additional function as a purely musical illustration of their dramatically superior status in the opera. Thus the freely developing accompanied recitative for the lovers and rustics is interspersed with more concise arioso passages for Oberon and Puck, the chief agents of the drama. In addition to this obvious contrast, the recitative styles of the lovers and rustics are subtly differentiated: the music associated with the former is tightly organized through ongoing motivic elaboration,[13] while that of the latter is essentially free. The presentation of the opera-within-an-opera, 'Pyramus and Thisbe', is therefore highly ironic because the rustics' comically inept adoption of closed vocal forms is complemented by the aristocrats' lapse into free recitative for their witty interjections, an irony already present in Shakespeare's play where the rustics adopt verse and the lovers revert to prose.

The symmetry of Act I is emphasized by the appearance of Lysander's and Hermia's accelerating rhythmic pattern in retrograde after the central point of the arch form (compare Figs. 25 and 73), and the enclosure of the entire act between two symmetrically corresponding arias sung by Tytania's fairy henchmen. The first of these ('Over hill, over dale') contains a scalic pattern which appropriately returns in inversion as the 'lullaby' refrain of the second ('You spotted snakes'). Both arias are partly accompanied by material from the instrumental ritornello employed throughout the act, and their function as a static outer framework is disturbed only by the final reappearance of Oberon, an intrusion calculated to arouse expectancy in the audience since it prophesies the disorder of Act II.

The ubiquitous ritornello reflects the predominance of the fairy world, serving not only as the principal binding element in Act I but also – by its association with the enchanted wood from the very outset – a symbolic unification for the act. Similar ritornello structures are common in Britten's music in the late 1950s and early 1960s and seem to derive from the strong desire for formal clarity which underlies all his mature work. Well-known examples include the recurrent string music representing troubled sleep which links the eight poems of the *Nocturne* (1958) – a work strikingly close to *A Midsummer Night's Dream* in both its subject-matter and musical techniques – and the string quartet's depiction of the passage of time in *Cantata Misericordium* (1963). In the latter case, Britten apparently resolved on the ritornello scheme before a word of the libretto was written.[14]

While associated in general with the supernatural forces at work in the wood, the ritornelli in Act I are more specifically linked with Tytania and her fairy attendants. The song 'Over hill, over dale' emerges from the first statement of the ritornello (Fig. 2^{-6}), while Tytania's 'Come now a roundel' is sung simultaneously with the fourth statement (Fig. 94). Throughout the act, Oberon is given sharply contrasting material to mark his temporary breach with Tytania and her fairy clique, and it is only in the seventh and final appearance of the ritornello that his spell motif – in both original and rhythmically diminished forms – symbolically mingles with the wood music (Fig. 103). This telling effect appears in Britten's composition sketch as an afterthought: he had copied out several bars of the ritornello in its original guise before deleting them and reworking the ending by continuing the spell motif so that both elements fade away together.

The ritornello itself consists of a sequence of the twelve major triads, although a preliminary sketch shows Britten to have been experimenting with a mixture of major and minor triads. The chords are linked by atmospheric string glissandi, an idea which may have been consciously borrowed from the music for the swaying trees in Ravel's opera *L'enfant et les sortilèges* (1925). The root notes of Britten's harmonic sequence are in no way treated serially, but an interest in the tonal possibilities of dode-caphony is evident in much of Britten's work from this period. Although in this instance the overall chromatic sequence remains largely unaltered when it recurs, each ritornello is slightly modified to establish the tonal region of the scene which follows it. These modifications are typical of Britten's ability to apply a simple and readily comprehensible musical technique which at once creates a feeling of unity and a sense of dramatic progression.

The four chords comprising the passacaglia sequence by which the musical structure of Act II is unified are also constructed by design from all twelve notes of the chromatic scale and once again represent the enchanted wood (Ex. 7.1). They are more specifically associated with the spellbound sleep through which Oberon's magic takes effect, and they make a significant reappearance at the mid-point of the act when Tytania and the transfigured Bottom fall asleep in each other's arms (Fig. 57⁻⁷) and at the end of the act when each lover lies down in turn to one of the four chords (Figs. 94–101). The act concludes with a fairy song con-structed over eight statements of the passacaglia chords, in which the fairies' lines 'On the ground, / Sleep sound' (III.2.448–9) ironically point not only to the symbolic function of the passacaglia but also to the musical technique (i.e. *ground* bass) itself.[15] Although the structure of Act II is neither as complex nor as closely integrated as that of Act I, it again fulfils the dual function of both musical and (by way of symbolic connotations) dramatic cohesion. The passacaglia's intentional use of all twelve pitches clearly corresponds to technical procedures in Act I, while the chords themselves are directly recapitulated in Act III as the accompaniment to Bottom's reminiscences of his supernatural adventure (Fig. 33⁻⁵). It is interesting to note that Britten's preliminary sketch for this chord sequence first arranged the twelve pitches into a pattern of four triads in which the gentle parody of the opening of Mendelssohn's famous overture to Shakespeare's play (composed in 1826) is much more explicit (Ex. 7.2).

The opera's most important vocal ensembles are also organized by a systematic exhaustion of all twelve possible triadic roots. The first occurs in Act I when Oberon and Tytania argue above an ostinato figure for timpani and double bass, the rapidly shifting harmonies in the harps encompassing twelve major and minor triads with different roots appear-ing in the order indicated in Ex. 7.3a. The roots are arranged in a chain of thirds (a Britten hallmark) so that the final two isolated chords (marked *a*) are those of B♭ minor and A major; the semitonal tension between these chords immediately becomes illustrative of the disagreement between the fairy King and Queen and provides an ostinato backdrop to their sub-

Example 7.1

Example 7.2

Example 7.3 (a)

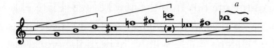

Example 7.3 (b)

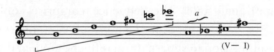

sequent discourse.[16] This material is recapitulated at the symmetrically corresponding moment in Act III, but with the order of the triads significantly altered to serve a new dramatic purpose (Ex. 7.3b). The fifth triad (C♯) is omitted to permit an extension of the chain of thirds and now becomes the penultimate chord, thus neatly serving as a dominant preparation for the diatonic F♯ major in which the opera's final fairy song is set.

When Lysander and Hermia vow 'I swear to thee' in Act I, they do so to each of the twelve major triads in turn in a simple but strongly affirmative duet. Britten departs from Shakespeare by dividing Hermia's speech (I.1.169–76) into stichomythia, each line accompanied by its own different triad. An examination of the composer's annotations to his proof dyeline full score reveals that the full sequence of twelve triads was only established immediately prior to the opera's publication. The composition sketch, manuscript full score and proof vocal and full scores all give a first-inversion C major triad as the accompaniment to Hermia's

Example 7.4

opening phrase (Ex. 7.4). Britten – presumably having suddenly realized that he had only used eleven of the twelve available roots – had his proof copies heavily corrected to instate the missing triad (A♭) at this point, both eliminating the pre-emption of the C major in which the section concludes, and conveniently completing the panchromatic scheme. The vocal line was adapted simply by inserting the necessary accidentals, not by transposition of the melody into the new key (see Plate 11).

When Lysander awakes *non compos mentis*, he proclaims his drug-induced love for Helena in a wildly hyperbolic vocal style to the accompaniment of a series of dominant-thirteenth chords strongly reminiscent of his earlier duet with Hermia, but now graphically illustrating his unstable emotional state. The sequence comprises only eleven different roots (Ex. 7.5a), the central chord of G♭ (enharmonic F♯) symbolizing his submission to supernatural influence. When this scene is resumed in Act II, the sequence is curtailed after only two chords by the insertion of the missing root D♭ (Ex. 7.5b). The dominant thirteenth on D♭ is treated as a major/minor dominant discord above a G root and can thus lead directly to C minor for Demetrius's ensuing solo.

Two sections of Act III constructed along similar lines are both organized to strengthen the role of F major as a unifying tonic throughout the first half of the final act. The quartet 'And I have found Demetrius like a jewel' (Fig. 20) exhausts all twelve triads in a fashion analogous to the procedure in 'I swear to thee' (providing a clear symmetrical correspondence with Act I), with the triad on F delayed until the end of the sequence. The march interlude which covers the change of scene to Theseus's palace takes the form of an extended development of the Duke's hunting calls above a quasi-ostinato bass: F is here retained as an implied pedal note while all the eleven remaining pitches of the chromatic scale are once more systematically introduced (Ex. 7.6).

At certain other dramatically significant points, the music freely encompasses all twelve pitch-classes. Oberon's first instructions to Puck

Plate 11 Britten's alterations to the dyeline full score of *A Midsummer Night's Dream*, p. 55

Example 7.5 (a)

central
point

Example 7.5 (b)

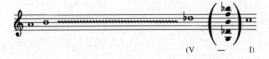

(V — I)

Example 7.6

[Quick March]

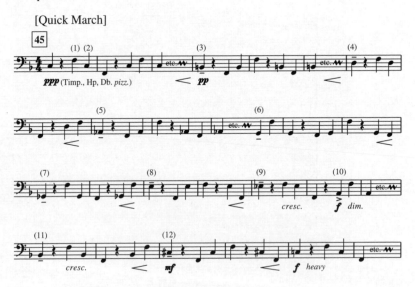

in Act I are accompanied by a celeste figure including eight different pitch-classes disposed in a pattern of alternating major seconds, the four remaining pitches added by the glockenspiel and vocal line (Fig. 19). Similarly, Tytania's invitation to Bottom to lie down on the bank in Act II is formed from a juxtaposition of the two whole-tone scales which between them include all twelve pitch-classes (Fig. 45). Britten's preoccupation with these simple dodecaphonic manipulations is graphically illustrated in his composition sketch by the appearance of twelve-note check-lists, the relevant letter name deleted by the composer as each note was employed. Although the absence of serial ordering precludes his method from achieving *per se* a significant structural function, the reservation of this technique for dramatic incidents dealing with the central theme of love ensures its effectiveness as a long-term referential symbol. Furthermore, Britten's clear distinction between those twelve-tone schemes used primarily to deploy roots of major or minor triads and those involving a more melodic conception often highlights the essential difference between the dramatic themes of genuine love and the doting induced by Oberon's magic herb.

The opera's formal clarity is strengthened by the subdivision of much of the music into smaller self-contained units, mostly simple ternary forms illustrating in microcosm the arch-like conception of the work as a whole. This is particularly emphasized when the recapitulation of the 'A' section is a free retrograde of its first appearance, as at the central point of Act II where the following symmetry is established: Puck's entrance (Fig. 60) – Oberon – Demetrius and Hermia – Oberon – Puck's exit (Fig. 68). Puck's exit music is a free retrograde of his entrance, recalling Britten's treatment of the outward and return flights of the dove in *Noye's Fludde* (1957); the device also shapes Puck's entrance and exit when he squeezes the magic juice on Lysander's eyes in Act I (cf. Figs. 78^{-2} and 80). The three component sections of Tytania's liaison with Bottom (Act II, Figs. 37–57) are each presented as discrete ternary forms. A satirical touch occurs in 'Pyramus and Thisbe' where Bottom's aria 'Sweet moon, I thank thee for thy sunny beams' includes an incongruous *da capo* to the words 'Now am I dead'. 'Pyramus and Thisbe' is distinguished by the structural clarity prevalent elsewhere in the work: recurrent passages for Wall and Flute serve as primitive ritornelli in the manner of Britten's designs for Acts I and II, and the entire performance is framed by two statements of a fanfare. Thus Britten's opera-within-the-opera parodies not only the Italianate conventions it so elegantly ridicules, but also the techniques Britten himself employs in the structuring of the work as a whole.

In addition to fairly conventional leitmotivic techniques, the opera's music is unified by a sophisticated scheme of key symbolism recalling the procedures already explored by Britten in *Billy Budd* (1951) and *The Turn of the Screw* (1954).[17] The four most important triads are stressed in the opening ritornello of Act I. G becomes associated with the mortal lovers, particularly in its guise as the dominant of C – a key which can be taken to represent love in its major form and resentment in its minor. In Lysander's and Hermia's first scene, C major is established at the line 'It stands as an edict in destiny' (Fig. 28^{+7}) and again at the conclusion of their duet 'I swear to thee' (Fig. 33). During their second scene, the disagreement over their resting place introduces the opera's first C minor triad (Fig. 75). The climactic points of Act II occur at Demetrius's abrupt and unwelcome avowal of love for Helena (Fig. 71) and the moment of rupture between Demetrius and Lysander (Fig. 86); both take the form of tutti C minor chords, the former reached via Lysander's protestations (see Ex. 7.5b above) and the latter marking the culmination of a lengthy quarrel scene of which the final section had also been cast in C minor.

Example 7.7 (a)

Example 7.7 (b)

Example 7.7 (c)

Example 7.7 (d)

F♯ is always associated with the fairies and Tytania. It provides the tonic for the two fairy arias framing Act I and becomes the predominant key towards the end of Act III for the fairies' closing benediction. We noted above that Oberon inhabits key regions quite distinct from those of Tytania before their détente in Act III, and he only adopts F♯ when communicating directly with his queen (Ex. 7.7a). When the fairies are absent from the action, their pitch-class is used for dramatic irony (Exx. 7.7b–d).

C♯ is the principal tonality in Act II in its enharmonic equivalent D♭ and is, as previously remarked, symbolic of the deep sleep that affects all within the act. It returns conspicuously during Act III in Lysander's observations upon waking (Fig. 18[-2]), and throughout 'Pyramus and Thisbe' to represent moonlight – a nocturnal association recalling Britten's use of the same key in the *Nocturne*. A major plays a far more

Example 7.8

subtle role: as in many other works by Britten, it is invested with a personal significance as a symbol for innocence and love.[18] Helena's pathetic little aria 'I am your spaniel' is mostly set in a diatonic A major, and this follows a passage in which Demetrius's attempts to evade her affections are graphically portrayed by the manner in which his tortuous chromatic lines attempt to escape from the pedal A which underlies the construction of the entire scene (Ex. 7.8, in which the square bracket indicates his adoption of the triad only when he openly rejects Helena – a device directly comparable with Ex. 7.7a above). When Lysander pursues her, Helena ironically assumes exactly the same musical stance as Demetrius, attempting to evade the G♭ (= F♯) pedal which indicates Lysander's bewitched state (Fig. 90^{-5}). Throughout the opera, the predicaments of Tytania and Helena are closely associated by their common use of A major and the close tonal relationship between A major and F♯ minor. There is also a strong similarity between the vocal style and diatonicism of their arias 'Be kind and courteous' (see below) and 'I am your spaniel', since both represent doting – the contrast between this and mature love forming an important theme in both play and opera.

Oberon's spell is, like the similarly coloured music for Quint's ghost in *The Turn of the Screw*, built around E♭: his commands to Puck are frequently issued on an E♭ monotone. When Tytania awakes under Oberon's spell, she does so to music reminiscent of that of her fairy henchmen but now firmly in E♭ major (Fig. 31). The 'disenchanted' music at the beginning of Act III is entirely diatonic for 69 bars until Oberon recalls his spell with an isolated E♭ ('I will undo / This hateful imperfection of her eyes'), and once his magic is terminated he never returns to that key. Act III is dominated by F major, hitherto sparingly used and no doubt intended to portray normality, since it is the key both of the diatonic string ritornello representing the cold light of dawn and of the transformation interlude to Theseus's court, and the key traditionally associated with the duke's prominent hunting horns.

The telling simplicity of Britten's tonal symbolism is perhaps best illustrated by a representative example from Act II. The principal section of Tytania's aria 'Be kind and courteous to this gentleman' is in a diatonic C major, indicating her abandonment of her fairy key (F♯) as she falls in love with a mortal. The only notes disturbing this serene diatonicism are the accented B♭, E♭ and A♭ on solo cello and double bass – the three accidentals which belong to the key of Oberon's spell music. At the climax of the central section of the ternary form, the reiterated F♯s and florid vocal line give a brief glimpse of her true character, but the spell returns with the *da capo*. Britten thus represents both the cause and effect of Tytania's position by the most economical of musical means.

A Midsummer Night's Dream exhibits all the formal clarity of Britten's music in the later 1960s but incorporates much of the richness of both sonority and technique typical of his earlier style. Chromatic and diatonic idioms are juxtaposed as effectively as the opera's dramatic and musical structures are interrelated. It is above all the equal status of musical and dramatic considerations that makes the work so impressive an achievement: as one critic observed in response to the first performance, it 'aroused instant admiration for the unity of ideas in the development of the music as an organic part of the comedy'.[19] Although Britten's innate musico-dramatic instincts undoubtedly contributed towards the work's quality, we have seen that many of his ideas arose from extensive and sure-footed calculation – most strikingly evident in his detached and clinical reworking of the 'I swear to thee' duet. The composer succeeds in setting one of Shakespeare's best-loved plays to a musical framework which not only imparts unity to the whole but also serves as a consistently appropriate and atmospheric representation of the plot's development. It was left to the Shakespeare scholar W. Moelwyn Merchant to isolate the work's most significant achievement, perhaps only to be appreciated by a drama specialist: 'it is one of the ironies of theatre history that this opera version is the richest and most faithful interpretation of Shakespeare's intentions that the stage has seen in our generation'.[20]

8 Eros in life and death: *Billy Budd* and *Death in Venice*

CLIFFORD HINDLEY

Billy Budd and *Death in Venice* between them cover many of Britten's fundamental concerns in life and art: the overriding commitment to artistic expression, the conflict between the individual and the constraints imposed by society, the awfulness of war, the role of homoerotic desire. While to a large extent the two operas are differentiated by their subject-matter – war and fate on the one hand, and art and the artist's vocation on the other – both are concerned with love between males, and on this point, two important differences between them should be noted at the outset. *Billy Budd* was written at a time when not only was society's rejection of homosexuality embodied in the criminal law, but when the British stage was still subject to censorship. It is one of several operas in which, I believe, Britten intended to make a statement about homosexual experience, but, because of the censorship, had to do so in coded form.[1] *Death in Venice*, on the other hand, was composed after the abolition of censorship in 1968, when its theme of same-sex love could be openly stated. A further, and important, difference is that while Tadzio is a teenage boy, Billy Budd is a mature man – a good deal more mature than the Billy presented by Melville.

Herman Melville's *Billy Budd, Sailor* was the great American novelist's last work. It was found among his papers when he died in 1891 in a form which still awaited final revision. It was perhaps in part occasioned by a historical incident in the US Navy, in which three innocent seamen had been executed in the interests of averting mutiny. Melville's cousin had been implicated in condemning the men, and the novelist may well have intended to devise 'a series of circumstances which would make a brutal hanging of a seaman inevitable and justifiable'.[2] There is, of course, much more to Melville's story than this. The 'natural depravity' of Claggart, the ship's Master-at-Arms, the almost perfect innocence of the young sailor, Billy Budd, the unbending severity of Captain Vere, all prompt philosophical reflection. E. M. Forster, who was to become the principal librettist for Britten's opera, had, years previously, perceptively weighed up Melville's work in his book *Aspects of the Novel*, where he describes it as 'a remote unearthly episode', which 'reaches straight back into the universal, to a blackness and sadness so transcending our own that they are undistinguishable from glory'.[3] This metaphysical dimension remains a powerful force in the opera, which demands to be treated as, in some sense, a 'parable of salvation'.[4]

The collaboration on the opera arose from Britten's friendship with E. M. Forster, whom he had first met in 1937. The friendship developed following Britten's return from America in 1942, and Forster was invited to deliver a lecture at the first Aldeburgh Festival in June 1948.[5] The possibility of working together on an opera seems to have been mooted at this time, and by the end of the year Melville's novel had emerged as firm favourite. In view of Forster's diffidence about entering the field of opera libretto, Eric Crozier as 'a man of the theatre' (who had worked closely with Britten on earlier operas) was brought in as co-librettist.[6] Despite Crozier's misgivings about the difficulty of the project, *Billy Budd* was decided upon, and by the end of 1949 the libretto was all but completed. Originally in four acts, the opera received its première on 1 December 1951. Britten revised the score to produce a two-act version for the l960 revival, and this is the version now generally used.[7]

The opera was written in response to a commission from the Arts Council of Great Britain in connection with the Festival of Britain in 1951, and there is some irony in the fact that for a commemoration of national reconstruction the choice fell on a narrative which represents so graphically the wretchedness of life below decks in Nelson's navy and the inhumanity of naval discipline. The implicit criticism of these evils as necessary concomitants of war would no doubt have commended the story to the pacifist in Britten. At the same time, the camaraderie among the men (in the shanty sequences) and the patriotic exhilaration at the prospect of action are positively portrayed.[8]

In the first scene the sailors are seen scouring the deck under the constant threat of the lash for any step out of line, and at the end of the opera they are driven cowering back into their quarters as, following the hanging, the incipient mutiny is quelled. The sense of being on the edge of a mutinous eruption is distinctly more prominent in the opera than in the novel. The famous opening phrase of the music betrays not only Vere's mist of doubt: its oscillation is between the keys of B♭ major (which, as we shall see, represents salvation) and B minor, the key of mutiny.[9] The latter danger is much in the minds of the officers as they discuss Spithead and the Nore over their wine in Act I scene 2. 'Spithead and the Nore' were the sites of mutiny in the British Navy in the very year of the *Budd* narrative, and these allusions give advance warning of the considerations that sway Vere in his decision to call Billy immediately to trial for the blow which kills Claggart.

The most moving image of repression is the capricious flogging of the

Example 8.1

Example 8.2

Novice in Act I scene 1. It gives rise to a dirge of searing melancholy (Ex. 8.1), which comes to symbolize the meaninglessness of the sailors' existence and its dominance by malign fate. Not only the sailors, but the principal characters and their mutually destructive actions are all touched by this fate-laden F minor and its related themes – in the fraught version of the dirge which overshadows Vere's move to convey the death sentence to Billy, or the strangely spaced version of the tonic chord of F minor which lacks the fifth degree of the scale (Ex. 8.2). Even Billy's stammer (when first hinted at in the Prologue as 'some imperfection in the divine image') is coloured by a reference to F minor. Indeed, the true significance of this stammer is simply (at least in the opera) as a symbol of the irrational fate which deals suffering and death to good and evil alike.[10]

Critics have tended to overlook the pervasiveness of fate in the opera. Yet this concept dominated William Plomer's interpretation of the story in his preface to the edition of Melville with which the opera-makers began. 'I see the story', writes Plomer, 'as Melville's final protest against the nature of things – that is to say against fate and against human institutions, of which the apparent necessity is itself ascribable to fate.'[11] Similarly, Forster spoke of 'fate' as 'Melville's main note'.[12]

It is this perception of fate which illuminates the opera's understanding of the 'salvation' which Vere anticipates in the Prologue and which, in the Epilogue, he claims to have experienced. 'Salvation' here does not relate to sin or guilt, but is seen as a way of getting the better of fate – courageously asserting oneself in the face of a hostile universe (in a manner akin to Stoicism[13]), through the support afforded by love. The path to this interpretation is laid out in a short note in Forster's hand-writing which has been preserved among the copious libretto drafts in the archives of the Britten–Pears Library at Aldeburgh.[14] The document is headed 'Librettist's Note on Dirge Libretto' and its first paragraph reads:

> I intended to convey not only that the men were lost, but *where*: – the infinite sea. First of four references to such a plight; the next being Vere's after [the] trial; the next Billy's solution when he sights the sail of love which isn't Fate; the last Vere's in the Epilogue when he sees what Billy's shown him.

The reference to love here is remarkable. It brings us to the libretto's most significant series of departures from Melville's story – the character of Vere, the love between him and Billy and a presentation of the young man as much more mature than Melville had conceived him to be.

In the novel, the physical attraction that Billy holds for Vere is hinted at, but the Captain remains aloof, at no point coming near to a personal rela-tionship with Billy. In the opera, not only is the physical appeal noted in Claggart's representations to Vere; one can also trace a series of changes in the libretto drafts which all point to a developing warmth between Billy and his captain: a commitment by Billy and recognition of goodness by Vere which, one feels, but for the exigencies imposed by the censor, would be openly expressed as love.[15] For Vere, the climax is reached in the aria on Scylla and Charybdis (inserted, it would seem, by Britten himself). It exposes the agony caused by his dilemma. 'My heart's broken, my life's broken', he cries at the prospect of having to order the execution of one who has come to mean more to him than an ordinary seaman. The situa-tion is a variant on Britten's recurring theme of the individual against the crowd, but here the conflict is not (as in *Peter Grimes* or *Albert Herring*[16]) between a desire for same-sex love and society's homophobia. The 'crowd', or the will of society at large, is here embodied in the whole structure of naval discipline and the necessities of war. Billy, however innocently, has killed a superior officer, and according to the Articles of War he must die.

Billy's character in the opera is far removed from the dog-like sub-ordinate described by Melville. In his concluding meditation he is able to reflect with great maturity on fate, his relationship with Vere and his vision of ultimate peace. He responds to the goodness he perceives in Vere with the promise to die for him, if need be, and whatever precisely trans-pired in the veiled interview, it is clear that it has left Billy with deep reserves of strength to accept what has to be done, and to bless the man who must order his execution.

There is of course another, and sinister, aspect of 'love' in the opera – Claggart's perverted desire for Billy. Forster, in a famous letter, refers to it as 'a sexual discharge gone evil'.[17] Claggart's desire, incapable of outward expression, turns inward and festers into a hatred which must destroy the unattainable object of love. These thoughts are given profound verbal and musical expression in the aria which leads up to Claggart's vow to destroy Billy (the fateful F minor again) and which has been likened to Iago's 'Credo' in Verdi's *Otello*.

The opera in fact presents us with a structure in which, in different ways, Claggart and Vere love Billy, and in which through the compulsion of fate both are led to destroy the object of their love. Yet such is the power of Billy's love for Vere that out of the agony can come a victorious confrontation with a hostile fate, which enables Vere to declare at the end of the work, 'But he has saved me, and blessed me, and the love that passes understanding has come to me.'[18] The structure I have traced is expressed and reinforced by a complex set of interlocking musical ideas, embracing intervals, themes, chords and tonal relationships.

There is, first, a broad pattern of contrast between the fourths in which Claggart's vocal line predominantly moves (as in Ex. 8.2 above), and the way in which Vere's line frequently reverts to thirds, often with a falling third at points of cadence. But when, in his agony, he reflects on the judgment of the court, he moves from his characteristic falling thirds to the fourths of Claggart, as he recognizes that fate has decreed that he must be the instrument of Billy's destruction (see Ex. 8.3, in which the tritone may be taken to symbolize evil, as so often in Britten's music). Then there is the 'fate' theme and its associated motifs in F minor to which reference has already been made. It may be contrasted with the jaunty arpeggio figure with which Billy comes aboard and which reflects his irrepressible spirit, a thought which movingly returns when Billy comes on deck to face execution, ready to cry 'Starry Vere, God bless you'. For Billy's farewell to this world and his perception of 'the far-shining sail that's not Fate', Britten provides a long-breathed melody harmonized in consecutive sixths (Ex. 8.4) – the concord which (along with consecutive thirds/tenths) has by a long musical tradition been associated with love and peace.[19] Similarly, the cabin dialogue between Vere and Billy had been emotionally enhanced by a harmony of consecutive tenths to sustain Vere's line. The symbolic use of the sixth reaches its apogee at the moment of Billy's death, where the excruciating dissonances of the hanging are transformed into an ethereal high B♮ and the G♯ a thirteenth (i.e. a sixth plus an octave) above: here, it seems to me, Billy's love transcends death.[20] It then falls to Vere in the Epilogue to pick up phrases from Billy's melody (with its harmonization in sixths) to demonstrate that, in Forster's words, he 'sees what Billy has shown him'.

Example 8.3

VERE

The an-gel of God___ has struck and the an-gel must hang   through me

Beau - ty,   hand-some-ness,   good-ness   it is for   me___   to des - troy you

[* Note the tritone]

Example 8.4

BILLY

But I've sight - ed   a   sail   in   the   storm

etc.

Fl., Hp,
Vn

B. Cl.

One feels that the basis for seeing this as the triumph of love over fate must lie in what passes between Billy and Vere as, behind closed doors, the sentence of death is communicated. Yet access seems barred. There are no words, only the mysterious sequence of 34 common chords – the so-called 'interview chords'. Are they a deliberate symbol of ineffability?[21] Are we to take refuge in ascriptions of 'profound significance' which convey no ascertainable meaning? Or should we risk attributing a reason-ably specific meaning (however subjective) to this unprecedented musical invention? Encouraged by Britten's belief that music could in some sense communicate ideas, I believe that it is worth making the latter attempt.[22]

In other works by Britten, sequences of triads occur in contexts por-traying love, whether homosexual or heterosexual.[23] The interview chords may naturally be interpreted in the same light. Similar triads (though with a more sinister flavour) appear at moments when Claggart, in his own perverted way, is drawn to Billy (Ex. 8.5). We seem, then, to have yet another example of Britten's assigning the same motif to opposed characters: it symbolizes the sharing of a common element, which is nev-ertheless susceptible of significantly different interpretations.[24]

The 'interview chords' also prompt reflections on tonality, particularly in view of the significance of tonal planning in this opera.[25] Granted that the key of F minor represents fate, it must be significant that, as Vere

Example 8.5

moves into the cabin under the shadow of the F minor 'dirge' theme, minor turns to major with the first of the interview chords, and that those chords themselves constitute different harmonizations of the notes of the common chord of F major. The implication is that as the major van-quishes the minor, so a victory over fate is achieved through the love between Billy and Vere, symbolized by the triads. Moreover, while F major has previously been the key of Billy's inner tranquillity, the interview chords may be heard as moving into C major, the key consistently used to represent Vere's positive qualities. The two keys thus bring the two men together. Finally, there is a repeated appearance of two chords which make up the 'Amen' of church hymnody: occurring always with the same orchestration, they convey a sense of assurance and well-being. The suc-cessive harmonizations of F major also, of course, introduce tonally remote and disturbing elements which might be taken to cast doubt on the whole idea of 'victory'. But these alien elements, while reflecting the strain under which the two men labour, do not deny the possibility of salvation at last.[26]

The chords are recalled three times. First, during Billy's monologue on the gun deck they powerfully express his strength of character which can somehow get the better of fate. Then, Vere is strengthened and reassured by the (brief) return of the chords to accompany his entry for the hanging, and again (in combination with Billy's 'far-shining sail' melody) in the Epilogue – notwithstanding his recognition, in retrospect, that he had made a grievous error. The assurance of the 'Amen' chords returns, and the passage moves through a tortuous harmonic resolution to burst forth with full orchestra into a triumphant chord of B♭ major. Musically, this dispels the ambiguity between B♭ and B minor of the opera's opening. Dramatically, it confirms for Vere in his old age the sense of redemption and victory over fate that Billy had bestowed upon him so many years ago.

Such a conclusion inevitably raises questions about the religious interpretations which have been offered. The simple parallel between the innocent suffering of Billy and that of Christ has often been drawn, but Melville scholarship has been much divided over what Melville himself intended by his often ironic references to Christian truth and practice. In the opera, virtually nothing of the novella's overt reflections upon Christian themes survives and what does appear has to a large extent suffered a sea-change.[27] The Christian myth concerns the sinless one as a *divine* saviour: yet Forster (however muddled his feeling for theology may have been) clearly and explicitly rejects this element. In his *Griffin* article (1951) he writes, almost brutally, 'The hero hangs dead from the yard-arm, dead irredeemably and not in any heaven, dead as a doornail, dead as Antigone, and he has given us life.'[28] For Forster the humanist, this gift of life meant a present experience of personal self-worth and the self-affirming reality of personal relationships if not of sensual love. He finds no place for the glancing vision of a transcendent Billy (hinted at by Melville, only to be withdrawn). Salvation in the opera remains a humanist experience.

There is nevertheless a universal aspect to the story, a reaching back into deeper levels of significance beyond the mere telling of a tale. As Forster expressed it in a letter to Britten at the outset of the project, his concern was with 'the ordinary loveable (and hateable) human beings *connected with immensities* [my emphasis] by the tricks of art'.[29] And it was surely with this in mind that he made Vere, in his final reflection, dissolve the link between Billy's story and the particularity of 1797. It is not just 'years ago', but 'centuries ago, when I, Edward Fairfax Vere, commanded the *Indomitable*'.

For what was to be his last opera, Britten turned yet again to a classic of world literature – Thomas Mann's novella, *Death in Venice*. Its theme is art and artistic inspiration, and in particular the risk that in pushing his experience to the limit, the artist may destroy himself. It centres upon the love of an ageing and highly intellectual writer for the beauty of an adolescent boy, and reflects an experience of the author's which had actually occurred during a holiday in Venice.[30] Mann himself said, 'Passion as confusion and as a stripping of dignity was really the subject of my tale.' Yet the homoeroticism cannot be disregarded, and its treatment led the poet (and austerely homosexual) Stefan George to say of the work that 'the highest is drawn down into the realm of decadence'.[31] Mann, for his part, insisted that he had not intended to disavow or denounce homosexuality as such, and it seems that only in the course of working on the story did Mann come to emphasize its pathological aspects, largely eliminating his earlier conception of noble possibilities in the Greek texts about boy-love upon which he drew.[32]

The novella (published in 1912) reflects Nietzsche's theory that art arose from the conjunction between, on the one hand, the intellectual quest for formal perfection (through an Apollonian order of individual self-discipline) and, on the other, the Dionysiac forces which emerge from passion and the submission to collective feeling. In reaction against the 'naturalism' then prevailing in German letters, Mann evolved a finely wrought poetical prose style, which was elegantly fitted to describe through symbol and irony a decline into artistic decadence which rejected Apollonian order and abandoned itself to the impulses of Dionysus.

While its brilliant deployment of language shows affinity with musical composition, the book's preoccupation with abstract ideas, its multiplicity of words and the virtual confinement of its narrative to the reflections of one individual upon his experiences, provide grave difficulties for the opera composer. When one recalls that the boy Tadzio never speaks, one can sympathize with the librettist Myfanwy Piper, whose first thoughts, when Britten mentioned his plan, were that it would be impossible. But, she added, 'if Britten said so, it could be done'.[33]

Britten's interest in the subject, according to Rosamund Strode, dated back at least to 1965, but only in September 1970 was the new collaboration with Mrs Piper set in train. Golo Mann, son of the novelist – who had been associated with Britten, Pears and others in an artists' commune in New York in 1940 – was helpful in securing the necessary agreement with the Mann Estate for the use of the novella. His father, he recalled, had said that had his novel *Doctor Faustus* ever been dramatized, Britten would have been the ideal composer to supply the music. Difficulties however arose with Warner Brothers over the Visconti version of the novella which was then being filmed. Agreement was only reached after nearly two years of negotiation, but Britten (acting on legal advice on the dangers of a charge of plagiarism) never saw the film.[34]

As was usual with Britten, the process of composition was pursued alongside a taxing load of other engagements and responsibilities. In August 1972 a medical check-up showed that a longstanding heart problem was deteriorating, and required surgery. The composer was, however, resolved to complete the work, which was likely to provide Pears with his last major role, and decided to postpone the operation until the score was completed (in March 1973). Sadly, the operation was not a complete success, and a long convalescence prevented Britten from participating (as was his wont) in the preparation of the opera for its first performance on 16 June 1973.[35]

Both in its subject-matter and in its musical structures, Britten's *Death in Venice* represents a summation of his own career as an artist, which must have become the more significant for him as the awareness of his own mortality grew ever more pressing. Its music incorporates not only the techniques which the composer had deployed throughout his life, but resonances drawn from a wide variety of styles. Particularly notable are his use of a Delphic Hymn from the second century BC to represent the Voice of Apollo, and the device of a rhythmically free form of pitch-notated recitative which (while deriving from Pears's rendering of the recitatives in Schütz's Passions) provides a brilliant solution to the problem of presenting Aschenbach's stream of consciousness.

As to subject-matter, the conflict between the Bohemian and the bourgeois (often epitomized as that between Dionysus and Apollo), and the need for a balance between them, had been challengingly put to Britten as a young man by W. H. Auden. Britten himself, shortly thereafter, wrote of his ideal as 'a carefully chosen discipline', and years later, Pears referred to Britten's lifelong concern with the questions asked by Aschenbach about knowledge, beauty, and love.[36] That they might be related to the Greek ideal of eros and the composer's own response to adolescent male beauty should hardly surprise us, and it was perhaps inevitable that Britten should be drawn to Mann's celebrated treatment of this subject, despite its negative account of homosexual experience. Indeed, it may well be that the ambiguities of the novella reflected Britten's own uncertainties and underlying guilt. At the same time, any intepretation of the opera must take account of the composer's statement to Donald Mitchell, '*Death in Venice* is everything that Peter and I have stood for.'[37] The affirmative tone of this remark is difficult to reconcile with the sombre picture of the disintegration of a fine mind painted by Mann. Perhaps, as often in studying Britten's operas, one may look for a solution in noting the differences between the opera and the text upon which it is based.

Mann's novella is a study in pathological decadence, brilliant in style, but pessimistic in its psychological analysis. Aschenbach is a distinguished writer, destroyed by his passion for a teenage boy. The story is one of inexorable decline, accelerated at the moment of the 'foiled departure', when the misdirection of his luggage forces Aschenbach to stay on in Venice, in the same hotel as his idol. This incident is the turning-point, when he begins to realize the nature of his affliction, and surrenders himself to it. He invests his attitude with a shimmer of Platonic idealism, but fails to convince us that this is more than an ironic cover for a desire to seduce.[38] Aschenbach's earlier devotion to an aesthetic of austere purity of form may be characterized as 'Apollonian', but the god is not mentioned in Mann's text, and the image of the sun (often in literature identified with Apollo) is that of a hostile seducer and destroyer. Its baleful influence works along with Dionysiac frenzy and the spread of the cholera epidemic towards the climax of the writer's disintegration and death.

The second act of Britten's opera, after Aschenbach has refused the opportunity of friendship with Tadzio, largely follows Mann's narrative of besotted decline. But the opera's first act substantially reworks and adds to Mann's material in a way which imparts to the whole a quite different significance. According to Myfanwy Piper, the aim was to present an amalgamation of Aschenbach with the character of Mann himself, and for this she and Britten turned to Mann's semi-autobiographical novel, *Tonio Kröger*. The novel tells of a would-be writer who feels himself excluded from the real world, reflecting a preoccupation of German writers with the role of the artist as a detached observer. But Tonio Kröger's search for 'life' concludes, not with Bohemian excess, but with the reality of everday, 'bourgeois', human relationships.[39] Also in the background are the classical Platonic texts which combine the ideal of love of male beauty as a route to the Absolute, with the need to develop moral relationships with the beloved. All this is summed up in Aschenbach's artistic 'credo' by the phrase (which has no counterpart in the novella): 'When genius leaves contemplation for one moment of reality' – surely a reference to Tonio Kröger's longing to close the gap between the artist and reality.

Equally significant is Britten's own earlier use of the symbolism of Apollo and the sun. One of his early works, the bravura piece for piano and string orchestra, *Young Apollo* (1939), was inspired not only by the brilliant North American sunshine, but also by a young man whom he had left behind in England.[40] He later was to set to deeply serious music one of the finest expressions of male love – Hölderlin's poem on Socrates and Alcibiades. These lines of thought prepare us for the displacement of Mann's ironic presentation of Hellenism as a mere façade. In its place we find an extensive new development – the Games of Apollo in which 'Apollo and the sun' are revealed positively as joint symbols of the Platonic ideal with which Tadzio is poetically identified. Then, as Tadzio emerges as victor in the Games, Aschenbach is challenged to make a decision. This is now the turning-point of the story. Will he dare to enter upon an open friendship with the boy? Will he, or will he not, engage creatively with the reality before him, and so re-kindle the dying spark of inspiration?

He fails to do so, while unable to suppress his 'I love you.' It is this failure which leads to the corrosive introversion of his passion, the undermining of his former skill as a writer and the disintegration of his personality. Had he chosen differently, the opera implies, an open friendship with Tadzio might have brought to fruition the hopes for artistic renewal which had led him to Venice. An interpretation along these lines (when coupled with what we now know about Britten's feelings for the adolescent male) enables us to approach an understanding of the composer's statement that *Death in Venice* 'is all that Peter and I have stood for'.[41]

The musical symbolism of the opera, I believe, supports this interpretation. It is about the quest for the Platonic 'Absolute Beauty', embodied in a theme (the 'vision' theme) which bursts upon us as Aschenbach is shown the view of the sea from his hotel window (Ex. 8.6). This seems to reflect Plato's words about the 'sea of beauty' as a symbol for transcendent reality.[42] The harmonization in triads may well also reflect Britten's use of such sequences to symbolize love (see above, p. 152), and hint at Aschenbach's coming discovery that the transcendent vision may be mediated through love for a beautiful youth. Certainly the 'vision' theme itself will soon become focused upon Tadzio, most dramatically when in Act II scene 9 Aschenbach suddenly comes upon the Polish family in his walk through the Merceria (Fig. 225). Tadzio himself is given a highly distinctive motif on the vibraphone (Ex. 8.7). Its derivation from the Balinese gamelan evokes, as does similar orchestral colour for Quint and Oberon in earlier operas, an other-worldly allure and carries particular weight since Tadzio never speaks (see p. 177). His combination of physical grace and silence, and that of his mother, is brilliantly conveyed in the opera through the medium of dance.

The Games of Apollo (Act I scene 7) present an apotheosis of Tadzio as the medium through which the Platonic form of beauty may be discerned. His motif is integrated into the philosophical milieu by having both Apollo and Aschenbach employ it at climactic moments in the scene, to suggest the boy's identification with the god and his embodiment of the writer's artistic ideal. Meanwhile, Apollo delivers his reflections on love and beauty in melodic lines derived from the Delphic Hymn.[43] Aschenbach follows the same melody for his creed which, with Tadzio as his model, will reveal that 'eros is in the word'. To draw upon classical Greece (and the cool temper of the countertenor voice) for its musical expression suggests the Apollonian ideal of formal perfection, while it is nonetheless inspired by 'love' – in a chaste relationship with the beloved.[44] When, at the end of Act I, Aschenbach refuses the opportunity for such a love, the sun, which hitherto has been a positive image, suddenly becomes suspect as the source of illness. Even more dramatically, a four-note

Example 8.6

Example 8.7

[The sign █║║⊪ indicates a tremolo with gradual ritardando]

Example 8.8

phrase (Ex. 8.8), sounded in the bassoon, reveals a threat – the origins of which we must now trace.

In the opera's opening scene, the Traveller had offered the disconsolate Aschenbach a renewal of inspiration through travel to the south. Yet his first words are set to Ex. 8.8, in which an interweaving of major and minor thirds is (as Peter Evans suggests) a recurring symbol for 'the worm in the rose' and similar concepts.[45] In Act II the phrase is revealed as a symbol of the plague. Moreover, the Traveller himself is the first of six characters who appear successively in ambiguous guise, carrying overtones of menace. All six are sung by the same singer, who also takes the Voice of Dionysus. Thus from the beginning seeds of disquiet are sown, to be reinforced by the idea of ambiguity applied to Venice itself – at once beautiful and corrupt.[46] Yet these hints of unease are balanced (and in the first act, more than compensated for) by positive themes, notably – as the Traveller's words open up a vision of pleasurable achievement – the rising figure of Ex. 8.9 (the 'anticipation' motif), which several times recurs.

But once the relationship with Tadzio is declined (and the menace of the 'plague' theme is heard), a new melody (the *Sehnsucht* theme) is introduced. *Sehnsucht* in German signifies unfulfilled yearning, particularly associated with the artist's quest for the ideal, which much occupied German writers who influenced Mann.[47] The *Sehnsucht* theme thus

Example 8.9

Example 8.10

Example 8.11

portrays Aschenbach's insatiable yearning and hopeless pursuit of the boy (Ex. 8.10). As Tadzio smiles, a sadly distorted form of the 'anticipation' motif recognizes that he is now unattainable, while (too late) Aschenbach ends the act with his declaration, 'I love you' (Ex. 8.11). Its closing major third points to another of Britten's musical symbols – the contrast between the fourth and the third which in previous operas had stood for the opposition of darkness and light.[48] Here it is the Lady of the Pearls, who is now brought on to remove her son from the older man's gaze. Her music (a woodwind variant of Tadzio's motif) is harmonized in *fourths*, combining her elegance with society's hostility to any friendship between the ageing writer and the boy. Aschenbach's phrase, with its concluding major third ('I love you'), continues into the second act, in increasing tension with a drone fourth in the bass – an after-glow (or, rather, after-chill) of the Lady of the Pearls' hostility.

The opening soliloquy of Act II suggests that, as a consequence of his failure to engage Tadzio in friendship, Aschenbach's inspiration as a writer has soured into introspective self-pity. Yet a positive note is still

Example 8.12

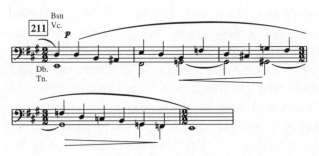

sounded – 'This "I love you" must be accepted' – accompanied by the triads which so often for Britten signify 'love'. Aschenbach's pursuit of Tadzio and his family through Venice is accompanied by a double passacaglia, which combines the *Sehnsucht* theme with a bass markedly shaped by 'I love you', with its rising figure of anticipation and falling third of love (Ex. 8.12). This longing brings him to the very door of Tadzio's bedroom,[49] where (another positive note) he recalls the honour accorded to the heroes of old among whom eros flourished.

The appeal to a past age indicates Aschenbach's increasing isolation from society. The Hotel Guests in Act I may have portrayed (not unkindly) the superficiality of bourgeois social life, but Aschenbach still had a share in it. In Act II, however, he sits apart, while the songs of the Strolling Players imply an uncomfortable cynicism about the conventions of heterosexual courtship and marriage. This milieu Aschenbach contrasts with the richer possibilities of keeping company with Tadzio, only to be overcome by thoughts of death. Such thoughts are confirmed by the Travel Clerk's revelations about the spread of the cholera epidemic, to the accompaniment of a full restatement of the Traveller's aria with the 'plague' theme.[50]

Aschenbach, however, fails to give any warning to the Polish family as the Mother, still harmonized in the fourths of hostility, passes him in the hotel. Instead, his love/death wish ('What if all were dead, and only we two left alive'), set to the 'I love you' motif, marks the point of no return. In the next scene, the 'anticipation' motif unveils its ambiguous nature by introducing the Dream and its contest between Apollo and Dionysus for Aschenbach's soul. Tadzio's motif (more ambiguity) now recurs as inspiration for the Dionysiac orgy, to which Aschenbach at last surrenders himself, at the cost of forfeiting his earlier vision. Thereafter the 'vision' theme makes several attempts to re-establish itself, but without success. Aschenbach repairs once more to the Barber, now to take on the role of the Elderly Fop which he had previously despised.[51]

The final visit to Venice leads to Aschenbach's physical collapse by the well-head, but also a reflection in music of surpassing beauty on the experience of the artist. Its melody derives from the opera's final allusion to ambiguity, 'O perilous sweetness', but apart from a momentary reminder of Tadzio's vibraphone chord, the boy is absent from this 'Socratic' meditation.[52] Despite its beauty, it is about the experience of an Aschenbach who has turned away from a creative relationship with the embodiment of his ideal. It now seems that both the way of passion and the way of 'form and pure detachment' lead to the abyss. There follows an austere statement of the 'vision' theme developed contrapuntally in a way which is both noble and detached, but which seems to suggest that the vision to which it points is no longer available to Aschenbach, at least in this life.

In the closing scenes, mundanity takes over as Aschenbach enters, still seeking Tadzio (reprise of the *Sehnsucht*/love theme), but then sees him playing on the beach as a very ordinary boy. Tadzio wades out to sea as Aschenbach slumps in his chair. The orchestra combines Tadzio's vibraphone motif with a recall of Aschenbach's statement of his artistic creed, but the absence of the 'vision' theme here suggests that the opera remains agnostic about the existence of any transcendental reality. What is affirmed is the self-justifying spectacle of beauty here and now, as, to an orchestral epilogue of quiet rapture, Aschenbach dies gazing upon it.

Billy Budd and *Death in Venice* constitute twin peaks in Britten's career as an opera composer. Despite their obvious differences, there are links between them, particularly in respect of the theme of eros or male love and the desperate dilemmas it poses for the two central characters. Both Captain Vere and Gustav von Aschenbach have attained positions of some public responsibility: and both find a conflict between their love for a younger male and what society expects from men in their position. The parallel in public position is given musical expression, when Aschenbach's monotone declamation ('famous as a master writer') echoes that of Vere ('I . . . Captain of the Indomitable') as he prepares to convey the sentence of death to Billy.[53] Yet the differences outweigh the similarities.

To begin with, the roles of eros as a response to beauty are to be differentiated. Tadzio is a symbol for physical perfection, but little more. He has no character, beyond that expressed in occasional flirtatious glances, and when Aschenbach fails to develop a relationship, eros moves from being a response to an aesthetic ideal to become an uncontrollable, destructive passion.[54] There is here a parallel with the effect of Billy Budd on Claggart, and in this sense one may speak of the power of beauty to destroy.[55]

But there is much more to Billy Budd. The young sailor is certainly handsome, and this constitutes part of his attraction for Vere as well as Claggart. But far more frequently the libretto emphasizes his moral qualities – beginning with an appreciation (from Claggart, no less) which quotes Christ's analogue for the Kingdom of Heaven.[56] The operatic Billy's maturity has already been noted, and the music given to him likewise seems to emphasize his positive, outgoing character (see above, p. 151). It is Billy's goodness and love (as well as beauty) which characterize the world from which Claggart knows he is excluded, and which is recognized by Vere just before the final confrontation with the Master-at-Arms.

The relationship between Billy and Vere is threatened not by society's hostility to unorthodox sexuality, but through the operation of law, authority and the need to preserve the ship from mutiny. Vere's dilemma, once the fatal blow is struck, is akin to that of the Queen in *Gloriana*, who is torn between her love for Essex and her obligation as ruler to order the execution of a rebel.[57] Whether or not (as has been argued) there is in Elizabeth an element of sexual repression, in Vere's case, it is his sense of duty as a naval commander that motivates his silence at the trial and his failure to intervene on Billy's behalf. His dilemma is set out in the Scylla and Charybdis monologue – in which he recognizes the harrowing choice of evils before him and reveals his human sensitivity. 'How can I condemn him? How can I save him', he cries. His silence about the need to enforce the Articles of War is as significant as his failure to raise the possibility of saving Billy. For he can neither condemn nor acquit, without repudiating a fundamental obligation, and must therefore leave the matter to the duly constituted court to decide.[58] It is Billy's love and acceptance of this that enable him to bless Vere, and confer upon him a sense of salvation. For his part, Vere, despite the agonizing realization in old age that he may have come to a wrong decision, is able to accept Billy's dying blessing, and allow his mind 'to go back in peace'. Thus in the tragedy of *Billy Budd*, eros comes to play a positive role.[59]

In *Death in Venice* the heart of any relationship between the writer and the youth is aesthetic rather than (as in *Billy Budd*) moral and personal, though in each case these qualities are to be seen as the twin foci of an ellipse rather than as mutually exclusive. In particular, *Death in Venice* reflects Britten's refusal (evident in his Aspen speech) to separate art and life.[60] The goal is a Platonic friendship, both moral and aesthetic, with the beautiful youth as a source of artistic inspiration. One cannot but surmise that the lyrical affirmation of this ideal implicit in the first act may have sprung from the composer's own friendships with teenage boys imbued, as it seems, with the resolve on his part to keep them on an idealistic plane.[61]

Thus far, eros has the potential to play a positive role (as it does in *Billy Budd*). But Aschenbach falters, unable to rise to his opportunity. The impediment to a maturing relationship between him and Tadzio arises not from the duty imposed upon a responsible commander of men (Vere) but from society's view of what is expected of its venerated intellectual leaders, and its rejection of same-sex relationships, particularly across the generational gap. Aschenbach's public position requires him to view the possibility of open friendship for Tadzio as a threat rather than an opportunity, and the Dionysiac element in the artist's life as disruptive rather than creative. The opera's second act, accordingly, presents the descent into the abyss which follows his self-abnegation. It remains ambivalent on the question whether the 'Dionysiac abyss' might be a price worth paying for artistic achievement. But if the aesthetic philosophy remains cloudy, one cannot mistake the personal disintegration which follows upon the repression of love. For Aschenbach, eros comes to mean death in the midst of life, whereas for Vere it had meant life in the midst of death.

Thus it appears that despite the obvious resemblances, the role and indeed the nature of eros are significantly different in the two operas considered in this chapter. It is true of them, as of all Britten's work in which (male) homosexuality is covertly or overtly present, that same-sex desire is not a one-dimensional stereotype, but a reality in some men's relationships with one another and with society as a whole, which, in its distinctive way, exhibits the nuanced subtleties which are to be found in any significant artistic reflection upon the human condition.

PART THREE

Perspectives

9 Distant horizons: from Pagodaland to the Church Parables

MERVYN COOKE

> Writing this work [*Canticle III: 'Still Falls the Rain'*] has helped me so much in my development as a composer. I feel with this work & the Turn of the Screw (which I am impatient for you to hear) that I am on the threshold of a new musical world (for me, I am not pretentious about it!) I am worried about the problems which arise, & that is one reason that I am taking off next winter to do some deep thinking. But your great poem has dragged something from me that was latent there, & shown me what lies before me.

Britten wrote these lines to Edith Sitwell on 28 April 1955, six months before the momentous concert tour which took him halfway across the globe for five months in the winter and spring of 1955–6 and provided him with the opportunity for 'some deep thinking'. The significance of those travels in exposing the composer to vivid firsthand experiences of various Asian musical traditions, and the surface impact these had on his own style, have long been recognized. But Britten's identification with Far Eastern music went far deeper than the obvious borrowings from the Balinese gamelan to be heard in *The Prince of the Pagodas* (1955–7) or the emulations of the Japanese Nō theatre in *Curlew River* (1956–64) would suggest. Britten's style was at a turning-point in the mid-1950s, as his remarks to Sitwell attest: the intense motivic economy and dodecaphonic techniques in *Canticle III* and *The Turn of the Screw* had clearly left him wondering in which direction his style would now develop. The Asian adventure, with perfect timing, opened his ears to other traditions of musical economy and structural clarity while his compositional thinking was clearly running along similar lines, and his travels strengthened a latent curiosity about exotic cultures that had originated many years before.

Britten's eclectic tastes during the 1930s had been sufficiently enterprising to embrace an incipient interest in non-Western music. Between 1933 and 1940 he encountered for the first time the three musical cultures with which he was to identify more closely in later years, those of Indonesia, Japan and India. His first recorded experience of ethnic music in live performance came on 6 May 1933, when he confessed in his personal diary to having been greatly impressed by a concert of Indian music and dancing he attended at the Ambassador Theatre.[1] Then, in 1938, he

became involved in Ezra Pound's eccentric attempt to mount a performance of a Japanese Nōplay.[2] Only in the sphere of Indonesian music
did Britten's early experiences bear almost immediate artistic fruit: his
encounter in 1939–42 with the Canadian composer and ethnomusicolo-
gist Colin McPhee (a frequent guest at the home of Dr William Mayer on
Long Island, New York, where Britten and Pears were based during their
transatlantic sojourn) gave him a basic introduction to the fundamental
principles of Balinese gamelan music that would later become absorbed
into his own compositional style.

McPhee had lived in Bali for many years in the 1930s, making a thor-
ough study of the island's musical traditions and distilling his knowledge
into a series of transcriptions for two pianos, some of which Britten and
McPhee performed in New York and subsequently recorded for Schirmer
in 1941.[3] Balinese influences are abundant in certain of McPhee's
compositions, most notably in his toccata for two pianos and orchestra
entitled *Tabuh-tabuhan* (1936), in which some of the orchestration is so
close to the procedures later adopted by Britten in *The Prince of the
Pagodas* that it comes as a surprise to discover that Britten probably never
heard McPhee's piece (although it seems plausible that he would have
been shown the score). McPhee's two-piano transcriptions, three of
which were published by Schirmer in 1940 under the title *Balinese
Ceremonial Music,* were of sufficient interest to Britten for him to mount
their first British performance with Clifford Curzon on 29 March 1944 at
the Wigmore Hall; the programme notes for this concert were provided
by Britten himself, heavily based on the introductory notes written by
McPhee for inclusion in the published scores.[4] Britten's copy of the
transcriptions was inscribed by McPhee in April 1940 with the words 'To
Ben – hoping he will find something in this music, after all',[5] a remark
clearly implying that Britten had not yet been convinced that Balinese
music ought to engage his attention, and all the more surprising in view of
the undeniable influence that McPhee's transcriptions appear to have had
on Britten's subsequent output.

McPhee's arrangements had furnished Britten with clear examples of
the principal styles and tuning systems of Balinese music, and the piece
entitled 'Taboeh Teloe' had an immediate impact on Britten's own music
by suggesting the scheme of colotomic (i.e. 'dissecting') punctuation
underlying the 'Sunday Morning' interlude which begins Act II of *Peter
Grimes* (see Ex. 9.1).[6] Britten appears to have transposed the pentatonic
Balinese *selisir* scale down a semitone and used this as the basis for the
layered ostinati of the upper parts of his orchestral texture, which clearly
owe much to his post-Debussyan awareness of stratified gamelan
polyphony. One of the dissonant triads used in McPhee's transcription to

Example 9.1

suggest the resonance of the gamelan's punctuating gong strokes is also transposed down a semitone and deftly transformed into a tolling Suffolk church bell. It seems unlikely to be coincidental that this derivation should occur in a work written while Britten was studying the *Balinese Ceremonial Music* with Curzon.

Britten's works from the period 1939–56 contain many further examples of such dissonant punctuating devices, and of motivic material corresponding to the intervallic contours of the two principal Balinese tuning systems (as standardized in Western notation in McPhee's transcriptions). Stratified counterpoint based on superimposed ostinato patterns and a notable fondness for metallic percussion sonorities are both widespread, the latter most obvious in the emphasis placed on the alluring celeste and gong associated with the ghosts in *The Turn of the Screw* (1954). An increasingly important equality between melody and harmony as different manifestations of identical pitch content was ultimately to reach its culmination in the sparse textures of the Church Parables under the direct influence of Japanese music, while heterophonic techniques which may be related to those of the Balinese gamelan occur as early as the Prologue to *Paul Bunyan*, composed in 1940–1 when Britten was collaborating with McPhee in the USA.[7] The use of this 'exotic' technique to depict a supernatural event is itself significant, since virtually all Britten's later applications of Balinese material were to fulfil strikingly similar musico-dramatic functions. Britten was clearly interested in such heterophonic techniques long before he met McPhee (see, for example, the superimposition of motivic fragments in 'Rats Away!' from *Our Hunting Fathers* in 1936), and between 1941 and 1955 Britten's use of heterophony significantly increased.

In November 1955, Britten and Pears left England on their five-month concert tour, which took them to Austria, Yugoslavia, Turkey, Singapore, Indonesia, Hong Kong, Japan, Thailand and Sri Lanka. The fortnight they spent in Bali in January 1956 was kept completely free from engagements, and was intended to be a holiday from the punishing recital schedule.[8] Whilst relaxing on the idyllic island, Britten found time to make a remarkably comprehensive study of the local gamelan music, visiting temples, attending dances and the shadow-play, and immersing himself in many different genres of Balinese music. On his return to England, the composer directly incorporated Balinese material into the score of his ballet *The Prince of the Pagodas* (see below), completed later in 1956 and his first work to make widespread use of specific oriental borrowings – although, as we have seen, by no means the first to demonstrate his latent interest in the music of the Far East.

Britten first experienced a live performance of Indonesian music in Bandung, Java, on 8 January 1956. Both Britten and Pears could easily distinguish between the basic melody of the composition and the embellishments added by the performers, and Britten delighted the musicians by accurately singing back their scale to them.[9] A diversion to Semarang proved to be of considerable interest, since the town is an important centre of gong manufacture in South-East Asia and Britten was thus provided with the opportunity to see gamelan instruments being made.[10] His enthusiasm for the instruments is revealed somewhat later by an undated postcard sporting a picture of typical gongs he sent to James Blades from Indonesia with the message: 'I've heard Gongs of all shapes, sizes and metals here – producing fantastic notes – you'd be very interested. I hope to bring back some tapes of the music here – fantastic stuff.' It was to Blades that Britten would later turn for specialized advice on the exact choice of Western percussion instruments to represent specific gamelan sonorities in *The Prince of the Pagodas*.

The tour party flew on to Bali on 12 January. Britten's visit was confined to the south of the island, the foothills of the volcanoes Gunung Agung and Gunung Batur marking the limit of his excursions northwards.[11] Most of his artistic experiences seem to have occurred during the few days he spent in the peaceful village of Ubud and its satellite community Peliatan, noted for its famous gamelan which had toured the West with the entrepreneur John Coast in 1952.[12] Britten availed himself of specialized instruction in the shape of Bernard 'Penny' IJzerdraat, who helped him to label the sketches he made during the visit with accurate Balinese terminology. Britten later wrote to Imogen Holst: 'We are lucky in being taken around everywhere by an intelligent Dutch musicologist, married to a Balinese, who knows all musicians – so we go to rehearsals, find out about and visit cremations, trance dances, shadow plays – a bewildering richness.'[13] IJzerdraat was director of the gamelan *Babar Layar* at the Royal Tropical Institute in Amsterdam, and was an expert on rhythmic patterns in gamelan music; he had contributed a transcription of West Javanese angklung music to Jaap Kunst's monumental study of Javanese music, first published in 1949.[14] John Coast recalls that Mr IJzerdraat played for a time in the Peliatan gamelan – an extremely rare privilege for a Westerner in those days.[15]

Britten compiled a set of manuscript sketches from the music he heard on the island, carefully labelled with details of dance genres and musical scales, the most significant of which originated from his time in the region of Ubud where he saw the famous *legong* dance. A representative page from Britten's sketches is reproduced in Plate 12. It was from Ubud on 17 January that Britten wrote his much-quoted remarks to Imogen Holst: 'The music is *fantastically* rich – melodically, rhythmically, texture (such *orchestration*!!) & above all *formally*. It is a remarkable culture . . . At last I'm beginning to catch on to the technique, but it's about as complicated as Schönberg.' In the light of Hans Keller's remark that Britten's interest in the heterophonic techniques of Asian music should be related to his equally strong involvement with twelve-tone procedures, Britten's mention of Schoenberg in this context is especially noteworthy[16] – and the parallel reminds us that it was precisely the dodecaphonic techniques with which he had been experimenting before his departure that had forced him to find the opportunity for 'some deep thinking' about general compositional issues during his world tour.

During the morning of 23 January, an event took place which provided important source material for the Balinese sections Britten had by this stage evidently decided to include in *The Prince of the Pagodas*: the making of a studio tape recording of gamelan pieces in which he was especially interested.[17] Sent to Britten in the UK after his return home, recordings from this session were edited by IJzerdraat onto a tape that included extracts from many other musical genres Britten encountered during his time in Indonesia. The most important item on the tape proved to be a performance of 'Tabuh Telu', the melody of which Britten incorporated more or less directly into the score of *The Prince of the Pagodas*.[18] It was on the day these recordings were made that Britten sent an optimistic telegram to Dame Ninette de Valois at Covent Garden to say 'CONFIDENT BALLET READY FOR MIDSEPTEMBER LOVE BRITTEN'.

The genesis of *The Prince of the Pagodas* dates back to January 1954, when the Sadler's Wells Ballet announced a forthcoming collaboration between Britten and the choreographer John Cranko. Britten had begun work on the ballet's music in the spring of 1955 and had reached Act II by mid-August, when it became apparent that (most uncharacteristically) he would be unable to complete the score on time. A new February deadline was scrapped, and the ballet's production was postponed until July 1956.[19] It was, in the event, highly propitious that Britten should have had Act II of the ballet in his mind when he arrived in Bali, since it was into this act that he subsequently incorporated material borrowed from the gamelan music he encountered there. Britten's ballet score contains several features that clearly parallel aspects of gamelan music he had

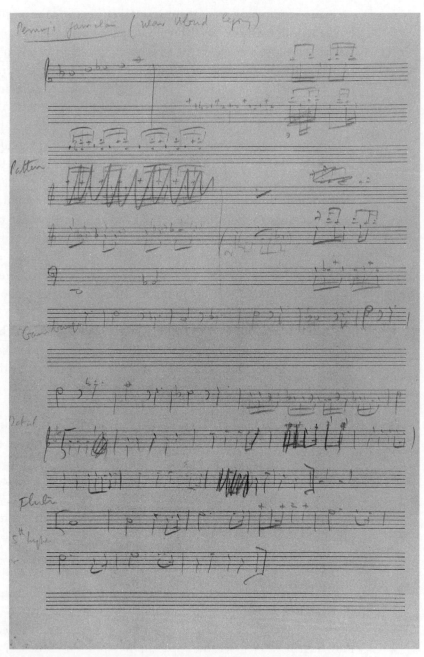

Plate 12 Britten's sketches from Bali, January 1956 (fol. 2ᵛ)

encountered through McPhee's transcriptions years before. Polyphonic stratification occurs in the Prelude (a late addition written well after the Balinese trip) and in the massive crescendo between Figs. 19 and 23 in Act III where all the themes associated with the Prince are combined as the lights come up on the Pagoda Palace. Familiar pentatonicism colours much of the ballet's music, but an equal debt is shown to the Russian ballet tradition with ubiquitous and affectionate echoes of Tchaikovsky, Prokofiev and Stravinsky: the score is finely balanced between East and West.

The direct appropriation of Balinese musical material in Act II presented Britten with the challenge of emulating gamelan sonorities strictly within the confines of the Western orchestra. The resulting 'gamelan' passages symbolize the attraction the supernatural Prince holds over Belle Rose in his guise as Salamander and as ruler of the exotic Pagodaland, an important parallel with the symbolic use of tuned percussion in several of Britten's operas. The Balinese sonorities were reconstructed with the aid of the sketches from Bali, four gramophone recordings of gamelan music which may have been in Britten's possession before his visit to the island, and the tape recording of miscellaneous Indonesian music made under the guidance of IJzerdraat. Two of the gramophone records are 78rpm discs (MO 104 and MO 105) which contain music from Java and Bali, and two are LPs (Argo RG1 and RG2) containing Balinese *kebyar* music performed by the Peliatan group during their 1952 tour. Britten filled both sides of a half-folio of eighteen-stave manuscript paper with sketches taken down from four of the recorded pieces.[20] The sketches from Bali provided Britten with a reminder of the popular *gambang* theme he first encountered in McPhee's second transcription, which he now decided to include in the ballet at Fig. 73 in Act II (Ex. 9.2 and Plate 12). The 'salamander' theme (Ex. 9.3) was probably added to the Balinese sketches at a later date from the tape recording Britten had made for him in Bali and sent on to the UK, since the composer wrote out the melody in a ballpoint pen quite distinct from the pencil used consistently elsewhere in the sketches. In addition to his memories of McPhee's transcriptions, he must certainly have had in mind Poulenc's Concerto for Two Pianos (1932), which he had recently performed alongside its composer on 16 January 1955 at the Royal Festival Hall. Poulenc and Britten first performed the concerto at the Royal Albert Hall in 1945, and the work's 'gamelan' material is also based on a Balinese *selisir* scale on B♭ – presenting precisely the same pitches as those used by Britten between Figs. 69 and 74 in *Pagodas*, and in McPhee's transcription of 'Taboeh Teloe' (cf. Ex. 9.1).[21]

Britten's orchestration in Act II of *Pagodas* demonstrates an intuitive grasp of the structure and instrumentation of gamelan music and an

Example 9.2

Example 9.3

astonishing ear for percussion sonorities. At Fig. 71, the piano, celeste and xylophone present a much simplified version of a cadenza for the reong (a rack of gong-chimes played by four musicians) which occurs shortly after the opening of Britten's LP recording of the Peliatan gamelan's 'Kapi Radja'. At Fig. 72, the gamelan's colotomic gong strokes are suggested by a conventional orchestral gong doubled with a sustained doublebass note of definite pitch (Ex. 9.4). The distinctive timbre of the kempli, a small hand-held timekeeping gong, is captured by a repeated staccato C♯ on piccolo timpano (played with hard sticks) and harp *près de la table*. The smallest Balinese metallophones are evoked by rapid figurations on the xylophone, with two dovetailed piccolo lines representing the popular Indonesian bamboo flute (suling), while the vibraphone and celeste provide the slowly moving ostinato of the deeper and softer metallophones. A small pair of clashed cymbals serves as their Balinese equivalent (cengceng), and throughout the passage a piano duet doubles most of the individual lines – undoubtedly signifying the renewed influence of the McPhee and Poulenc precedents. Three tom-toms represent the kendang (the Balinese double-headed drum), and at several points the vibraphone solo recalls the melodic function of the trompong, a rack of gong-chimes played by a soloist (e.g. first- and second-time bars before Fig. 73 and Fig. 74^{-2}). The music then launches into a brilliant and extended free reconstruction of one of the toccata-like sections from 'Kapi Radja', cul-

Example 9.4

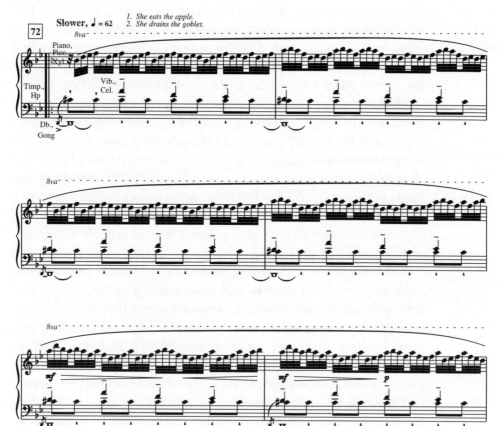

minating at Fig. 73 in the authentic *gambang* melody, scored for glockenspiel, celeste, harp harmonics, piano and solo violin in an uncanny imitation of the sonorities of the suling and bright, high metallophones (Ex.
9.2 above).

At Fig. 74, the trumpet fanfares which began the ballet's Prologue are
modified to reflect the intervallic contours of the *selisir* scale, and the
music is now transposed down a semitone. The 'gamelan' then enters with
a tutti chord at the new pitch level in a gradual, unmeasured accelerando.
Such cluster chords are a strong characteristic of the Balinese *kebyar* style:
the accelerating rhythm is also typical, and Britten would have heard it
with particular clarity towards the end of the *legong* dance on the second
side of one of his Peliatan records (RG1) and in the shadow-play music on
his reel-to-reel tape recording (track 5). At this stage he had not yet developed the special notation for this accelerating or decelerating pattern
which was to become a prominent feature of many works composed in
the 1960s and 1970s. (For an example from *Death in Venice*, see Ex. 8.7,

p.159.) The transposition of *selisir* at this point not only relieves the potential monotony for the Western ear: it also allows Britten to incorporate the Prince-as-Salamander theme at Fig. 75^{+5} at the same pitch level at which he had encountered it in Bali and on IJzerdraat's tape recording (see Ex. 9.3 above). Britten relaxes the stringently applied *selisir* scale at Fig. 77^{-4} to effect a transition to the entry of the full orchestra in an emphatic C major. The theme announced by the trumpet at this point represents the Prince-as-Human, and the contrast between the thoroughly Western key of C major and the preceding *selisir* is an obvious musical comment on the dramatic situation. Nevertheless, the interjected clusters from the 'gamelan' remind the listener of the duality in the Prince's character; and when Belle Rose flees at the end of the Act, slowly followed by the Prince-as-Salamander, Britten superimposes a recapitulation of his gamelan music over a dissonant C♮ in a typically economical and graphic reminder of the Prince's dual nature.

The incidence of heterophonic techniques, polyphonic stratification, colotomic percussion patterns and scales resembling the two Balinese tuning systems in Britten's music composed before 1956 could in many cases be viewed as a product of the composer's subconscious. Those features recalling the early stimulus provided by McPhee's *Balinese Ceremonial Music* were equally well inherent characteristics of Britten's compositional style well before his initial contact with Balinese music. One reason for his intense involvement with the gamelan in 1956 must therefore have been his realization that certain Balinese musical procedures paralleled his own stylistic preoccupations at the time. There seems little doubt, however, that the notable intensification of these devices after *The Prince of the Pagodas* represents a more conscious application of Balinese devices on the composer's part, especially in cases such as *Noye's Fludde* (1958) where adumbrations of his later Japanese-inspired Church Parable style co-exist with quasi-gamelan sonorities and pentatonicism. Heterophony and the derivation of both harmony and melody from identical pitch content become more widespread from the *Nocturne* (1958) and *Missa Brevis* (1959) onwards, and stratified polyphony culminates in the superimposed textures of the *War Requiem* (1962) – which in places looks directly ahead to the free metrical alignment of the Church Parables. Colotomic gong strokes occur in virtually every post-1956 orchestral score and are especially prominent in the first movement of the *War Requiem*. Equally notable is Britten's increasingly systematic use of quasi-gamelan sonorities as a consistent musical response to comparable dramatic situations in different stage works: the tinkling allure of the ghosts in *The Turn of the Screw* is recalled by the fairy 'gamelan' in *A Midsummer Night's Dream* (1960), while the percussive sonorities in *Owen Wingrave* (1970) are disconcertingly associated both with the martial heritage from which the protagonist attempts to escape, and with the attractiveness of the peace that eludes him (see pp. 190–5).

The gamelan influence on Britten reached its final fruition in his last opera *Death in Venice* (1971–3), in which Balinese procedures and sonorities were allocated to the beautiful Polish boy Tadzio and his associates in a deliberate attempt to provide the maximum possible contrast to the music associated with Aschenbach. As the opera's librettist Myfanwy Piper put it, 'the type of melancholy gaiety in the Balinese sound is in total contrast to the rather Germanic character of Aschenbach's self-absorption and underlines his feeling of alienation'.[22] In contrast to the direct reconstruction of specific Balinese prototypes in *Pagodas*, Britten's empathy with gamelan techniques allowed him in *Death in Venice* to compose in his own synthetic 'gamelan' idiom in which pentatonic scales were treated less rigorously, and both percussive sonorities and scale configurations were transformed and deployed in economical and effective moments of musico-dramatic symbolism. While the music for the children's beach games directly recalls the scoring of *Pagodas* (compare, for example, *Death in Venice*, Act I, Fig. 82, with Ex. 9.4 above), the music for Tadzio is provided by the vibraphone in the manner of a trompong solo, and remains resolutely on a *selisir* scale based on A – and inevitably suggesting a parallel with Britten's habitual key of innocence and purity. On the Polish boy's first appearance, this pentatonic configuration is treated as part of a dodecaphonic pitch collection in a striking fusion of Eastern and Western musical procedures.[23]

Shortly after their memorable stay in Bali in January 1956, Britten and Pears flew on to Japan, arriving in Tokyo on 8 February. Three days later, another inspiring artistic experience awaited Britten in the shape of a performance of Nō theatre, which his librettist William Plomer – who lived in Japan in the 1920s – had strongly recommended him to see for himself.[24] In preparation for the event, Britten had acquired a copy of Faber's reissue of Ezra Pound's Nō-play translations before his trip.[25] A detailed description of the performance seen by Britten is to be found in the travel diary written by Prince Ludwig of Hesse (who, together with his wife, accompanied Britten and Pears during the latter stages of their tour): it concentrates on the verbal unintelligibility of the genre, but notes that the drama nevertheless exerted a profound impact on the composer.[26] That Britten's imagination was principally fired by the play *Sumidagawa* was revealed by his desire to see the performance once again (on 19 February), just before his departure from Tokyo; he subsequently acquired a tape recording of the play for his own use.[27] In a special radio message broadcast to the people of Japan on New Year's Day 1958, he declared:

> I count the [Nō theatre] among the greatest theatrical experiences of my life. Of course it was strange to start with, the language and the especially curious kind of chanting used; but we were fortunate in having excellent literal translations to follow from, and we soon became accustomed to the haunting sounds. The deep solemnity and *self*lessness of the acting, the perfect shaping of the drama (like a great Greek tragedy) coupled with the strength and universality of the stories are something which every Western artist can learn from.[28]

An excursion to Kyoto in the period 12–14 February had meanwhile brought an amusing encounter with D. J. Enright at a geisha evening, an event recorded by the poet:

> The most highly-regarded samisen [*sic*] players and singers were brought in to entertain the guests. As they performed, Britten scribbled down the musical notation while Pears (an even greater feat, I should think) swiftly made his own transliteration of the words. Then Britten borrowed a samisen and plucked at it while Pears sang – the result being an uncanny playback. The effect on the geisha, a race who tend to be excessively conscious of their inimitability, their cultural uniqueness, and aggravatingly assured of the pitiable inability to understand their art inherent in all foreigners, was almost alarming. They paled beneath their whitewash. A more violent people would have seen to it that their guests' throats were cut the moment they left those sacred halls. This was one of the few indubitable triumphs for British art or artists which I noticed in Japan – and probably the most striking.[29]

The shamisen referred to by Enright is a three-stringed banjo played with a large plectrum, the traditional accompanying instrument for geisha singing; unfortunately, Britten's jottings from this extraordinary evening have not survived. The composer was by this stage becoming familiar with the relevant musical idiom, having already heard a similar performance in Tokyo. The distinctive heterophonic techniques of shamisen songs, in which the single instrumental line 'shadows' the vocal melody, were later to exert a far greater influence on the contrapuntal procedures of the Church Parables than the music of Nō, which is notoriously complex and virtually impossible to express adequately in Western musical notation.

Perhaps the most significant event of the three-day excursion to Kyoto was Britten's purchase of a shō, the mouth-organ employed in traditional Japanese court music (Gagaku). After his return to Tokyo, Britten paid what was probably his second visit to the Music Department of the Imperial Household Agency on 18 February to hear the haunting hetero-

phonic textures of the court orchestra, which were also to leave their mark
on the innovative idiom of the Church Parables. As a result of his interest
in Gagaku, Britten obtained two Columbia long-playing recordings (BL
28–9) made by the Music Department of the Imperial Household and a
volume of printed transcriptions from the Gagaku repertory.[30] After his
return to England, Britten received a warm letter from his Japanese host,
Kei-ichi Kurosawa, sent on 31 March 1956 as a covering note with an
article specially written for the composer by Leo Traynor and wittily entitled 'A Young Britten's Guide to the Shō'. Britten had already received
instruction on the instrument while in Japan, as shown by a photograph
taken in Tokyo (Plate 13).

Britten's fascination with Nō and other traditional Japanese genres
was to lead to the composition of the first Church Parable, *Curlew River*
(completed in 1964 after an eight-year gestation), a work which embodies
an unconventional dramatic aesthetic created from a combination of elements borrowed from Japanese theatre and the mediaeval English
mystery play, and which spawned two successors: *The Burning Fiery
Furnace* (1966) and *The Prodigal Son* (1968).[31] The composer communicated his enthusiasm for Japanese theatre to Plomer immediately upon
his return from Japan, singling out *Sumidagawa* for comment in a letter
dated 13 May 1956. Correspondence between the two men surviving from
the summer of 1957 reveals that the possibility of an operatic adaptation
of the play had been discussed but temporarily shelved, but in the autumn
of 1958 Plomer went ahead and produced his first draft libretto in the
shape of a straightforward paraphrase of the authorized English translation of the play.[32] On 2 October, Plomer wrote to Britten to communicate
his desire to retain various Japanese details, including names, to which the
composer responded six days later: 'I am very keen on as many nice evocative Japanese words as possible!' Plomer duly handed over his completed
libretto, and Britten thanked him for it in a letter dated 16 November in
which he declared: 'The more I think of it, the more I feel we should stick
as far as possible to the original style & look of it – but oh, to find some
equivalent to those extraordinary noises the Japanese musicians made!'
Plans were made to mount the new work in 1960, but the reopening of the
Jubilee Hall at Aldeburgh in that year necessitated a change of direction
(see p. 129).

On 15 April 1959, Britten wrote a long and carefully considered letter
to Plomer in which he advocated a radical rethinking of the work's
content: having resolved to perform the piece in a local church setting, he
had conceived the idea of Christianizing the story and removing the 'little
bits of Zen-Bhuddism [*sic*], which don't mean much to me'. He continued:

Plate 13 Britten playing the shō in Tokyo, February 1956

The story is one which stands strongly wherever it is placed. I have been *very* worried lest the work should seem a *pastiche* of a Noh play, which however well done, would seem false & thin. I *can't* write Japanesy music, but might be led into trying if the rest of the production (setting, clothes, moves) were Japanese . . .

. . . if we made it Mediaeval, or possibly earlier, it would be accurate that no women should be used; also if the style were kept very artificial, very influenced by the Noh, then it wouldn't seem so odd for a woman to be played by a man, especially if the dresses were very carefully & strongly designed . . . we might get a very strong atmosphere (which I personally love) if we set it in pre-conquest East Anglia . . .

Working on a typed version of the earlier libretto, Plomer accordingly set about transposing the action of *Sumidagawa* to mediaeval England, making ingenious emendations in ballpoint pen. The most significant alterations were the provision of a new and strongly cathartic ending, in the sharpest possible contrast to the bleak conclusion of the Japanese original, and the addition of a narrative frame in order to present the tale as if enacted by a group of Christian monks. Heavy compositional commitments prevented Britten from resuming work on the project until Christmas 1963, when Plomer completed his libretto in time for Britten to compose the bulk of the music in Venice in the following February and introduce the work at the 1964 Aldeburgh Festival.

Clearly, Britten's decision to Christianize the plot of *Sumidagawa* marks a radical departure from the aesthetic effect of the Japanese original. To the uninitiated Westerner, many Nō plays seem highly static in their dramatic effect because stage action and plot developments are less important than the philosophical contemplation expected from cognoscenti of the genre. Britten's Western approach to the story has a dramatic cogency equal to that of *Sumidagawa* if based on entirely different aesthetic principles: *Curlew River* may be viewed as a spiritual progression towards a single climactic and cathartic moment (a familiar scheme in the composer's operatic output), this simple and tangible dramatic momentum greatly aiding the Western audience's appreciation of the story. In spite of this significant shift in dramatic emphasis, the first production of *Curlew River* reflected the original Japanese stimulus in numerous respects, although Colin Graham (the work's producer) has recalled that Britten requested him not to see a genuine Nō play lest his ideas should be too heavily influenced by the genre.[33] The Nō theatre evolved in mediaeval times specifically to suit the tastes of the aristocratic warrior class (Samurai), which forbade the uninhibited expression of emotions: this consideration was clearly crucial to the formulation of an art famously characterized by extreme stylization and restraint, both of which left their mark on the dramatic style of all three Church Parables. The economical and versatile stage set evolved by Graham for the trilogy perfectly captured the unelaborate functionality of the Nō prototype, and emulated the special ramp along which characters enter in Nō (and which symbolically links the real world with the supernatural), Britten responding in his score to the Nō convention of providing entrance music specifically associated with each actor. The function of the Nō mirror room, where the principal actor dons his mask in order to study its reflection and where the instrumentalists play a sacred prelude before processing on stage, is replaced in Britten's parables by the initial procession and subsequent on-stage robing ceremony (suggested to Britten by an ecclesiastical ritual he witnessed in Venice while at work on *Curlew River*). Many details of set design, masks, costumes, props, stage directions and stylized acting gestures were directly modelled on the Japanese original and further developed in the two later Church Parables.

On the evidence of the score of *Curlew River* and Britten's correspondence with Plomer, it seems incontrovertible that the composer was primarily attracted by the dramatic qualities of Nō and not by its musical idiom: the latter is emulated at a fairly superficial level, chiefly in matters of sonority (exclusively male voices, with a predominantly monophonic chorus and prominent flute and drums – the only instruments used in Nō) and in a clear preoccupation with quasi-Japanese vocal portamento. Although Britten made no attempt to study or emulate in specific detail the complex rhythmic procedures of Nō music, it nevertheless seems likely that his liberation of rhythm in *Curlew River* was inspired by the sense of rhythmic freedom which will strike any Westerner listening to a Nō play for the first time (the product of a complex theoretical system 'following the fluid rhythm of life and avoiding mechanical arrangement'[34]). Much more seminal Japanese influences on the musical style of the parables were Gagaku, which showed him how to organize heterophonic textures on a grand scale and which may have provided a model for the dense canonic writing in certain passages,[35] and the simple style of two-part heterophony to be found in traditional vocal music with shamisen accompaniment (both that performed by geishas and in the Kabuki theatre, which Britten attended in Tokyo on 17 February 1956). Gagaku drumming provided a model for the accelerating drum patterns heard in the narrative frames of the first two parables (transferred to a suspended cymbal for variety in *The Prodigal Son*), and Britten had previously encountered similar accelerating repeated notes in the Balinese *kebyar* style; these were directly recalled in the 'Sanctus' of the *War Requiem* (and indicated by an innovative notation).[36] The gamelan parallel was retained in *Curlew River* where the accelerating rhythms appear on the set of small bells at Fig. 87.

Example 9.5

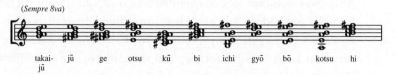

Example 9.6

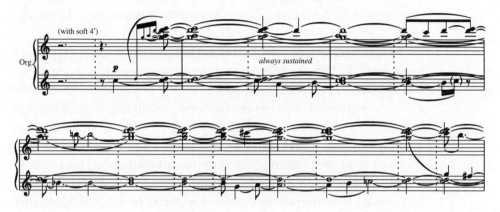

Britten's understanding of the shō (three of which participate in the Gagaku ensemble) contributed significantly to the unusual style of the music for the chamber organ in the three parables. The Japanese instrument can play eleven different chords of five or six notes each, termed *aitake* ('complementary bamboos'), the lowest notes of which are heterophonically related to the thematic material of the melody instruments. These chords, which are given in Ex. 9.5, are linked in performance by subtly blurred transitions, faithfully reproduced by Britten in the chamber-organ part of *Curlew River* (Ex. 9.6).[37]

The initial eight-year gestation period which had led to the creation of the new idiom allowed the subsequent members of the Church Parable trilogy to be conceived and executed at a far greater speed. The Christianized Nō play was followed by an Old Testament story in *The Burning Fiery Furnace* (1966), with the New Testament parable of *The Prodigal Son* completing the triptych in 1968. The *Furnace* managed to achieve a high degree of instrumental colour and dramatic vitality, perhaps in part reflecting Britten's and Pears's memories of Kabuki, while adhering closely to the dramatic and musical conventions of *Curlew River*.[38] *The Prodigal Son* deftly combined the austerity of the first parable (for the tranquillity of the family environment) with the hedonism of the second (in the nightmarish city scenes), while leaving some commentators with the feeling that the initial impulse behind the trilogy had now grown somewhat tired.[39] The function of the chorus as the principal commentator on the action in *Curlew River* – a feature directly inherited from Nō – was one of many elements to undergo significant transformation. Britten had already made his chorus participate directly in the action of *Curlew River*, in sharp contrast to their strictly sedentary narrative function in the Nō prototype, and the still greater participation of the chorus in the dramatic action of the two later parables (as courtiers, workers, revellers and beggars) is a further move away from the aesthetic principles of the Nō theatre towards a more Westernized operatic conception.

The Prodigal Son provides an isolated but striking example of Britten's response to the Indian music which he had first encountered as a student. During the 1955–6 world tour, he was greatly impressed by the Indian music he witnessed on several occasions – including a dazzling performance by Ravi Shankar in Delhi on 22 December 1955 which Pears described in his travel diary as 'brilliant, fascinating, stimulating, wonderfully played' – and on the return leg westwards from Japan, Britten added a tape of virtuoso Singalese drumming from Kandy (Sri Lanka) to his growing collection of ethnic source material. In the 1958 Aldeburgh Festival, the Asian Music Circle presented a programme of Indian music and dance at the Jubilee Hall.[40] Although Britten was never to return to Bali or Japan after 1956, he did find the opportunity to travel once more to the Indian subcontinent for a holiday in the spring of 1965 (and a programme of Indian dance was again included in the Aldeburgh Festival later that same year).[41] Amongst the fragmentary sketches for *The Burning Fiery Furnace* he made at the end of 1965, there exists a curious passage marked 'Toda welcome song'. This theme was not incorporated in the second parable, or apparently anywhere else in Britten's output, but it was certainly derived from Indian sources since the Toda are a southern Indian people whom both Britten and Pears had described in correspondence written during their 1965 trip.[42]

Britten possessed a gramophone recording (EALP 1252) of the Indian flautist Pannalal Ghosh performing two Ragas: *Yaman* and *Shri*. Britten was so captivated by *Raag Yaman* that he notated parts of it in his sketchbook and subsequently incorporated sizeable portions of Ghosh's melody in the music for *The Prodigal Son*: a comparison of representative extracts is given in Ex. 9.7. Transferred to the alto flute (the Western instrument closest to the sonority of the mellow Indian flute), the languid and repetitive patterns conjure up the tranquil, pastoral atmosphere at the father's estate. At some point in 1968 Britten purchased a copy of Alain Daniélou's newly published study *The Râga-s of Northern Indian Music*, in which the raga is described as 'joyful and contented'.[43]

Britten's sustained involvement with Asian music is significant on at

Example 9.7

Raag Yaman Sketches

The Prodigal Son
[Page references correspond to the published full score.]

least three different levels. In its most straightforward manifestation, the composer reconstructs and reinterprets specific techniques in certain works where the influence of Asian music is both precisely definable (the relevant source material having survived) and unequivocal; in doing so, Britten continued to reveal the astonishing technical facility that had characterized his work since the 1930s, when he had shown himself capable of imitating virtually any style of music that attracted his attention.

On a more general level, many characteristics of the composer's style before his world tour in 1956 suggest that various developing technical preoccupations offer a plausible explanation for his growing interest in Balinese and Japanese musical procedures. In some cases, however, the extent to which the appearance of a particular musical technique may be attributed to a process of 'influence' is clearly open to question. (One is reminded of Jaap Kunst's remark that the final phrase of the Javanese theme *Plenchung Wetah* is virtually identical to a cello melody in the finale of Beethoven's String Quartet in F major, Op. 135.[44]) But Britten's early compositional style was well suited to the admixture of more explicit Asian material, and the success of his combination of Eastern and Western elements was undoubtedly made possible by a degree of inherent stylistic affinity. As with Debussy before him, Britten's experience of the gamelan acted as a catalyst by throwing up fortuitous musical parallels that focused his attention on the more radical aspects of his own style – to reapply the composer's own words to Edith Sitwell, it had 'dragged something from me that was latent there, & shown me what lies before me'. Neil Sorrell's remarks on Debussy's interest in Javanese gamelan music may be applied to Britten with equal relevance: 'The key word is *influence*, with its suggestion of bringing about a change of course. With Debussy a much more fruitful word would be *confirmation*. It seems far more plausible that what he heard . . . confirmed what he had, at least subconsciously, always felt about music, and this experience went far deeper than a desire to imitate something new and exotic.'[45]

Finally, the precise nature of the personal significance with which Britten appears to have invested his Asian borrowings is likely to prove a source of ongoing interpretative fascination. Philip Brett has been the first to explore the close connection between the phenomena of orientalism and homoeroticism in Britten's operas in a groundbreaking essay.[46] Although it transfers McPhee's own (and explicitly confessed) erotic view of Bali too unquestioningly onto Britten without supporting evidence, Brett's research nevertheless offers much food for thought in its perceptive account of the musico-dramatic function of those disquieting 'gamelan' sonorities in *The Turn of the Screw* and other stage works. From the disturbing allure of Quint's celeste and Miss Jessel's gong, through the exotic attraction of Pagodaland and its supernatural Prince to the sexual chemistry dispensed by Oberon's spells in *A Midsummer Night's Dream*, from the ritualized restraint of the Church Parables to the invocation of peace in *Owen Wingrave* and the celebration of adolescent beauty in *Death in Venice*, Britten's transformation of Far Eastern techniques proved to be the basis for a remarkably flexible and suggestive musical language.

10 Violent climates

DONALD MITCHELL

Any account of the evolution, chronology and documentation of Britten's pacifism will, I believe, benefit from first acquiring a familiarity with what I would describe as his creative awareness of 'violent climates', when we may be a shade surprised by the persistence and sheer volume of it. This means a scrutiny, brief in some instances, more extensive in others, of those works in which that creative response shows itself.

Its manifestations were various, varying indeed according to aim, utility and genre. This in itself will entail breaking the broad generalization down into categories, to the first of which, 'documentary', I assign to film, the so-called 'Peace' film of 1936 – *Peace of Britain* – and the *Pacifist March* (a unison song) that was written in 1937 for the Peace Pledge Union. These and others like them are works or collaborative projects that, literally and liberally, document Britten's pacifist convictions and his political and social sympathies. They speak for themselves; indeed, the need for simplicity and clarity – for the clear articulation of a 'message' – defines the 'documentary' mode and its necessary limitations. These 'documentaries' are in fact close to propaganda; and it is worth remembering that they belong to a period when Britten was highly active in collaborating in the creation of a genre of film, with its own aesthetic, that was to become known as 'documentary film'. It was an aesthetic, incidentally, that incorporated a very powerful element of social propaganda. These were films with a 'message', undisguisedly, but executed with such sophistication and so imposing an array of innovative techniques that a reference to 'propaganda' seems singularly inappropriate. However, while John Grierson's GPO Film Unit – if not in the business of propaganda – was certainly committed to propagating information about matters of social or communal importance, Peace and Pacifism (whatever the convictions of the creative participants may have been) were not on the Unit's agenda; for which reason, when it came to the making of the famous 'Peace'[1] film it had to be undertaken by a private film company of which the *animateur* was Paul Rotha, a strikingly independent-minded director. Thus, while the documentary films for which Britten wrote the music can certainly be produced as evidence of his general social concerns – typical, one might think, of a 1930s artist on the left of the political spectrum, though none the less important for that – it is elsewhere that we must look for manifestations of the composer's preoccupation with violent climates altogether more complex than the *Pacifist March*, the poster for Peace that was Rotha's film or the plea for trades union solidarity that was Ralph Bond's.[2]

Curiously enough, it was perhaps in another area of Britten's pre-war composing, one often loosely associated with his composing for films, for the radio, for the theatre – the whole area of 'incidental music' – that we encounter the first substantial signs of what was to become, in my estimation, one of the fundamental preoccupations of his art: acts of violence, their consequences and the 'climates' that unleash them.

This has been one of the results of the investigation of Britten's huge legacy of unpublished music, much of it written for what we now know as the 'media'. His incidental music, commissioned in the main by the BBC, shows how vivid a presence in the young Britten was the issue of violence. The issue, in these early scores, is raised and debated by various means, both musical and textual – the emphasis goes one way in one work, is placed differently in another. In *The World of the Spirit* (1938), for example, it is the voluminous texts, their character and their subject-matter, that spell out the twin messages of peace and reconciliation, which the music, in a diverse and intriguing patchwork of forms and styles, attempts to mirror. There are undeniably moments of a transfiguring beauty, for example the last number of all, 'Come, O Creator Spirit, Come'. What there is not, is any attempt to find a *music* that would match up with the images of war and death – the First World War, remember – that so remarkably punctuate the narrations; I write 'remarkably' simply because the range of topics and narrated incidents reveals a liberalism, a freedom of implied comment, that even in the 1990s one finds arresting. Would a British team working before the inception of the current 'peace process' in Ireland on a comparable feature for television, say, have given much serious consideration to including an account of the last hours of one of the heroes – James Connolly – of the Easter Rebellion in 1916? (We may be sure, in any event, that a *composer* would have had no major role to play in the programme.) Already, however, in December 1935 Britten had written some of the incidental music for a documentary play by Montagu Slater (the future librettist of *Peter Grimes*) entitled *Easter 1916*, in which James Connolly's involvement in the rising is documented. The music has been lost but Slater's play includes a dramatization of the last hours of Connolly's life, the very incident that is narrated in *The World of the Spirit*, while an epilogue for a (spoken) chorus records the actual moment of his execution by firing squad. It is interesting that Michael Tippett (in the 1930s) had seriously considered writing an opera on the Easter Rebellion of 1916. This further confirms the resonance the event had for the 1930s and continues to have for our own time.

The World of the Spirit, while it does not integrate its texts and its music(s) or attempt parallels between musical numbers and narrated incidents, none the less very clearly anticipates at least one compositional mode that Britten was to employ in a much later work, composed to mark the twentieth anniversary of the founding of the United Nations, *Voices for Today* (1965). This last work opens with a series of moral injunctions and exhortations, drawn from a score of worldwide sources, each one of which relates to the idea of Peace, for example 'Love your enemies; do good to those that hate you' or 'Burning stakes do not lighten the darkness'. I doubt very much if Britten were still conscious of the precedent that had been established in *The World of the Spirit* when he came to work on *Voices*; but though he may have banished his old BBC feature of the 1930s from his memory, the mode of address he adopted there, which may have had its roots in the settings of biblical injunctions that formed part of his church-going experience as a boy, at home and at school, undoubtedly left its mark on the later work. In other words, the exploration or excavation of a particular area of feeling (or, in this instance, conviction or commitment) gave rise to an identifiable compositional mode.[3]

The evolutionary link between *The World of the Spirit* may strike some as too casual to be taken seriously, but for me it is powerfully confirmed if one makes a time-leap forward to *Owen Wingrave*, Britten's penultimate opera composed for television in 1970. The centrepiece of the work, almost everyone would agree, is Owen's 'Peace' aria in Act II (at Fig. 246); and it was well described by Jeremy Noble in his review of the première of the work in 1971: 'a characteristic Britten inspiration,' he wrote, 'simple in essence, but absolutely right in context – and unforgettable'.[4]

Perhaps not all *that* simple, in fact, though undeniably unforgettable. But what must detain us here is its demonstration of a clear line of descent, in compositional principle, from *The World of the Spirit* and *Voices*. What a chronology of these works will reveal despite a diversity of genres is a succession of statements accompanied in each work by music consistent with the mode or style of the work in question: pastiche Bach in *The World of the Spirit*, Britten's own freely conceived recitative in *Voices*, and, in *Wingrave*, a remarkable synthesis of the compositional techniques he was to deploy in the 1960s and 1970s. Owen's fervent apostrophe to Peace combines a layered texture in which a rotation of triads, major or minor, spanning all twelve pitches, accompanies Owen's freely floating vocal line, while superimposed on this conjunction of a melody and its harmonization(s) is a halo of radiant, gamelan-engendered per-

Table 10.1 *The World of the Spirit*

Sentences*	
(No. 6a)	'A voice within our souls hath spoken, And we who seek have more than found'
(No. 6b)	The Fruit of the Spirit is Love The Fruit of the Spirit is Peace The Fruit of the Spirit is Gentleness
(No. 6c)	The Fruit of the Spirit is Faith
	and sim. to
(No. 6f)	And the Fruit of the Spirit is Joy

[* The sentences shown here are taken *verbatim* from the script of the original broadcast on the National Programme of the BBC, 5 June 1938, 9.05–9.50 pm.]

Table 10.2 *Voices for Today*

Sentence No. 1	'If you have ears to hear, then hear!' (Jesus Christ)
Sentence No. 2	'The Beloved of the Gods wishes that all people should be unharmed, self-controlled, calm in mind, and gentle' (Asoka)
Sentence No. 3	'Love your enemies; do good to those that hate you' (Jesus Christ)
Sentence No. 4	'Where is the equal of Love? Where is the battle he cannot win?' (Sophocles)
	sim. until
Sentence No. 18	'The world's great age begins anew, The golden years return' (Shelley)
Sentence No. 19	Recapitulation of No. 1: 'If you have ears to hear, then hear!'
	followed by
Sentence No. 20	Virgil: Eclogue IV 'Ultima Cumaei . . .' (*tutti*)

cussion in largely heterophonic patterns. An altogether typical manifestation of late-style Britten, one might suppose; and one would be right.

But fascinating though the textural make-up of the aria is, and tempting though it is to dawdle over the details of it, it is rather the motivating principle that gave rise to the aria's specific layout and formal build that I find particularly revealing, especially of how the composer's mind worked if challenged by a dramatic or poetic situation when the idea of Peace was, so to say, centre-stage. In short, how to find a 'voice' for Peace? Britten had been here before in *The World of the Spirit* and *Voices*; and, while it scarcely needs emphasizing again that in the acquisition of compositional techniques and resources he had since travelled a vast distance, when, nonetheless, he wanted to take up a moral stance – to put his work's (more than that, *his*) 'message' across (thus *Wingrave* too, though it may seem far removed from Paul Rotha's film or the Peace Pledge Union, has its propagandist profile) – he returned to the formula that, it seems, came naturally to him. For the 'Peace' aria – 'Owen's lonely *Credo*' in William Mann's words, who judged it to be 'conceivably the finest monologue Britten ever composed'[5] – is in fact constructed out of a series of *statements*, each

9a.

Owen (alone)

O Peace! what have you brought me?
Rejection, Ignomeny, Hatred.

I was surrounded with love
nursed in hope
bathed in admiration.
Now I am a stranger.

But they loved me in the image they had made of me.
Their hope, their admiration was for the man they
planned to make of me
Now I am nothing to them.

Peace! you have brought me my own image
you have brought me myself.

In peace a man can rejoice to be amongst men
and yet walk alone
And in peace he must watch over this difficult balance
so that it is not broken

For peace is not lazy, but vigilant.
peace is not acquiescent, but searching
It is not weak, but strong like a bird's wing
that bears its weight in the dazzling air.
Peace is not silent, it is the voice of love.

O you with your bugbears, your arrogance, your
intolerance your greed, your selfish morals and
petty victories, peace is not won by your wars

Peace is not confused, nor sentimental, not afraid;
It is positive, passionate, committing, like war itself

Only, in peace there is no waste.

Plate 14 Three pages from the draft text for Owen's 'Peace' aria, the first an early revision by Myfanwy Piper in her own hand, the second and third an early typed version of the text with Britten's corrections in his own hand. The crucial amendment here (see the facsimile on p. 194) is the composer's own substitution of 'And at last I shall have peace' for his librettist's 'At last I am alone'. These characteristic refinements show how intimately related the composer's suggestions were to the specific music he had in mind.

for
But all ~~&~~ the image they made of us,
for the war they planned to make of me.

Owen
(Cont'd)

~~But they loved me in the image they had made of me.~~
~~Their hope, their admiration was for the man they~~
~~planned to make of me,~~
Now I am nothing, ~~to them.~~ I bid you all farewell -
~~And so I bid them~~
~~And I bid you all~~   *away from*
~~Farewell~~   (turns ~~to~~ the portraits

I have found my image,
~~In~~ Peace ~~m~~ ~~You have brought me my own image,~~
~~You have brought me myself.~~ I have found myself.
In peace I can rejoice ~~to be~~ amongst men and yet
    walk alone,
In peace I will guard this balance so that it is
    not broken.

For peace is not lazy, but vigilant:
Peace is not acquiescent, but searching:

Peace ~~It~~ is not weak, but strong like a bird's wing, *bearing*
~~That bears~~ its weight in the dazzling air.
Peace is not silent, it is the voice of love.

O you with your bugbears, your arrogance, your *greed,*
your Intolerance, ~~your greed,~~ your selfish morals and
Petty victories, peace is not won by your wars.

Peace is not confused, not sentimental, not afraid:
Peace ~~It~~ is positive, passionate, committing, more than
    war itself. *can I be free*
Only, in peace, ~~there is no waste.~~

And I am finished with you all

Plate 14 (*cont.*)

15

Owen
(Cont'd.)   Yes. I am free,
                I have finished with them all.

The apparitions of the ballad slowly walk across the hall, up the stairs

(Owen)   Not yet -
                There are two more.

                Come on,
                Come on, I tell you.

                This is the last time you will ever walk for me.
                I am rejected -
                The Wingraves have turned me out,
        and   You don't belong to me,
                Nor I to you.
To the young boy Poor boy,
                You made your stand too young -
                But I have done it for you - for us all.
                Tell the old man, tell your fearful father,
                Your fate and his no longer frighten me.
                Tell him his power has gone
                                we have
                And peace has won,

Apparitions disappear into the room
                And at last I shall have peace.
                At last I am alone.

        And he sinks into a chair — the shadows

Plate 14 *(cont.)*

Table 10.3 Owen's 'Peace' aria

Sentence 1	'In peace I have found my image, I have found myself'	B♭
Sentence 2	'In peace I rejoice amongst men and yet walk alone'	D (minor)
Sentence 3	'in peace I will guard this balance so that it is not broken'	F
Sentence 4	'For peace is not lazy, but vigilant'	C
Sentence 5	'peace is not acquiescent, but searching'	E (minor)
Sentence 6	'peace is not weak but strong'	G
Sentence 7	'Peace is not silent, it is the voice of love'	B
Sentence 8	'peace is not won by your wars'	E♭
Sentence 9	'Peace is not confused, not sentimental, not afraid'	F♯ (minor)
Sentence 10	'Peace is positive, is passionate, committing more than war itself'	A
Sentence 11	'Only in peace can I be free'	C♯ (= D♭)
	Fig. 259: spoken (to the ghost of the boy): 'Tell the old man, tell your fearful father, Your fate and his no longer frighten me. Tell him his power is gone and I have won'	
Sentence 12	'and at last I shall have – peace'	A♭ (= G♯)

one of which is anchored to one of the twelve triads forming the series of accompanimental chords (see Table 10.3). The rotation of the triads represents by virtue of its totality of all twelve pitches the ideal of 'wholeness', of a world, not without contrast (major/minor) or inner tension, but one in which everything (everybody) is interrelated: the possibility of an ideal integration is at least hinted at by the comprehensive commitment of all available pitch resources to the unfolding of Owen's message.[6]

It is thus – with the percussion band magically divested of its militancy, its gamelan-like figuration providing a horizontal complement to the vertical conflations of the triads – that Britten promotes Peace in *Wingrave*, as he had by similar means suggested the restoration of order to the troubled Wood at the close of Act II of *A Midsummer Night's Dream* (1960). As even the simplest of descriptions suggests, it is a highly sophisticated and elaborate exercise; and yet, I repeat, behind it stand the principles, both compositional and philosophical, already adumbrated in works like *The World of the Spirit* and *Voices for Today*.

It is surprising, indeed, how prominent the idea of sentences, of a series of compact moral exhortations, was in Britten's thinking, perhaps especially in the incidental music for radio from the 1930s which now turns out to have been not so incidental after all. In fact in *The Company of Heaven* (1937), the immediate predecessor of *The World of the Spirit*, there is also a corresponding series of sentences. The difference lies in the choice of images and objectives, in the case of *The Company of Heaven* a scrutiny of angels rather than the pursuit of peace (which is not to say that the two were not related in Britten's imagination). But there is a yet more prophetic manifestation of the composer's preoccupation with acts of violence. The movement entitled 'War in Heaven', for strings, timpani and chorus (the latter singing a kind of *Sprechstimme*) remarkably antici-pates, albeit at far remove, the drums of war that punctuate the central song – the setting of Wordsworth – in Britten's last orchestral song-cycle, *Nocturne* (1958), the grim human consequences of which are then depicted in the ensuing Owen setting, 'The Kind Ghosts':

> She sleeps on soft, last breaths; but no ghost looms
> Out of the stillness of her palace wall,
> Her wall of boys on boys and dooms on dooms.
>
> She dreams of golden gardens and sweet glooms,
> Not marvelling why her roses never fall
> Nor what red mouths were torn to make their blooms.

In Britten's setting the poem's unforgettable images of the dead are imag-ined with high originality as a *dead march*. From Wordsworth's dream of 'September Massacres', lent vivid reality by Britten's erupting timpani obbligato, it is only a step to the monumental timpani interjection in *War Requiem* (1961), the setting of lines from Owen's sonnet, 'On Seeing a Piece of Our Artillery Brought into Action'. (One might, while one is about it, take a further step forward and suggest that it is indeed the cycle of Owen settings incorporated, in *War Requiem*, into the setting of the Requiem Mass (*Missa pro defunctis*) that authentically represents Britten's final orchestral song-cycle.)

Even this incomplete list begins at least to hint at how continuous a pre-occupation of Britten's was the threat of war and violence – how *persistent and invasive a presence* was that threat even in works that outwardly were dedicated to quite other areas of feeling and description. An important example is the *Spring Symphony* (1949), at the very heart of which resides the setting of Auden's remarkable poem 'Out on the lawn I lie in bed' and the sudden vision of conflict (muted brass fanfare and percussion) that shatters the nocturnal scene – 'Vega conspicuous overhead':

> To gravity attentive, she
> Can notice nothing here; though we
>   Whom hunger cannot move,
> From gardens where we feel secure
> Look up, and with a sigh endure
>   The tyrannies of love:
>
> And, gentle, do not care to know,
> Where Poland draws her Eastern bow,
>   What violence is done;

Nor ask what doubtful act allows
Our freedom in this English house,
   Our picnics in the sun.

It reminds us, retrospectively, in a work with its roots in Britten's love of
spring (the season he loved most, he told me once), of the threatening
atmosphere (the poem was written in July 1933) of the 1930s which
exploded into the Second World War, part of the history of Britten's own
times, a history in which he was himself involved and by which he was
enveloped. It is worth a moment's consideration to reflect on the oddity,
though that's not the right word, of a hymn to spring, which the symphony ostensibly is, invoking the threat of war as a central reference in the
movement that constitutes the most important stretch of slow music in
the main body of the work; while *Nocturne*, ostensibly dedicated to sleep
and dreams, to the evolution of a final dream of the loved one of one's
dreams, releases, at its rupturing climax – when the sleeper momentarily
surfaces into consciousness of the (real) world – potent, savage images of
death and destruction. Violent climates, it seems, were ever at Britten's
elbow.

The consistency and persistency of Britten's preoccupation with violence, enacted on many different levels in different contexts, shows up in
the violent imagery that plainly haunted his imagination. One thinks for
instance of the *blow* with which Peter Grimes fells Ellen Orford in Act II of
the opera (1945) and sets in motion the sequence of events culminating in
the final tragedy, a blow that is itself engendered by the *blow* that caused
the ugly bruise on the apprentice's shoulder. The successor to *Grimes* was
the first of the chamber operas, *The Rape of Lucretia* (1946), a new
medium, maybe, but it shows a continuing preoccupation with an act of
violence and its consequences. No less significant, perhaps, is the
incorporation into the opera of the image of the hunt, the pursuit: the
mob hunting Grimes gives place to Tarquinius on horseback in pursuit of
his victim, Lucretia. The 'hunting' imagery of 1936, to which I shall return
– its first substantial surfacing was in *Our Hunting Fathers* – was still
potent in 1946.[7] Again, to jump ahead to *Owen Wingrave*, one recalls that
it is a savage *blow* which, in the Ballad that opens Act II, represents the
gruesome ancestral burden of spilled blood that is Owen's inheritance:

He struck him on his tender head,
His tender head with blood did flow,
Until a corpse upon the floor
He never ran nor breathèd more.

It is a *blow*, likewise, that constitutes the single most important dramatic event in *Billy Budd* (1951, Act III; revised version, 1960, Act II) and

results in the twin, intertwined tragedies of Vere and Billy; and yet again it is the vicious coming to blows of Tadzio and Jaschiu in the final minutes of *Death in Venice* (1973) that constitutes the final *blow* that precipitates Aschenbach's death (an assault on his *heart* for sure). It is a *blow*, or hail of blows rather, that hastens the death of the abducted child in *Curlew River* (1964). To be sure, although it is not a lethal blow that is the culmination of all the acts of violence that are gathered together and scrutinized in *War Requiem*, it is hand-to-hand – worse, face-to-face – combat and the cold thrust of the bayonet with which the dialogue of the dead in 'Strange Meeting' concludes:

> I am the enemy you killed, my friend.
> I knew you in this dark; for so you frowned
> Yesterday through me as you jabbed and killed.
> I parried; but my hands were loath and cold.

Nor do I overlook in the 'Offertorium' the ironic inversion of the Abraham and Isaac parable, as a consequence of which the youth is ritually slaughtered with a knife. 'And half the seed of Europe, one by one.' The consistency of the preoccupation is more often than not matched by the consistency of the image.

I have mentioned above, albeit in passing, Britten's involvement in the history of his own time, especially in the 1930s and after. One of the new formats in which acts of violence materialized in those years was death from the air, the development of aerial bombing and its inevitable consequence, death by the thousands of civilians, among them many children. Britten, as his diaries show, was particularly aware of the horrors and terrors of the Spanish Civil War; indeed it was during that conflict that the potentialities of assaulting cities from the air were seriously explored. A famous – infamous – example was Guernica (27 April 1937), but Barcelona and Madrid were also frequently bombed; and I have often wondered if these particular incidents, about which Britten must have read,[8] made a particular impression on him, since the image of the air raid plays a specific role in his oeuvre, from early works to late. There is, to take an impressive mid-span example, *Canticle III*, '*Still Falls the Rain*' (1954), settings of Edith Sitwell for tenor, horn and piano, the subtitle of which is explicit: 'The Raids, 1940, Night and Dawn'. The unrelievedly sombre character of this work, the virtuosity of which is indication of its dark, seething passion, and the formal complexity of which mirrors the unique formal build of the immediately preceding opera, *The Turn of the Screw* (1954), can leave us in no doubt whatsoever of the power of Britten's response to the idea of death from the air. (He had experienced air raids himself after his return to England from America in 1942.)[9] But it is intriguing to roll back the years and recall the incidental music he wrote in 1938 for Auden's and Isherwood's *On the Frontier*, a year in which Spain was in flames and Europe on the brink of the Second World War. In the opening number it is the wail of air-raid sirens that forms the accompaniment to Auden's brilliantly graphic text:

> The clock on the wall gives an electric tick.
> I'm feeling sick, brother; I'm feeling sick.
>
> The sirens blow at eight; the sirens blow at noon;
> Goodbye, sister, goodbye; we shall die soon.

A marvellous idea to have converted the sirens summoning the workers to start their shift into the sirens which warned against death from the air (hence, of course, the conclusion of Auden's second couplet, 'Goodbye, sister, . . . we shall die soon').

Possibly one should not be surprised by consistency of gestures inhabiting a composer's imagination over a very long period, but one is surprised momentarily, nonetheless, to encounter those self-same sirens at work, articulated again with Britten's customary and impeccable accuracy, in a late song-cycle, still far too little known, *Who Are These Children?* (1969). The surprise wears off as soon as one realizes that the cycle – the very last Britten was to compose – focuses on the slaughter of innocents (in the Second World War) during raids from the air: it is these very images of violence, blood and children which prompted William Soutar's remarkable poems (e.g. 'Slaughter', 'Who Are These Children?' and 'The Children'); and it is not only the destruction of human kind that is central to this late ('late', too, in every respect of style[10]) masterpiece but also, as Paul Banks has perceived, the mindless destruction of the Earth, characteristic of the century now coming to an end (e.g. 'A Riddle (The Earth)', 'Nightmare' and 'The Auld Aik'). How supremely ironic that the death, felling or collapse of the ancient tree – 'Twa hunner year it stüde, or mair, But noo it's doun, doun, doun' – should be memorialized in a majestic procession of – for the most part – timeless triads, the most intense concentration of triads since *Budd* and *Wingrave*. Furthermore, how remarkable and revealing that in one respect this very last song-cycle casts a retrospective look at the preoccupation which, like non-violence, was a feature of Britten's schooldays and earlier youth. The title song of the cycle, 'Who Are These Children?', has as its central image 'foxing folk', fully apparelled, riding through a village street in wartime, stared at by children 'out of the fire and smoke' created by a random bomb. Once again, after the passage of over thirty years, one hears the calls of huntsmen's horns in Britten's music, affirming an indissoluble link with that terrifying first orchestral song-cycle of 1936, *Our Hunting Fathers*. The image of the hunt, it seems, was never to be erased from Britten's imagination.

In fact the concept of a violent hunt, or pursuit, on one occasion took the shape of a 'wild dance' in an ambitious score he wrote for the BBC in 1937: *King Arthur*, for a radio drama written by D. Geoffrey Bridson and produced by Val Gielgud. Britten took a very dim view of Bridson's contribution,[11] rightly so in so far as one can judge from wading through an irredeemably fustian script. Nonetheless there was clearly something in the drama or in certain incidents generated by it that fired Britten's imagination, especially the hunting of Lancelot by the baleful Mordred. I include here (Plate 15) a reproduction of the page from the script during the course of which the hunt – the 'wild dance' – erupts. On reading what there is on the page of the Second Narrator's long commentary – a further thirty-one lines, but this time from the First Narrator, follow on p. 45 of the script – one cannot but be reminded of the central event in *Lucretia* and Tarquinius' stealthy approach to Lucretia's bedroom. Of course there is no rape in *King Arthur*, but the device of the Narrator (an embryonic Male Chorus?) and the illicit character of the episode seem to anticipate the similar contrivance in Ronald Duncan's libretto for the opera of 1946.

If there were an overspill into *Lucretia* from *King Arthur*, then this would only strengthen the claim the radio drama makes on our attention as a source of music in later works that is of specific relevance to any consideration of violent climates. For a start, the 'wild dance' re-emerges only a couple of years later (still in G minor!) as the central Scherzo of *Ballad of Heroes* (1939), now acting as accompaniment of a setting of Auden's famous pre-war text, written in 1937 just before the poet's departure to Spain, 'It's farewell to the drawing room's civilised cry...' Yet more significant, in the choral and orchestral *Ballad* – written to honour the members of the British Battalion of the International Brigade who had fallen in the course of the Spanish Civil War – the brilliant 'wild dance' of 1937 is identified as a 'Dance of Death'. Auden, in the wake of Britten's *Ballad*, was himself to give his poem the title of 'Danse macabre' when including it in his *Collected Poems* of 1945.

This extensive redeployment of a set-piece from *King Arthur* shows that the incidental music for what became a forgotten radio drama from the 1930s had remained a vivid presence for the composer; which makes it less surprising that in 1945, when intent on putting together a new slow movement for his Piano Concerto of 1938, it was again to *King Arthur* that he had recourse, from which he looted the so-called 'Grail' theme, magically re-harmonizing it.

But this is by no means the end of the continuing narrative *King Arthur*

- 44 -

MORDRED: Sir Agravaine and I will take with us)
twelve Knights. It is more than time)
enough that they be taken.)
)
ARTHUR: Have a care, Mordred. He will not be)
taken easily ...)
)
MORDRED: Let us deal, sire. He shall be taken.) (Music)
)
AGRAVAINE: Tonight, sire. Before midnight.)
)
MORDRED: He shall not escape us again, sir.)
Let us deal.)
)
AGRAVAINE: Before midnight, sire. Tonight.)
)
ARTHUR: Peace, peace.)
)
MORDRED: We shall not fail, sire.)
)
ARTHUR: Leave us. Leave us alone ... Oh,)
Lancelot, Lancelot ....)

(The music surges in again,
whirls on, and after
making its suggestion of
the letting loose of every
demon in hell, fades slowly
down to silence before the
following narration)

(MUSIC: The wild dance once more.
1 minute)

FOURTEENTH LINK

2nd NARRATOR: The hunt is up. And when the hood
Of darkness draws across the wood
Where Arthur follows hound and horn,
Is purport of a message borne
Back to the Queen that he will sleep
Once more abroad.
And when the deep
Full silence of the midnight falls
On Camelot's deserted halls,
Quietly has Lancelot made his way
By corridor and secret stair
To the remoter turret where
In all her loveliness she lay.
And silent fingers lift the latch
Of the Queen's chamber, and the patch
Of moonlight on the chamber floor
Is darkened as he stands before
Her bed and whispers it is he.
And in his arms all nakedly
He takes her and lies down to love.

Plate 15 The script of D. G. Bridson's radio play *King Arthur*, showing the 'wild dance'

Table 10.4 'Dances of Death'

1936	*Our Hunting Fathers* (3. 'Dance of Death')	[E minor]	6/8
1937	*King Arthur* (Scherzo ('Wild Dance'))	G minor	6/8
1939	*Ballad of Heroes* (2. Scherzo ('Dance of Death'))	G minor	6/8
1939	*Violin Concerto* (2. Vivace [scherzo])	[E minor]	3/8
1940	*Sinfonia da Requiem* (2. 'Dies irae' [scherzo])	D minor	3/4
1945	*Peter Grimes* (Act III, Fig. 41 [lynching chorus])	A♭	3/4
1961	*War Requiem* ('Dies irae')	G minor	7/4

had initiated. There are too those other sonorous images of violence and strife: fanfares. These play a vivid role, naturally enough, in the scenes of combat in *King Arthur* and especially in the 'wild dance' itself, but are then incorporated, though in a more elaborate acoustic form – off-stage trumpets and percussion – into the ensuing *Ballad of Heroes*; and then they roll on through time, surfacing again in 'Out on the lawn I lie in bed' in *Spring Symphony* of 1949, and most powerfully and extensively of all in *War Requiem* of 1961. Fanfares, along with the concept of a hectic, frenzied *dance*, in which violent passions are released, are virtually basic components of Britten's materials whenever he is bent on creating the most violent of violent climates. Death and Dance, indeed, if one may thus personify them, often dance hand in hand in his music.

Between them, *Our Hunting Fathers*, *King Arthur* and the *Ballad* initiated a 'tradition' that was then to evolve in diverse works in diverse incarnations across a whole span of Britten's creative life. It may be helpful to set out how I see that 'tradition' developing by means of a simple list of works, noting however one particular amendment: the transformation of the initial 'Dance of Death' idea[12] into a 'Dies irae'.

It will be remarked upon, no doubt, that the first item in Table 10.4 is *Our Hunting Fathers* of 1936. Though it is into a 'Dance of Death' for orchestra alone that the last song explodes – one of the most virtuosic in instrumental conception and tonally attenuated of any orchestral 'interlude' by Britten – this first in the series of 'wild dances' had its origins in the pursuit of animals by men. In short, the *hunt*; and as I have already mentioned this was an image that was unforgettably to re-surface in the final song-cycle of 1969, *Who Are These Children?*[13] Then, what one might have thought was a 'domestic' issue, i.e. resistance to blood sports, was converted by a brilliant analogical transposition into a terrifying commentary on one of the most monstrous acts of violence in the twentieth century, the persecution and annihilation of Jews by the Nazis. The 'domestic' horror is re-drawn as a symbol of international terrorism. Just two words do it: the juxtaposition of 'German, Jew' at the end of the song.

Next in sequence – and what we witness here, surely, is the evolution of a unique type of Scherzo? – is the 'wild dance' in *King Arthur* which, despite its overtones of battle and feudal conflict, is again associated with the idea of a *hunt* (this time, the pursuit of Lancelot); in this respect, *King Arthur* sustains not just the impetus but the generating impulse that had created the innovating, independent scherzo for orchestra in *Our Hunting Fathers*. The critical moment of transition from 'domestic' issues to matters of prime concern to humanity as a whole was effected in the *Ballad of Heroes* when what had been the 'Wild Dance' in *King Arthur* was not only revived but, harking back to the precedent of *Our Hunting Fathers*, newly entitled 'Dance of Death'; this time, however, serving a work which for the first time unequivocally affirms that it is War, and the sacrifice of life that it exacts, that heads the hierarchy of Britten's public concerns.[14]

Thereafter, I submit, the 'tradition' continued, unmistakably so in the scherzo of *Sinfonia da Requiem*, the only match perhaps in virtuosity for the scherzo of *Our Hunting Fathers*. A 'Dance of Death', in truth, but this time – and it is again a significant modification of nomenclature – re-titled 'Dies irae'. Inevitably so, one might argue, when a scherzo is pre-ceded by a 'Lacrymosa' and followed by a 'Requiem aeternam', and the work itself conceived as a Requiem. To be sure, as Britten himself made clear, the *Sinfonia* was not only written in memory of his parents – and there is no reason to doubt the genuineness of that commitment – but should also be read as his response to the threatening political events in Europe that were soon to engulf large areas of the world in war. The scherzo, in any event, would have been an odd way of 'remembering' his parents (it was an even odder way of celebrating the ruling imperial dynasty in Japan, the commission which facilitated the writing of the work).[15] The *Sinfonia*, in short, was a Requiem for a deeply troubled world on the brink of an explosion of violence, the like of which had not been seen before and some manifestations of which (e.g. the atomic bomb of 1945)[16] could not have been foreseen. The 'domestic' had now become the universal and the transformation was registered in the adoption of a 'universal' language, Latin.

There was, then, a hidden logic behind the evolution of the 'Dances of Death' of heretofore into the 'Dies irae' of 1940; hence too, of course, the 'Dies irae' of twenty years later, in *War Requiem*, the 'universality' of which has been much commented on and perhaps even become something of a burden that the work has to bear, along with its reputation.

But while the long line of succession from the *Sinfonia* to *War Requiem* is obvious enough, there remained too *en route* those features that had attended the birth of the idea of a 'Dance of Death': the concept of a *dance*, however much transfigured, and a *hunt*, a *chase*. It is for this reason that I include in my inventory the man-hunt – Grimes-hunt – 'lynching' chorus from Act III of the opera. I have written about this extensively elsewhere[17] and will content myself here with repeating that it was no

accident that this arousal of a collective bloodlust should have been conceived as a dance (a *Ländler*). The roots of this remarkable association, as
I hope I may have shown, are to be found way back in his creative development.

The 1930s, undoubtedly, represented the seed-bed period when very
many of Britten's attitudes to violence and the threat of violence were
formed and when his own adherence to Pacifism itself would have been
further defined and resolved. There are works from that period, up to
Sinfonia da Requiem, that are altogether less explicit in their articulation
of climates of violence; and yet who can doubt that the strangely parodistic finale of the Piano Concerto (1938) was not a kind of gesture – thumb
to nose – aimed at militarism? (The movement to my mind is better comprehended in this light if it follows the original slow movement, the
'Recitative and Aria'.)[18] Or there is the Scherzo, the second movement of
the Violin Concerto (September 1939), a work which surely makes reference to the Spanish tragedy, just concluded in March, with Franco triumphant. The Scherzo may not be a dance of death, but it is a restless,
ambiguous movement and one is aware of something unnerving and
unsettling when the tuba, almost always the messenger of bad news in
Britten's music, enters at Fig. 29.

All of this, it might be claimed, was exactly what one might have
expected of a composer of Britten's generation as socially conscious and
involved as he was. But what I hope this scrutiny of mine may already have
suggested – and I have deliberately refused to impose something falsely
schematic on a body of work that is distinguished by its diversity – is the
extraordinary continuity of the preoccupation with climates of violence.
It was there early on and it was there until the end of his life, as *Who Are
These Children?* (1969) unequivocally proclaims.

One might have thought that with the creation of *War Requiem* in
1961 Britten would have discharged his sense of duty to the anti-War
cause. But on the contrary there was not only *Owen Wingrave* to follow
but also a number of important smaller-scale works in which he continued to press home unremittingly his analysis of the dark, destructive
deeds which humankind is so adept at inventing. One could be forgiven
for thinking that as he grew older so his pessimism increased. Even in *The
Golden Vanity*, the vaudeville written as an entertainment for the Vienna
Boys' Choir in 1966, the Cabin Boy's heroic efforts are rewarded by
treachery and a poignant watery death. *Children's Crusade* (1968), to a
text by Bertolt Brecht, is of quite a different status and stature. It inhabits
without relief the bleak landscape of total war and the impact of it on a
group of lost children. This is not a work *for* children, although it was conceived for young performers – nine solo voices, chorus and a percussion

orchestra. One may ponder on the supreme irony of instruments often associated with childhood replicating the sounds of war – bomb, bullet and shell – and played by young performers of an age comparable with the lost tribe whose misfortunes the team of soloists recount. Or to take another example, what do we find at the heart of *Songs and Proverbs of William Blake*, composed for Dietrich Fischer-Dieskau in 1965? It is a setting of Blake's 'A Poison Tree', distinguished by a contrapuntal accompaniment of exceptional and accumulating intricacy. The climax of the song unfolds as a kind of stretto, each entry of the repeated-note motif extrapolated from the main theme treading on the heels of the preceding entry. The result is a graphic representation of the poison[19] – Hate and Wrath, the annihilating hatred of one human being for another – that leads to the final image of violence and death:

> In the morning glad I see
> My foe outstretch'd beneath the tree.

In the light of what I have written above I believe that the wealth of music touching directly or indirectly on acts of violence constitutes the creation of a genre *without parallel elsewhere in the history of twentieth-century music.* Can one, in fact, name other composers of matching purpose and principle? Shostakovich inevitably comes to mind, but there is not, I suggest, the same preoccupation with and indictment of violence over a comparable span of time. It is no belittling of his stature to observe that while he may have often wished to create in a similar vein he was obliged to keep his mouth shut in order to survive. He was indeed a victim of the violent political and social climates that obtained in the USSR for much of his lifetime and his music, to those with ears to hear, told of the terrors of oppression. Britten was more fortunate.

The one truly comparable figure, I think, was Michael Tippett. No one who reads the lapidary account he gives in his autobiography of his own life and work in the 1930s can fail to be struck by the many parallels between his life, activities and beliefs and Britten's.[20] Tippett was not only a convinced pacifist but responded to the assassination of Ernst vom Rath in Paris in 1938 and the subsequent assault on the Jews in Germany with the composition of his oratorio, *A Child of Our Time* (1939–41). Ian Kemp suggests that in writing this work 'Tippett was following the conviction that a composer has a moral responsibility to address himself to the problems of his time',[21] and without doubt the significance of Tippett's achievement, both musically and morally, was not lost on Britten. In this specific context, too, one should remember a later work of Tippett's, *The Heart's Assurance* (1950–1), first performed by Pears and Britten and composed with their encouragement – a song-cycle that commemorated 'all those who lost their lives and loves in the brutality of battle'.[22] These two remarkable works alone are evidence of Tippett's commitment to causes that were also Britten's; and from the 1930s onwards there can be no questioning the strength of that commitment to humanitarian concerns and ideals, whether in works for the stage or the concert hall – an altogether singular creative history. But there was an important difference. Ian Kemp, I think, touches on it when he mentions, in the context of *A Child of Our Time*, Tippett's wish that the oratorio should not only be representative of 'the contemporary situation' but also of 'an archetypal pattern in human existence'.

I am far from making a qualitative judgement here, but I think Britten's obsession with clearly defined acts of violence – the *blow*, for example – or, to put it another way, the *intensity of the focus*, was distinctive and unique, and distinguishes him from Tippett. It remains the case, however, that it is only Tippett's oeuvre that, in the context of the issues raised by violent climates, can be mentioned meaningfully alongside Britten's.[23]

Despite the focusing, I believe it is impossible to gather together all the works I have laid out under the banner of Pacifism; one ideological description simply will not suffice. If a generalization may be risked at all, then perhaps the most appropriate is Owen's description of the haunted room at Paramore in *Owen Wingrave*: he cries out to Kate, 'The anger of the world is locked up there, the horrible power that makes men fight.' This may be the original curse of humanity, while war – its greatest scourge – represents the release of 'the anger of the world' on a mass scale. In *War Requiem* Britten took on the challenge of a face-to-face confrontation with war; not only a confrontation but a condemnation of it. If there is one work of his that one might point to as a classic statement of Pacifism it is *War Requiem*. It was Tippett who commented in 1977 that this was 'the one musical masterwork we possess with overt pacifist meanings'.[24]

Because of the extraordinary reception of the work in 1961 – which certainly surprised the composer at the time, and was to trouble him and eventually dismay him because it led to a multiplicity of routine, underpowered performances – it has often been overlooked or at least underestimated how much *War Requiem* owed to those works that in effect constitute the work's *ancestry*, a creative history that was to continue as innovatively and vigorously as ever, long after *War Requiem* was done.

It is true, of course, that the sheer scale of *War Requiem* marks it out as something special, a scale that reflects the comprehensiveness with which Britten brought into play all the signs, images and sonorities that he had developed since the 1930s to represent the idea of violence. He had, so to say, assembled a whole vocabulary with which and through which he could communicate intelligibly on the issue of violence, tribal or individual, with a 'mass' audience.[25]

I have already mentioned some of the specific imagery – fanfares and drums of war – that were the furnishings of Britten's commentaries on or evocations of violence from the 1930s onwards. They are, so to say, apotheosized in *War Requiem*. But there are, as I have attempted to point out, much profounder and more crucial influences and anticipations, as in the *Nocturne* of 1958, in which there are not only direct intimations of the sounds of battle but chamber-orchestral settings of texts, including Britten's first setting of Wilfred Owen, that in sophisticated character and style clearly form the bridge between the last orchestral song-cycle and the realization of an integral chamber-orchestral Owen cycle *within* the framework of the Requiem. The latter constitutes the most arresting and original feature of *War Requiem*, but one, I fear, that after more than three and a half decades since the work's first performance is seriously underplayed (and I mean that almost literally), perhaps because the function of the Owen settings is still not fully comprehended and thus not fully articulated in performance.

The innovative incorporation of a chamber-orchestral song-cycle into a 'traditional' large-scale choral work is typical of the gathering together of all the resources of relevance to his purpose, his own and sometimes indeed his eminent predecessors', Verdi pre-eminent among them.[26] In *War Requiem* we find two principal channels of cross-over and fertilization: the works that I have specifically mentioned in this chapter which, in retrospect, we can see formed a kind of preparation for the Requiem that was to come, and a whole swatch of genres (not only genres but techniques), perhaps especially those in which the vocal dimension predominates, for example song-cycle, motet, cantata, oratorio, opera, canticle, mass, music for boys' voices, etc. (It is much along these lines that, after all, Mahler compiled his Eighth Symphony.)

I have written above of the 'frame' into which the Owen cycle is incorporated; and perhaps that description seriously underestimates the role and function of the chamber-orchestral song settings. For a start, it implies a passive relationship (almost) that I believe to be remote from the composer's actual intention. The truth is, surely, that the Owen settings which continually interrupt – better, disrupt – the majestic flow and momentum of the Requiem (I am thinking particularly of the 'Dies irae') should provide a caustic commentary on the 'values' with which unthinking tradition blandly and blindly, and above all solemnly, associates the grand old, age old, Latin text. Perhaps 'commentary' is too tame a word: 'subversion' might be altogether nearer the mark. What the ideal performance of *War Requiem* should achieve is an unmediated confrontation with the horror, terror and pity of war. A principal factor in this must be a razor-sharp articulation of Owen's words (singers take note!): the settings should leave *us* wounded and bleeding. Further, these disruptive interruptions, interjections and interpolations should be heard to question – contradict, even – the 'culture' that the setting of the Latin text of the Requiem represents; or at the very least to question the values that seemingly permit a conciliation between mutually exclusive agenda, a traditional affirmation of civilization and system of belief versus the actuality of barbarity.

The absolutely fundamental role played by the Owen settings in *War Requiem* as agents of doubt and scepticism even within the 'frame' that holds them together – and this surely adds to the irony of their function – is unequivocally demonstrated by the 'Agnus Dei', where, as I have often pointed out in the past – but I believe the significance of it still to be insufficiently recognized – the relationship of the internalized song-cycle and the framing Requiem is precisely *inverted*. It is the setting of Owen's text for tenor solo – 'One ever hangs where shelled roads part' (the poet's wartime image of a Christ-figure hanging shattered on a Cross) – that takes the lead, accompanied by the chamber orchestra. At Fig. 97 the main orchestra (though much reduced) now accompanies the subdued setting of the Requiem text, 'Agnus Dei qui tollis peccata mundi...'; and the alternation – the inverse, I must emphasize, of the formal principle that has been maintained to this point – continues until the very end of the movement (Fig. 100), when all the forces that have been involved combine for the final bars, a passage to which I shall return.

This unique formal reversal is remarkable enough. So too is the unequivocal insistence on the baneful tritone (C–F♯), the Requiem's unappeasable and all-pervasive leading motif, a scalar version of which comprises without relief the accompanying ostinato. (Incidentally, the 'Agnus Dei' shows Britten's continuing preoccupation with the potentialities of heterophony: see also p. 333, note 10.)

The music, then, spells out for us the special importance of the 'Agnus Dei'. But the text is of especial significance, not just for the image of Christ on a wrecked Cross as a victim of violence, but for the contempt the words disclose for the established priesthood, those who stood near Golgotha:

And in their faces there is pride
That they were flesh-marked by the Beast
By whom the gentle Christ's denied.

We should note here Britten's scrupulous accents on 'flesh-marked' and a few bars later (Fig. 99⁻⁴) the use of percussion – the *only* percussion intrusion (side drum) in the entire movement – to drive home the ensuing indictment, 'The scribes on all the people shove / And bawl allegiance to the state'; the side drum, undoubtedly, serves as a reminder of the weapons to which an oppressive state will have recourse (an echo too of the machine-gun stuttering of the side drum that has been a feature of the second Owen setting in the 'Dies irae', 'Out there, we've walked quite friendly up to Death ... He's spat at us with bullets ...'). Here again the ideal interpretation of the Requiem will make absolutely clear the systematic organization in terms of sound of parallel images throughout the work. The composer's fanatical attention to detail is often neglected by lazy conductors who find it easier to make an impression with the big gesture.

There is no question to my mind that one should be shocked, brought up short, by the (righteous) anger that erupts in the 'Agnus Dei'. Furthermore, the objects of that anger were to attract Britten's indictment again in the future. The choice of the parable of the Good Samaritan as text for the *Cantata Misericordium* of 1963, written to mark the occasion of the centenary of the International Red Cross, speaks for itself: it is the representatives of established religion who pass by on the other side. While in *Owen Wingrave*, years later, it is lines by Shelley that Owen reads over to himself as he sits in Hyde Park. They begin:

> War is the statesman's game, the priest's delight,
> The lawyer's jest ...

And end:

> Look to thyself, priest, conqueror or prince!
> Whether thy trade is falsehood ...

That 'falsehood' (clearly, as these citations suggest, a prime concern of Britten's) has often been disguised by – indeed, expressed in terms of (the state has seen to that!) – ceremony and ritual; and I believe the tension that, in *War Requiem*, is consciously generated by the juxtaposition of ritual and *actualité*, finds expression at its most economical and most searing in the 'Agnus Dei'. It is in that movement that the heart of the Requiem – its 'message', if you prefer – resides. Not even the atomic explosion of G minor (G minor yet again!) in the extraordinary 'Libera me' exceeds the impact of the 'Agnus Dei'. I hope to have already put the centrality of the movement beyond doubt by describing the most significant of its purely musical features. But it is the composer himself who clinches the matter in its final bars, to which I have already referred. They vouchsafe a statement of the classic pacifist position – the only one of its kind in Britten —

> But they who love the greater love
> Lay down their life; they do not hate —

while, in the last three bars, when the ostinato frees itself from its perpetual rising and falling motion, the ascending scale for solo voice (the tritone of course is still embedded there) delivers the only words that do not form part of the *Missa pro defunctis*, 'Dona nobis pacem' ('Give us peace').[27]

I make no apology for comments that here and there might appear to be more appropriate to *interpretation* than to description of the music itself. On the contrary, I want to emphasize that in the particular case of *War Requiem* and for the sake of its reception in the years ahead it is vital to remind ourselves of its origins in the long-standing history of Britten's preoccupation with acts and climates of violence and, above all, not allow the work to be overlaid – stifled, smothered – by an interpretative tradition associated with oratorio, the concept of the 'big' choral work. It is there, perhaps especially when English forces are involved, that a dangerous temptation resides. In short, the protesting Owen settings are overwhelmed by an encompassing choral ritual that can seem to be mitigating, exonerating even, the brutal realities of war. Britten, for sure, would have hoped that the combatants in 'Strange Meeting' found peace, or at least the peace he imagined for them, in the slumber song that concludes the setting; for the composer, as we know, sleep and death were often inextricably compounded. But he was certainly not in the business of making Peace with War. It is the tritone indeed that is tolled again by the bells, albeit for the last time, in the seven-bar coda that brings *War Requiem* to an end; and it is that chilly *memento mori* that we should take with us as we leave the church or concert hall, not the act of conciliation implicit in the lullaby, which belongs to the combatants, the *victims* of war, and is addressed to *them*, not to us. I have heard too many performances of *War Requiem* in recent years in which the audiences, so to say, appropriate the lullaby to themselves, and misinterpret its principal text, 'Let us sleep now . . .', as if it were a consolatory injunction.

The pain of the Owen settings should not be masked, but proclaimed; and no member of the audience should leave *War Requiem* without fully comprehending the inversion of relationships between ritual and reality in the 'Agnus Dei', the movement in which Britten himself, in unforgettable music, takes a very close and uncomfortable look at the consolation and exorcism offered by the convention of ritual. An interpretation that takes full account of the *climax* that 'Agnus Dei' represents, for all its chamber-orchestral character and (relatively) muted dynamics, and also – to return to one of the earliest manifestations of the 'Dance of Death' concept, the (G minor) scherzo in *King Arthur* (see also Plate 15) – succeeds in fertilizing the ritualistic ritornelli of the (G minor) 'Dies irae' of

1961 with the hectic spirit and invasive fanfares of the 'wild dance' of 1937 – 'The music surges in again, whirls on, and after making its suggestion of the letting loose of every demon in hell, fades slowly down to silence . . .' – will stand a chance of revealing *War Requiem* in the *livid* light that I believe in many of its most significant parts is its most appropriate form of illumination.

An untidy reckoning, all of this? Perhaps; but if so, necessarily so. The untidiness reflects the extraordinary diversity of the works of all shapes and sizes which in one way or another and at one time or another, marking very different occasions and functioning in very different contexts, comment on, or are directly related to, acts of violence. The sheer sprawl of the music thus generated may create problems for the commentator; on the other hand it speaks volumes for the centrality of the basic preoccupation to Britten's creativity. Significant swathes of his music were touched by it or wholly ignited by it. It may not be possible to pin down one tidy, logical, evolving thread that one can identify as Pacifism, on which all the works hang. They don't. But there is instead a profound consistency of motive sustained over decades, the more profound perhaps because so variously expressed. It is not just a statement and re-statement of pacifist conviction that we encounter but, from the 1930s onwards to the very last years of Britten's life, a consistent indictment (and, not infrequently, analysis) of violence, its causes and its consequences. It is a record that does honour to him, as an artist and a man.

Epilogue: prohibited immigrants

Did Britten and Pears suffer for their Pacifist convictions? In one unexpected way – not the only way but probably the most bizarre – yes, they did. It may not be generally known, but in the post-war years they were both categorized as 'prohibited immigrants' by the United States, a consequence of the tide of McCarthyism that swept America in the 1950s. (McCarthy, in the current *Cambridge Biographical Encyclopedia* (1995) is aptly described as 'US Republican politician and *inquisitor*' (my emphasis).) However, as a remarkable letter dated 5 February 1942 shows (Plate 16) – it was signed by the then Director of the FBI, J. Edgar Hoover, no less – what later came to be recognized as McCarthyism was already actively in operation.

Britten and Pears would hardly have been aware of the fact that the FBI was keeping an eye on them in 1942, though they certainly would have

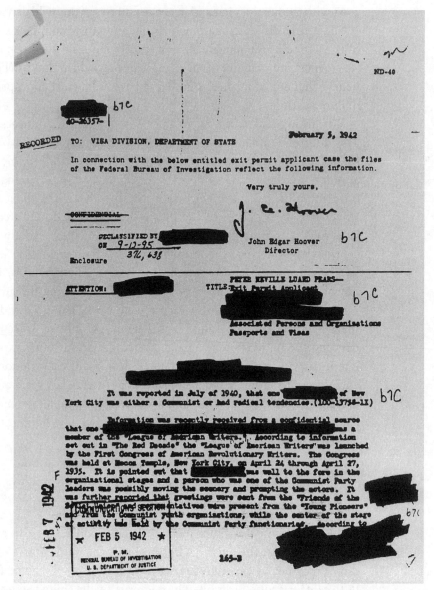

Plate 16 FBI documentation relating to Pears, signed by J. Edgar Hoover and dated 5 February 1942

know that liberal activists were all too readily identified as 'Reds'. Rather amusingly, it is precisely with that term of abuse that the Old Trees in the Prologue to Britten's and Auden's *Paul Bunyan* (1939–41) respond to the Young Trees' plea, 'We do *Not* want life to be slow'. (I guess that bit of incriminating evidence went unremarked by the FBI.)

In any event, Britten and Pears were not backward in making their convictions known when the occasion demanded; and in 1949, when on a recital tour of Canada and the States, the text shown in Plate 17 was

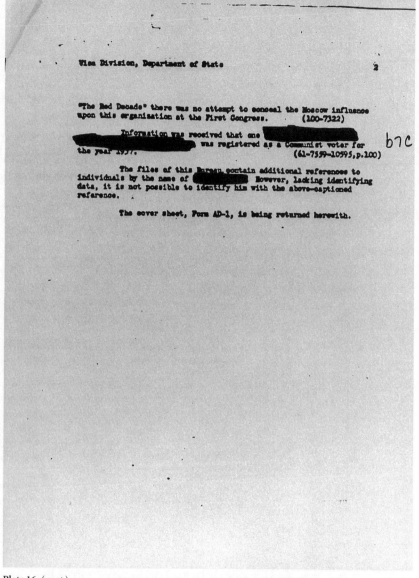

Plate 16 (*cont.*)

printed in the programme they gave on 8 December at Community Church Auditorium (probably located in the vicinity of New York).

It was precisely this kind of statement of and support for 'pacifist ideas' that caught the attention of the now proactive McCarthyite agents of state; as a result of which both Britten and Pears were declared to be 'prohibited immigrants'. (I have not yet established exactly when the prohibition came into effect but it must have been introduced in the 1950s.) This meant that whenever Britten and Pears, whether singly or jointly,

The governments of the world have declared in the Charter of UNESCO: "Since wars begin in the minds of men, it is in the minds of men that the defenses of peace must be constructed."

One of our leading English writers, the historian of art, Mr. Herbert Read, has pointed out what the scientists and the military also in effect declare, namely, that with the advent of atomic and biological weapons, war and armaments no longer provide any defense. Power in the military sense has become an illusion and it is indeed "worse than an illusion —it is an hallucination which invites suicide." Herbert Read says that under these circumstances young Englishmen who agree to be drafted "are engaging in a gigantic conspiracy which can only end in the obliteration of their island home" and adds that "the case is not different for young Americans, young Frenchmen, young Russians—for the youth of any nation."

Not only is modern war completely irrational and suicidal; it is also completely immoral. Recently Rear Admiral Ralph A. Offstie, U.S.N., at a Congressional hearing, raised the question, in a denunciation of atomic and "obliteration" bombing, what people mean by "survival." He declared: "If we mean the survival of the values, the principles and traditions of human civilization, we must insure that our military techniques do not strip us of our self-respect."

In these circumstances the first act of sanity for any nation is to break with war. The first patriotic, sane, morally decent step for the youth—any youth of any nation—is to withhold himself from military service.

Once we have decided not to slip over the precipice into atomic war, we can train ourselves to use higher and truly effective means to resist evil and possible aggression. If our democratic peoples maintain a vigorous health in their economic life, in relations between the nations, in education and art, health will gradually be instilled into the whole community of nations. Gandhi has shown how nonviolent resistance can be "a living reality among the practical policies of world politics."

It is because we believe these things and have in our own country been connected with movements which promote these pacifist ideas that we gladly give this performance under the sponsorship of two organizations which in this country seek to advance the same cause—the Fellowship of Reconciliation and the War Resisters League.

BENJAMIN BRITTEN
PETER PEARS

Plate 17 Pacifist statement printed in the programme of a recital by Britten and Pears in North America in 1949

were invited to visit the United States, they were obliged to apply for a visa on each occasion, visit the Embassy for an 'interview', and await the granting of the necessary permit – the latter was often not confirmed until very shortly before their planned departure. Had they turned up at a port of immigration without the authorizing paper work, they would not have been allowed entry. Permission, however, was invariably granted.

It seemed intolerable to me that this grotesque and, above all, secret indictment should still be in force long after McCarthyism itself had been abandoned and in 1983, with the help of good friends in the States, we

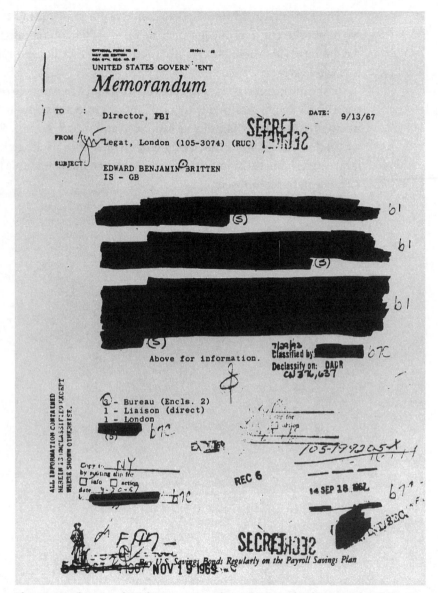

Plate 18 Heavily censored FBI documentation relating to Britten, dated 13 September 1967

succeeded in removing Pears from the register, itself a long and – for a by then old man – exacting procedure. To the best of my knowledge, however, Britten himself never made any effort to get the ban lifted. He died in 1976 still officially prohibited.

Pears's 'release' generated an attempt to wrest from the FBI (under the Freedom of Information Act) the relevant papers that would tell us what it was that had led to his and Britten's impeachment. Despite our lawyers' best efforts what was produced was scarcely informative. Plate 18 – a document dated as late as 13 September 1967 – speaks (if that's the right word) for itself.

There seemed little point in (expensively) pursuing the matter further. No doubt the 'truth', if one may use the word at all in this context, will one day be revealed. There is certainly room for further dogged research in this whole area.[28]

In the meantime the episode provides a strange footnote to our survey of Britten's Pacifism, along with a rare insight into a disreputable feature of twentieth-century politics in America (and nearer home). Perhaps it was in this context alone that it might be claimed that an altogether singular though shameful manifestation of a violent climate was able to take its revenge on the composer.[29]

11 Britten as symphonist

ARVED ASHBY

Britten originally thought of using the designation 'First Symphony' for his first large-scale, purely orchestral score – the composition, sketched and completed in the spring of 1940, that would instead carry the final title *Sinfonia da Requiem*.[1] But within seven years the momentous premières of *Peter Grimes* and *The Rape of Lucretia* and subsequent formation of the English Opera Group channelled his energies in different and ostensibly non-symphonic directions. The variety of music that followed, most of it involving text and the voice, shows a composer consistently ambivalent about those ideas central to symphonic traditions – tonal hierarchies, authorship and genre writ large, the grand and universal statement, and the classicist and folklorist ideas that spawned a symphonic renewal in the decades after the First World War. Perhaps it was to be expected, then, that Britten's symphonic works would be few and undoctrinaire: the *Sinfonietta* (a student composition written in 1932), *Sinfonia da Requiem* (1940), *Spring Symphony* (1949), and Cello Symphony (1963) differ extremely in tone, instrumentation, structure and symphonic morphology. Like the contrasting 'symphonies' and symphonic attempts by those who influenced Britten's early development most directly – Mahler, Schoenberg, Berg and Stravinsky – his four symphonic scores define the post-tonal symphony, and things post-tonally 'symphonic', in at least four different ways.

The variances to Britten's essays in this most generic of forms – that is, the form saddled since Beethoven with the heaviest conventions of structure, instrumentation, and manner of performance and reception – also point to a non-generic and non-serial quality to this composer's output that goes beyond issues of genre and structure. Even Mahler's symphonies, which invite a collective hearing in series as some kind of autobiographical meta-symphony, obey certain laws of genre that Britten's symphonies and operas and canticles do not.[2] (One could say the same of Tippett's symphonies, which describe a fairly linear path from Hindemithian classicism to more improvisatory structures, not to mention Walton's essays in more consistent four- and three-movement symphonic forms.) In this respect, Britten's evasion of the simple English title 'symphony' – and his relative avoidance of symphonic works more generally – becomes symptomatic of larger, compositional evasions in all genres.³ But then an uneasiness with genre conventions becomes apparent in many of Britten's titles, which tend toward neologism. For example, the unique stringing-together of nouns for the titles *Spring Symphony* and *War Requiem* differs from the usual parenthetical or characteristic descriptions – such as Mahler's original heading *Symphonie ('Titan')* for his First Symphony, Vaughan Williams's *Sinfonia antartica*, or Delius's use of the indefinite article and preposition for *A Mass of Life*.

If Britten's four 'symphonies' do have something in common, it is their nonconformity with the classic Viennese legacies of Beethoven and Brahms, the defining presences in any history of symphonic music and compositional presences in England even into the 1920s and 1930s. Britten was an outspoken critic of these two composers, which in itself might have been nothing more than an alibi against their influence.⁴ But his music and methods of working corroborate these distastes: he consistently compared his process of composing to an architect's labours – imposing form from without – thereby invoking contrast with the Brahmsian organic form described by Dahlhaus as 'development or elaboration, both logical and rhetorical, of a process of thought' – which is more like letting a natural form grow from within, unwilled.⁵ A listener might also hear Beethovenian and Brahmsian symphonic teleologies subjugating momentary pleasure to long-term cumulative effect, giving them historical value as tropes on the Hegelian division between *werden* and *aufheben*. By contrast, critics both sympathetic and fault-finding are often struck by Britten's ear for things momentary – fleeting and memorable nuances of sonority and affect, moments that are *sui generis* and therefore non-symphonic.⁶

Britten's *Sinfonietta* for ten instruments, which he wrote in 1932 as an eighteen-year-old student at the Royal College of Music, documents his thoughts on symphonic composition at a time when he was still enthusiastic about Beethoven and Brahms, seeking out their music on the radio and playing them at the piano for his own pleasure. To be more precise, the concise *Sinfonietta* shows an apathy toward the various Brahms and Beethoven legacies heard in the music of Parry, Stanford, and Vaughan Williams, and an unfashionable fascination with Schoenberg's reconception of Beethoven's and Brahms's symphonic legacies in his early chamber music. This Schoenbergian work, Britten's Op. 1, must represent a similar stepping-stone in what he later called his 'struggle . . . to develop a consciously controlled professional technique. It was a struggle away from everything Vaughan Williams seemed to stand for.'⁷ Britten's form, instrumentation, motivic writing, and polyphony were clearly influenced by Schoenberg's First String Quartet and especially the First Chamber Symphony, Op. 9. Like many composers beginning with Webern, Britten was fascinated and stimulated by Schoenberg's attempts to contrive a kind of symphonic meta-unity – a large-scale and organic structure that would, in Schoenberg's words, 'include all the four characters of the sonata type in one single, uninterrupted movement'.[8]

Schoenberg's Chamber Symphony is a feat of structural virtuosity, an increasingly extreme – indeed, dangerous and exhilarating – steeplechase of development, episode and recapitulation. With Britten's *Sinfonietta* as with the Schoenberg, a running-together of movements works with a thematic-motivic teleology to help the composer postpone any real sense of recapitulatory satisfaction until the very end of the composition. Britten ends his first movement with only tenuous and abbreviated restatement, layering the opening theme with an augmented version of the second subject (first heard at Fig. 8, transposed for the recapitulation) and leaving a listener open to the more definitive restatement of this material heard at the end of the finale. Any sense of arrival or relaxation is doubly tenuous here because Britten does not state the first theme in the distinctive form heard at the very opening, but in the telescoped form heard later, at Fig. 2. (In Ex. 11.1, compare bars 1–8 with bars 20–4. Ironically, this kind of selective recapitulation of the opening subject is also prominent in Brahms – compare Britten with the first movement of the Clarinet Quintet, Op. 115, for example.) He also cuts off the recapitulation abruptly and prematurely: after a mere 22 bars of reprise (to be compared with 89 measures of introduction and exposition), Britten ends the movement on a repeated major-seventh chord on B♭ without a third. This chord acts as a formal signpost, referring back to the piled B♭–A sevenths of the introduction and forwards to the end of the slow movement and to the beginning of the third movement, where the chords, instrumentation, and voicing pick up precisely where the first movement had left off.

Despite these long-range, pitch-specific connections, Britten seems to identify with his Schoenberg exemplar – and with the idea of an end-weighted symphonic teleology – less and less as the music proceeds. The development in his first movement (Figs. 10–19) recalls fragments from both thematic areas but has clearer and more stable tonal leanings than the exposition and offers little if any climactic and comprehensive working-out. It is also thinner in texture than the second subject area and saves any imitative counterpoint for the lengthy retransition, concentrating instead on simple sequential manipulation of the opening figure of the second theme. A rigorously intervallic as opposed to functional-harmonic language makes Schoenberg's aggressive organicism possible, and by Britten's second movement – with its surprising 'English pastoral' tone – one hears him straining against this borrowed language. Likewise, in the final 'Tarantella' one might hear the composer escaping to a more

Example 11.1

characteristic, highly rhythmic *moto perpetuo* and more relaxed functional-harmonic trappings.[9] And Britten's patient reassembly here of the
original form of his first subject from the first movement sounds more
forced than teleologically satisfying – the work of an ambitious student
using a Schoenbergian model in some ways incompatible with his language.

The *Sinfonietta* is conspicuously Schoenbergian in its motivic thinking: the first movement cogently reconfigures and expands upon a small
number of motifs, all of them stated within the first eight bars. Yet
Britten's score also comes across as only selectively organic. Three ideas
from the first movement reappear in the introductory opening of his
second movement, with changes of tempo and affect that suggest the

Example 11.2

thematic transformation of Liszt and Tchaikovsky more than Schoenberg's motivically based techniques of 'developing variation' (see Ex. 11.2): (1) the secondary theme now reappears in flute and bassoon; (2) the emphatic and highly rhythmic pentatonic horn call leading up to Fig. 2 now appears as a loosely canonic figure in the strings; and (3) the opening of the very first subject is now recalled in flute and clarinet (bars 5–7). With their original phrasing, articulations, contour and rhythm retained, the first and third of these become less motivic entities or motto-themes than themes to be recalled literally but at a different tempo and imbued with a different character.

Much of the particular urgency and import of the symphony since Mahler stems from the problem of just how to maintain or revitalize this author-heavy, grandiose form – its status as a proving-ground of compositional competence and artistic vision inescapable even in the modernism of Schoenberg's Op. 9 – when the functional harmonic inter-relationships that had grown symbiotically with it had eroded or been thrown out altogether. This challenge must have been particularly impos-ing for the young Britten, whose structuralist thinking and intrinsically diatonic but non-hierarchical harmonic language lay uneasily alongside his appreciation of Mahler's large and 'cunningly contrived' symphonic forms, where 'every development surprised one and yet sounded inevitable'.[10] Britten answered the challenge with his *Sinfonia da Requiem*, a work that creates a truly symphonic dialectic by pitting tonal uncertainty against tonal certainty. In Arnold Whittall's words, 'Britten's answer [to the post-tonal symphonic dilemma] was to let the strong assertion and elaborate prolongation of the tonic itself justify – indeed, make inevitable – the non-diatonic motions which remain subordinate to that asserted tonic.'[11]

The tonal assertiveness of the *Sinfonia da Requiem* lies in an almost oppressive insistence on D at the middle-ground level in all three movements. This D tonality is enforced in the 'Lacrymosa' by an insistent and inexorable bass-line, which dwells on this tonic and twice ascends the octave from the opening D – an ascent the final 'Requiem aeternam' movement will answer with its own twofold *descent* over the D octave. The regularity of this bass motion in the 'Lacrymosa' promises a processional, non-dialectic kind of formal logic more like the passacaglia than sonata-allegro precedents. (The formal dynamic of this movement, and of the *Sinfonia da Requiem* as a whole, bears the imprint of Britten's interest in ground-bass forms; in this, it also shows his propensity for writing sonata forms that, as Peter Evans describes the first movement of the *Sinfonietta*, 'continue to rise after the mid-point' instead of tracing a dynamic arch.[12]) At the same time, Britten accommodates this processional structure to certain expectations of sonata-allegro form. Confronting the tonal insistence and certainty of the bass-line are passages of harmonic uncertainty arising from two interruptions in the bass-line. The second of these episodes, moving away from the tonic D minor and toward the tritone axes F–B and C–F♯, displays the kind of conflicted and uncertain tonal structures common to Britten's years in America (1939–42).[13] The bass arrives on the diminished-fifth degree (A♭) at the onset of this passage, setting off a new turn toward flat keys, and the interruption in the bass ascent and the new chordal texture make the series of juxtaposed chords starting at bar 3 of Fig. 5 sound like the onset of the classical second subject. But Britten does not present any harmonic pole – or harmonic duality, even – as a counter to the firmly defined tonic D minor. According to tradition, ostensibly new themes would appear here to articulate and fix a turn toward a new harmonic area. Instead, Britten offers a series of ambivalent and restless chord juxtapositions, the profusion of unresolved tritones defusing any sense of stable functional relation – he downplays the point of furthest harmonic and thematic 'remove' that is intrinsic to the traditional sonata-allegro shape, preferring instead to trace a uniform and more dramatically convincing dynamic line.

One could find Britten's pointed avoidance of any clear-cut thematic and harmonic duality non-symphonic, but then the *Sinfonia da Requiem* shows especially clearly the necessary interrelationship between Britten's non-teleological, non-hierarchical harmonic thinking and his incapacity – at least as Hans Keller would have it – for symphonic development in the conventional thematic-motivic sense.[14] Like Liszt, Britten replaces exposition, working-out, and reconciliation of thematic and harmonic contrasts with 'thematic transformation' and the linearity of a simple extramusical idea or character transformation: Britten's final 'Requiem

Example 11.3

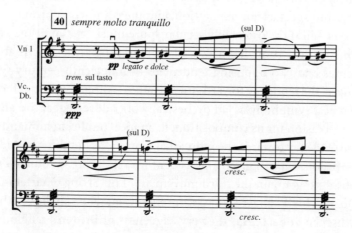

aeternam', which Auden described as 'a movement of peace and quiet rejoicing',[15] resolves the conflicts of the 'Lacrymosa' and allays the scarifyingly numb atomization of the 'Dies irae' by bringing back the initial material – anxious in those earlier movements, where it had been laden with semitones, minor sixths and minor sevenths, but now hopeful and finally ecstatic (Ex. 11.3). Liszt spoke of a 'progression of soul-states' in discussing his own symphonic poems, and works like *Tasso* and *Les préludes* trace a will to apotheosis, dramatic outline *per aspera ad astra*, movement from darkness to light, that is linear without being teleological.

The slowly moving bass pattern of 'Lacrymosa', and insistence on D throughout the entire work, creates and enhances extra-musical associations: the funeral march and religious sub-text, two trademarks of Mahler's symphonic thinking. Britten borrows many of Mahler's gestures – among them his juxtaposition of conflicting major and minor third degrees, the irony of purposefully banal material, the thematic use of rhythm, and certain ideas on orchestration.[16] But the more fundamental affinities between Britten and Mahler are less immediately audible – characteristics that have more to do with the symphonic accomplishments than the immediate styles of these composers.[17] Like Mahler in his Second and Fifth, Britten begins his symphony with a funeral march and uses this to create an especially symphonic structural tension and breadth. This particular conflation of extra-musical illustration and high formalist traditions of absolute music – a collusion of theatrical gesture and concert-hall periodicity – was one of Mahler's most original and indelible contributions to twentieth-century symphonic music. A processional rhythm and tempo also help Britten introduce an indistinct spiritual or religious programme – as arranged from the Requiem Mass, a linear and dramaturgically effective juxtaposition of the sinner's guilt, the dreadful spectacle of damnation, and the comforting promise of eternal peace – into the ostensibly secular, 'pure music' realm of the symphony. This in turn provided a way of bringing together church and secular genres and two opposing tendencies of nineteenth-century symphonic music: the tendency towards universality – Alfred Einstein referred to the classical symphony as 'an orchestral work addressed, above and beyond any occasion for its composition, to an ideal public, to humanity'[18] – and the tendency towards the individual or even the autobiographical.

Beethoven had given a precedent for rendering spirituality within an 'absolute' genre in the third movement of his String Quartet in A minor, Op. 132, his 'Heiliger Dankgesang eines Genesenen an die Gottheit, in der lydischen Tonart'. But the very vagueness of Britten's religious ethos in the *Sinfonia da Requiem*, its universality and non-sectarian nature, more directly recalls Mahler – for both the *Sinfonia da Requiem* and Mahler's 'Resurrection' Symphony, in which that composer had broken off his setting of Klopstock's *Resurrection Ode* at its first mention of Jesus, are really no more specifically Christian than they are Judaic or Buddhist. This non-denominational quality makes doubly ironic and bizarre the tale of how the Japanese authorities who commissioned the *Sinfonia da Requiem* came finally to reject – and profoundly misunderstand – Britten's work as 'purely religious music of a Christian nature'.[19] In fact, the *Sinfonia da Requiem* is like a Mahler symphony or later example such as Honegger's *Symphonie 'Liturgique'*, in that the contrast between its nebulous extra-musical programme and its emotional specificity send the curious listener back to the composer's biography rather than to any theological issues. Those seeking reason or context for the *Sinfonia da Requiem* turn not to Catholic or Anglican belief but to biographical events: the deaths of Britten's parents, his recent life-threatening illness, fascist victories in Europe, and his self-exile from a country that was at war and besieged.

With his next large-scale orchestral work, the *Spring Symphony* of 1949, Britten demonstrated a more enigmatic creative relationship with the symphonic oeuvre of Mahler – and also a more enigmatic idea of what a symphony could be in the late 1940s. Commentators have called the *Spring Symphony* a cantata, a song-cycle, and a latent opera. In truth, the work is all and none of these: in some ways a profoundly non-Mahlerian composition, it nevertheless represents a playing-out of some of the formal ambiguities and genre-allusions of Mahler's symphonies. Britten's own description of his piece – 'a symphony not only dealing with the Spring itself, but with the progress of Winter to Spring and the reawakening of the earth and life which that means'[20] – might suggest the vocal symphonies of Mahler, especially *Das Lied von der Erde*. Like Mahler, Britten emphasizes orchestral colour but usually breaks his ensemble into a variety of chamber groups. Britten also uses solo voices in the 'concise' and 'specific' – operatic as opposed to instrumental – style that Mahler heard in his own early symphonies.[21] More precisely, we might turn to the fifth movement of Mahler's Third Symphony – his setting of 'Es sungen drei Engel' from *Des Knaben Wunderhorn* – or to a Purcell opera to find similar dance rhythms, onomatopoeic vocal effects, alfresco lustiness, and changeable collusions between soloists and choruses.

The operatic cast to the voices in Britten's *Spring Symphony* might suggest Mahler, but Britten goes further than Mahler in suggesting the operatic stage.[22] Though unnamed, his singers are as much characters as they are voices – like Lukas in Haydn's secular oratorio *Die Jahreszeiten* or Mahler's wandering penitent in 'Urlicht', but unlike Doctor Marianus in Mahler's Eighth or the heartsick wanderer in *Das Lied von der Erde*. Already a consummate composer for the stage, Britten emphasizes the individuality of each character by plumbing and complicating their individual psychologies. The tuba line in the outer sections of 'The driving boy', grinding repetitiously through the same II–V–I progression in E♭ and asserting a low brass tone-colour that always connotes morbidity in Britten, hints surreptitiously that the pubescent male might not find spring to be all strawberries and cream (or cakes and ale, to take an expression from the finale). Likewise, the bristling and polytonal string and harp ostinati of 'When will my May come' take us beyond the impatience and unrequited arcadian love of Richard Barnefield's text and into something more Stravinskyan, almost animalistic – thereby injecting a sense of irony and frustrated sexuality into the naive, strophic setting of the inner two stanzas.

The *Spring Symphony* actually comes across as the least Mahlerian of Britten's symphonies if one searches it for Mahler's manner of bringing theme, programme, voice and text together into one linear and symphonic structure. In contrast with Mahler's symphonies, vocal or purely instrumental, Britten's movements contribute to no real cumulative hyper-plot, apart from seasonal passage from late winter to early summer.[23] Accordingly, the *Spring Symphony* is also non-Mahlerian in the important fact that it is not end-directed. Mahler often connects his movements – especially first and last – with reminiscence themes, while Britten's finale concentrates on tying off the material of its own ternary form. The *Spring Symphony* also differs from *Das Lied von der Erde* and Mahler's vocal Second, Third, Fourth, and Eighth Symphonies – and from Mahler's own exemplars in Beethoven's Ninth, Mendelssohn's Second and Liszt's *Faust Symphony*, not to mention such twentieth-century examples as Scriabin's First and Shostakovich's Second and Third – in that it builds no particular structural relationship between vocal music and purely instrumental music. Dahlhaus categorized these nineteenth-century works as 'symphony-cantatas', works in an intrinsically romantic sub-genre where the vocal section emerges as a kind of combined summary, apotheosis, and recapitulation of the instrumental.[24]

Britten owes the number and variety of texts in the *Spring Symphony*, and therefore the large-scale, cumulative structure of the work itself, less to Mahler's influence than Auden's – and specifically, to Auden's love for the literary anthology.[25] For his twelve songs Britten collated more texts than Mahler did in any one symphony, and culled them from far-flung sources – but on the other hand he did not do this in a purposefully provocative way, as Mahler did in his Eighth when he juxtaposed a ninth-century Pentecost hymn with the final scene from *Faust*. Britten fashioned his twelve songs into what he called 'the traditional four movement shape of the symphony',[26] yet the remarkable differences of colour and affect between the individual songs tend to de-emphasize or detract from that larger symphonic shape. Passing from one song of the *Spring Symphony* to the next is much like emerging from the string-dominated chiaroscuro of the fourth movement of Mahler's Third (his setting of Nietzsche's 'Midnight Song') to the brightly lit, percussive, and more strictly metrical world of Mahler's fifth movement (colours more appropriate to the child-folkish Christianity of the *Wunderhorn* text 'Es sungen drei Engel'). Britten's fusion of instrumental colour and vocal style for each individual text becomes delightfully obvious in 'The driving boy', for example, where tambourine rolls and cross-accented roulades in the woodwinds echo the changing metres and relentless consonants of George Peele's 'When as the rye reach to the chin, And chopcherry, chopcherry ripe within'.

If the *Spring Symphony* owes its anthologistic structure to Auden, should not the choral aspect also point to British influences rather than more distant Austro-German traditions? The *Spring Symphony* was preceded by two works that struck common ground between British symphonic and choral traditions, and which Britten would undoubtedly have known: Vaughan Williams's *A Sea Symphony* (1903–9) and Holst's *Choral Symphony* (1923–4). But Britten's vocal–orchestral relationships and the operatic immediacy of his vocal writing relate more readily to early Mahler. The Vaughan Williams and Holst, diametrically opposed in the intercessions they propose between choral and symphonic music, are both resolutely non-operatic. Holst's orchestra either gives the most tentative of accompaniments or simply doubles the voices, his vocal writing itself is highly improvisatory and often – as in the striking opening pages

– monotonal, and the work owes much of its failure in the concert hall to its lack of drama and non-symphonic lack of structural or dynamic development. Vaughan Williams, on the other hand, justified his frequent repetition of Walt Whitman's words and phrases in *A Sea Symphony* by describing this work as 'symphonic rather than narrative or dramatic … the orchestra [also] has an equal share with the chorus and soloists in carrying out the musical ideas'. Holst's orchestra is often dispensable, while Vaughan Williams's textures are grand and colourful enough, and his four-movement design sufficiently symphonic, that his work would suffer relatively little if one replaced the voices with instruments. Either measure would utterly defeat the *Spring Symphony*, just as it would Mahler's vocal symphonies.

The *Spring Symphony* effects operatic tableaux and the localized, moment-to-moment references and pitch relations of the song-cycle more than it does the thematic relations and latent harmonic narrative that spread across the larger whole in the classical symphonic repertory (and in the Vaughan Williams just mentioned). In this, the *Spring Symphony* is less symphonic than the *Serenade, Nocturne, Les illuminations,* or the 'symphonic song-cycle' *Our Hunting Fathers.* But the constructive principles of the song-cycle are known for ranging wide between the intuitive and the rigorous, and in the *Spring Symphony* Britten does not devise local relations at the expense of the larger structure. The capstone-like length of Britten's first and last songs also serves to underline any linear and symphonic qualities heard in the *Spring Symphony* as a whole. Despite the fact that Britten moves consistently along a series of fluid pitch-entries, one could hear the C major of the finale as the logical, long-range result of the G proposed cumulatively by the opening three songs – with the A centre of the first two immediately re-interpreted at the opening of the third as secondary dominant of a new, tentatively tonicized G major.

The finale, the longest song of the twelve, ends the *Spring Symphony* on a note of summation but leaves open-ended the thematic and harmonic structure of the work. When the boys come in at the close with 'Sumer is icumen in' in an almost glaring C major (in the *Nocturne* and elsewhere the concluding key of transcendent purity, beyond consciousness, time, or place), it becomes clear that Britten's work is not dialectic in the classic symphonic manner – a paradigm still audible in the interrupted I–V–I background of the first movement of the *Sinfonia da Requiem.* Instead, the new tune symbolizes a kind of formal accomplishment that is different from the accustomed 'symphonic' kinds of teleological harmonic accomplishment. Britten leaves his large-scale harmonic motion purposefully open-ended to suggest arrival at new spiritual states and instrumental colours, much as Mahler did when he ended his Fourth, Fifth, Seventh, and Ninth Symphonies in keys different from those in which they started. Britten's ongoing play between sharp and flat key-centres, and – at the very end – his using the original key-centre A as an added-sixth to a close on C major, might even recall the structural tactics of the nineteenth-century *Liederkreis*.

While the title of the *Spring Symphony* originally caused debate among Britten's critics, no one has questioned his use of the word 'symphony' for the Symphony for Cello and Orchestra, his final large-scale orchestral work. Indeed, writers have embraced this title and singled out this score as a kind of vindication of Britten's seriousness as a symphonic composer, a final refutation of the adroit but superficial cleverness he was accused of earlier in his career (see p. 2). Evans, for one, declared the Cello Symphony 'Britten's most considerable achievement in the field of purely instrumental music'.[27] We owe such a verdict in part to the fact that this is seemingly Britten's most abstruse essay for the orchestra, and one that apparently carries no extra-musical allusions. But the air of summation and mastery that surrounds the work can also be attributed to Britten's much-discussed classicism of structure. There is a particular classical symmetry to the sonata-allegro design of the first movement: exposition and development are precisely the same length (95 bars each), and the recapitulation in conjunction with the coda is not much longer (total of 113 bars). The second subject is recognizably 'thematic' because of its periodic phrase-structure, and is also centred primarily on A major, a fifth above the D minor key centre for the opening theme. In the recapitulation, this second subject returns to the tonic D (major, this time), as one would expect in classic examples of sonata-allegro form. The development section is also quite straightforwardly developmental with its imitative textures, stretti of inverted motifs from the opening two pages, and truncated reworkings of the opening subject. It even ends with nine bars of dominant preparation.

Between them, the third and fourth movements of the Cello Symphony also suggest a classical sonata-allegro structure by relating contrasting themes to a calculated return of the tonic. The Adagio actually introduces the theme of the following passacaglia movement as its own second subject, in A major, and then restates its own first theme in A (at Fig. 57) before leading into the cello's cadenza. Immediately stating the passacaglia theme in the tonic D, the passacaglia movement thereby acts as a consequence, even a completion, of the Adagio.

Britten's democratic sharing of material between orchestra and soloist is often cited as evidence of the classic-symphonic bearing of the Cello Symphony – and here we approach the question of why this work is a symphony with soloist and not a concerto. To cite but one example, the roles of solo and orchestra are reversed when the theme that opened the first movement returns in the recapitulation (Fig. 17): in the recapitulation it is the soloist who states the ground while the orchestra provides the upper rhythmic-harmonic pattern. When Evans contrasts the Cello Symphony with a hypothetical, highly soloistic counter-example, something more akin to the 'bravura Concerto with orchestral accompaniment' that Britten essayed in his earlier Piano Concerto,[28] he seems to compare this work to the Brahms concertos. In Evans's estimation, Britten transcends any concerto-like conflicts between individual roles of orchestra and solo instrument or any structural confrontations of timbre. With the Cello Symphony, Evans seems to say, Britten wrote a Bach-like piece of 'pure' music or perhaps something like the 'symphony with solo obbligato' that Hanslick heard in Brahms's Second Piano Concerto.

There are many things wrong with such a classical reading of the Cello Symphony, and by extension the view that this composition represents a stepping-back from the world of vocal music into something necessarily more 'absolute' and instrumental in conception.[29] For the Cello Symphony is powered and enriched by the colouristic, narrative and cognitive devices of the experienced opera composer – and is therefore one of Britten's most profoundly Mahlerian compositions. The Cello Symphony offers a feast of new and unique timbres despite its only moderate orchestra of seventeen players plus the strings – and despite Britten's unusually modest use of percussion and violins. The very first sound – a roll on the bass drum with the tonic D doubled at the unison in tuba and double-bass – presents an unforgettable colour, one as far from the world of absolute music and as much a promise of dramatic, stage-worthy event as any opening in Mahler. Like Mahler and Shostakovich, Britten also deploys textures so varied and unbalanced as to pull work and listener out of the timbral-semiotic world of the absolute-symphonic and into the realm of narrative and theatre: note the bottom-heavy opening of the first movement, the interplay of spiccato strings against muted brass in the second, or the 'hole-in-the-middle' texture where contrabassoon appears with higher registers of the B♭ clarinet and oboe (first movement, Fig. 13).

The opening pages, where Britten immediately creates and exploits expectations of 'symphonic' and 'non-symphonic' sounds, are too conflicted to create the sense of structural downbeat appropriate to the beginning of a thirty-minute symphonic work: the tonic emphasis and element of rhetoric are fairly strong, but more important are irrational, just-beyond-earshot qualities of rhythm and timbre. The *style-brisé* entrance of the cello is inevitably an exercise in rhythmic irrationality, especially when the ear comes across the high-string-to-low-string direction for the sixth chord. Britten also gives the scalar bass figure (bars 4, 8, and 14) to the contrabassoon with selective doubling in tremolo *piano* double-basses, creating a highly indistinct sound – one that is virtually inaudible in some halls. By the recapitulation these timbral and rhythmic qualities are 'corrected', made more concrete and resolute. (The exchange of solo and orchestral material that transpires between exposition and recapitulation in one sense marks a 'symphonization' of the first movement – an agent of linearity working in tandem with the composer's holding off on a restatement of the first theme in the tonic D minor until the coda at Fig. 24.) But the process is gradual, and – significantly for the Cello Symphony's classicism of structure – is enacted over the development section (Figs. 8–17). By the beginning of the development, the original *style-brisé* chords have been given – now unbroken and in strict rhythm – to the winds. The scalar figure, however, emerges only slowly as something more distinct and more obviously thematic than it was at the opening: an inversion rises in register and clarity through the voices of bassoon, clarinet, and finally the solo cello itself. The figure appears uninverted in the recapitulation, sounded precisely and prominently by the soloist. By the recapitulation the chordal idea and the scalar idea have not become self-actualized – at least in the sense that the main theme of the first movement of the *Eroica* eventually finds harmonic closure – but have revealed themselves only gradually in a way that is more auditory than inherently musical.

The second aspect of the Cello Symphony that removes it from the realm of the absolute-symphonic is its vocabulary of gestures borrowed from vocal music – some of the same gestures, surely inspired by the cello's particular brilliance as it approaches the higher 'A-string' registers of Britten's favoured tenor voice, that are also to be heard in the Cello Sonata and Cello Suites. These gestures would seem out of place in an organically conceived piece of absolute music. But they are perhaps closer to the baroque concept of cognitive-semiotic rhetorical figures than to the suggestions of standard lyric styles and vocal phrase structures that Joseph Kerman found in the late Beethoven quartets.[30] Britten's 'tranquillo' second subject is a particular lode of cognitive-semiotic gestures (see Ex. 11.4). The falling two-note phrases seem to enact the classical 'sigh' topos. But the repetitious – even obsessive – interest in the rising semitones C♯–D, B–C, and G–A♭ suggests cadences in the recitation tones of ecclesiastical vocal music, thereby invoking the unspoken presence of both extra-musical import and worded 'text'. A revealing link can be established between Britten's second theme and the archaic ecclesiastical gestures of *Curlew River*, written the following year under the influence of plainsong. In a passage from *Curlew River* very similar to that in question

Example 11.4

from the Cello Symphony, the Madwoman recounts her son's disappearance ('Near the Black Mountains there I dwelt . . . Far, far in the West') in
abbreviated and formulaic phrase-fragments so full of cadential motion
through seconds that the larger disjunctions *between* phrases can seem
extreme. The cello line takes on a comparatively specific, recitative-like
scansion – a series of understressed and end-accented lines that, punctuated by trochaic two-note phrases, seem to comprise a continually disrupted monologue. Especially when the interrogative phrases begin to
spin farther and farther away from their consequent 'replies', rending the
line with multi-octave breaks, our 'singing' character takes on a surreal,
pathetic, even mad character. Britten had created a similar quality
through incantatory pitch repetition in the *Sinfonia da Requiem*, establishing a link between that work and Messalina's pathetic homilies in *Our
Hunting Fathers*.

The 'vocal', allusive elements in the Cello Symphony force us to recon-
sider a persistent refrain in Britten reception: that the composer found his
true métier with *Peter Grimes* and quit the world of symphonically conceived instrumental composition for the more appropriate and fulfilling
worlds of opera and vocal music. Keller spoke of Britten's non-symphonic
'naïvety' and allergy toward development as though they were inborn
qualities, and Whittall concluded from Britten's instrumental works of
the late 1930s that 'it was becoming increasingly clear – and, with hindsight, it was inescapable – that he could give a more natural melodic
articulation to his instincts about harmonic structure when setting
words'.[31] But exclusively 'vocal' and exclusively 'instrumental' or 'symphonic' forms and techniques, for that matter, become painfully artificial
constructs when one tries to turn them on Britten's music. (Or on that of
his friend and fellow Mahler-disciple, Shostakovich. As Eric Roseberry

has observed, 'with Britten the term "symphonic" is as applicable to his operas as the term "operatic" is frequently applicable to Shostakovich in his symphonies. The fact is – and this is part of their innovatory conservatism – that both gave new meaning to the established generic forms through their very mixing of genres within them.'[32]) The non-Mahlerian abstractions of the *Spring Symphony* and the vocal allusions of the Cello Symphony suggest that Britten conceived his texted vocal music and his symphonic works with few assumptions and few givens: in the former, we find harmonic relations that are at the same time simple and symphonic in scope, and in the latter he created vocality and extra-musical reference in his most restrained and classical orchestral structure, without words or a singing voice.

The question as to why Britten did not write more 'symphonies' then begins to sound like the old question of why Mahler wrote no operas. If there is an answer to both queries, it can be found in Britten's indebtedness to Mahler and Mahler's conciliation of a symphonic posture with an operatic inclusiveness. After the Viennese composer's late expansion of symphonic structures and styles, useful divisions between symphony and opera begin to break down: the symphony, and Britten's examples in particular, came to represent a style posing as a form.

12 The concertos and early orchestral scores: aspects of style and aesthetic

ERIC ROSEBERRY

It is tempting to speculate on the kind of composer Britten might have become if he had gone on to write that second piano concerto, composed a successor to his 'rather serious'[1] Violin Concerto, or followed along the path of symphonic, purely instrumental composition opened up in 1940 by his *Sinfonia da Requiem*. In the event, the student of Britten's music has to be satisfied with the Cello Symphony of 1963 as a long-postponed return to the preserve of 'absolute' music – a preserve from which Britten may seem to have become creatively estranged since his well-nigh total commitment to opera and song-cycle after *Peter Grimes* in 1945. Yet this divorce from 'abstract' sonata form, from the so-called 'sonata cycle' and its three or more movement musical 'plot' was by no means confrontationally hostile and – to say the least – a covert relationship continued. In 1945 (at the instigation of Curzon) he revisited his Piano Concerto – by now seven years old – and replaced the original third movement ('Recitative and Aria') with a fine reflective passacaglia that managed to integrate thematically and stylistically with the other three movements. Moreover, the achievement of the Second and Third String Quartets as well as the concentrated Sonata for cello and piano of 1961 testify to a significantly recurring need for the committed opera composer (who at times found himself not beyond critical reproof for the apparent over-reliance of his music upon words) to test himself in the arena of the 'absolute' – albeit through the 'private' world of chamber music.

Nevertheless, it is apparent that the nineteenth-century concept of 'absolute' music was abhorrent to Britten. His sharply negative attitude towards Beethoven and Brahms[2] – the very embodiment of the 'absolute' in music, as it were – and the counter-attraction for him of Purcell, Bach and Mozart in the shaping of his aesthetic accorded fully with what may be designated his neo-baroque-classical tendencies. This orientation is demonstrated amply enough in his frequent recourse to passacaglia and fugue, canon, suite and variation, the vocal-instrumental forms of recitative and aria, mass, motet and cantata, and in the classical symmetry and balance of his forms, always faithful to the principle of recapitulation. It becomes therefore all the more intriguing to examine a body of work that on the face of things runs counter to the aesthetic of the later, vocally orientated Britten.

Britten's lifelong commitment to the string orchestra officially begins with the *Simple Symphony* of 1934, but it goes back at least as far as the two Sketches for strings from 1930 that have recently come to light (see pp. 29–31). In view of the discovery that the later *Variations on a Theme of Frank Bridge* were originally conceived as a composite portrait of their dedicatee,[3] it is significant that these two pieces are also portraits, one of a school friend, the other as Britten saw himself. Of the two, by far the more substantial and progressive in style is the first – an extended, mono-thematic *poco presto* that suggests the influence of the early post-romantic Hindemith in its winding atonality and dense counterpoint. Its expression is dark and serious, and though it may lack the conciseness one associates with Britten's mature style it is an impressively sustained exploration of the implications of its main theme, with passages of considerable intensity. The other piece, for solo viola (Britten's own instrument) and strings, is slighter in comparison, in a somewhat conventional folk-like style, a *pastorale* that shares kinship with the kind of English inbreeding from which Britten turned away in his later work. None the less, it is interesting that Britten's 'self-portrait' is of a melancholy, introverted character, and takes the form of a set of free variations on its folk-like theme. The *Simple Symphony*, composed only four years later, is an altogether different proposition. Prophetically,[4] Britten blends the idea of the four-movement sonata 'cycle' with that of the baroque suite, and each movement underplays the idea of sonata as a monumental/transcendental genre in favour of a dance sequence. If highly stylized parody is here of the essence, we may note how this same element is at times absorbed into a deeper, more self-absorbed intensity of feeling. There is already a hint of this process in the dark seriousness of the main theme (G minor) of the Sarabande – a piece that looks forward to the 'Funeral March' of the *Frank Bridge Variations* in the pedal-grounded sense of tragic feeling it conveys.

As an orchestral composer Britten's preoccupation with chamber textures had been apparent from his Op. l, the *Sinfonietta* (a chamber symphony for solo strings or, alternatively, a small body of strings). His next work for orchestra, the suite of five movements from Rossini entitled *Soirées Musicales* began life as a smaller collection of pieces for a chamber group that accompanied a short silhouette film called *The Tocher* produced by the GPO Film Unit in 1935. The young highland hero of this film has a fat Post Office Savings Account which wins him the hand and the dowry ('tocher') of the approving chieftain's daughter. Britten's 'film ballet' score is for boys' voices, flute (doubling piccolo), oboe, clarinet, piano and percussion. The exquisite instrumentation has something of the innocence and freshness of Tchaikovsky's in *The Nutcracker* – a comparison that is further enhanced by the use of (wordless) boys' voices. Britten later re-orchestrated three of these pieces for both small and large orchestras and added two new items, 'Tirolese' and 'Tarantella'. The companion second suite from Rossini, *Matinées Musicales,* was composed in America in 1941 in response to a commission for a ballet for the American Ballet Company. These dashing and piquant adaptations from Rossini are in the spirit of all Britten's arrangements – there is no false reverence for a past style, no attempt to imitate Rossini's orchestral manner. Preserving only the tunes and original harmonies intact, the composer feels free to give rein to his own creative exuberence in exploiting the expanded wind and percussion resources of the twentieth-century orchestra, occasionally adding his own sly parodistic asides here and there.

Britten's next work for string orchestra, the *Variations on a Theme of Frank Bridge,* is the first in a clutch of four major scores that form the core of his orchestral legacy. The remaining three are the Piano Concerto, the Violin Concerto and the *Sinfonia da Requiem.* Britten's socio-political engagement in the 1930s is sufficiently well documented; it would be uncharacteristic if his orchestral music of the war years did not reflect the anxiety, the contradictions, the pain of a sensitive young genius on the threshold of self-imposed exile in wartime. The *Sinfonia da Requiem,* openly programmatical, proclaims itself as a document that bears witness to the time in which it was composed and has long been recognized as an important statement in the line of Britten's protests against war that culminated in the *War Requiem* and *Owen Wingrave.* But it is difficult to avoid a sense of hidden programmes in the symphonic works that precede it, conceived as they were in an epoch of violence and atrocity on a world-wide scale. Thus the Violin Concerto, with its formal anticipation of the musico-dramatic plan of the *Sinfonia da Requiem* and valedictory passacaglia finale, seems no less of a requiem than its successor. The expressive significance of Britten's use of a Mahlerian progressive tonality in these works is noteworthy. And in this connection the progressive tonality of the (pre-war) *Bridge Variations* gives cause to ponder on a possible sonata-like sub-text (with its own implicit 'narrative agenda') lurking somewhere behind this sequence of character variations. If the work was intended as a portrait of Bridge, its aspiration towards what could be taken here as Britten's 'own' key of D major suggests a symbolic synthesis of the identities of teacher and pupil.

If Beethoven decisively changed the course of a form that had hitherto inclined towards the merely decorative, Britten in his variations was already feeling his way towards grouping his separate parts together into a quasi-symphonic entity. This technique was also to stand him in good stead in the genres of song-cycle, symphony and opera, where his feeling for the large-scale grouping, contrast and sequence of smaller units enables him to impart a larger tonal-rhythmic sweep. It is thus not just Bridge's theme that guarantees unity, fascinating though Britten's motivic-harmonic derivations prove.[5] The ground-swell of the music has to do with tempo – much of it slow and reflective – as well as a key progression that, starting out in Bridge's tonally ambiguous E minor, takes the listener towards Britten's consummatory D major. (D may in fact be taken as the 'other' key seeking to gain some sort of foothold from the start – there are no fewer than three variations in this key, beginning with the 'allegro' march that leads the listener out of the initial slow music, and around which the others may be heard as grouping themselves. We shall see this same expressively motivated progress from one tonality towards another at work in the first movement of the Violin Concerto.) The 'narrative' may be summarized as follows: first the slow introduction and theme; growing out of this, the reflective recitative that leads into the active rhythms of the first part (march and dance, corresponding to first movement and scherzo of traditional symphonic procedure) towards a more contemplative state of being (the grief of the slow funeral march); then the finale preceded by a slow introduction ('Chant'). Finally, the transfigured return (coda) of Bridge's theme in an incandescent 'adagio'. (Could the influence of Mahler's slow symphonic perorations already be showing its hand here?) Every available sound effect is brought into play – pizzicato, harmonics, sweeping open-string effects, and the most subtly devised groupings. The fugal finale (with its tarantella-like subject, derived from the opening notes of Bridge's theme, figuring in paradoxically monophonic polyphony!) is a *tour de force* of sonority for a multi-divisi orchestra, with the composer bringing back Bridge's theme first as a viola cantilena against the busy fugue (shades of the forthcoming finale of *The Young Person's Guide to the Orchestra*) and then as a deeply eloquent transformation in D major (the E pitch orientation of Bridge's original theme still prominent as an added note).

To appreciate to the full the expressive ambiguity of the Piano Concerto (1938) we have to turn to the original version – and Britten's own unusually full programme note for its first performance.[6] As I have argued elsewhere,[7] Britten's substitution of a passacaglia third movement in 1945 for the original 'Recitative and Aria' would seem to blunt the point of the burlesque false triumph of the finale's martial display.[8] In the original version, the romantic tune of the third movement (after previous attempts to subvert its emergence) is made to appear a 'false dawn' that is ruthlessly brushed aside by the arrogant, Lisztian glitter of the triumphant main tune of the ensuing finale. This contradicts the progress of the first movement where instability of mood, caricature (see especially the Poulenc-like treatment of the second subject in the development) and menace are finally put to rest after the solo cadenza in a glowing transformation of the uneasy, restless second subject. Britten unifies the whole conception with a semitonally inflected motto that comprises two chords, and which is ultimately derived from the piano's opening toccata figuration (see Ex. 12.1a below). This first surfaces menacingly towards the beginning of the first movement in a tutti climax and thereafter puts in several appearances in different guises – even underpinning certain thematic and developmental processes. Notable derivations are the middle section of the 'Waltz' (Fig. 30), the angry outburst of the brass at Fig. 43 in the 'Recitative and Aria' and the threatening second subject of the finale at Fig. 54, led into by a pungent fanfare progression. The second movement (a kind of half-cousin to the 'Wiener Walzer' of the *Bridge Variations*) hovers – as Constant Lambert was the first to observe – 'cynically and convincingly' between 'straight' and cod.[9] But its eeriness and sharp sense of caricature (its Viennese allusions seem now to take on a sinister significance in the light of Hitler's Anschluss the same year) effectively prolong the unease of the first movement and transport us into the 'sport' of the 'Recitative and Aria' (note the baroque 'stylization' of this title) which offers a kind of parody of Beethoven's search for a finale theme in the prologue to the Finale of the Ninth Symphony.[10] (Here we encounter pre-echoes of the soloistic introductory links in *The Young Person's Guide to the Orchestra*.) It culminates in a romantic tune that in the end appears unsure of how to take itself, ending in a shy waltz which Britten incorporated into his later passacaglia substitution. Existing commentaries appear deaf towards the tonal-thematic irony of the finale.[11] The note of false, 'evil' triumph sounded in its main theme and the menace and anxiety of its continuing sonata 'narrative' are grounded in a larger structural irony – the (A major) estrangement of the whole movement from the home key of D major – until the perfunctory twist (at Fig. 64) of the recapitulation, that is. Nonetheless, Britten's final thoughts have to be respected, and the 1945 substitution of the so-called 'Impromptu' movement given its due. The reflective calm it introduces is undoubtedly effective even if it does neutralize somewhat the burlesque element implicit in the music of the finale. Britten took the theme from music composed at the same time for a radio play *King Arthur* and – whether by accident or design – its contour of falling thirds anticipates the shape of the finale's main theme, as well as indirectly referring (in the characteristic false relations of its paired harmonies) to the all-pervasive twin-chordal motto of the concerto.

In the three-movement Violin Concerto that immediately followed the Piano Concerto the element of burlesque is confined to a percussive second-movement scherzo of considerable ferocity and menace. (The furious onslaught from timpani and down-bow solo violin that drives on to the dark transitional climax suggests a parallel with the corresponding place in the second movement of the *Sinfonia da Requiem.*) Framing this *danse macabre* is a moderato sonata-form first movement and an epic passacaglia slow-movement finale shot through with tragic expression – the first of a memorable sequence of passacaglia finales that sound a note of high seriousness in Britten.[12] The form of the first movement is as polished, as admirably concise as its predecessor in the Piano Concerto. Once again Britten makes a point of transformation and thematic condensation in a telescoped recapitulation that scorns the idea of unnecessary repetition. Acting as a bridge between scherzo and finale is a cadenza for solo violin bringing back material from both first and second movements. (Here Britten anticipates by nearly twenty years Shostakovich in his First Violin Concerto of 1947–8 and himself in his own Cello Symphony of 1963.) The Violin Concerto is undoubtedly a more tightly knit work that its predecessor for piano, with admirably consistent thematic workmanship that ultimately derives from the stepwise progression of its first movement's main theme. The arrival of this theme is prefaced by a timpani motto-rhythm on C and F (shades of the opening of Beethoven's Violin Concerto!) and an epigrammatic, deeply felt falling sequence on the strings made up of two chords (a homely 6/4 followed by a piercingly anguished fourth-plus-tritone) that seem a distant derivation of the motto of the Piano Concerto (see Ex. 12.1b). This sets the basic elegiac tone of the concerto. A likely 'mood' model for Britten could be that of Berg's Violin Concerto, the world première of which was heard by Britten (who was deeply moved) at the ISCM Festival in Barcelona in 1936 where he was giving the first complete performance of his own Suite for Violin and Piano with Antonio Brosa, who performed the solo part in the Berg and later gave the first performance of Britten's Violin Concerto in New York in 1940. Certain correspondences between the Berg and Britten concertos are unmistakable, especially the conception of a slow (variation) finale; a thematic connection with Berg suggests itself in the main theme of the first movement, its falling shape and tonic-dominant accompaniment corresponding strikingly with the theme of the famous 'Adagio' interlude in D minor after the death of the title character in *Wozzeck* (see Ex. 12.2). The use of imagery with Spanish associations (castanet rhythms, flamenco-like guitar sonorities, the slow sarabande rhythm of the section beginning at Fig. 36 in the finale) together with pre-echoes of the *War Requiem* (fanfares, threatening trumpets and drums) would seem

Example 12.1

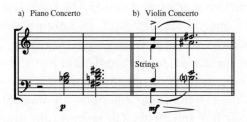

Example 12.2 (a)

Example 12.2 (b)

to point towards a Spanish Civil War sub-text. The hidden agenda suggested by such imagery links the work with Britten's contemporaneous tribute to the victims of the Spanish Civil War, the *Ballad of Heroes* (1939).

Iberian associations of a happier nature had already been broached in *Mont Juic*, a suite of orchestral arrangements of Catalan dances undertaken in collaboration with Lennox Berkeley in 1937. In his essay on Britten's light music, Berkeley does not indicate precisely how the work was apportioned between Britten and himself.[13] Yet (as Christopher Palmer notes[14]) Britten's involvement can be sensed in No. 3, the menacing 'Lament' (subtitled 'Barcelona 1936') with its doleful alto saxophone solo (an instrument which – again following the example of Berg's Violin Concerto – Britten puts to pungent use in the *Sinfonia da Requiem*) and the melancholy depth of feeling involved in this simple tune. This surely is the number that qualifies the suite as a fitting memorial tribute for the composer's friend, Peter Burra.

The experience of the Violin Concerto undoubtedly led directly into the cyclic conception of the *Sinfonia da Requiem*, which if anything

displays an even more tightly knit thematic-motivic continuity and dazzling skill of transformation than its predecessor. The *Sinfonia da Requiem*
is Britten's untitled Concerto for Orchestra, an extraordinary display-
piece for orchestra which reaches its apogee in the terrifying 'Dies Irae',
another of those *danses macabres* so characteristic of Britten's work from
Our Hunting Fathers on. Britten's imagination is often at its most incandescent in music at the extremities of emotion – in moments of great
serenity and beauty, or fear and terror. The terror of the disintegrating
climax at the end of the 'Dies Irae' – in which the music as it were dashes
itself to pieces – is a case in point. This frenzy may seem sheer sound and
fury at first hearing, but Britten's control of its subsidence, its gradual
transformation into the measured tread of the 'Requiem Aeternam', is
masterly. If composition is (according to Wagner's dictum) 'the art of
transition' then the *Sinfonia da Requiem* proves itself as a masterwork in
this respect.

An uninhibited delight in sonority and pianistic virtuosity *per se*
would appear to be the *raison d'être* of *Young Apollo*, a short occasional
piece for piano and strings composed for the Canadian Broadcasting
Corporation in 1939. The composer's decision to withdraw the piece after
initially giving it an opus number (16) does not seem without foundation,
for here – if we are to evaluate the music from a sonata standpoint – the
thematic invention and tonal scheme are little more than a glittering pro-
traction of a characteristically Lydian-inflected A major.

It cannot be long before the *Canadian Carnival* becomes popular with
audiences. The excitement, brilliance and tuneful accessibility of this
orchestral fantasy, composed during Britten's sojourn in Canada in 1939,
deserve better than to be consigned to the meretricious genre of the 'pot-
pourri'. Instead of the teleology, the development of themes, the whole
process of 'becoming' inseparable from sonata form, we have here a
mosaic of perpetual immediacy that suggests parallels with the
Shrovetide music of Stravinsky's *Petrushka*. (The association is especially
close in the central slow waltz episode, which suggests an analogy with
Stravinsky's hurdy-gurdy music.) It is an early example of Britten the
compulsive arranger, the Britten for whom homely tunes from near and
far remained a perpetual stimulus. But the placing and pacing of these
tunes, the smoothly engineered transitions and bald juxtapositions,
and the brilliantly clear chamber-style orchestration go beyond mere
'arrangement'. If Stravinsky comes to mind there is also a close parallel
with the fresh, open-air verve and panache of Copland's ballet scores or –
to take another contemporary close to Britten – with Shostakovich's
handling of popular material (the revolutionary songs in the first movement of the Eleventh Symphony, for example). The frame for all this

activity consists of a thrusting, fanfare-like tune, now evocative, now stir-ring, treated in the manner of an atmospheric prelude and postlude that fades in and out off stage. (This is an early example of a characteristic device in Britten that was to become famous via the *Serenade*.) Here, again, the influence of Mahler on Britten is self-evident – the posthorn solo of the Third Symphony, perhaps, or the fanfares of the second ('Nachtmusik') movement of the Seventh Symphony.

If the Violin Concerto and *Sinfonia da Requiem* remain the out-standing masterpieces of these years, two shorter works for piano and orchestra do not suffer in comparison. These are the elegant *Diversions* (1940) and the *Scottish Ballad* (1941) for piano left hand and two pianos respectively. The *Diversions* mark a return to Britten's perennial fascina-tion with variation form. In a sense they are offshoots of both the *Bridge Variations* and the Piano Concerto – suite-like, dramatic, highly informed by an element of burlesque that is in places used to serious expressive ends. Although, unlike the Piano Concerto, they are in no way sonata-like, they offer at the same time a more compact unity and continuity in variety – a chain of brilliantly contrasted variations that keep close to the epi-grammatic harmonic structure of the theme. The work, as its title sug-gests, is of course intended primarily as entertainment, but there are fleeting beauties and reflective depths to be encountered on the way. Britten's theme is something quite new: a quasi-march invention based on the interval of a fifth[15] cadencing at each of its resting points on a lumi-nous triad (major or minor). For all the parody of this (again somewhat Coplandesque) statement there is a touch of something not quite benign – and it is possible to trace a connection here with the similar intervallic construction of the twelve-note theme of *The Turn of the Screw*.[16] Thus the cadential woodwind and brass chords can seem to smile sardonically and the parodied classicism of the repeated chords of the C major coda with its thumping tonic-dominant timpani is unmistakably subversive. Such an ambiguous invention yields a closely knit yet contrasting sequence of variations that encompasses a wide range of expression: tender, brilliant, eloquent yet at the same time epigrammatically reticent (a case in point – the chordal chant in Variation V that looks forward to the 'Concord' choral dance in *Gloriana*), nocturnal, menacing, playful, sumptuously sonorous, irresponsibly cheerful. Amongst the notable contemporary influences on this score are those previously encountered in the Piano Concerto – especially that of Prokofiev (the third March Variation) and Ravel (the gloriously sonorous 'Adagio' which contains near-quotations from *Daphnis and Chloe*). The scoring for large orchestra, though massive enough in effect when necessary, is at the same time lithe and frequently soloistic; the virtuosic piano part a challenge to two hands, let alone one.

The *Scottish Ballad* for two pianos and orchestra juxtaposes the genres of strathspey and reel in what is, in effect, a Mahlerian funeral march in C minor (with a central F major Trio) followed by a hectic *moto perpetuo* highland fling. Once again we encounter Britten as arranger, for the whole work is based on three Scottish tunes: the hymn tune 'Dundee', the lament 'Turn ye to me' and 'The Flowers of the Forest'. In the funeral march (after the awesome solemnity of the hymnal/chordal introduction) the pianos make intense drum-rhythm contributions, loading the biting, wailing orchestral texture with tropes of menace and doom. The atmosphere of this dirge with its motivic concentration on the scotch snap (a favourite rhythmic motif) can be linked to two other north-of-the-border laments in Britten – the 'Lyke Wake Dirge' in the *Serenade* and the folksong setting 'Ye Highlands and ye Lowlands'. As in the 'Lyke Wake Dirge', the element of the grotesque is pressed into the service of the macabre. There is an exquisite sense of consolation in the shift to a higher tessitura for the cantilena of the trio, but the delight in sonority (after all, this is a display piece) – glissandi not excluded – continues unabated. A short, casual transition leads straight into the whooping gymnastics of the finale. Here is a piece that brilliantly combines elements of display, both orchestral and pianistic, with musical expression of a high order.

Dating from the same period is the last of Britten's American-period works for orchestra – the *American Overture* (1941), commissioned by the Cleveland Orchestra but not performed at the time. One has no hesitation in describing this overture as inspired and thoroughly characteristic – inspired in its eclectic response to 'American-ness', characteristic in what was to become familiar through later stylistic fingerprints. The brilliantly sonorous scoring is concerned with three main blocks of material, two slow and the third fast: a long-drawn-out processional fanfare over pizzicato stalking bass (with harp) of the type that the composer later utilized in, for example, *Gloriana* and *The Prince of the Pagodas*; a grandly sweeping chordal-triadic gesture, Coplandesque in its fresh simplicity (and linked to the kind of imagery that presents itself in the 'Chorus of Trees' at the beginning of *Paul Bunyan*); and a swirling arpeggio/fanfare allegro configuration punctuated with aggressive chords, recalling the Stravinsky of both *The Firebird* and the 'Sacrificial Dance' of *The Rite of Spring*. The bite and jazzy rhythms of the 'allegro' development lead to the triumphant return of chorale and fanfare in slow tempo. It has to be admitted that this overture possesses a drive and freshness of material, an excitement and sense of spaciously controlled climax, that the later – and arguably more perfunctory – *Occasional Overture* (1946) in the same vein seems unable to recapture.[17]

Example 12.3

Fugue subject entries at beginning of 'Allegro energico'

On Britten's return to England in 1943, a new work for string orchestra appeared amidst the clutch of beautiful vocal pieces immediately preceding *Peter Grimes* (including the incomparable *Serenade*, with its own inspired handling of the string orchestra). This is the *Prelude and Fugue for 18-Part String Orchestra*, composed for the tenth birthday of the Boyd Neel Orchestra in 1943. The piece (lasting a mere 8½ minutes) is not on the scale of the *Bridge Variations* but it achieves an impressive formal concentration and elegance that impart classical balance to a virtuoso exploitation of the medium. The work is in that characteristic 'frame' form which appears in other works of the period (e.g. *A Ceremony of Carols* and the *Serenade*) and the frame here is a rhetorical prelude marked 'Grave' which, when it returns at the end, interestingly transforms (and reverses the order of) its material. Its austere two-part texture (solo violin in counterpoint with orchestral octaves) deliberately contrasts with the effortlessly built up sonority of the eighteen-part fugue in which both harmonic/tonal plan and texture are astonishingly simple and clear by virtue of a reliance on triadic harmony – a feature prominently anticipated in the Prelude. As in the fugue of the *Bridge Variations*, Britten introduces a contrasting (and here canonic) cantilena for middle voices (second violins and violas), its shape deriving from the alternating falling steps and rising fourths of the fugue subject (see Ex. 12.3). The fugue (with its C major/A minor-orientated subject) heads finally for Britten's ever-beckoning D major but the prelude insists on D as a Mixolydian seventh in E major and the latter key wins out.

The choice of a theme by Purcell for *The Young Person's Guide to the Orchestra* (1946) has a certain resonance at this stage of Britten's development, for he had begun to feel a strong sense of identity with the great English composer (the 250th anniversary of whose death had been saluted in the Second String Quartet of the preceding year). The theme itself has that triadic, fanfare-like character which, standing in strong contrast to the modal meanderings of the English folk school, seemed to

Example 12.4 (a)

Example 12.4 (b)

attract the composer. In these variations Britten's mastery of the orchestra in all departments – percussion (which has a separate variation to itself) not excluded – is displayed, in conjunction with his considerable flair for sharp characterization and thematic transformation. To take but a single instance, the conversion of Purcell's theme into a Mahlerian cello cantilena is a miraculous piece of reshaping (by inversion and interversion) of the original motifs of the theme (see Ex. 12.4). Notable too are the cunningly devised transitions over which the speaker in the original film version introduces each new section – here is the 'operatic' film composer at work in the creation of witty, linking instrumental recitative. As in the *Bridge Variations*, fugue (more precisely a fugue-cum-passacaglia) is once again conscripted into service as a clinching finale, with Purcell's theme triumphantly reappearing in conjunction with Britten's lively fugue subject at the climax.

In a sense, this happy work brings to an end an important phase in Britten's career. From now on, the orchestra (in particular the chamber orchestra), with no less brilliance and subtlety, was to join forces with the vocal Britten, the Britten of opera and song-cycle, the Britten of *Saint Nicolas*, the *Spring Symphony* and the later choral cantatas. Yet the early orchestral repertoire holds its place and is gaining increasing recognition. Far from being a youthful corpus that was overtaken by the 'mature' opera composer, it survives as a brilliant achievement in itself, fully consistent with Britten's devotion to music as a language of human feeling.

13 The chamber music

PHILIP RUPPRECHT

This chapter examines Britten's relatively few mature works for conventional chamber ensemble – just three numbered string quartets – and four pieces written for the artistry of a single virtuoso instrumentalist: the Sonata in C, and the three solo Suites, all for the cellist Mstislav Rostropovich. The small number of works under discussion need not imply a lack of sympathy for purely instrumental composition on the part of a composer whose career was dominated by opera. Britten's precocious boyhood compositions include numerous chamber works (in 1926–8, for example, he wrote four pieces under the title 'String Quartet'), and this early involvement with chamber music – continued as a student at the Royal College, where Britten played piano trios regularly – was certainly reinforced by his contact with Frank Bridge. Much later in life, Britten wrote publicly of his debt to his teacher: 'He taught me to think and feel through the instruments I was writing for: he was most naturally an instrumental composer, and as a superb viola player he thought instrumentally.'[1]

The cello works for Rostropovich (and also the haunting *Nocturnal* for guitarist Julian Bream) are solitary, private statements, and they do not offer the chamber-musical interplay of voices within a group. In clarity of line and textural transparency, though, they encapsulate that aesthetic ideal of chamber music – in the composer's words, 'a subtlety, an intimacy . . . usually lacking in grander forms'[2] – that informs all of Britten's work.

Ideas for a string quartet appear alongside those for the *Sinfonia da Requiem* in Britten's 1940 sketchbook, but it was not until July 1941 that he could report to Elizabeth Mayer the final shape of his Quartet No. 1: '4 movements (Rondo–Scherzo–Andante–Finale) & in – would you believe it? – D major!!'[3] The first movement's 'Rondo' title (dropped in the published score) points to its ingenious form, and to the distinctiveness of Britten's previous approaches to the dialectical drama of sonata form in works of the early 1930s.[4] The quartet's alternation of strongly contrasting themes does suggest rondo procedure; but a characteristic sonata-form drama underlies the main formal return, with its synthesis of both themes.[5]

Arresting in its brilliance of sonority,[6] the canopy of shimmering

Figure 13.1 String Quartet No. 1/I: formal plan

	Andante sostenuto	Allegro vivo		Andante	Allegro			Andante	Allegro–Andante–Allegro		
Theme 1		2	3	1	3+2	1+2	1		2	1	2
	Introduction	Exposition		2nd Group *or* Rondo	Development	Return *or* Development	Rondo		Coda		
Tonic	D	(F)		D		F		(D)	D		D	
Bar	1	13		25	61	82	96	119	179	190	195	197

high-register pitches in the opening 'Andante' tempo is the timbral opposite of its successor, a questing 'Allegro vivo', poised on the more gutsy
sound of the cello's low C string. Typically for Britten, the ensuing dialogue, in what sounds like an exposition, effects a traversal of this vast,
ringing registral space. The form is delightfully hard to pin down (Fig.
13.1 summarizes main landmarks): the opening sounds at first like a slow
introduction, in the home tonic D major, but soon returns in F, apparently as a contrasting second thematic group. A brief developmental discussion dissolves abruptly, and suddenly we are surprised by familiar
gestures. It is now (bar 119) that the listener perceives, almost sub-
liminally, synthesis of the earlier dichotomy: below a twinkling registral
ceiling evoking the brilliance of the opening (back in D, though bright-
ened by Lydian G♯s), the more forthright questing theme reassembles
itself, at the same time spinning fresh melodic shapes. Is this development
or return? It is both; labels fail to capture the dynamic quality of a gradually dawning return, one that revisits earlier events but flows smoothly on.
Traversing the registral gamut from bass to treble in a single motion (bars
160–78), we are suddenly back to the opening andante premiss, the third
reprise of which now leads to a coda.

The compactness of the Rondo, and of the volatile and highly stylized
march-scherzo that follows, focuses attention on the third movement as
the quartet's emotional core. After the angular scherzo, one appreciates
the smooth melodic continuity of the 'Andante calmo' (based on a theme
in Britten's 1940 sketchbook). 'Calm' here is more than a reflective distance from surrounding animation: this is a return to a stasis that, in the
first movement, was glimpsed only for isolated moments, its spell continually broken by the allegro's rhythmic drive. The warm major-third
sounds opening the third movement establish the cyclic link, and allusions become more explicit in its central section, with a reworking of the
shimmering 'canopy' texture and a move sharpwards, back to D major.[7]

The movement's calm rests on placid tonic pedal points – a bed of
sound over which solo lines hover, suggesting quite independent tonal
claims within a single texture.[8] The result is kaleidoscopic in its tonal allusions. While cello and viola ascend smoothly within an enhanced B♭ major
mode, the violins range more widely, straining sharpwards (Ex. 13.1):

Example 13.1

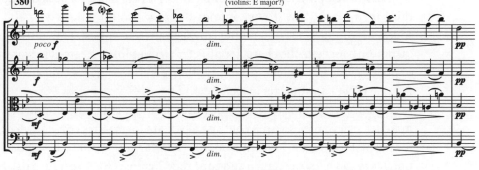

In the slow movement, Britten amalgamates divergent tonal strands to achieve an opulent density of sound; in the finale he reverts to more clear-cut assertions of tonal stability. The opening fugue is only mock-serious; the commanding presence is a sweeping melodic line given out in stirring unison. It is at such boldly direct moments, in fact, that one senses the stylistic change, a 'new confidence in simplicity',[9] that signals the close of Britten's American years.

If the First Quartet of 1941 represents a stylistic watershed, Quartet No. 2 in C, written four years later, confirms Britten's own perception of a stylistic 'advance'.[10] This is heard above all in the work's expansive conception, both within individual paragraphs, and in the cumulative effect of the entire three-movement span. And while the Second Quartet is only slightly longer in performance than the first, a full half of its length comes in the monumental finale, a chaconne with twenty-one variations. Once more, then, the form of each movement is best understood as part of a larger unfolding pattern of events.

Britten's title already hints at the quartet's quasi-cyclic status. All three movements are 'in C', and this monotonal anchoring, in fact, plays a role in those features of the first movement's sonata allegro that have attracted critical comment: its unorthodox opening, and its very concise conclusion. The opening departs from both tonal and thematic conventions by stating not one, but three distinct thematic groups in rapid succession, asserting not only the home tonic, C (with an eleven-bar tonic pedal point) but also the dominant key area, G, and *its* dominant, D (in pedals of equal duration). As Hans Keller remarked in a lucid analysis, we hear 'an exposition *within* the exposition'.[11] That impression is confirmed by the developmental caste of the subsequent argument, with elaborately worked counter-statements of all three opening themes – the second theme proper, for example (bars 80–111), has the first as its accompaniment.

Compared with the elaborately contrapuntal double-exposition, Britten's development section sounds loose, for its main focus is on the third theme only. The drama unfolds by stark confrontation: lyric episodes, 'tranquillo', are interrupted by 'agitato' outbursts. This musical dichotomy suggests the character of Peter Grimes himself, given to states of poetic calm and violent instability (the opera's scoring was finished by February 1945, the quartet in October).[12]

Britten's rethinking of the relationship of statement to development – in Keller's view, the essential contrast of sonata form – has consequences for the first movement's conclusion, which is startlingly brief (the exposition takes 148 bars; the return and coda together just 68). The return itself is more development than statement, for it conflates the three main themes in a dense contrapuntal web over a firm tonic pedal in the cello. A full sense of tonal balance arrives only in the coda, where Britten transforms the shifting modulatory pattern of the opening into a gesture of absolute tonal stability. Again, we hear three sustained pedal points, but all three now rest on the purest C major tonic.[13]

Adorno's cryptic remark about Beethoven – that one hears the music 'forward and backward at the same time'[14] – is suggestive in considering the suddenness of the first movement's ending, and the character of the following Scherzo. Timbrally, string mutes set this movement at a strange distance from framing events. Thematically, its hushed discussion combines memories of earlier events with gestures that prefigure future happenings (see Ex. 13.2). The cyclic links are effective precisely because they are shadowy; themes of a similar shape (a rising or falling fourth) sound oddly familiar, even when otherwise 'new'.

The finale's 'Chacony' title reflects both Britten's well-known admiration for Purcell and the specific occasion of the quartet's commission, the 250th anniversary of his death. The Chacony theme itself is Purcellian in its asymmetrical nine-bar plan, and its internal tonal mechanism – a journey from B♭ to C major – offers the potential for strikingly varied har-

Example 13.2

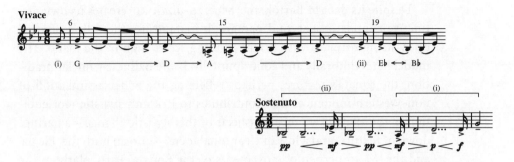

monic inflection within the extended variation sequence. Britten's own summing up – a 'review [of] the theme from (a) harmonic, (b) rhythmic, (c) melodic, and (d) formal aspects'[15] – describes the movement's layout, but not the impressive coherence of its fifteen-minute span, or the inevitability of its triumphant C major homecoming.

The theme is introduced in a plain unison, and a first group of six variations explore diverse harmonic settings, only resolving directly to C major in the cello cadenza ending variation 6. The six rhythmic variations continue to evade home-tonic emphasis. The viola cadenza, then, points the way for a journey back to tonal clarity. Variations 13–18 establish our distance from that goal by a pronounced textural separation into tonally discrete strata (the effect is more sustained and intricate than in Quartet No. 1). With the Chacony theme hidden as an inner voice, a new melodic outpouring appears in the violins. Tempo and mood relax in this brief slow movement, laying the ground for the spectacular triumph of the violin cadenza and final three variations. The closing tutti's brilliance is all the more magnificent in a piece in which the earlier movements have both vanished into silence.

The Sonata in C for cello and piano, completed for Rostropovich in January 1961, marks Britten's return to instrumental composition after a decade dominated by texted music. Britten referred to the piece as a Sonatina[16] and its modest dimensions – five short movements, under 20 minutes in all – reflect a certain precision of utterance. The opening sonata form is, in Britten's description, a concentrated 'discussion of a tiny motive of a rising or falling second', and the title, 'Dialogo', is apt for such a carefully balanced exchange of melodic phrases and dramatic roles between the two instruments. Animated triplets appear first in the piano, then in the cello; the tranquil second theme balances prime and inversion phrases almost as clearly as does the boys' choir at 'Te decet hymnus' in the *War Requiem* (written in the same year). Formally too, exposition and return are balanced in a sonata scheme closer to classical models than any in the quartets.

Despite its debt to Bartók, the 'Scherzo-pizzicato' creates its own distinctive sounds in a second paragraph juxtaposing the cello's plucked open-string ostinato with bright running scales high in the piano. The model here, timbrally and contrapuntally, is the Balinese gamelan tradition, the sonata's textures perhaps reflecting the wider assimilation of non-Western influences that contributes to Britten's stylistic reorientation in the 1960s. Two related aspects of this stylistic change – a paring-down of texture, and a loss of clear tonal focus – inform both the 'Elegia' and the 'Moto perpetuo' movements of the Sonata. Particularly in the 'Elegia', voices are essentially thickenings of a single, monodic line; when these acquire rhythmic independence, the result is as close to Balinese heterophony as to European note-against-note counterpoint. The intervening 'Marcia' recalls the satire prominent in Britten's works of the 1930s, here renewed with vehemence on the eve of his most public statement on the malice of war.[17]

The three Suites for Cello (composed in 1964, 1967 and 1971) belong with the Sonata as products of Britten's friendship with Rostropovich. The Suites continue, in the self-imposed austerity of the solo medium, Britten's experiments in the Church Parables with textures built around a single melodic line. A more elusive quality, too, growing from the ritual of performance itself, seems to link the Suites with the Parables. The Parables reduce thematic activity to a few simple, stylized gestures, repeated almost obsessively, but creating in the process the 'intensity and concentration' of effect Britten so admired in Japanese Nō drama.[18] In the Cello Suites, such intensity grows from the additional rhythmic freedom open to the solo player. Though Britten scrupulously notates dynamics and phrasing, much of the music is non-metrical (bar lengths vary). In movements such as the 'Ciaccona' of the Second Suite, and the 'Introduzione' to the Third, Britten employs the fermata pause – a sign indicating an event of deliberately unspecified duration – at numerous phrase endings. The notation aspires, paradoxically, to the absolute spontaneity of an improvisation.

In the character pieces of the First Suite, the musical atmosphere evolves from the pacing of brief, repeated gestures: guitar-like chords in the 'Serenata'; in the 'Marcia', *flautato* arpeggios and *col legno* taps on the open strings. The static drone of the 'Bordone', likewise, risks monotony unless the player pushes the music on towards the rhythmic and tonal release of the succeeding 'Moto Perpetuo'.

Formally, the First Suite is all of a piece: six contrasting instrumental scenes follow one another without pauses, and are framed by a recurring 'Canto'. The Second Suite uses a simpler groundplan (five self-contained movements), but in the Third, Britten again favours cumulative progression by linking together nine short movements without a break. The melodic ideas in each movement derive from a common pool of three Russian folksongs and an ancient hymn tune, sources unveiled only at the conclusion. Britten here amalgamates his own earlier reverse-variation practice (in *Lachrymae* (1950) for viola and piano and the *Nocturnal* (1963) for guitar, both based on songs by John Dowland) with the formal procedure of Shostakovich's later quartets, which he greatly admired.[19] Another kind of thematic return will form the crux of Britten's final chamber work.

Quartets Nos. 1 and 2 were both occasional works, composed to commission. String Quartet No. 3, on the other hand, was written under the difficult circumstances following Britten's heart operation in 1973; almost the last score he completed, it is a piece of considerable personal significance. By adding a subtitle, 'La Serenissima', to the Finale, Britten drew attention to five thematic self-quotations from the opera *Death in Venice*; evocative titles for the preceding movements – 'Duets', 'Ostinato', 'Solo', 'Burlesque' – likewise hint at a dramatic context for the work's varied mood sequence. Britten initially called the piece a 'Divertimento', and while titles and thematic references set the Third Quartet apart from its more abstract predecessors, its five-movement arch creates the sense of inevitability common to works of high formal integrity. With its suppleness of gesture, stunning control of instrumental sonority, and sheer expressivity, the Third Quartet is, simply, Britten's most moving chamber work.

Britten's consciousness, while composing *Death in Venice* in 1972, of failing health ('I wanted passionately to finish this piece before anything happened'[20]) had lent the opera's plot an uneasy topicality. Work on the quartet, in October and November 1975, was marked by still greater urgency. As Donald Mitchell suggests, Britten's quotation of Aschenbach's agitated Act I melody – 'While this Sirocco blows / Nothing delights me. My head is heavy, My eyelids ache' – has clear autobiographical overtones.[21]

My discussion of the Third Quartet takes the Finale's *Death in Venice* quotations as only the most explicit among many links between opera and instrumental work. I begin with the Finale, where the quotations are explicit, and where there is a close link to the ending of the opera's first act.

Subsequently, I explore ways in which earlier movements, 'Duets' in particular, establish, by more subtle and indirect operatic allusions, a context for the Finale's literal quotations.

The listener who knows *Death in Venice* will certainly sense its reflection in the quartet. Intertextual resonances, though, do not imply that one must hear in the later score some new chapter in Aschenbach's biography. Precisely because the quartet's quotations are 'mute' (no words appear in the score), its relationship to the opera is best understood at the level of gestural resemblances rather than as a translation of dramatic details. Britten's comment on the quartet's final bars – 'I want the work to end with a question'[22] – on the other hand, does affirm the quartet's gestural kinship with the opera: the music of the quartet, like Aschenbach's, is music of searching.

Self-quotation is rare in Britten's music, and – unlike the reworking in the *War Requiem* of Canticle II (see p. 268) – the quartet's operatic quotations do not exploit verbal meanings in creating their dramatic effect. The local setting of their appearance, though, does suggest an intrusion from 'beyond' the immediate context: edgy cluster sonorities surround each thematic fragment, keeping it at a distance from the here-and-now of the quartet. Only in the final, tutti gesture does the atmosphere clear, making way for the Beethovenian paradox of an instrumental *voice*: a speaking presence without words.

Each of the quoted melodies is associated in the opera directly with Aschenbach, and each is heard, in the quartet, in a different solo 'voice'.[23] As a group, they present a Recitative fantasy leading into the Passacaglia proper: the 'Serenissima' barcarolle of Aschenbach's gondola trips (cello); the melody of his pursuit of Tadzio (violin 2); a phrase from Tadzio's Act I solo dance, recalled in the Act II 'Phaedrus' aria (violin 1); the 'Sirocco' theme mentioned above (viola, pizzicato); and, in climactic tutti, the 'ridiculous, but sacred' vow ending Act I – 'I love you' (see Ex. 13.3).

The order of these quotations defies the opera's plot sequence, but their presence, and a further recollection of the 'Phaedrus' melody late in the Passacaglia (violin 1, bar 89), has prompted a programmatic interpretation of the quartet's overall plan.[24] David Matthews hears in the work a continuation, 'on a purely musical level', of Aschenbach's 'quest for transcendence'. 'The quartet is about the rediscovery of stability', Matthews suggests; the finale returns to E major, Aschenbach's personal key in Act I of the opera, and that of his 'I love you' vow, as the completion of his redemption.[25]

The musical link between quartet and opera traced by Matthews is evident in a further parallel between the scores, one of formal scheme. In *Death in Venice*, Britten captures the reckless obsession of Aschenbach's pursuit of Tadzio with a passacaglia, its bass chromatically distorting the

'love' motif (see p. 161).[26] But whereas the revolutions of the operatic passacaglia chart spiritual decadence, the quartet presents its *alter ego*, a
process of reconstruction. Restoration of Aschenbach's E major comes
about by dawning tonal clarity (see Ex. 13.3): a sustained pedal C, hanging
provisionally in the inner voices, is gently displaced by the E tonality
(major mode, but with Mixolydian D♮ inflections) of the theme and its
melodic counterpoint.[27] Britten literally 'marks' the return to E major: its
key signature reappears only by stages, underlining its association with
'La Serenissima' and with Aschenbach.[28]

The Passacaglia's decisive restitution of Aschenbach's E tonality itself
reworks the rhetorical and tonal sequence concluding the opera's first act.
There, a vast orchestral crescendo, on C, gives way to Aschenbach's unaccompanied 'I love you' over an E pedal-drone. The tonal motion from C to
E corresponds to Aschenbach's sudden realization of his erotic feelings for
Tadzio. The quartet's passacaglia emerges in a comparable moment of
musical truth, an epiphany in its harmonic transfiguration of the 'love'
motif: in Ex. 13.3, x is octatonic, y diatonic. And the deeper logic is tonal,
for the tonal pairing of C and E major is prominent elsewhere in the
quartet and throughout the opera.

Britten's keys always bear highly characteristic ambiences, and the
quartet's pairing of C and E has precedents throughout *Death in Venice*.[29]
In Aschenbach's feverish thoughts of union with Tadzio (Ex. 13.4), for
instance, the rising-third aspect of the 'love' motif appears on both E and
C tonics (a reversal of Ex. 13.3) in a melody of uncertain mode. As the
opera unfolds, the tonal and motivic shape of such moments is increasingly familiar, establishing numerous musico-dramatic associations for
the listener. Returning to the Third Quartet – in particular, its first movement, 'Duets' – one hears in the music's darting key changes and sudden
realizations a close affinity to the opera's gestural world.

Within the sonata-like scheme of 'Duets',[30] a compact exposition is
dominated by tonally diffuse music recalling Aschenbach's intellectual
exhaustion at the opera's opening. The point-like sequence of isolated
high and low pitches that forms around the opening duet is, like
Aschenbach's music, a twelve-note unfolding, and a creeping second
theme (bar 19) reworks the contour of Aschenbach's melody, 'My mind
beats on', with its precise balancing of prime and inversion phrases.[31] A
second twelve-note row appears, but its chromatic saturation is banished
by the surprise of richly diatonic C major sonorities, anchored by a sustained viola C.

But is the C major of 'Duets' really a continuation of that in the opera?
Ex. 13.5 shows a second move from amorphous chromaticism to C major
clarity, soon after the movement's recapitulation is under way.[32] The
arrival of the added-sixth chord here (Ex. 13.5, second bar) is perhaps the

Example 13.3

Example 13.4

Example 13.5

most arresting event in the movement, both tonally and timbrally – chordal warmth comes after a passage of glassy-sounding harmonics. It is also a recollection of a specific moment late in the opera's second act, Aschenbach's imaginary Socratic dialogue by the well ('Does beauty lead to wisdom, Phaedrus?'). In the quartet, as in the opera, the C^6 chords are a vision of tranquillity amid chromatic surroundings. In both scores, this vision fades. In the quartet's opening movement, though, the disappearance of C makes way for another luminous diatonic presence: E major (see Ex. 13.5, last bar).

Plate 19 String Quartet No. 3, composition sketch; first movement, pp. 4–5

Britten's attention to the C/E major pairing in 'Duets' is evident in the manuscript itself (Plate 19). Remarkably, his first notation of the passage was not directed towards E major at all; the crossed-out draft cadences a semitone higher, to an F major tonic (the faint pencil sketch – top system, last bar – shows an A/F double stop in the viola). But it is Britten's revision, moving from C to E major, that corresponds directly to the harmonic idiom of the opera, at the same time prefiguring the tonal progression of the entire quartet. The sketch process here strikingly recalls that of the opera's Act I finale, also notated first in F, and then transposed down a semitone.[33] Aschenbach's first stage appearance in *Death in Venice* establishes a tense fluctation between both keys, and Britten's later hesitancy, when composing 'Duets', underlines both the movement's tendency to evade direct tonal affirmation, and its closeness – at the level of harmonic and tonal syntax – to the world of the opera.

Colin Matthews, who assisted Britten on 22 and 23 October 1975 as he checked his sketch of the quartet's first two movements, recalls the com-

Plate 19 (*cont.*)

poser's thoughts about this passage in relation to the quartet's larger scheme:

> Ben originally considered cutting [bars 64 to 75], on the grounds that the movement was too long. . . Ben was, however, rather reluctant to make this cut and, when the finale [completed in November] proved to be much longer than he had expected, he was ready, without much prompting, to restore the passage so that the first movement would 'balance' the finale.[34]

Britten's choice of a direct motion from C to E major in the closing moments of 'Duets' establishes a balance that is architectural and tonal. The decisive motions from C to E in the quartet's outer movements are symmetrically arrayed about the radiant C major celebration concluding the third movement ('Solo'), the keystone of the composition's formal arch (Fig. 13.2).

Fig. 13.2 suggests, in précis, ways in which Britten's five-movement scheme builds towards the arrival on C major concluding 'Solo', and away

Figure 13.2 String Quartet No. 3: prominent tonal references

Movement:	Duets	Ostinato	Solo	Burlesque	Recitative and Passacaglia
Tonal definition:	C, E allusions	E/C strata	A♭–F–A–F–A♭–C	A–E♭ ('Trio') – A ('maggiore')	initial E pedal
	C-to-E motion (Ex. 13.5)	–	–	–	C-to-E motion (Ex. 13.3)
	ends on V of C	ends on V of C	ends in C	–	ends 'with a question'

from it, towards Aschenbach's E major in the Passacaglia. In 'Solo', we at last reach the tonic glimpsed in 'Duets', yet side-stepped at the movement's close (a half-cadence to V), only to reappear as an assertive bass-register presence throughout 'Ostinato'. Only in the fourth movement 'Burlesque', in A minor, is the tonal force of C dormant. Britten had used the title 'alla Burlesca' in a quartet as early as 1933 (the piece became one of the *Three Divertimenti* of 1936), but the Third Quartet's 'Burlesque', in its key, thematic character, and in overall strenuousness of mood, refers quite directly to the 'Rondo-Burleske' of Mahler's Ninth Symphony. In the sardonic tone of its 'Trio', amid the disconcerting whistlings of a viola bowed on the 'wrong side of the bridge', Britten pays another homage: to Shostakovich, who had died in August 1975.

An interpretation of the Third Quartet's tonal resonances would be incomplete without some comment on the Passacaglia's celebrated lack of cadential repose. On one level, Britten's decision 'to end with a question' might be understood as a defamiliarizing gesture – a way of drawing attention to the arbitrary quality of any halt to the flow of musical time. The Quartet ends – as does *Death in Venice* – with a single note, sustained in the act of disappearance: 'dying away', as the verbal markings in both scores read. In the wider context of the complete Quartet, though, the Passacaglia's 'non-end' (Hans Keller) prompts the listener to re-evaluate the nature of what has gone before. The eloquence of the Passacaglia's closing 'question' resides in its effect on one's understanding of the form of the piece as a whole. Evading any definitive signal for ending, the Third Quartet imbues those earlier moments of C major warmth – in 'Duets', and, most brilliantly, at the end of 'Solo' – with a closural significance that is all the more poignant because in some sense retrospective.

The specific colouring of the C major triads in 'Duets' and 'Solo' with the added sixth, A (as in Ex. 13.5, second bar), looks back, I have noted, to the visionary clarity of Aschenbach's 'Phaedrus' aria. In the opera, Britten distances the first C/A major sixths (before Fig. 308) from surrounding reality by a timbral shift to muted string harmonics. In 'Duets', the C^6 chords themselves are restored to a fuller string tone, and it is the final chordal sonority – a shimmering cloud of harmonics, spanning every register – that signals a perception detached from the everyday. Beyond the quite direct musical links between opera and quartet, though, the reference is to a more distant precursor: the final, unresolved chord of 'Der Abschied' in Mahler's *Das Lied von der Erde*.[35] (See Donald Mitchell's remarks on p. 333, note 6.) Traces of that unmistakable sonority accompany the moment of Phaedra's death in the cantata Britten completed immediately before the quartet.[36] What is remarkable, in the Third Quartet, is Britten's decision to place Mahler's original symbol of departure at the heart of his score, not at its end.

14 Music for voices

RALPH WOODWARD

From his early boyhood, Britten seems to have been fascinated by the musical possibilities inherent in words; as he later explained, he was initially exposed to 'a catholic choice of poets'.[1] Several early de la Mare settings were revised and published in 1969 as *Tit for Tat*, and he also set French poetry, amplifying his comment to Murray Schafer that he was 'not a linguist, but I pride myself that I have a feel for languages'.[2] While still at school, he began to write music for vocal ensembles. *A Wealden Trio*, *Sweet was the Song the Virgin Sung* and three de la Mare settings (all for women's voices), as well as *The Sycamore Tree* (for SATB), were revised for publication in the 1960s, but *A Hymn to the Virgin* (for double choir) was released with minor changes (including transposition down a semitone) as early as 1934.[3] The text is a modernized version of a fourteenth-century macaronic original; although the setting is largely syllabic, the melody is increasingly allowed to blossom for the Latin phrases which cap each line of verse. If Britten's 'Englishness' is often overlooked, in choice of text at least he follows the example of Vaughan Williams, Holst and Warlock, as he does in the recently unearthed *Thy King's Birthday* (1931).

Mediaeval lyrics were also to be the starting-point for his first extended choral work, *A Boy was Born* (1932–3). This is a set of choral variations on a theme which is itself an unfolding of a basic three-note cell (z), subsequently subjected to the intense motivic working demonstrated in Ex. 14.1a–j. Several features of the work relate to aspects of the mature Britten. First, his handling of the texts: it is a bold stroke to superimpose the fifteenth-century *Corpus Christi Carol* and Christina Rossetti's *In the Bleak Midwinter*, but Britten does not shrink from the stylistic contrast, drawing attention to it through a differentiation of colour (between boys' and female voices) and variety of metre (boys in 12/8, women in 4/4). A fascination with details of colour is also evident in the 'Glory to God on high' of the finale, when the choir explores changing timbres on a unison middle D, heralding a return to the tonic key and the work's theme; in 'The Three Kings', a quasi-instrumental 'Ah' provides rhythmic and harmonic support for the melodic strands. The reprise of earlier thematic ideas in the finale indicates a composer already seeking to organize his vocal music along absolute lines.

Britten's next choral work, the *Te Deum* in C, posed a different set of

Example 14.1
© Oxford University Press, 1934

challenges. It is a long text, and much set, so that to choose it is to invite comparison with Stanford, Elgar and others. Britten's response is typically direct: to impose a firm musical structure onto the words, in fact a clear derivative of sonata form – complete with a 'second subject' in the submediant, and tonic recapitulation thereof. The tonally assertive function of a 'first subject' is fulfilled by the extended exposition of C major triads at the opening (the same idea is reprised later, with the predominantly homorhythmic texture transformed into pealing Monteverdian polyrhythms); not until the E♭ at bar 54 does a note alien to C major appear.

While the subject of the 1936 orchestral song-cycle *Our Hunting Fathers* is ostensibly animals, there can be no doubt that the message is fundamentally about man's inhumanity in general. Britten's mentor and collaborator was W. H. Auden, who had introduced him to a wide variety of artistic, political, social and, perhaps, sexual thought, and whose relationship with the composer is examined in more detail elsewhere (see Chapter 2).[4] The work is unified by a five-note cell, its juxtaposition of major and minor infiltrating many structural moments; Peter Evans points to the intensive use of this shape and to the work's quasi-symphonic structure as evidence of Britten's 'determination . . . to brace his word-settings by some "absolute" principle'.[5] A significant model for Britten in this respect may have been Alban Berg, with whom he nearly studied, and whose opera *Wozzeck* uses absolute forms, so that Act II, for instance, is a 'symphony' in five movements; the concept of an orchestral song-cycle reveals Britten's spiritual kinship with the Mahler of *Das Lied von der Erde* and the *Kindertotenlieder*. An aspect of *Our Hunting Fathers* which must have struck its first audience more forcibly is the virtuosity of the writing for soprano solo, foreshadowing that in the following year's major Britten–Auden collaboration, *On This Island*.

The five songs of *On This Island* established features common to many Britten song-cycles; they do not (unlike, for instance, Schubert's *Die schöne Müllerin*) present a narrative, but instead offer contrasts of mood and, indeed, technique. This in itself may reveal the influence of Auden, for, as Peter Porter has stated, 'Britten's song-cycles of mixed origin show a poetic taste which reflects Auden's many popular compilations . . . [they] are much more like Auden's vision of poetry than any other literary person's.'[6] The first song opens in an opulent, neo-baroque, triadic D major, complete with fanfare figures for the piano, before turning to an even more overtly Purcellian G minor in 6/4. Debussy is arguably recalled in the third song, Fauré in the fourth and Walton in the fifth: Britten's deliberate eclecticism here surely highlights the mercurial spirit of Auden's verse. 'Fish in the unruffled lakes' springs from the same year and the same partnership, and its piano part is a typical Britten response to watery imagery.

Auden's advocacy of the works of Rimbaud may have resulted in Britten's use of them for *Les illuminations* (1939). Harmonically, much stems from the conflict between B♭ and E, which is presented in the most explicit terms at the opening. Having twice dissolved into C major, the clash is finally sounded six bars before the end of the cycle and allowed to 'resolve' onto E♭ major. Various reminders along the way keep the structural dissonance active; for instance, 'Antique' ends on a serene B♭ major, immediately gainsaid by the forceful E major of 'Royauté'. As would become common in the operas, a voiceless Interlude dwells on some of the thematic material midway through the cycle. Paul Hamburger[7] has written eloquently about the hermeticism of Britten the composer and of many of the poets whose work he set: Auden, Rimbaud, Blake and Donne, for example, to which list could be added Christopher Smart, Edith Sitwell, William Soutar and T. S. Eliot. Britten shows a preference for poets whose language is mystical, even abstruse, partly because they tend to draw on a wide range of images that are highly beneficial to a composer, but also because such verse aptly counterpoints the understated and cerebral nature of Britten's own creative personality. The use of foreign texts fits into this picture; as Porter has said, 'the foreign language brings out an answering hermeticism, a command to the oracular'.[8] So it is fitting that Britten's next major vocal work, in 1940, should be the *Seven Sonnets of Michelangelo*, in Italian; he felt that these two works 'were necessary for me in order to shed the bad influences of the Royal College. With both the French and the Italian I was perhaps responding to Nietzsche's call to "mediterraneanize music".'[9]

The Michelangelo settings were another departure for Britten. Here the essence is unfolding melody, with phrases inverted, abridged, extended and otherwise modified, as distinct from the Germanic approach of harmonically based forms with which Britten had been brought up. Britten himself may have provided a clue to the work's genesis when he wrote of Verdi's 'long, casual lines, a succession of apparently unrelated phrases, which repeated hearings discover to have an enormous tension deep below the surface'.[10] It would be a mistake to think, though, that Britten eschews harmonic planning in these songs. Not only are harmonic contrasts effectively deployed and harmonic ambiguities exploited to match the text's ambivalence (notably at the end of the fourth song), but a clear harmonic design is always in evidence, while the ritornello form of the final song anticipates Britten's later use of ground basses. This was the first song-cycle to be written expressly for Peter Pears, and the influence of Pears's voice can be heard in the frequent use, especially for long notes, of high E, which might be regarded as Pears's 'best' note – and around which Britten would later construct the whole of the aria 'Now the Great Bear' in Act I of *Peter Grimes*.

In the period 1942–3, during the gestation of *Grimes*, Britten composed two major choral works: another Auden setting, the *Hymn to St Cecilia* (for unaccompanied choir) and *Rejoice in the Lamb* (with organ).

The happy chance of Britten's sharing a birthday with the patron saint of music doubtless contributed to Auden's composition of his Cecilian poem, and its numerous musical references permit Britten to indulge in vocal imitations of the violin, drum, flute and trumpet; these are not merely naive word-painting, but are related to motivic material elsewhere in the piece. Britten makes Auden's structure more coherent by treating the 'Blessed Cecilia' section as a refrain, to be repeated once reharmonized and once to the music which opened the *Hymn*; this re-alignment of text and lyrics is a particularly deft touch. A highly original choral scherzo sets the text 'I cannot grow', while there is overall a careful weighting of harmonic areas to let the C/E ambivalence function and ultimately be resolved in favour of E. Some transitional harmonies have a duality of function which seems to be a musical counterpart to Auden's reverberant text.

The seemingly disparate movements of *Rejoice in the Lamb* are unified by the motifs of an oscillating perfect fourth, and a rising scale (x) followed by a falling triad (y): see Ex. 14.2a–g. The Purcellian verse-anthem is evoked in the dotted-note, contrapuntal 'Hallelujah'. Describing Purcell's songs, Britten spoke of their 'independent, short sections mysteriously linked by subtle contrasts of key, mood, and rhythm' and the 'firm and secure musical structure which can safely hold together and make sense of one's wildest fantasies',[11] words equally applicable to *Rejoice in the Lamb*.

With the *Serenade* of 1943 we reach one of Britten's most famous pieces, and it is consequently easy to forget how original was the idea to take six poems from different authors, spanning four centuries, and link them into a single piece; for a precedent, one would have to look to Mahler's *Kindertotenlieder*, but here Britten celebrates his English literary heritage in contrast to his earlier song-cycles. This is an instance of what Christopher Palmer has called Britten's ability 'to find connections between poems not intended by their creators to be linked in a chain'.[12] The identical Prologue and Epilogue for solo horn by which Britten lends the cycle a rounded shape are to be played on natural harmonics only; this means that some of the notes sound 'out of tune', obviously an idea that fascinated Britten (compare the similar cow-horn effect in the *Spring Symphony*). In Blake's 'Elegy', the horn's falling semitone figure, which generates the twelve-note melody of the introduction, is an apt musical illustration of the blight in the rose, and is eventually played in the final bars using horn handstopping, a magical idea which lends the flattened third an additionally eerie timbre. The G/G♯ oscillation is then picked up by the tenor as G/A♭ for the 'Lyke Wake Dirge', in which the voice unfolds the same six-bar theme nine times over an instrumental fugato in which

Example 14.2

irregular phrase lengths do not come into focus until the horn's dramatic entry. In setting Ben Jonson's 'Hymn to Diana', Britten chooses a form and manner akin to a baroque aria, and then rests the horn for the concluding Keats Sonnet, which commences with four chords bearing a well-documented similarity to those that open Act II of *A Midsummer Night's Dream*.[13]

The Holy Sonnets of John Donne were written in 1945 after the successful première of *Peter Grimes*, and a great seriousness pervades the cycle, which builds to a confrontation with death inspired in part by Britten's recent recital tour of Nazi concentration camps with Yehudi Menuhin. The unifying idea is an opposition between B and C minors, implied when the voice sings a C minor triad over a dominant pedal of B minor in bars 5–7 (see Ex. 14.3). This key defers to C minor for the second song, in which the chromatic central section reaches B minor before a swift return to C, and the direct opposition continues in the third, which is built largely on an oscillation between the notes B and C. The two following sonnets then expose the minor dominants of the two keys (F♯ minor and G minor) and Nos. 6, 7 and 8 juxtapose their mediants (D and E♭); E♭/D♯ appears to be victorious, for the final song is in B major. And, just as Britten closed his Michelangelo cycle with a repetition-based form, so this cycle ends with a passacaglia over a five-bar ground. Even the way Britten moves between the songs enhances their impact. The piano's repeated G–F–E♭ figure at the end of No. 5 sets up an expectation which makes the voice's decorated G–F–E♮ at the start of No. 6 all the more to be savoured. The first dyad of the final song (F♯ and D♯) is ambiguous, following as it does an E♭ minor triad, so that the new tonality is not immediately assured. Certain features remind the listener of *Peter Grimes*: the Lydian D major and piano flourishes in No. 7 are strongly reminiscent of the opening to Act II, while No. 8, pitting D against F♭ in the context of E♭ minor, takes us back to the start of the Storm Interlude. The contrast between syllabic and melismatic treatments is masterly, allowing Britten to vary phrase lengths at will. Music, of course, functions across a time-span, unlike written poetry, and to neglect the changeable pace implicit in great poetry is to diminish it. This is what Hans Keller meant when he said that Britten's 'verbal inspiration was intimately bound up with his ability to create tensions between musical and verbal rhythm; these tensions were of a magnitude that made it possible for him to create extended structures with comparative ease'.[14] One need look no further than Purcell for a model; if we consider the opening of *I Attempt from Love's Sickness to Fly in Vain* (realized by Britten in 1960), we can see how skilfully Purcell transforms a rather four-square verse into two phrases of five and seven bars' length respectively, by means of repetition and melisma.

In 1947, Britten wrote his first Canticle, a form which he acknowledged to be 'a new invention . . . although it was certainly modelled on the Purcell *Divine Hymns*'.[15] We should not forget that Britten's declared aim was to 'restore to the musical setting of the English language a brilliance, freedom and vitality that have been curiously rare since the death of Purcell'.[16] In this piece, Purcell's example is followed by the imparting of a musical structure to a poem which, despite its recurrent refrain, was not ideal for setting to music. While using the interval of a sixth to unify the work, Britten strongly differentiates its sections by various harmonic and textural means. In the recitative section, Britten creates a blurred piano texture by the superimposition of black notes in one hand onto white notes in the other; this device, reminiscent of both Berg and Bartók, was seen in the 'Seascape' movement from *On This Island* and appears again in the first song of *A Charm of Lullabies*, though its most important usage is in the recitatives in *Death in Venice*, where it creates twelve-tone aggregates.

Example 14.3

A Charm of Lullabies is, like the Serenade, a diverse collection of poems dealing with aspects of the same subject. The placid outer songs enclose a darker core, in particular Thomas Randolph's threatening 'Charm', which grafts a memorable 7/4 rhythm onto the text as if the poet had intended it; the 'Lydian' D minor of its close anticipates 'Welcome Maids of Honour' from the Spring Symphony. The shape of the final song's recurrent opening owes something to the 'Lyke Wake Dirge' in the Serenade, but the harmony is much more stable; modulations are brief and unthreatening, and lyricism is allowed to blossom.

Having completed Billy Budd in 1951, the next work upon which Britten embarked was the second Canticle, Abraham and Isaac, which deals with a similar subject: the unwilling sacrifice of an innocent youngster because it appears to be ordained by a higher force. In the Canticle, that higher force is given speech, in the homorhythmic combination of alto and tenor to depict the voice of God – a brilliant solution to the problem of performing a three-character piece with a cast of two. The interval of a third is a vital constituent of almost every phrase; the sequentially falling thirds which the alto sings at 'For aught that may befall' return ingeniously as the bass-line at the start of the recitative 'O! My heart will break in three', a passage which includes triads on ten of the twelve possible roots with very little repetition, the eleventh (F♯) appearing melodically a few bars before, and the twelfth (E♭) a few bars after. This reflects Britten's growing interest in dodecaphony at this time, which had discernibly touched his technique in *Billy Budd*, leading to the repeated near-exhaustion of all twelve triadic roots in the 'Mist' Interlude (Act II, Figs. 50–7) and the twelve-note chord before Vere's 'Scylla and Charybdis' (Act II, Fig. 73⁻¹).

In the wider context of Britten's oeuvre, however, the most striking thing about *Canticle II* is the way he later re-used much of it in the *War Requiem* when dealing with Wilfred Owen's chilling parody of the same story. The phrase 'Make thee ready, my dear darling' from the Canticle becomes 'Quam olim Abrahae promisisti', and at Fig. 69 in the Requiem the chamber orchestra imitates the piano texture at that point in the Canticle. The Requiem's 'Father, Behold the preparations' borrows from the Canticle's 'O! My heart will break in three', and the passages depicting the binding of Isaac are closely related. God's intervention in the Canticle produced a return to the work's fifthless opening chord of E♭ major; in the Requiem, the angel's intervention produces the same chord, now sounding, through its transposition to C major, even more like the end of Stravinsky's *Symphony of Psalms*. The angel's voice is represented by homorhythmic writing for the tenor and baritone, and ultimately the sequential melody from 'For aught that may befall' is inverted. For those who are familiar with the Canticle, there is certainly an extra sardonic edge to those moments in the Requiem when we hear the earlier piece twisted, as Owen's Abram slays 'half the seed of Europe, one by one'.[17]

Throughout these years Britten produced a number of choral works in response to commissions. The *Festival Te Deum* (1945) takes as its principal technical feature the non-alignment of rhythm between choir and organ. The organ progresses in a steady 3/4, while the choir's bar-lengths vary constantly. The quicker central section abandons non-alignment and invents some effective syncopated rhythms for the words; a treble solo ushers in a reprise of the earlier texture, now with an active, chromatic pedal line, until at 'O Lord, in Thee have I trusted' all the forces converge rhythmically into 3/4, and harmonically onto the tonic, E major. *A Wedding Anthem* (1949) is a rarely performed but nonetheless enjoyable piece; the soprano and tenor soloists have some attractive music and the harmonic plan is simple but well contrived.

The *Five Flower Songs* are almost universally undervalued; as demonstrations of how to write twentieth-century madrigals they could scarcely be bettered, particularly in the diversity of their choral textures. 'To Daffodils' pairs soprano rhythmically with bass, and alto with tenor. The second Herrick setting ('The Succession of the Four Sweet Months') sounds at first like a four-voice fugue; in fact, the entries are subtly modified to lend unique character to each of the four months (April to

July) described. 'Marsh Flowers' adopts the more conventional partner-ship of soprano/tenor versus alto/bass; the rising glissandi are an original touch and the canon 4-in-2 gracefully conceived, while the seaweeds' rolling is conveyed by a circular phrase heard against its own inversion. The lyrical harmonies of the John Clare setting ('The Evening Primrose') give it a particularly intimate air; yet the implications of 6/8 over the underlying 4/4 avoid predictability and the song closes with a highly expressive double canon by inversion. The final, tongue-twisting number is a joyous romp which audiences love.

The *Hymn to Saint Peter* (1955) is based on the plainsong 'Tu es petrus', which is stated on the organ and then imitated by the choir while the pedals play an eleven-quaver ostinato derived from its second phrase; a central scherzo takes the music up to the mediant (D) for a return to the opening texture, but the tonic re-emerges as a treble solo sings the plain-song in full, in Latin. The *Antiphon* (1956) which shares the same opus number is more adventurous harmonically, but perhaps less interesting, despite a pseudo-baroque fugue near the end based on the opening melody. The particular timbre of George Malcolm's choristers at Westminster Cathedral inspired Britten's *Missa Brevis* in D (1959) and the composer sets the Latin text with the freedom that characterizes his English works. Anthony Milner has suggested that, as Stravinsky did in *Oedipus Rex*, Britten treats the Latin words as 'phonetic material',[18] to be subject to whatever rhythmic treatment seems appropriate: the words are savoured more for their form than for their content. The witty, syllabic 7/8 'Gloria in excelsis' is a good example of this, which compares quite closely to the 'Laudate Dominum' in Stravinsky's *Symphony of Psalms*. This is a pervasive tendency in Britten's music, of which extended melis-mata on single words (notably on 'Rats' and 'Fie' in *Our Hunting Fathers*) are also an example. Equally of interest is the twelve-note row which opens the 'Sanctus', while the work's three treble lines look forward (par-ticularly in the reiterated F♯s of the 'Kyrie') to the fairies in *A Midsummer Night's Dream* (see p. 144).[19] The *Jubilate Deo* (1961) is a characteristic Britten miniature, although so different in style as to be a slightly uncomfortable partner for the much earlier *Te Deum* (1934) which it was written to complement. The *Hymn of St Columba* (1962), on the other hand, is one of Britten's most straightforward pieces for choir, and con-tains a characteristic feature: triads on all twelve roots are played by the organ reeds at 'Diesque mirabilium'.

The Hardy cycle *Winter Words* (1953) uses a highly triadic language, as had the two previous operas, *Billy Budd* and *Gloriana*; like *Billy Budd*, the cycle as a whole progresses from a clash of opposing triads at the opening to the resolution on a major triad at the end. The second song opens with

Example 14.4

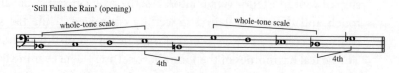

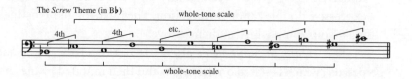

juxtaposed triads of C minor and B major (to suggest the Doppler effect of a passing train), before minor triads on all twelve roots are heard at 'What past can be yours . . . ?' These two details are entirely in line with Britten's practice as developed in *Billy Budd*. Just as, here, C minor and B major triads share a common Eb/D#, so the opera's two crucial key centres, B minor and Bb major, share a common D♮. The fifth song harmonizes the hymn-tune 'Mount Ephraim' (mentioned in the poem) with parallel triads, in a manner reminiscent of the 'Old Hundredth' setting in *Saint Nicolas*; the limited span of the vicar's phrases superbly implies his lack of imagination. The piano in the sixth song suggests the mood of the text rather than literally imitating the birdsong described – another instance of Britten's resisting the temptation to depict superficial details, preferring instead to seek out what Gerard Manley Hopkins would have called the 'inscape'. The final song reasserts the role of the triad in symbolizing innocence, as it had in *Billy Budd* and *Canticle II*: an obvious metaphor, in a way, but no less satisfying for that.

Just as *Billy Budd* has been shown to have affected the vocal works that followed it, so *The Turn of the Screw* had a marked influence on the subsequent third Canticle, *Still Falls the Rain*. The opera is cast in paired variations and scenes (see pp. 106–11), and the Canticle is a set of variations, each beginning with a voiceless interlude, so that the aural experience is similar. Ex. 14.4 illustrates the kinship between the opera's 'screw' theme (cf. Ex. 5.6) and the first two horn phrases of the Canticle; the row from the opera exhausts all twelve pitches, as does the opening section of the Canticle, albeit less systematically.

In the Canticle, the theme is developed through the systematic alteration of its tones and fourths into other intervals. Inspiration is thus drawn from purely musical details. This is surely a baroque inheritance: just as Purcell could base a Fantasy on a recurring textural pattern or even a single note, so Britten can sustain the music from within itself, so that he 'expresses' not only the text but music itself. Similarly, in the *Songs from the Chinese* (1957) for high voice and guitar, Britten demonstrates his command of the instrument by deliberately exploiting various clearly technical features such as glissandi, lute-like figures and, in no. 5, a chord based on the guitar's open strings (E, A, D, G, B, E).

With the *Nocturne* (1958), we return in some ways to the world of the *Serenade*,[20] but with the major difference that in this work the poems are incomplete, linked by a drowsy string ritornello, so that one appears to drift in and out of consciousness; this lends impact to the completeness of the Shakespeare sonnet with which the work ends. The work has a carefully organized tonal structure; the C major of the opening is contradicted in the third bar by a dominant of D♭, and though C reappears as the least ambiguous tonality on a handful of occasions (particularly on the word 'Sleep' in the Keats setting), the Shakespeare sonnet is in a mode which could be interpreted as Phrygian C or Lydian D♭. The voice ultimately cadences onto C major, but the final chord is a dyad of D♭ and F, which both preserves the ambivalence and provides an explicit link with *A Midsummer Night's Dream*, in which can be found examples of the C/D♭ opposition. The four chords which open Act II of the opera move from a D♭ major triad to a high dyad of C and E (see Ex. 7.1, p. 139); later, in Act III, Starveling's mention of the word 'Moon' brings about a high dyad of D♭ and F. The aural link between these two moments is strong, strengthened by an understanding that in the *Nocturne* this same D♭/F dyad, with a similarly bright scoring, was the outcome of a conflict with C. As in the opera, dodecaphonic techniques help to illuminate the structure of the work. At 'Nurslings of immortality' the tenor sings a long melisma, the first four notes of which pick out a C major triad with added major seventh (as heard in the first bar of the work), and which covers eleven of the twelve notes in all (see Ex. 14.5a). The twelfth note, A, arrives with the first pizzicato chord of the second poem, and remains an irritant against the prevailing B♭ minor of the ground bass, brilliantly highlighted by its being an open string which is left to ring while the other, stopped, notes of the four-note chords are immediately damped. This same A then becomes the tonic of the third song. The eleven-note melisma reappears, shared between tenor and horn, at 'mew! mew!' in the fourth song, before the bass shifts down a semitone to F♯ for the Wordsworth setting, another tense song in what is generally a much darker work than the *Serenade*. When the eleven-note melisma has closed the Keats setting, the ritornello directly contrasts C major with dyads of D♭ and F, in preparation for the start of the Shakespeare sonnet. Juxtaposed dominants of C and D♭ underly its climax, and then the eleven-note melisma appears in inversion, beginning with A♭ and D♭; the twelfth note is B, which appropriately appears as a major seventh dissonance in the C major chord which accompanies the singer's last note, echoing the first bar of the piece and the first four notes of the melisma (see Ex. 14.5b). As both the *Midsummer Night's Dream* chords and the subject-matter seem to connect the *Nocturne* with the *Serenade*, it is intriguing to observe that this same note, B, is the one pitch missing from the four chords with which the final number of the *Serenade* opens.

The *Sechs Hölderlin-Fragmente* of the same year show Britten tackling yet another foreign language, this time the German of his beloved Schubert. The two-stanza question-and-answer form of the third poem ('Sokrates und Alkibiades') is beautifully suggested in its setting; the pianist's right hand in the first stanza plays a bare melody, which in the second stanza the singer takes up, accompanied by all twelve major triads which again symbolize beauty and perfection. In 'Die Jugend', Britten gives an irregular rhythmic shape to the vocal line, at odds with the implied metre of the poem itself. This nevertheless allows the poetry to speak all the more clearly, as with his setting of 'You spotted snakes' in *A Midsummer Night's Dream*, and is one of the great paradoxes of setting verse. Hans Keller explored this approach by citing Schubert's 'creative aggression towards the text': often it is the setting which seems to pay the least heed to the poem's exterior that most plumbs its depths.[21]

1965 saw the composition of two new song-cycles, neither for Pears. The first was the *Songs and Proverbs of William Blake*, written for Dietrich Fischer-Dieskau. As in the *Nocturne*, a unifying ritornello links the Songs, forming the accompaniment to the pithier Proverbs, so that the cycle is played without a break. This ritornello exhausts all twelve pitches in the course of its first three phrases, each phrase concentrating on four pitches which are made harmonic by the use of the piano's sustaining pedal. The threefold segmentation of the row passes ultimately into the voice at, appropriately, the final and most all-encompassing Proverb ('To see a World in a Grain of Sand'), and then generates the chordal accompaniment for the last song. Many other details confirm Britten's interest in dodecaphony at this time: the twelve triads that end the phrases in 'London' and the twelve-note melody at the start of 'A Poison Tree' form part of a complex web of thematic relationships. The pessimistic slant of much of this cycle links it in substance with the similarly philosophical Hardy and Hölderlin cycles, but the Blake work is darker and less accessible. Britten's quasi-serial verticalization of linear material is pursued in his next cycle, *The Poet's Echo*, written in Russian for Galina Vishnevskaya. Its first song witnesses a heterophonic unfolding of melodies arising from the piano's spread chords, which may reflect the influence of Indonesian and Japanese music. In the final song, Britten evokes the ticking of a clock,

Example 14.5 (a)

Nurs — — lings of im-mor-tal — — i - ty, of im-mor-tal — — i — ty!

Example 14.5 (b)

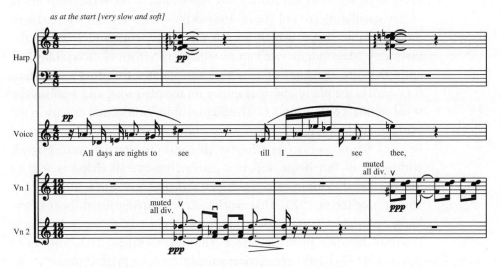

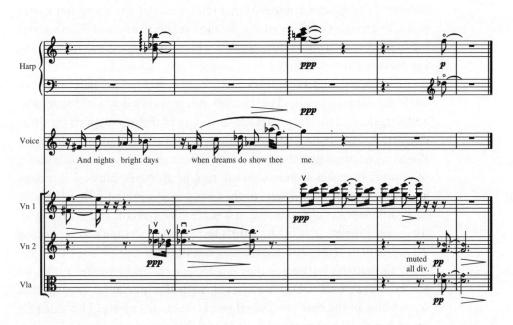

and it is an interesting comment on the way his music plays with time and eschews the superficial that the pulse is deliberately and significantly quicker than $\mathbf{\downarrow} = 60$ (the same can be said of the similar passage in Act II of *Owen Wingrave*, Figs. 280–94).[22]

The fourth Canticle, *The Journey of the Magi*, was written in 1971 for the unusual combination of countertenor, tenor, baritone and piano. T. S. Eliot's style seems to suit Britten; the repetitions in the verse result in the voices' oscillating second chord. Indeed the first two chords give rise to the intervallic shapes which govern the entire work and relate to the plainsong 'Magi videntes stellam' by which Britten, more successfully and aptly than in *The Rape of Lucretia*, consolidates the story's Christian framework; the piano epilogue muses on the plainsong and resolves the tonal conflicts onto Lydian G. The themes of innocence and cruelty in the William Soutar cycle *Who Are These Children?* (1969) relate it to many of Britten's major works (see Chapter 10), and the alternation of English with Scots dialect helps impart a convincing overall shape as well as looking ahead to his more relaxed, lyrical *Birthday Hansel* written for the Queen Mother in 1975. That work's accompanying instrument is the harp, to which Britten increasingly turned in later years as illness thwarted his own pianistic career. The fifth Canticle, *The Death of St Narcissus* (1974), has harp accompaniment and is a brief, intimate work, reflecting the greater compositional refinement of the composer's later years. Britten responds to all the detailed suggestiveness of Eliot's verse, but within a controlled structure in which thematic cross-referencing supports the overall effect.

Britten's last solo vocal work was *Phaedra*, written for Janet Baker in 1975; as well as strings and percussion, he employs a quasi-baroque cello and harpsichord for the recitatives. A variety of themes suggests the three characters and their states of mind, and Britten reprises these on Phaedra's death to give the work a satisfactory shape in an absolute sense; of course, it makes dramatic sense too, as Britten's musical impulses always do, in that the themes (or the forces they represent) are what have caused Phaedra's suicide in the first place. The passion and economy of the cantata makes it as fitting a final testament to Britten's song-writing art as *Death in Venice* had been to his stage output.

With Britten's last major choral work, *Sacred and Profane* (1975), we are in a sense back where we started, with the mediaeval English that served him in the first two choral works discussed above. This music is more demanding of performer and listener than were many of his earlier scores, but the old knack of inventing original rhythms for word-setting is very much alive, as the openings of the third and fourth movements demonstrate. The naive repetitions of the 'Carol' draw forth from Britten a sophisticated re-invention of an earlier style, to be performed 'with parody!'. The repetitive phrases and tonic/dominant harmony of the opening give way to a wider chromaticism, suggesting a fusion between a sixteenth-century English carol (e.g. the Coventry Carol) and the choral style of Ravel (as seen in the *Trois chansons*) or Poulenc. The final section of the work harks back to the last of the *Flower Songs*, but expressing a very different sentiment: 'Of al this world ne give I it a pese!', a strange valediction from this most compassionate of composers.

PART FOUR

The composer in the community

15 Britten and the world of the child

STEPHEN ARTHUR ALLEN

Robin Holloway has commented that there exists a 'two-sidedness' in Britten's 'primeval' harmonic language:

> Britten's 'new start' [as opposed to the romantic ones of Beethoven, Schubert, Mahler by way of Wagner's *Rheingold* Prelude and Bruckner] is quite different from such conscious primevalization; it is rather the natural extension of tendencies implicit in his brilliantly wayward mastery of traditional harmony, which, when pressed, *can run quite counter to it though still alongside*.[1] [My italics]

One possible key to this essential stylistic dichotomy may be summarized as the simultaneous co-existence of progress and regress in his musical aesthetic. These apparently conflicting states were bound together by Britten throughout his creative life by an artistic quest for Beauty. This may be viewed as a highly personal interpretation of an essentially Platonic position: Plato's pre-Christian philosophy revolved around the concept of god-like invisible archetypes ('Forms') standing outside creation yet partially revealed through the contemplation of it.[2] Thus, classically, in the association of Platonic epistemology with Greek homoeroticism the 'Form' of Beauty could be most perfectly perceived by encountering it through the beauty of a young boy.[3] For one to whom the beauty of childhood meant so much, the appropriation of this philosophy would be virtually intuitive. Britten's most overt public revelation of the personal significance of this theme is explored in his final opera, *Death in Venice*.[4]

There is clearly a darker and more dangerous aspect to this, acknowledged in Plato's writings: the danger of physical attraction interfering with the contemplation of metaphysical transcendence. This is a temptation with which Britten, as an unusually sensitive person, appears to have been frequently confronted. Humphrey Carpenter's biography of Britten (HC*BB*) would seem to indicate that Britten the man was able to overcome this temptation when it concerned young children (see p. 6 above). More recently, Carpenter has stated:

> it is the darkness of his private urges, *and their assimilation into technically brilliant music*, that gave Britten's work its originality and force, and if we do not discuss them candidly we will not get very far in understanding his huge achievement.[5] [My italics]

Technically, the appropriation of such metaphysics by Britten into his musical aesthetic resulted in a special network of significances ('secret meanings') that, although necessarily over-generalized when expressed in prose, are nonetheless essential to consider if a deeper comprehension of his art is to be achieved.

What we hear on a technical level as the key of A major in Britten's music may, for example, also be 'read' to imply the ideas of beauty and nescience.[6] His frequent combination of major and minor thirds in both this key (involving the semitonal tension between C♯ and C♮) and other tonal regions creates a certain complex of mood inherited from Mahler but employed for his own purposes. In passages from *Peter Grimes* (Interlude I) and *The Rape of Lucretia* (Act I scene 2) it would appear that chains of thirds are associated generally with women and femininity, and at least one critic has speculated that the minor third in Britten's art may signify homosexuality.[7] Stemming from this is another interval that seems from different contexts (notably in the *War Requiem*) to assume some kind of special signification, that of the tritone. This can be sub-divided into two superimposed minor thirds, and was historically out-lawed by the Catholic Church as the Devil's interval (*diabolus in musica*).[8] For Britten, chromaticism often implies a sense of unease, sin, tension and distress, which generally manifests itself in the tension between the semi-tone and the whole tone. The latter, with its pentatonic associations linking it to the emergent use of orientally derived materials – another sign of nescience – in Britten's music from *Paul Bunyan* on (see Chapter 9), is contrasted with the semitone by signifying 'naturalness'.

Beyond this, it is well known that Britten was addicted to schoolboy puns, and it is not beyond the bounds of possibility that phonetic inter-pretations of pitch-classes such as B♭ (= 'Be flat!'), B♮ (= 'Be natural!'), C♭ (= 'See! flat') or C♯ (= 'See! sharp') as codes and signals were not lost on him. Certainly the contrasts between flat, natural and sharp key regions often seem to carry special significance for the composer. One has only to hear the 'flat' regions inhabited by the Borough and its values in *Peter Grimes* (e.g. Act II scene 1), or by the ghosts in *The Turn of the Screw*, to detect this.

These significations could be taken to absurd and ridiculous extremes, and it is not my intention to advance any form of inflexible interpretative doctrine. However, in responding to Britten's music for children the lis-tener might well be advised to 'read' several layers of meaning simultane-ously: these layers are synthesized and diversified by the composer with characteristic resourcefulness, and often belie the apparent simplicity of the music's surface (e.g. in *A Ceremony of Carols* and 'The Birth of Nicolas' from *Saint Nicolas*).

The *Three Two-Part Songs* (1932) and better-known *Friday Afternoons* (1935) are both sequences of songs written for boys' voices and piano while Britten was in his late teens and early twenties – virtually still a boy himself. The round 'Old Abram Brown', the final song in *Friday Afternoons*, is an early indication of Britten's obsession with the theme of death. His use of material with the character of a nursery rhyme in this funereal context invokes the Mahler of the *Wunderhorn* songs and the slow movement of the First Symphony. Apart from the delight children gain from singing the increasingly sophisticated permutations of the round tune – composed simply from repeated notes, an octave leap and a descending sequence – any danger of banality is prevented by the sheer intensity of the piano accompaniment.

A Ceremony of Carols (1942), for treble voices and harp, is Britten's first mature work for boys' voices (although prior to publication it had been conceived for – and first performed by – women's voices).[9] The use of the harp as an accompanying instrument in this context was considered radical at the time of the première. From this point on in Britten's work, the harp seems additionally to signify the dilemma between beauty/nescience and temptation (cf. the association of the harp with the Tempter in *The Prodigal Son*). Throughout *A Ceremony of Carols*, it specializes in 'child-like' ostinato patterns and generally evokes dance-like rhythms that enhance the quality of innocence and nostalgia for lost childhood.

Britten's adoption of the plainsong antiphon *Hodie Christus natus est* from the Christmas Eve Vespers as processional and recessional is typical of his habit of employing framing techniques, perhaps most notably seen in the three Church Parables where plainsong is employed not only as a symmetrical frame but as the basis for the musical fabric throughout. In *A Ceremony of Carols*, the plainsong and 'Wolcum Yole!' are both in A major; the tritone is introduced in the plainsong as the Lydian fourth (D♯, alternating with D♮). After the lush harmonies of 'There is no Rose' (sharing its F major key with the central section of 'Wolcum Yole!'), we are suddenly brought into a different world. This is partly because 'That Yongë Child' – added, along with the harp interlude, by Britten just prior to the work's publication in 1943 – and 'Balulalow' illustrate respectively the ('wrong') song of the nightingale and the (implicitly 'good') song of Mary described in the text of 'That Yongë Child'. The accompaniment centres upon a semitonal ostinato (D♭/C) – which may symbolize the impoverishment of the nightingale's song – at first harmonized in F minor but enharmonically reinterpreted in A major/minor at the beginning of the second verse. In 'Balulalow' the major/minor ambiguity is now painted across a broader canvas (F♯ major/minor, i.e. relative of A major) where its Mahlerian echoes (e.g. the fourth movement of the Third Symphony) resonate more openly. Semitonal tension persists in 'As Dew in Aprille', while 'This Little Babe', a text describing Christ's battle with Satan, is projected as a *con fuoco* chase, the canonic writing so commonly found in Britten's music for children here accentuating the mood of tension and insecurity.

The Phrygian G minor of 'In Freezing Winter Night' shifts to G major for the central section with obvious textual relevance, but the 'freezing' tremolos continue on the harp and the tritone is soon introduced. The layered use of ostinato in imitation and of dissonance centred on the tritone serve both practical and illustrative purposes. The range of the final solos – featuring low G – is also a darkly effective use of the boys' timbre, and poignantly illustrative of the price paid for man's fall. After 'Spring Carol', the A major/minor ambiguity returns for the final 'Deo Gracias', an excellent example of Britten's 'strange' nescience. The moment the apple of the Tree of the Knowledge of Good and Evil is taken, the music flowers into a symbolically pure A major in a gesture of extreme irony: the (Catholic) text explains that if sin had not entered the world, the Virgin Mary would never have become heaven's Queen.

Many of the techniques discussed above are common to all Britten's music for children, notably the use of canon to create an impression of contrapuntal sophistication from a single melodic line. Canons and rounds are both fun to sing and, especially in the context of *A Ceremony of Carols*, such imitation tends to produce an impression of timelessness, enhancing the effect of non-development. Ostinati also abound, from the opening march rhythms of the harp in 'Wolcum Yule!' to the bell-like tollings of the accompaniment in 'There is no Rose'.

Saint Nicolas, written for the centenary of Lancing College in 1948, is not purely a work for religious digest. A duality of narrative may be perceived through the dilemma between Nicolas's public and private worlds:

> Our eyes are blinded by the holiness you bear,
> The bishop's robe, the mitre and the cross of gold.
> Obscure the simple man within the Saint.
> Strip off your glory, Nicolas, Nicolas, and speak! speak!

The dirge-like music of the opening religious chorus, captivating though it is, could not contrast more strongly with that of the individual Nicolas, which begins in an explosion of C major (Fig. 3) with scalic runs strongly reminiscent of those Britten had used in *Young Apollo* (1939). The tritone (F♯) is heard in Nicolas's cry of 'I come to stand in worship with you', and helps pull the music away from C into A major. In the final movement ('The Death of Nicolas'), an ambiguous nescience may be detected in the orientally derived 'otherness' of gamelan-like sonorities: high, fast, percussive figuration in the piano and deep, gong-like effects (conjured from doubling the gong with pedal notes in the organ and lower strings) form a brief prelude and postlude frame to the movement. The 'Nunc dimittis' is sung by the choir, doubled in octaves by lower strings and piano. This repeated phrase forms a cantus firmus in the manner of a passacaglia theme. The calmness of the biblical text is contrasted with the solo tenor music which belongs to the inner world of Nicolas's previous arias: his music, although ostensibly a hymn to 'CHRIST' the 'LORD', is also a hymn to 'DEATH', which is invoked at the beginning of the text. The chains of thirds gives added resonance to the tenor's vocal line. In this dual context, the significance of the final hymn *London New* ('God moves in a mysterious way') is surely heightened, not only as an act of praise, but also as a key that unlocks the binary paradox lying at the core of the work:

> God moves in a mysterious way
> His wonders to perform;
> He plants His footsteps in the sea,
> And rides upon the storm.

Between these movements are arranged a number of different incidents from the various legends and myths surrounding Nicolas. The transparent nescience of 'The Birth of Nicolas' is reinforced by its A major setting. The presence of the tritone, governing the stepwise movement of the sequence in each phrase (Ex. 15.1), demonstrates that Britten is able to write music that children can engage with and sing easily, while embodying sophisticated intervals and a symbolic dimension that offsets generic expectations otherwise associated with such material. The non-development of the melodic line is also enhanced by the 'progress' of the instrumental accompaniment: Britten's use of variation form (in contrast to organic 'development') is again illustrative of his childlike musical aesthetic.[10] A hint of autobiographical significance may be detected in 'Nicolas devotes himself to God'. The insinuating oscillation of the final tritone and perfect fifth on a B major triad to the words 'And Love was satisfied' resolve onto an unexpectedly melancholy E minor, leaving an air of considerable ambiguity. The serious and introverted tone of this movement and its counterparts in the second half of the work, 'Nicolas from Prison' and the solo music in the final 'The Death of Nicolas', belongs to the world of *The Holy Sonnets of John Donne* (1945), and draws us to the inner world of 'the man within the Saint'. 'Nicolas from Prison' is cast as a neo-classical and nervous piece that can be interpreted as much as the protest of a repressed homosexual community in the Britain of the late 1940s as that of the persecuted church in the fourth century.

'He journeys to Palestine' is the most overtly dramatic movement of the work. The storm of the text is illustrated musically by the contrasting

Example 15.1

of white-note and black-note configurations that, in combination with the metallic scoring for piano duet and percussion, give the movement something of an oriental tang. The children's music, contributing to the exchanges of the central section, is related to the climax of the storm: their spatial separation (singing from the gallery) in this dramatic context, and that of the later 'Nicolas and the Pickled Boys' – with its liturgically related procession for the three resurrected boys – clearly anticipates the similar distancing of the boys' choir in the *War Requiem*. Once again, this music for children is sophisticated in effect and belies the simplicity of its memorable melodic shapes, in which difficult leaps are avoided.

The 'public' aspects of Nicolas's religious role (contrasted with the 'private' moments of the tenor arias) are parodied in two sections: 'Nicolas comes to Myra and is chosen Bishop' (an academic and wilfully interminable Handelian prelude and fugue, the prelude featuring the naivest of children's tunes), and 'His piety and marvellous works' (an affectionately tedious parody of the nineteenth-century religious romanticism of Fauré or Elgar). The setting of Psalm 100 is particularly interesting from this perspective, and contradicts the arrangement of 'The Old Hundredth' by Vaughan Williams and the tradition to which that belongs. Britten's harmonies are full of mischief with traditionally 'illicit' second inversions and unprepared dissonances. The orchestral cadential decorations in the third verse, based on the fugue's counter-subject, enable Britten to introduce the tritone (C♯ in G major) to accompany the text 'His [God's] mercy is forever sure'; and a shift into C minor unsettles the affirmation of 'His truth at all times firmly stood.'

It was Hans Keller who first referred to *The Little Sweep* (1949) as 'a children's *Grimes*'.[11] The work has its origins in William Blake's poem 'The Chimney-sweeper', one of his *Songs of Innocence* later set by Britten in *The Songs and Proverbs of William Blake* (1965). Each of the four 'audience songs' – equivalents to the interludes of *Peter Grimes* and *The Rape of Lucretia* – are themselves subtle parables (inspired perhaps by the success of the hymns in *Saint Nicolas*), permitting the audience to participate in or comment upon the drama. The opening 'Sweep's Song', set in D minor, uses the major and minor second (exploiting the false relation between C♯ and C♮) at the cry of 'Sweep!' to suggest the resonances of pain in Blake's original poem. Both this and the irregular metre (5/4) once again insure against banality. Irony is suggested as the curtain goes up on the evil Black Bob and Clem, not only singing the audience's music, but concluding their sadistic theme in D major – the key of the triumphant finale of the work. The second audience song, 'Sammy's Bath', is also more complex than its 'innocent' swinging waltz (an idiom associated with baths and baptism in *Saint Nicolas*) would superficially suggest. As Sammy is plunged into the bath symbolic of his salvation (verse three), the music surges waywardly off in resistance, it would seem, to the implied dramatic scenario (is Sammy being 'saved' or not?).

The strangeness of the audience's 'Night Song' is also palpable. Describing the passing of the night, it is the only completely independent item in the opera. The sometimes savage, sometimes sensuous imagery of night and death is enhanced by the 'exotic' tolling gong and the death-rattle of the castanets. The apparent nature of the concluding 'Coaching Song' is also questioned when one realizes that the image of the galloping horse often carries a sexual connotation in Britten's texts: examples include Tarquinius's ride to Rome in *The Rape of Lucretia* ('Now who rides? Who's ridden?') and the corrupt Peter Quint's calling to the boy Miles in Act I scene 8 ('At Night') of *The Turn of the Screw* ('I am all things strange and bold, The riderless horse Snorting and stamping on the hard sea sand'). This may appear too dark an ambiguity for such pantomime to bear until we recognize that the horse bearing Sam is driven by a whip-flourishing coach driver (Tom) – played by the same actor who earlier played Black Bob.

The overt theme of compassion in this tale of the rescue by children of a sweep boy from cruelty is paralleled by a less obvious theme questioning the nature of 'possession' (i.e. what we think we possess but do not) and a linked theme of things not always being what they seem. This can be perceived in the song which forms the emotional heart of the work ('Run poor sweep boy!'), where the burning sincerity of the compassion expressed is offset by our knowledge that the boy Rowan believes to have disappeared into a cruel world, and whose fate she is lamenting, is hidden from her in the same room. The 'Finale', with its three-tiered ensemble set over a rising D major scale treated as a passacaglia theme, parodies not only the feigned collapse of Juliet, but also (like the Threnody in *Albert Herring*) the frequent association between passacaglias and death – both real and imagined – in other Britten works.

Britten not only introduces both children and audiences to the different forms and manners of operatic convention in *The Little Sweep* (which is a kind of 'Young Person's Guide to the Opera'), but also to the subversive and powerful irony of which the genre is capable. This recommends a re-evaluation of what many critics have considered the limitations of the rather twee middle-class Victoriana of the opera's surface narrative.[12]

If in *Saint Nicolas* the distinction between 'private' and 'public' pre-occupations was deliberately polarised, then the greater popular success of *Noye's Fludde* (1957), Britten's setting of the Chester Miracle Play, can at least be partly attributed to a far greater degree of integration (by virtue, again in part, of its being through-composed). Britten's decision to retain the original Old English guaranteed that a greater degree of linguistic stylization would ensure a higher degree of universality than in either the earlier cantata or the children's opera. The more direct relevance of the texts of Britten's imported hymns to the dramatic situation in *Noye's Fludde*, along with the transference of two of them to his favourite 'framing' position, ensures that everybody gets a good sing at the beginning and end, as well as a greater degree of audience participation *in* the dramatic situations than had been the case in *Saint Nicolas* – where they tended (like a Greek chorus) to comment *on* them. The blending of sacred and profane elements in the vernacular text and the central theme of 'salvation at sea' both partly account for the attraction of the miracle play to Britten.

The spirit of the explicitly communal purposes of the original play is retained by Britten in a score that calls for a core band of professional musicians, a veritable plethora of untrained children and almost everyone in between. The work is distinguished by its sheer tightness of construction (clearly anticipating the Church Parables), flexible scoring and the cunning distribution of musical content for the professional forces; the straightforward but far from unsophisticated material for the amateurs and children ensures a remarkably democratic aesthetic as well as an inbuilt guarantee of successful effect in performance. The leading roles for children recall the range and sophistication of those in *The Little Sweep* (see, for instance, the handling of the ensemble between Figs. 8 and 15). The orientally derived music suggested in the frame of the last movement of *Saint Nicolas* is vastly expanded in *Noye's Fludde*, prompted specifically by Britten's and Pears's Far Eastern tour of 1956: the overt inclusion of music derived from these sources lends the work its strange uniqueness and a possible second narrative that subtly subverts the surface story, most notably in the ambiguity of the work's closing moments.

From the opening false relations between the Phrygian minor second (F♮) and the major second (F♯) in E minor in the hymn *Lord Jesus, Think on Me*, such strangeness is self-evidently at work. It can also be heard in the intensely dramatic and effective central setting of the hymn *Eternal Father, Strong to Save*, anticipated by a parody of yet another liturgical

Example 15.2

Noye's Fludde: 'Storm' Passacaglia theme

The Turn of the Screw: Theme

Example 15.3

processional as scores of young children (representing the animals) pour down the aisles and fill the ark to cries of that favourite Britten text from *Peter Grimes* to *Curlew River*: 'God/Lord have mercy upon me' (*Kyrie eleison*). Britten shrewdly sets these cries to a lively, instantly memorable rhythm centred on the interval of a tone (F – E♭), easy enough for the smallest of children to sing. The hymn is set in the context of a 'storm' passacaglia, based on a twelve-note theme many have related to that of *The Turn of the Screw* (see Ex. 15.2), made up from minor seconds, minor thirds, the tritone (the influence of which is omnipresent in the work), and phrases slowly rising by whole tones. Against this the hymn material struggles for and against integration: although we hear Dykes's original harmonization of the hymn in verse three, it is (like verse two of Psalm 100 in *Saint Nicolas*) accompanied by a descant that at times borders on shrill parody. This is the only verse we hear without the storm music's resonance, which, though ebbing after this point, never entirely vanishes from the music (e.g. the music of the Raven and Dove, the recessional cries of 'Alleluia!' and the diminished triad that crowns the bugle chords at Fig. 110 as part of a dominant-seventh chord: see Ex. 15.3).

The final paragraph of the work incorporates, after the spirit of

'Old Abram Brown' from *Friday Afternoons*, Tallis's canon *The Spacious Firmament on High*, which is set against the 'otherness' of the music that gathers around it with a strongly nescient flavour (orientalized bells and childhood bugles, class-room recorders and nursery-like slung mugs). Both Peter Evans and Humphrey Carpenter have commented on the strangely jarring effect of the organ outburst before the last verse of the hymn (Fig. 117⁻⁷).[13] The oriental splashes at the conclusion, when heard from the traditional perspective of Tallis's music, leave an air of doubt hanging over the certainty of orthodox Christian faith expressed in the hymn.

The *Missa Brevis* in D (1959) for boys' voices and organ anticipates the sound-world of the *War Requiem*, on which Britten worked soon afterwards – especially in the plangent writing for treble voices and a mystical sensibility which, while enhancing the liturgical texts, also seems to stand outside them. Clearly the demands of writing for the choristers of a professionally trained cathedral choir required a different approach to that adopted for the untutored extras of *Noye's Fludde*: Britten uses the opportunity to write music of greater vocal virtuosity, employing more challenging intervals while retaining many technical features (e.g. canonic imitation) found in his earlier children's music. This is further demonstrated in *The Golden Vanity* (composed for the world-renowned Vienna Boys' Choir) and *Children's Crusade* (first performed by the exceptional Wandsworth Boys' Choir under Russell Burgess).

In setting Latin texts, Britten strove for relative 'naturalism', ignoring Stravinsky's more ceremonial and ritualistic disregard of natural stress and syllabic weight. The 'Gloria' of the *Missa Brevis* is based directly on the tenth-century plainsong from the Mass *Dominator Deus*, to which the motivic structures of the other movements are related – recalling procedures in *A Boy was Born* (motivic tightness, also based on major seconds and perfect fourths), *A Ceremony of Carols* (plainsong), and the later intense motivic use of plainsong in the three Church Parables.

The opening 'Kyrie' (one of Britten's favoured texts) is not 'in D' at all, but centres on the ambiguity between F♯ major and minor. F♯ is the dominant of B, relative minor of D, which is heard at the climax on 'Christe eleison'. The 'Gloria' anticipates the vibrancy of Britten's well-known *Jubilate Deo* (1961). In the 'Sanctus', above the solid D major triad in the organ, the boys intone the text with a twelve-note proposition laid out in overlapping entries: a scheme fully in keeping with Britten's interest in twelve-note collections in works composed after *The Turn of the Screw*, and here resulting in challenging melodic intervals which could only have been conceived for professionally trained children's voices (see Ex. 15.4). False relations between F♯ and F♮ in the 'Benedictus' create a new conflict

Example 15.4

between modal regions on C and D, the semitonal tensions between these notes being heard both as fourth/Lydian fourth in C (tritonal subversion once again), and as major/minor third in D. In the final chord of G major, the tension between these two pitches is heard in a new tonal perspective as the sharpened and flattened seventh degrees. Throughout the 'Agnus Dei' ('O Lamb of God, who takest its away the sins of the world') semitonal tensions destabilize the tonic key of D minor, the closing second-inversion triad sounding designedly inconclusive: this final questioning gesture is characteristic of the endings of other Britten scores (cf. p. 258).

Psalm 150 (1962) returns us to the rougher (though not unsophisticated) musical world of *Noye's Fludde* and is scored for children's voices and whatever instruments happen to be to hand – an eminently practical scheme in the school setting for which it was conceived (Britten's old preparatory school, South Lodge). The opening music is an orchestral exposition contrasting a boisterous march theme with darker, more chromatic material that again seems to lie outside the nature of the biblical text. The central 7/8 section illustrates the instruments cited in the psalm, while giving the children repeated notes and step-wise figures to sing – as well as a loud shout at the word 'Cymbals', an effect guaranteed to captivate any otherwise uninterested children. A brief section is followed by very lively music (in A) contrasting triplet and duplet figures before a sequence of chords leads to the concluding doxology, set to a recapitulation of the opening march theme.

As *The Little Sweep* had been a *Peter Grimes* for children, so *The Golden Vanity* (1967) – a vaudeville for boys and piano after the old English ballad, to a text by Colin Graham – is a children's *Billy Budd*: the piece even includes a direct reference to its 'parent' opera (the firing of the canon at Figs. 17–21). If *Noye's Fludde* was about redemption through the sea, this vaudeville is about death in it. Arnold Whittall has commented that

> in spite of being written for the determinedly lovable young professionals of the Vienna Boys' Choir, *The Golden Vanity* gave [Britten] ample scope for his special technique of providing simple, even folk-like tunes with *disruptive if not actually destructive accompaniments*.[14] [My italics]

In *Billy Budd*, Captain Vere allows his 'public' sense of duty to destroy the 'private' individual (Billy), whom he loves and whom he subsequently considers to have 'saved' him.[15] Some critics have interpreted *Billy Budd* as a parable of homosexual love (see Chapter 8). In *The Golden Vanity*, the relationship between the Captain and the Cabin-boy is more assertively sadistic, and it is this destructiveness that is present in the accompaniment: the ballad becomes a vehicle for a set of variations – again the theme (regress) and variations (progress) aesthetically reflect the roles of Cabin-boy and Captain respectively, and create an air of obsession. Minor seconds and chromaticism now become part of a taut frenzy along with a perverse cultivation of dissonance that seems to invite repulsion rather than sympathy.[16] The final two-bar phrase of the work – the ballad's principal motif changed to imply A major – is too perfunctory to resolve the accumulation of dissonance throughout the piece.

In *Children's Crusade* (1968), darker themes are further explored. Bertolt Brecht's text acted as a near-perfect catalyst for Britten's metaphysical impulses of compassion and its simultaneous subversion into an anger that saturates the musical fabric. Britten himself referred to the work as 'a very grisly piece', and after its first performance in St Paul's Cathedral, he wrote to William Plomer to say:

> the boys' (singing & hitting) made a tremendous impression of passion & sincerity along side the assinine [*sic*] pomposity of the established church ... I react strongly to the roughness of the Brecht.[17]

The 'hitting' Britten refers to is the work's predominantly percussive sonority: he had difficulty notating its stark and rhythmically free music for boys' voices, keyboards and percussion, a freedom derived from the Japanese influences found in the idiom of the Church Parables. The story describes the wanderings of a lost group of Polish children during the winter of 1939 in their war-ridden country. They all die, along with a dog they find. The undiluted vernacular of the text, with its near-contemporary theme (unlike those of *Saint Nicolas*, *The Little Sweep* and *Noye's Fludde*) perhaps played their part in liberating Britten's darkest musical responses. The score caused Peter Evans to comment that 'the work ... is not related to the rest of Britten's output either in genre or in the manner of the musical discourse'. As in *The Golden Vanity*, the final and ultimate disintegration of A major at the conclusion is perhaps symbolic of the central theme of the work: the total violation of innocence.

The last composition to which Britten gave an opus number, *Welcome Ode* (1976) for young people's chorus (SAB) and orchestra, represents something of a return to the brightness of his earlier music for children. Composed as an occasional piece (in the tradition of Purcell's royal Welcome Odes and Birthday Songs) to celebrate Queen Elizabeth II's Silver Jubilee visit to Ipswich, the piece is a miniature summary of the compositional worlds of Britten's past. 'March' evokes the *Spring Symphony* and the piano writing of 'Lacrymosa' in the *Sinfonia da Requiem*, while 'Jig', a Scottish dance for orchestra alone, echoes the nursery rhyme 'Girls and boys come out to play'; the mood – like many such rustic moments in Britten (cf. 'Pantomime' from *The Little Sweep*, and 'Cakes and Ale' from the *Suite on English Folk Tunes, 'A Time There Was . . .'*) – is aggressive rather than jolly. 'Roundel', the last example of Britten's long fascination with round songs, has echoes of both Miles's song 'Malo' (*The Turn of the Screw*) and *Noye's Fludde.* The brief instrumental 'Modulation' leads to the final 'Canon' and another open-ended conclusion.

Throughout his life, Britten took delight in the innocence of childhood for its own sake, in spite of his darker personal struggles (about which commentators will doubtless continue to speculate), testified by many acts of unconditional personal generosity as well as the virtually unrivalled quality and quantity of the music he produced for children's entertainment and edification. Because of his refusal to 'write down' to the child performer, although drawing on his considerable technical expertise to tailor his music to the appropriate level of skill, there can be little doubt that this body of work contributes significantly towards what Carpenter termed Britten's 'huge achievement'.

16 Old songs in new contexts: Britten as arranger

ERIC ROSEBERRY

Britten's folksong arrangements – mainly from the British Isles, with their gallery of lovers, soldiers, sailors, characters and genre scenes drawn from rural life – are strongly representative of the 'English' Britten and span a working life that extends from the time just before the return to England (and *Peter Grimes*) in 1942 to the stricken composer's last summer in 1976. Here is the composer who worked with the English language, whose feeling for oddity, humour and peculiar sentiment – for *particularity* – was rooted in a sense of place, in what remained (despite a widely travelled artist's sophistication) a villager's sense of local character: the kind of curiosity that prompted Forster to write on Crabbe or William Plomer to lecture on 'Old Fitz'. Much of this feeling was strongly linked to an attraction towards – perhaps even a kind of nostalgia for – what might be termed the 'expressive character and modes' of life in eighteenth- and nineteenth-century England (the period settings, after all, of *Peter Grimes*, *Albert Herring*, *The Little Sweep*, *Billy Budd*, etc.). Britten's own native Suffolk – with its strong Victorian sea-side associations, its buildings and maritime history – still visually recalls this period, that saw the accumulation and collection of folk and 'national' songs dealing with a rapidly vanishing rural way of life. What makes this oeuvre distinct, however, is its absolute removal from the kind of 'Englishness' that may be associated with the Edwardian pomp and pageantry of Elgar, or later characterized in the watery meadows and 'gaffers on the green' modal meanderings and rustic frolics of the school of the English folklorists. Britten's was altogether a sharper, less complacent, more quizzical, personally sensitive 'national' temperament, alert to the expression of his chosen texts, both verbal and musical. But Britten was also a European, responsive to the new music of the twentieth century, and it is the extraordinary achievement of these arrangements that he made of them a unique blend of the innovative and the traditional, the insular and the international. In one important respect – that of harmonic 'appropriateness' – they are sharply interrogative of the Brahmsian influence on English music which, via Stanford (in, for example, the *National Song Book*) and Vaughan Williams, had taken a stranglehold on folksong arrangement.[1]

[292] Britten's first volume of seven folksong arrangements from the British

Isles for voice and piano was published in 1943 and was prepared shortly before the composer's return to England. Evidently they came into being in the American years through the early days of Britten's voice-piano duo with Pears.[2] In selecting his 'folk' material Britten was no purist – the sources of the tunes in this volume are not given, and in later volumes he was content to rely on the 'secondary' sources of collector-arrangers like Sharp and Vaughan Williams. 'Down by the Sally Gardens', the very first song in this collection (on the perennial folk theme of lost love) is in fact something of a hybrid for it is itself an 'art' adaptation of a near-pentatonic Irish tune (AABA) that appears in the Petrie collection under the title 'The Maids of Mourne Shore' to a quasi-folk poem by W. B. Yeats. It is revealing to compare the original in Petrie with Britten's adaptation: clearly the romantically 'appoggiaturized' adaptation of the tune attracts Britten in a treatment that comes near to Schubert in taking its introductory motif from the song itself (a favourite device with Britten), its pulsating quaver thirds and quasi-cadential falling bass figure. In short, this is the first of many 'art song' transformations in these volumes, and it shows Britten as a composer-arranger (rather than a folksong collector) who is concerned in the first place with realizing the emotional content of his text and taking the tune as he finds it from whatever available source, 'authentic' or 'corrupt'.

The other important point to keep in mind in this (as in so many of Britten's folk settings) is his subtle use of what I shall call non-cadential diatonic harmony, a treatment that keeps the tune buoyant and floating. The 'flavour' is a characteristic blend of the familiar and the unfamiliar – an unforced avoidance of cadential cliché that manages at the same time to allude to traditional practice. The normal V–I close is here delicately subverted by means of a gentle Db–Eb–Gb dissonance over the Ab bass before it comes to rest on pure Db harmony. Similarly, the touching Cb–Eb *pianissimo* harmony on the word 'foolish' is a conventional enough move in the direction of the subdominant Gb, but the chord in itself is pure Britten, hinting as it does at his characteristic penchant for piling up thirds. In its artful simplicity this beautiful, sadly reflective setting is archetypal.

The other song in this collection that deserves special comment is 'The Ash Grove',[3] once again a song of lost and remembered love. Here is the first instance of what was to become Britten's self-confessed addiction to 'canonizing'.[4] Britten's setting of this familiar (AABA) tune, with its characteristic stepwise descent through a fifth, is through-composed to take in the emotional intensification of the second verse. Setting out with a simple two-part, freely 'canonizing' accompaniment always flowing in diatonic thirds – so far so good, one might say – the tranquillity is disturbed in the bitter regrets of the second verse by means of a seemingly off-key development in the piano part that relocates the original tune in a mixed-modal/bitonal context. The phrase 'seemingly off-key' is used here because it should be noted that the harmony remains basically straightforward and functionally 'in key' (as a playing of the left hand only with the tune reveals), while the counter-melody in the right hand sets up the conflicting modal inflections, with their painful false relations. The climax is a touching A minor, as unexpected as it is a perfectly logical alternative to dominant harmony at this point (beautifully rendered, by the way, in Britten's recording with Pears). The peace and tranquillity of the opening are then restored, but it is the ironic peace and tranquillity of the death of the beloved. The almost passacaglia-like effect of this setting with its six repetitions of the 'A' part of the tune and (via the bitonal dissonance of Britten's piano accompaniment) its seamless build-up to a forlorn climax ('in search of my love') places the well-known melody in a completely new perspective. As Arnold Whittall writes: 'The social genre [of the folksong] is disorientated by the overmastering assertiveness of the aesthetic genre, and a narrative that, in the unaccompanied folk song, might appear, on musical grounds at least, to be recollected in tranquillity, is shown in the art song to be the source of persistent pain.'[5]

Regarded as a 'suite' of arrangements, this first volume establishes a number of characteristic categories for Britten. The 'aria' ('The Sally Gardens' and 'The Ash Grove'), the 'ballad' or 'narrative' ('Little Sir William' and 'The Trees They Grow So High'), the Scottish lament-cum-funeral march with its distinctive rhythmic 'snaps' ('The Bonny Earl of Moray'), the cradle song ('O Can Ye Sew Cushions?') and the terse scherzo-cum-nonsense song ('Oliver Cromwell' – a favourite encore). Of these, 'The Ash Grove' and 'The Trees They Grow So High' are notable for their more formally ambitious, cumulative, through-composed treatment, the latter suggesting a further parallel with the 'Lyke Wake Dirge' through its layer-by-layer, ostinato-like growth from unaccompanied beginning towards a climax and gradual subsidence to its starting point – an arch form much favoured by Britten, whether vocal or instrumental. Of note too is the subject of 'Little Sir William' – the innocent boy murdered by the Jew's wife. The theme is characteristic, and Britten gives it further point by singling out the repeated motif of the second line, symbol of a young life cut short, in his final comment on the piano.

Reviewing the first volume of folksong arrangements in the year of their publication, Vaughan Williams showed a generosity of spirit towards his young colleague that makes interesting reading:

Are we old fogeys of the folksong movement getting into a rut? If so, it is very good for us to be pulled out of it by such fiery young steeds as Benjamin Britten and Herbert Murrill. We see one side of a folksong, they see the other. They probably think our point of view hopelessly dull and stodgy, but that is no excuse for us to label them self-conscious or deliberately freakish.

Personally I am delighted to see these rockettings come to a sound *terra firma* from which I believe all flights of fancy must take off – beautiful melody, spontaneous melody, melody which belongs essentially to us.

The tune's the thing with which we'll catch the conscience of the composer. Do these settings spring from a love of the tune? Then, whatever our personal reaction may be we must respect them.[6]

In the second volume of folksong arrangements from France (1946) we enter the world of legend and romance – a world akin to that of Mahler's *Knabenwunderhorn* songs. Here are a Christmas carol in the manner of a drone or 'drumming' song, a spring song, two contrasting spinning songs, a hunting song that tells a simple tale of true love that spurns riches, a pastoral idyll, another love song – anxious in its fear of fickle-heartedness – and finally (perhaps closest of all to Mahler in its macabre theme) a young shepherd's dance-song (a *Ländler*) about a flute made from the bone of a sheep that has died of starvation, grinding out its mirthless tune.[7] The spring song, 'Voici le printemps', is a gem of simple artifice, and strophic repetition suffices to acclimatise the ear to its harmonic subtlety and originality. The idyll, 'La belle est au jardin d'amour' – in which a rocking chordal piano introduction and link suggest the chaste harmonic simplicity of a Fauré chanson – is seemingly more straightforward, yet it too contains a subtly overlapping cadence that leaves the key open to double meaning. Are we in B♭ major or Mixolydian F? The question may sound academic, yet the deception, the delicious modal ambiguity, is surely at the root of the listeners' pleasure in this setting. The genre of turning-wheel songs in Britten looks back, perhaps, to Schubert, to Gretchen or the imagery of brook and millwheel in *Die schöne Müllerin*. Of the two spinning songs, 'Il est quelqu'un sur terre' is a touching example of Britten's ground-bass treatment (the ground bass becomes the image of the turning-wheel) and onto this is projected a Purcellian chain of changing figurations and harmonies. The other spinning song ('Fileuse') reserves its change of harmony for the last verse, the cessation of the turning wheel, where the shift of harmonic perspective suggests a debt to Bartók in romantic-nostalgic vein (see Ex. 16.1).

The first song of the third volume (published in 1947), which returns to the British Isles, was the encore every audience hoped for in any Britten–Pears song recital. This deft setting of Shield's 'The Ploughboy', with its 'cynical insouciance' (in Lennox Berkeley's phrase)[8] has a stroke

Example 16.1

of genius in Britten's provision of a simple whistling tune (at whistling pitch – a touch of realism on the composer's part!) that introduces the song and then, Schubert-like, complements the refrain in each verse. It is interesting to note that Britten had already made an arrangement of this melody in a film score using folk and traditional tunes for a documentary *Around the Village Green*.[9] Yet another turning-wheel song comes up in 'The Miller of the Dee', in which a clashing diminished-fifth ostinato (half-cousin to 'Fileuse' in the previous volume) jars persistently in the piano against the song's open fifth – a rough fellow, this miller. Not, perhaps, Britten's least unforced invention, but the other three ostinato-based arrangements are wholly successful. The cradle-like simplicity of the brief 'There's None to Soothe', with its arching extension of the bass to underpin the sense of mounting grief, is complemented by two more highly wrought settings. In the sorrowful 'O Waly, Waly' the accompaniment is limited to a three-note 'dirge' rhythm taken from a motif of the song itself ('neither have') and alternating two chords, and the harmonic changes rung on this simple device give the setting poignancy and economy. The coldly distant harmonies on the final words of each verse form a climax of quiet despair. In more cheerful vein, the strict bass ostinato (a pair of fourths) of 'Come You Not from Newcastle' turns into an enchanting echo song with bitonal touches as Britten loosens the strictness of the line sequence to incorporate the effect. No such harmonic liberties are taken in the notorious 'Foggy, Foggy Dew', where the ironic guitar strummings of tonic and dominant are slyly displaced by an unexpected touch of naughtiness – the slightly syncopated doubling of the vocal line in the bass. Which leaves for final comment what is perhaps the gem of the collection – 'Sweet Polly Oliver'. This is the first of Britten's full-blown canonizing settings, and the wit and point of its through-composed invention give the song a narrative drive that – allowing for an 'interlude' in the temporary set-back and suspense of the fourth verse – sweeps on in mounting triumph to the final perfect cadence. The mastery of this arrangement lies in Britten's power to weld the strophic (and essentially static) narrative form of the original into a living entity, a complete drama in miniature. After an introduction that enlarges on the arpeggiated thirds of the song (a Brittenish figure in itself that becomes a telling link between verses), the strictly canonic first verse sets what might be designated the basic *Affekt* of the song, capturing the image of Polly enlisting as a soldier and following her love. Thereafter the canonic idea is developed as the narrative proceeds: in the treble, accompanied by march-style fourth ostinati in the bass (another characteristic device in Britten); in the bass with strutting right hand chords; finally – and after its temporary suspension in the fourth verse while the outcome hangs in the balance, so to speak – as a plaintive canon at the fourth in the right hand with subtly displaced arpeggiated chords in the left hand. With the piano's final falling thirds and clinching V–I 'that's that' the song reaches its goal. Britten's treatment of the momentary set-back and mounting optimism of the fourth verse is an epigram in itself. The strict canon breaks off; beginning in the minor, the heavy chords of the initially doleful accompaniment move back towards the major in a perfectly orthodox progression; at the same time the falling thirds now take over as the dominant motif in the piano, and are hopefully inverted.

Created for the English Opera Group in 1948 (and thus continuing the line of chamber opera established with *The Rape of Lucretia* and *Albert Herring*), *The Beggar's Opera* remained unique in Britten's output. Not only is it a compendium of his folk/national song-arranging techniques as discussed above, but it becomes a Britten opera in its own right through the composer's more or less 'free' treatment of his material, combining, reshaping it into duets, ensembles, whole scenes and the provision where necessary of his own music – link passages, melodrama, introductions, codas and the like. In short, the eighteenth-century loose ballad style becomes musico-dramatically organic. The task had already been undertaken by Frederick Austin, whose arrangement (first given in 1920) was an eighteenth-century pastiche scored for baroque orchestra with harpsichord. Britten in his new musical version of 1948 dispenses with pastiche. The sound, with its sharply characterized edge, is very much indebted to

Britten's absorption (beginning in *The Rape of Lucretia*) of the neo-classical Stravinsky in its clear-cut chamber orchestra conception (single
strings, solo wind and percussion) – a debt that is further incurred in
Britten's pandiatonicism, seasoned with his love of false relations (features, incidentally, of both Purcell's style *and* that of Stravinsky). The
latter technique, audible in the lively fugal introduction, derives from a
counterpoint of diatonic melody that takes scant account of traditional,
cadence-bound functional harmony, and owes much of its rhythmic pro-
pulsion (again as in Stravinsky) to ostinato. The overture, rejecting the
traditional Handelian overture of Pepusch (and Austin's own pastiche)
with its brilliantly devised presentation of the main characters through a
pot-pourri of their first songs, becomes a kind of invitation to refocus our
ears in receiving these familiar melodies, preparing the audience for what
is to come in musical as well as dramatic terms.

I propose to re-examine briefly three excerpts representative of
Britten's musico-dramatic adaptation of the genre. Once again we note
the composer's close attention to words, to meaning as much as tune, the
latter stripped of its purely eighteenth-century (i.e. figured-bass) harmonic connotations, though some vestiges of baroque allusion may
remain. Then there is the placing of the tune in its dramatic context,
which may or may not involve the provision of further music. First,
Britten's interesting treatment of the two Purcell songs – interesting in
view of his other, more 'strict', Purcell realizations. Second, his much-
admired treatment of the Scottish tune 'A Miser Thus a Shilling Sees'; and,
lastly, his brilliant musico-dramatic solution to the musical problem of
the condemned-cell scene.[10]

No. 6 ('Virgins are like the fair flower') is shared between Polly and her
father Mr Peachum, whose surname derives from his trade – to impeach
and live off the proceeds, having brought up his daughter to serve as a
useful accomplice to lure his victims. Unfortunately for business, she has
fallen in love with (and secretly married) the highwayman Macheath, and
is having to explain herself to her father. In this aria she attempts to
conceal from him the truth and show herself an obedient daughter.
Britten prepares the aria in the shape of speech over music (melodrama)
based on a free variation-paraphrase of Purcell's tune in five phrases that
moves unstably (reflecting Polly's shifting frame of mind) through a
number of more or less remote keys. There is no attempt here to use a
baroque figured-bass harmonic style; Britten is tonal but highly evasive.
(The syntax may sound 'wrong-note' at first hearing, but in fact has its
own coherence.) The aria itself is based almost literally on Purcell's
figured bass, more faithfully so in fact than in the once popular Austin
version,[11] and – apart from an occasional harmonic licence (e.g. of chord

position or casual seventh harmony) – sticks fairly closely to the baroque norm. (Britten's chamber orchestration and texture represents, of course, a more radical departure.) In the last phrase of this single-verse aria Britten the musico-dramatist in his own right takes over from Purcell. By means of counterpointing the last line of Polly's song with a variant of Purcell's first line, Britten sets in motion a further – and increasingly sinister – development. The instruments now continue their quasi-canonic overlap in a version of the last line of the tune that moves towards what Hans Keller has called the opera's 'fatal' key of E minor. As Peachum threatens Polly, the line is expanded in its halting descent over an obsessive pedal E–D♯ and the last line of Purcell's tune is left hanging in the air to form an accelerando link into the next number.

In No. 18, the appearance of the tune 'The Miser Thus a Shilling Sees' (dropped in Austin's version) once again shows Britten's attachment to the Scottish lament genre, with its funereal tread and 'snap' (iambic) rhythms. The latter are frequently a characterizing agent in Britten (see, for example, the Piano Concerto, the *Scottish Ballad* and the *Serenade*) – caught, perhaps, from Purcell who was no less addicted to it in his word-setting. It is not altogether surprising that this is one of the high spots of Britten's score, with the rhythm becoming obsessive as an accompanimental feature (initially on solo clarinet). Harmonically, Britten's style is simple, economical and even thoroughly traditional in being limited to a handful of closely related diatonic chords, with special insistence on I–V^7, a cliché which less gifted composers would seek to avoid. This leads to an especially poignant placing of V^7 at the climactic G of the song (Ex. 16.2). The scene is a farewell duet between Macheath and Polly. Each sings a verse apiece and in a final (unison) duet Britten adds an extra verse (supplied at his request by Eric Crozier) so that he can introduce a fading canonic farewell and recharge the climax with a different – but no less simple – G major (mediant major) harmony.

In the concluding prison scene in the condemned hold (No. 53), Macheath, 'in a melancholy posture', reflects on his fate and consoles himself with wine. His mounting anguish at leaving his two 'pretty hussies' leads into a bitter lament, directed against those more fortunate than himself. Here Britten hit upon a brilliant solution to the problem of giving unity to the 'bits of tunes' he was presented with in this scene. Having fitted a descending ground bass (Purcell again!) to the last – and only complete – song, 'Since laws were made for ev'ry degree', he takes it out of its local context and uses it as an introduction and recurring link between the fragments, always at the same (F minor) pitch, so that it comes as a climax to the whole scene when it finally fulfils its predestined role. Nothing could be simpler, more dramatically apt and – for Britten –

Example 16.2

characteristic (Ex. 16.3). (The whole scene occupies emotional ground shared by 'Billy in the Darbies' in *Billy Budd*.)

The ten settings of Moore's Irish melodies appeared in 1960 – the time of *A Midsummer Night's Dream* – with work on the *War Requiem* already in progress and the exquisite *Nocturne* recently composed. There is a time gap here of thirteen years since the publication of the previous volume, during which the highly successful Britten–Pears duo continued to feature the folksong arrangements as a regular part of their recital programmes. A detailed chronology of this collection has still to be established – and some of these settings may date back as far as 1942.[12] This is a substantial volume that features no less than three night pieces, an ornately decorated 'aria', three contrasted war songs and three further patriotic numbers in Moore's companionable 'after dinner' vein of high, noble – if somewhat pontifical – sentiment. Throughout them all runs the harp motif, so that arpeggiation becomes a characteristic feature of the piano accompaniments. (The harp was amongst Britten's favourite sonorities and the Welsh harpist Osian Ellis a highly favoured colleague – leading to a late volume of song arrangements with harp accompaniment when the composer was no longer able to play the piano.) 'The Minstrel Boy' and 'The Last Rose of Summer' are eloquent, harp-like settings of well-known ditties. The former is turned into an agitated march, underpinned with a characteristically displaced drum-beat ostinato in fourths; the latter treated in the manner of a passionately nostalgic aria accompa-

Example 16.3

nied by richly strumming chords, and the second verse is freely
ornamented in the voice part, giving quasi-baroque rein to Pears's expressive virtuosity. Another (strictly canonic) setting is the calm, gently
moving 'Rich and Rare'. Here Britten varies the interval and register of the
canon in the piano part from verse to verse, with the return of the original
interval of a second in right-hand piano octaves in the last verse. The textural effect is not unlike that in his setting of Hardy's 'Before Life and
After' in *Winter Words*. In the war-song genre the lively fanfare/drum-
inspired 'O the Sight Entrancing' is a tense ostinato piece that brilliantly
captures the mood of patriots in pre-battle array. Both this and its
companion 'Avenging and Bright' with its fierce false relations are suggestive of the baroque martial genre (and Britten's own keyboard realisation
of it) in Purcell and Handel. Amongst the 'nocturnes' of this set is the pentatonic imagery of 'How Sweet the Answer Echo Makes' – another setting
in which Britten joins hands with Purcell in the 'echo song' genre
(launched in 'Come You Not from Newcastle') and looks forward to one
of Britten's own echo songs, the first setting in the Pushkin cycle *The Poet's
Echo* (1965). Even more characteristic of Britten the composer is 'At the
Mid Hour of Night', in which a stepwise falling shape evokes a typical
scalewise descent of gentle diatonic discords of fourths and displaced
seconds (Ex. 16.4). (Cf. 'Sailing' in the early *Holiday Diary* suite for piano.)
Britten's fifth volume of folksong arrangements – which contains a

Example 16.4

larger proportion of well-known tunes than hitherto – seems to have
actually pre-dated the Moore's Irish melody collection, being collected
over a wider period of time. As Philip Reed has pointed out, the settings
cover a period of eight years (1951–9).[13] The first song, 'A Brisk Young
Widow', is based on the *Affekt* of a playfully contrived canon – in the
'dotty' false relations of the piano introduction/links (using a motif taken
from the last line) and in the actual accompaniment to the song itself,
where the piano in canon at the octave always follows close on the heels of
the tune. Canon surfaces (parodistically?) again in the bracing hunting-
style setting of 'The Lincolnshire Poacher' where in the final verse the
piano right hand veers off into no less than three different (and increasingly 'off-key') intervallic relationships with the tune, before returning to
the 'normality' of the octave. The harmonically piled-up thirds and
fourths (a hunting-horn image) are a further stimulating feature of this
lively setting, as is Britten's impish (one could almost describe it as perverse – even harmonically outrageous) delight in finding a different chord
for each of the five pauses on the 'O' prefix to ''tis my delight on a shining
night, in the season of the year'. In euphonious contrast, the harmonically
rich and sonorous 'Ca' the Yowes' offers an atmospheric effect of canon
through treating it as a diminution of the tune in the guise of accompanimental figuration. This song is a fine example of Britten's resourceful harmonic palette – not a single harmony is repeated in the richly concordant
sequence of root positions and occasional seventh chords, sympathet-
ically supporting the quasi-pentatonic (Aeolian) melody. Of the remain-

ing two arrangements in this set, 'Sally in Our Alley' (the tune and words are by the early eighteenth-century English composer Henry Carey) is remarkable for the way in which Britten intensifies the theme through an increasing concentration on its leading motif – the rising sixth of 'Sally' – so that by the time we have arrived at the last verse it has become obsessive and all-pervasive. The other characteristic of Britten's setting is the arpeggiated thirds – a fingerprint of his melodic style, of which the piano flourish to the Prologue of *The Turn of the Screw* furnishes a famous example. Here it serves as an ever-intensifying interlude between verses. To a lesser extent this same arpeggiated figure is characteristic of the piano 'cradling' of the tune of 'Early One Morning' – a setting notable for the purity of its diatonicism, with only an occasional chromatically expressive alteration to point up the pathos.

Appearing in close proximity (1961) to the preceding two volumes were the *Six English Songs* for voice and guitar, the first performances of which had taken place in the late 1950s at song recitals given by Pears and the guitarist, Julian Bream. The first of these, 'I Will Give My Love an Apple' – taken as it is directly from the Vaughan Williams source – offers an interesting nose-to-nose confrontation with the 'old fogey' who had so generously saluted Britten's idiosyncratic embrace of folksong back in 1943. Where Vaughan Williams sticks to cadential harmony based on traditional chord sequences derived purely from the (Aeolian) mode and unambiguous triple metre of the tune, Britten invents a somewhat perplexing 'non-cadential' ostinato figuration in changing cross-rhythms that strays uncompromisingly into territory alien (but not unsympathetic) to the mode. The setting is not as perverse as it would at first seem, for Britten is again responding to the riddle of the *words* here; it is the *text* rather than the tune that is responsible for Britten's 'strangeness', his seemingly unsophisticated interrogation of its modal purity embodying a musical pun on 'without any key'. Britten leaves the ear in doubt about the true key-centre before confirming it in a final *tierce de picardie* that teasingly clashes with the tune's minor third. Whatever our aesthetic response, the setting of the familiar folksong challenges pre-conditioned ears – and persuades us to consider its meaning afresh.

The stimulating 'composed background' to the next song, 'Sailor Boy', is an instrumental piece in itself, perfectly detachable from its context, capable of being served up (or 'dished up', as Grainger might have said) on its own as a 'walking song' without words. The fascination of this setting is precisely this independence of the guitar part – a jaunty countermelody brimful of modal ambiguities in the context of the tune's Aeolian B minor, developing its own characteristic motif in free asymmetrical cross-rhythms that disregard the cadence points of the original tune. Only when we reach the refrain does the guitar accompaniment become a swinging ostinato, and there is a spry cadenza-postscript for solo guitar to round off. Slight and unpretentious though the next song, 'Master Kilby', may be, Britten's harmony gives the tune a quizzical slant, for the cliché of imperfect cadence is subverted by means of an unexpected prolongation of dominant harmony, and the leading note of the tune lands on I instead of V.

Characteristic touches in the remaining songs include such things as the harmonic changes rung in the tipsy 'Amen' of 'The Soldier and the Sailor', the simple guitar-tuning (fourth-chord) inspired ostinati of 'Bonny at Morn' (with their fearlessly intricate 'false relations') and 'The Shooting of his Dear' – serenely decorative in the former, tragic and palely spectral in the latter. In each there is a fine, precarious balance maintained between traditional functional/cadential harmony and a more disjunct sense of ostinato-derived chordal colour.

The touching spirituality of the music of Britten's final period, when his frail state of health prevented him from playing the piano, is epitomized in the three valedictory works for high voice and harp written for Peter Pears and Osian Ellis. These are *The Death of St Narcissus* (words by T. S. Eliot), *A Birthday Hansel* (words by Robert Burns), and the *Eight Folk Song Arrangements* – the latter Britten's last completed vocal work, finished in the summer of 1976. (That folksong still mattered intensely to him is confirmed by another work from this late period, the suite on English folksongs for orchestra, *A Time There Was.*) It is in the context of these works that Britten's last volume of folksong arrangements is best understood. The sonority of the harp is a characteristic motif in Britten – from the evergreen *Ceremony of Carols*, through the *Nocturne*, with its memorable imagery in the Coleridge setting of the 'beauteous' boy plucking fruits to its rarefied collaboration with the strange words of the early T. S. Eliot in *The Death of St Narcissus*. In the wild cadenza-like commotion of 'Birdscarer's Song' in the *Eight Folk Song Arrangements* there is high art and admirable economy in Britten's free treatment of folk vocal line and harp accompaniment – wildness in the quasi-inversion of the tune implicit in the opening harp octaves, a whirring of wings in the partial heterophony of the harp tremolo that accompanies 'Shoo arlo birds', tension in the simple yet dramatic (mixed modal B major-minor versus pentatonic B♭) bitonality. One notes in both works a characteristic involvement with the rhythmic disturbance attendant on word repetition – something that is peculiar to, indeed becomes a motif of, the setting of Eliot's words in *The Journey of the Magi* ('a cold coming we had of it') and *The Death of St Narcissus* ('drunken and old'). For example – the nagging rhythmic dislocation of 'killed' at the end of 'Ma Hoggie' in the *Birthday*

Hansel or the spiteful 'wife', 'life', 'work' of 'Lord, I married me a wife' in the *Eight Folk Songs*. An uncanny hypnotism develops in the strange, hauntingly repetitive ballad of 'The False Knight upon the Road', as if the child's gaze becomes transfixed on its hapless victim. Although there is humour, an engaging feeling for oddity ('Wee Willy Gray' or the wild flappings of 'Birdscarer's Song') and vitality to be encountered in both works, certain songs stand out for their sadness and lyrical poignancy – for example, in 'Now the Winter it is Past' in the *Birthday Hansel* and 'She's like the Swallow' – with its motivically derived accompanimental figure – in the *Eight Folk Song Arrangements*. In the simple yet (harmonically and canonically) personal setting of the well-known 'David of the White Rock' ('Life and its follies are fading away' – set, like its predecessor, in Welsh), this poignancy catches something of the tone of impassioned despair that informs Schubert's *Winterreise*. A close look at this arrangement is not without its rewards, for here we confront one of those 'conditioned reflex' problems of acceptance of Britten's harmony, a problem highlighted by the comparatively traditional harmonic treatment of the preceding two settings. Britten's starting point is a sonorous F minor 6/4, octave led, and these octaves continue to provide a parallel-octave chord sequence which runs contrary (and how!) to text-book rules of functional harmony. The peculiarity of Britten's cadence-less background is all the more striking in view of the strongly defined traditional harmonic implications of the tune. Gradually, however, the new harmonic background falls into place and the ear becomes satisfied with the new, seemingly nonfunctional chord progressions (note the avoidance of F minor dominant harmony in the strange D♭ major-minor inflection of bar 3!), which are just sufficiently in line with the tune's F minor–D♭–A♭ orientation to keep faith with tradition. Less easily assimilated, perhaps, are the modal clashes/false relations Britten introduces further on: F♯ in bar 8, 'Dorian' D♮ in bar 11, and, most striking of all, 'Mixolydian' E♭ (= D♯) against leading note in bar 16 – but in the end this 'estrangement' of the tune serves to give fresh point to the forlorn message it carries. Finally, the middle verse is a fine specimen of Britten's free canonic treatment – the piano now echoing, now anticipating the tune – as in the motivically propelled flow into the 'recapitulation' of the last verse.

This fragile late-winter flowering of Britten's art is a precious bequest to the marriage he effected between music and words. In their fresh simplicity, restraint and economy, these last settings for voice and harp form an unpretentious yet memorable farewell to a genre he made completely his own.

17 Aldeburgh

JUDITH LEGROVE

> But I belong at home – there – in Aldeburgh. I have tried to bring music *to* it
> in the shape of our local Festival; and all the music I write comes *from* it. I
> believe in roots, in associations, in backgrounds, in personal relationships.[1]

There could be no clearer expression of Britten's artistic creed than that of
his thoughtfully worded speech on receiving the Aspen Award, in which
he spoke of his belief in 'occasional music', of an artist's role in society and
that music should demand of a listener 'some effort, a journey to a special
place, saving up for a ticket, some homework on the programme perhaps'.
Here already we have three ideas which, given the right circumstances,
could be made to flourish in the shape of a festival. The fourth ingredient
necessary for the formula was that 'special place', Aldeburgh; a place
which Britten was to regard as his home. As he memorably said in the
1964 speech, 'I do not write for posterity – in any case, the outlook for that
is somewhat uncertain. I write music, now, in Aldeburgh, for people living
there, and further afield, indeed for anyone who cares to play it or listen to
it. But my music now has its roots, in where I live and work.'[2]

It was while driving to Lucerne in 1947 for performances with the
newly formed English Opera Group that Pears turned to his companions
Britten and Crozier and suggested, 'Why not . . . make our own Festival?'[3]
The idea was prompted by the absurd hardship and expense of travelling
abroad to find audiences for new English operas that were not being supported in their country of origin. Although it was gratifying to present
Albert Herring and *The Rape of Lucretia* to packed houses at festivals in
Lucerne and Holland and to feel that English opera was once again
making its mark, it appeared uneconomic for the English Opera Group
tour to be repeated.[4] From this point of view a local festival including
opera certainly made sense.

On their return, Britten, Pears and Crozier started making enquiries
about the feasibility of an Aldeburgh Festival. It had already been decided
that if the Jubilee Hall were large enough to house a simple opera production, plans would be made for a small-scale festival in June 1948. At this
stage the practical help of Elizabeth Sweeting was enlisted in examining
potential venues.[5] Preliminary findings were positive: the Jubilee Hall,
seating 290, was just large enough for opera and the Vicar of Aldeburgh
was happy for the Parish Church to be used for concerts. Yet there still

remained the problems of financing the festival and of determining whether local feeling would be for or against the project, since without popular support the venture would be virtually impossible. A public meeting was held at which Britten and Pears, genuinely fond of Aldeburgh, put forward a persuasive case, and (perhaps surprisingly) the public was won over. Fears that the festival would amount to an unwelcome 'invasion' were allayed so that by the end of the evening promises had already been made against financial loss, outright offers of help received and, far from rushing away, people even stayed behind to discuss the idea further. It was this local support which was of crucial benefit to the early years of the Aldeburgh Festival.[6] As for the financial side, a 'guarantee' system was set up which produced a sum of £1,400. In addition to £500 made available by the Arts Council, this was deemed sufficient for the festival to go ahead.

Pears's original vision of an Aldeburgh Festival had been a 'modest [one] with a few concerts given by friends'.[7] The festival was to be built around the English Opera Group, both practically and artistically: the Group would provide the singers and instrumentalists necessary for recitals and chamber music, while opera (central to Britten's output) would be at the heart of the proceedings. Since it was very much an experiment, this first festival was limited to a week and two weekends with a programme largely consisting of chamber concerts and recitals to minimize rehearsal time. Britten gathered around him not only some of the finest British performers of his day but also a daunting line-up of figures from the literary world. There were lectures on subjects ranging from literature (William Plomer on Edward FitzGerald and E. M. Forster on George Crabbe and *Peter Grimes*), to theatre (Tyrone Guthrie on 'The Theatre Today'), music (Steuart Wilson on 'The Future of Music in England') and art (Sir Kenneth Clark on 'Constable and Gainsborough as East Anglian Painters'), in line with the founders' concept of the Aldeburgh Festival as a festival of 'Music and the Arts'. Exhibitions – *Peter Grimes* stage models and designs, contemporary East Anglian paintings, Suffolk writers' manuscripts, John Constable's paintings – were held throughout the town to tie in with the lectures and give the festival a local flavour. It was this individuality to which E. M. Forster alluded when he wrote that 'a festival should be festive' and 'it must possess something which is distinctive and which could not be so well presented elsewhere'.[8]

Musically the festival also had a unique character. At its centre in 1948 was *Albert Herring*, which was given three performances in the Jubilee Hall (see Plate 20). The opera was a resounding success: the intimacy of the small stage brought out the comedy of the piece and nowhere else could the references to local people and places have been better appreciated. The première of *Saint Nicolas* took place in the first concert of that festival, and was another landmark.[9] It was the first of what was to be a long line of Britten works given their first performances at the Aldeburgh Festival, and involved – together with professional singers – the local community, in the shape of the Aldeburgh Festival Choir. This brought together singers from all over east Suffolk, from choral societies, schools and church choirs. Entry to the choir was by audition, with preliminary rehearsals being held by local conductors before forces were joined for the last few practices. By all accounts those first two performances of *Saint Nicolas* were particularly magical: E. M. Forster described how 'the sudden contrast between elaborate singing and the rough breathy voices of three kids from a local "Co-op" made one swallow in the throat and water in the eyes'[10] and Imogen Holst recalled that 'the crowning glory of the work came at the end, when the listeners were drawn into the singing of "God moves in a mysterious way", and the "frozen hearts" in the audience-congregation became unfrozen'.[11] *Saint Nicolas* was repeated frequently at subsequent festivals.

Britten's and Pears's practical involvement was such that during the first festival they gave performances every day except one and twice took part in two concerts per day. Apart from Pears's role in *Saint Nicolas* (which was conducted by Leslie Woodgate), he sang the title role in the three performances of *Albert Herring* which Britten conducted; there was a recital of English and German song, a concert by the Zorian String Quartet in which Britten played the keyboard parts of Bridge's *Phantasy Quartet* and Purcell's *Golden Sonata*, an 'Aldeburgh Serenade' concert devised by Basil Douglas in which both Britten and Pears were involved, and a chamber concert in which Britten shared the conducting with Arthur Oldham. Even with these heavy performing commitments, Britten and Pears held 'open house' at their home in Crag Path – thus creating for themselves what could easily have been a punishingly hectic schedule. In retrospect, though, Pears was adamant about Britten's enjoyment of it: 'In fact, those early festivals were among the happiest years of Ben's life . . . because there was something to do: I mean, he liked to do things, he liked to work. He liked to have an aim and an object. He liked to work for people and he liked to be useful, to be serving the public.'[12]

If the first Aldeburgh Festival had been an artistic success, and judging from the favourable reviews it certainly was, from a financial point of view good ticket sales had made it nowhere near as disastrous as might have been expected – there was even a credit balance in the accounts. This was largely due to the economical use of a small number of performers for several events, but one other important factor should not be overlooked: the hidden subsidy from Britten and Pears themselves, who took no fees.

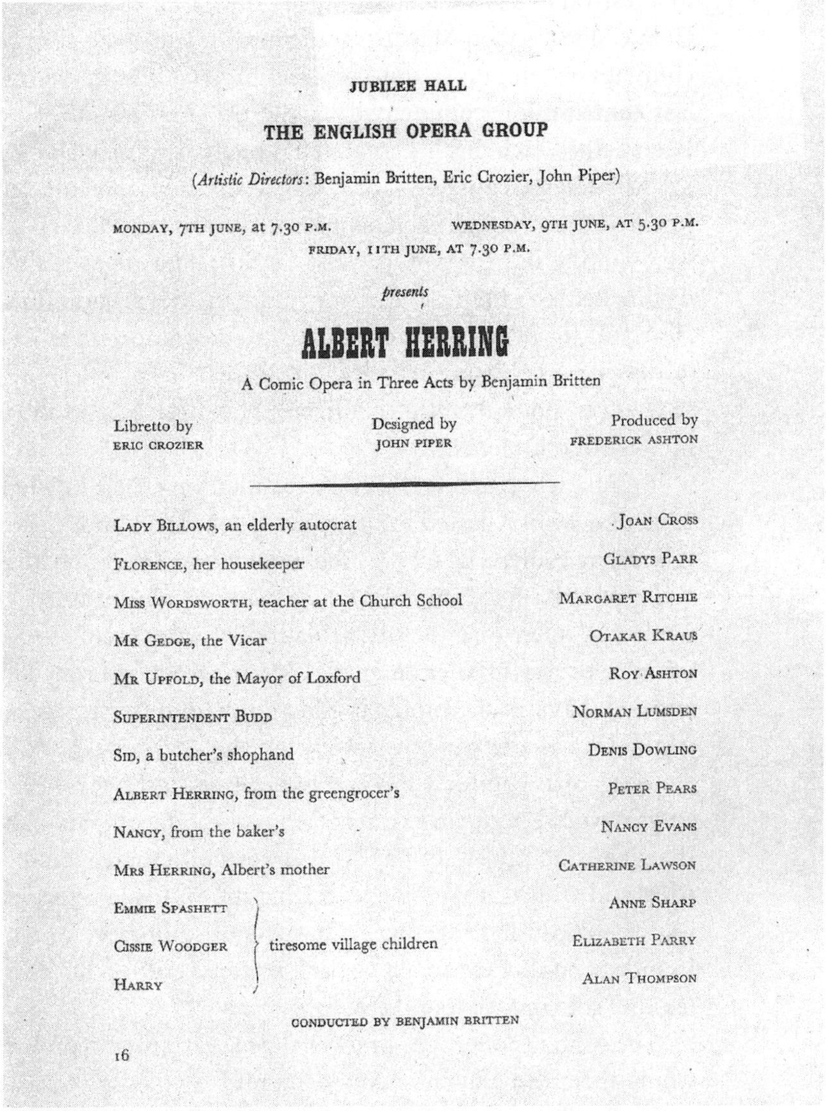

JUBILEE HALL

THE ENGLISH OPERA GROUP

(*Artistic Directors*: Benjamin Britten, Eric Crozier, John Piper)

MONDAY, 7TH JUNE, at 7.30 P.M.   WEDNESDAY, 9TH JUNE, AT 5.30 P.M.
FRIDAY, 11TH JUNE, AT 7.30 P.M.

presents

ALBERT HERRING

A Comic Opera in Three Acts by Benjamin Britten

Libretto by	Designed by	Produced by
ERIC CROZIER	JOHN PIPER	FREDERICK ASHTON

LADY BILLOWS, an elderly autocrat	JOAN CROSS
FLORENCE, her housekeeper	GLADYS PARR
MISS WORDSWORTH, teacher at the Church School	MARGARET RITCHIE
MR GEDGE, the Vicar	OTAKAR KRAUS
MR UPFOLD, the Mayor of Loxford	ROY ASHTON
SUPERINTENDENT BUDD	NORMAN LUMSDEN
SID, a butcher's shophand	DENIS DOWLING
ALBERT HERRING, from the greengrocer's	PETER PEARS
NANCY, from the baker's	NANCY EVANS
MRS HERRING, Albert's mother	CATHERINE LAWSON
EMMIE SPASHETT	ANNE SHARP
CISSIE WOODGER — tiresome village children	ELIZABETH PARRY
HARRY	ALAN THOMPSON

CONDUCTED BY BENJAMIN BRITTEN

16

Plate 20 Programme book to the first Aldeburgh Festival (1948), detailing the first performances of *Albert Herring*

At the post-festival meeting of the Executive Committee, of which Lord Harewood was President and Felicity Cranbrook Chair, a 'universal desire that the festival should be repeated from year to year' was minuted; and so what had started as an inspired idea became the tangible reality of an annual event.

In terms of content and programme planning the second year was similar to the first. A strong focus on local issues was retained and the programme book, beautifully produced with photographs and black-and-white illustrations, once again contained topical essays: an account of the first festival by E. M. Forster, a survey of coastal erosion at Aldeburgh by C. E. Colbeck (then Mayor of Aldeburgh), an article about east Suffolk churches by John Piper and a piece about Bach and Purcell by Pears. This last contribution commented on the programmes of Sacred Music & Poetry, in which Bach cantatas, anthems by Purcell and readings of English religious poems of the seventeenth and eighteenth centuries were featured. Purcell and Bach, along with Dowland, Mozart and Schubert, were among the composers most performed at the Aldeburgh Festival during Britten's lifetime, and from studying the programmes it becomes clear that there was a nucleus of favoured composers. As Crozier stated, 'We hoped, by pleasing ourselves, to please many people: if we had tried to please everybody, the result could only have been a timid and half-hearted mixture of oddments.'[13]

In the early years the festival expanded very little in length (between 1948 and 1959 it lasted either nine or ten days) and a pattern of programming evolved which was remarkably consistent. There was always a large choral concert in the Parish Church on a Saturday afternoon, flanked by opera on either the Friday or Saturday evening and at least two other concerts of the 'Serenade', chamber or solo-recital type. This ensured that anyone coming to Aldeburgh for only the weekend could be guaranteed a variety of musical fare. During the week, in addition to other concerts, opera performances or 'opera evenings' (where Pears and other singers would perform extracts from operas accompanied by Britten at the piano and introduced by Lord Harewood), there would be films, lectures and wine tastings, not forgetting the Sunday Festival Services – an important coming together of locals and visitors in which two of the founders would take an active part, Britten reading the lesson and Pears taking a solo in a verse anthem.

The contents of programmes changed very little: an orchestral concert would include a Haydn or Mozart symphony and a Mozart piano concerto as well as a more modern work; a chamber concert almost invariably featured works by Mozart, Schubert or Haydn as well as a piece by Janáček, Bridge or a less familiar twentieth-century composer; and a Britten–Pears recital often began with German Lieder (usually Schubert) and after the interval featured Britten's or other English songs, ending with Britten's own folksong arrangements. As for opera, in 1949 Britten composed a specifically 'Aldeburgh' piece for the festival: *Let's Make an Opera*, with a libretto by Crozier. Set in Iken Hall, not far from Snape, the girls and boys of the cast were given the names of 'the Gathorne-Hardys of Great Glemham, Suffolk'.[14] Daringly Britten invited the audience's participation in the songs which framed the three scenes of the opera (see pp. 284–5). Also revived in 1949 were *Albert Herring* and *The Rape of*

Lucretia, while in 1950 Britten's realization of *The Beggar's Opera* was staged in the Jubilee Hall and *Let's Make an Opera* repeated.

In 1951 Aldeburgh was chosen as a centre for the Festival of Britain but, despite an increased grant from the Arts Council, a heavy loss was incurred. This was perhaps surprising since there were only four opera performances – two double-bills of *Dido and Aeneas* with Monteverdi's *Il Combattimento di Tancredi e Clorinda* and two performances of *Albert Herring*. Looking back on 1951 and the following years Stephen Reiss, Elizabeth Sweeting's successor, blamed the financial plight on 'false economies and a mistaken belief in the guarantee system as the most effective form of subsidy'.[15] The tide began to turn in 1955, when covenanted subscriptions were introduced, but it was not until 1957 that the festival's fortunes really began to improve. In this year the first late-night concerts were held, in conjunction with the BBC Transcription Service, at 10.45 p.m. in the Parish Church. The five-part series featured Buxtehude's *The Last Judgment*, a cycle of cantatas with related texts, and was performed by singers from the English Opera Group with the Aldeburgh Festival Orchestra, conducted by Charles Mackerras. Late-night concerts (this time early settings of the Magnificat) were again included in the 1958 festival[16] and thereafter were financially supported by the BBC Transcription Service until 1971. The driving force behind these concerts was Imogen Holst, who had come to work for Britten in 1952 and became a mainstay of the festival for the next twenty-five years. Early music was a particular passion of hers, as can be seen from the phenomenal range of music featured – from Osbert Parsley (a little-known sixteenth-century Norwich composer) or Pérotin to a programme of eighteenth-century Spanish chamber music – and for these concerts Holst conducted the Purcell Singers herself. There were also regular appearances by leading figures in the early-music scene: Ralph Downes, the Deller Consort and David Munrow's Early Music Consort. Imogen Holst's contribution as an artistic director from 1956 until her retirement in 1977 was invaluable, as was her help in so many practical and advisory ways. For her own part, she recalled that at the programme-planning meetings Britten was always the one to think most quickly and clearly, 'always aware of the difficulties of organizing a festival'.[17]

The popularity of the Aldeburgh Festival brought its own problems. The Jubilee Hall and Parish Church were simply not large enough to accommodate the number of people applying for tickets, and it seemed ludicrous to forgo potential extra income simply because of lack of space. Plans for a new theatre or opera house in Aldeburgh itself were tentatively discussed for some time before being made public in the October 1956 report from the Chair, Fidelity Cranbrook. A plot of land was bought at

Adair Lodge, not far from the Parish Church, and in February 1957 estimates were drawn up for the cost of the building work. The programme book of that year contained 'Notes On An Opera House For Aldeburgh' by H. T. Cadbury-Brown (rather fancifully comparing the project with Wagner at Bayreuth), together with an aerial photograph showing the precise location of the proposed Festival Theatre. In retrospect it is easy to see that the siting of the theatre would have been disastrous for Aldeburgh, causing terrible problems of parking and traffic congestion, so it was perhaps fortunate that the project came to nothing.

In the mean time, the lack of space was solved by moving away from Aldeburgh to larger churches further afield. 1956 was the first year in which Blythburgh Church was used, for a concert of unaccompanied sacred music from the Purcell Singers and Pears, conducted by Imogen Holst. The first performance of *Noye's Fludde* in 1958 was presented in Orford Church,[18] which had the advantage of having no large or heavy fixed pews so that the back of the church could easily be cleared to accommodate staging. *Noye's Fludde* was another of the festival's landmark compositions, following very much in the tradition of *Saint Nicolas* and *The Little Sweep* in its involvement of the audience, but with the opportunity for far greater numbers of Suffolk children to take part.

Although Orford Church was to be used again for the three Church Parables in the 1960s, it was no answer to the problem of where to perform larger-scale secular concerts or opera. A temporary solution was found in the expansion (at a cost far below that of the projected new theatre) of the Jubilee Hall, which reopened in time for the 1960 Festival. For the occasion Britten composed *A Midsummer Night's Dream*, a full-length opera, but written very much to suit the limitations of what was, even with the enlarged stage, still a small auditorium.[19] Britten was determined that a larger venue should be found in order that a more varied repertoire could be heard at the festival. After much thought Stephen Reiss, then Festival Manager, suggested Snape Maltings as a candidate for possible conversion. In October 1965 Reiss wrote to Ove Arup, a distinguished civil engineer whose work had included Coventry Cathedral and the Sydney Opera House. Shortly afterwards Derek Sugden was sent by his employees, Arup Associates, to look at the Maltings – a group of traditional nineteenth-century buildings constructed from local brick with timber roofs now covered with mossed asbestos tiles. The original plan was to take out the central wall of the large kiln to allow seating for 750, to replace the charcoal timber roof, to provide a removable proscenium for opera and to make the auditorium suitable for use by Decca as a recording studio. It was a tall order, particularly as Britten initially wanted to limit expenditure to £50,000.[20] Paramount was the need for a good acoustic: the building would be a concert hall first and foremost with facilities for recording, and if opera were also possible it would be a bonus. Work began in May 1966 and the programme book of that year's festival included both photographs of 'Snape Malt House' before its conversion and a picture of the architect's model of the stage.

Remarkably, the transformation was completed in time for the 1967 Festival, when the concert hall was formally opened by the Queen. A new era now dawned for the Aldeburgh Festival: gone were the days of hearing a recital of Wilbye's madrigals sung by the English Opera Group in the Tudor Brandeston Hall, or of listening to ad hoc 'Music on the Meare' at Thorpeness. These smaller, more informal events gave way to concerts where there were no longer problems of transport to remote churches or worries over seating arrangements. With the concert hall and its excellent acoustic came new possibilities for expansion: the first festival in which it was used lasted twenty-four days, and included ten opera performances and fifty other events. There were also casualties. Setting aside the unhelpful criticism that the festival was no longer the intimate 'family affair' that it used to be, with the extra work-load it was not possible for the festival administration still to promote the highly successful 'Bach at Long Melford' weekends which had run annually in September since 1962.

1968 saw the addition of a new Artistic Director, Philip Ledger, to the existing trio of Britten, Pears and Holst for an even more ambitious festival of twenty-three days with eleven opera performances (including Birtwistle's *Punch and Judy* in the Jubilee Hall). Then, in the following year, disaster struck as fire gutted the Maltings Concert Hall on the first day of the festival. Britten, ever practical, immediately began to discuss contingency plans for the remaining concerts and vowed publicly that the hall should be rebuilt – a relatively easy task in that the basic plan had already been approved and most of the walls survived intact. The problem of fund-raising proved less straightforward, however. As the building had been comprehensively insured it was assumed that no further funds were needed, yet Britten wanted to take the opportunity to correct certain drawbacks which, as with any new building, had become apparent only through use.

Besides venue, the other most important aspect responsible for shaping the course of the Aldeburgh Festival was Britten's collaboration with other artists. Its effect can most readily be traced through the succession of first performances of works inspired by these musicians: *Lachrymae* (1950) written for the violist William Primrose, the *Six Metamorphoses after Ovid* for oboist Joy Boughton (premièred on Thorpeness Meare in 1951), *Songs from the Chinese* (1958) and *Nocturnal after John Dowland* (1964) for guitarist Julian Bream, Sonata in C (1961) and the first two Suites for cello (1965 and 1968) for Rostropovich, *Songs and Proverbs of William Blake* (1965) for Dietrich Fischer-Dieskau, *Gemini Variations* (1965) for the Hungarian Jeney twins, *The Golden Vanity* (1967) for the Vienna Boys' Choir, the Suite for Harp (1969) for Osian Ellis and *Canticle IV: Journey of the Magi* (1971) for Pears, James Bowman and John Shirley-Quirk. As well as Pears, who was in any case central to Britten's creativity, among the most important of these friendships were those with Bream, Ellis and Rostropovich. Bream and later the harpist Osian Ellis[21] both accompanied Pears and were the inspiration for folksong arrangements by Britten; in addition, the Julian Bream Consort frequently performed at the festival. George Malcolm was another mainstay, devising and conducting concert programmes and accompanying singers or instrumentalists. Above all, the Russian connection – Britten's friendship with Mstislav Rostropovich, his wife Galina Vishnevskaya and with Sviatoslav Richter – had a strong bearing on the character of the Aldeburgh Festival in the 1960s. With boundless enthusiasm Rostropovich immersed himself in the festival and all it had to offer, to the extent that after Britten's death he was willing to continue his support by becoming an Artistic Director in 1978.

By the time of the restoration of the improved Snape Maltings Concert Hall in 1970, the Aldeburgh Festival had been moulded to a form which, broadly speaking, corresponds with that of today. Britten's achievement in establishing an internationally renowned festival, with its own concert hall, is clear; what is perhaps not so obvious is his relationship with the festival – the interaction between composer, performer and public. To return briefly to the founding of the festival, there was certainly more to the idea than merely cutting the cost of touring with the English Opera Group. From the early post-war years onwards there was a gradual but steady stream of festivals being set up throughout Britain, of which that in Edinburgh, founded in 1947, was the first and largest. Peter Diamand, secretary to the Holland Festival from 1947 until 1965 when he joined the Edinburgh Festival, referred to this as part of a 'healing process' by which the country could begin to make amends for the cultural starvation of the war years.[22] Britten had a strong sense of duty, so there may have been a sense in which he wanted to be actively involved in this resurgence. Above all, though, Britten *enjoyed* the idea of a festival, so much so that in 1964 he described it as 'the musical project I have most at heart'. While he had no need to provide a platform for his own work – his growing reputation was sufficient to ensure performances elsewhere – he threw himself wholeheartedly into making the venture a success,[23] ultimately by providing a steady supply of new works to be premièred at the festival. This was vital both for his creative development and for the festival: Britten would write works for specific performers to tempt them to Aldeburgh, where they might take part in a number of concerts; the festival would in turn benefit from the attraction of a new piece and the presence of its eminent dedicatee.

As Britten's life became increasingly crowded with commissions and concert engagements it required careful planning to avoid clashes with the festival period. The winter was kept largely free for work on new compositions but rehearsal schedules for the festival could be worked out as early as January to save time later. Other work, such as programme-note writing, planning programmes, booking artists and marking-up scores could also be done in advance. Inevitably, though, as each festival approached time became scarce and last-minute crises, such as Rostropovich's illness in 1963, brought increased pressure. Rehearsal time was at a premium, so programmes would feature works which were already being prepared for a recording. Importantly the new concert hall, for which Britten had striven so hard, allowed him to put on or perform any work of his choosing and removed the necessity of travelling to London for recording sessions.

Imogen Holst recollected that the Aldeburgh Festival was essential in allowing Britten the opportunity to conduct and so learn the technique of conducting.[24] It was largely due to the experience gained during the late 1940s and 1950s that Britten was able to produce such a legacy of fine recordings with the English Chamber Orchestra during the 1960s and 1970s, as for example his superb interpretation of Elgar's *Dream of Gerontius* or his own *A Midsummer Night's Dream*. In these recordings it is Britten's ability to view the work from a composer's point of view which gives them that special quality – the taut dramatic pacing of an opera or the structural insight into a symphony – and while Britten may not have felt confident of his conducting technique there is no doubt that he communicated clearly with his orchestras, drawing from them unforgettable performances.[25]

After Britten's death, Pears continued as an Artistic Director, joined by Rostropovich, Ledger, Colin Graham, and Steuart Bedford; and, as was inevitable, the character of the festival gradually began to change. These days it is rare to hear the Bach cantatas or Mozart symphonies of the earlier festivals, but this is as much due to the modern authenticity movement as the festival administration: it no longer seems acceptable to play such works without period instruments or to include them in programmes with music from different periods. Innovations have included the performance of Japanese and Thai music, acknowledging the importance of Eastern influences in Britten's music. As early as the 1973 Festival, Colin Graham had given a lecture on 'The Classical Theatre of Japan', and in the evening a Japanese cast had performed two Nō plays (*Sumidagawa* and *Funa Benkei*) in the Snape Maltings. After 1976, the oriental connection was kept alive by Donald Mitchell, who devised a weekend of Thai music and dance at Snape in October 1977 and – as Guest Artistic Director – based a series of concerts, lectures and Japanese drama around two performances of *Curlew River* as part of the 1991 Festival. Yet the Aldeburgh Festival retains its identity. Britten's works are at its heart, and even now there are still works – early incidental music or unpublished songs – being heard for the first time in concert performance.[26] Recent Artistic Directors, Oliver Knussen and Steuart Bedford (with Colin Matthews as a close associate), have ensured that a good deal of contemporary music is heard as well as unusual or rarely performed works, though it should not be forgotten that this was also the case in Britten's time.

New generations are bringing fresh vitality to the festival. The Britten–Pears School for Advanced Musical Studies at Snape, established through the vision of Britten and Pears, has developed from a study weekend of lectures and masterclasses for singers in 1972 into a flourishing training centre, attracting high-calibre students from throughout the world and offering tuition by leading musicians. There is a well-established tradition of concert-giving by young musicians at the Maltings, and the Britten–Pears School's opera productions and Britten–Pears Chamber Orchestra's programmes are among the best-supported events in the Festival. The Hesse Student scheme is another valuable way in which young people can participate in the musical life of Aldeburgh. Initiated in 1959 by Margaret, Princess of Hesse and the Rhine, a bursary enables students to attend festival events in return for their help with selling programmes, arranging chairs or running errands. A thriving Education Department at the Aldeburgh Foundation involves schoolchildren in performances (of works such as *Noye's Fludde* and *Saint Nicolas*) during the festival, and in creative workshops throughout the year. Britten's encouragement of younger composers (among those to receive his advice were Oliver Knussen, Robert Saxton, Jonathan Harvey and Alexander Goehr) is continued in the regular feature of a showcase concert in the Jubilee Hall,[27] in two composition awards[28] and in the recent inclusion of a composition course at the Britten–Pears School.

Not least of all, Britten's heritage is safeguarded by the unique archive at the Britten–Pears Library, which has at its centre the corpus of Britten's manuscripts. These were preserved as an entity after Britten's death by a unique arrangement in which manuscripts belonging to the national collection at the British Library were deposited on permanent loan at The Red House, his home in Aldeburgh. The archive also contains an extensive collection of correspondence, photographs, sound recordings and printed ephemera, constituting a research institute which attracts interest from scholars worldwide.

The musical life that has grown up around Aldeburgh bears witness to Britten's strong commitment to a local community. The Aldeburgh Festival brought him into contact with his performers and public, the two other corners of that 'holy triangle',[29] and helped him to flourish creatively; today it remains an international event when performers, composers and audience alike can be refreshed both artistically and intellectually – and be sure of learning something new.

Notes

Introduction

1 Peter Evans, 'Instrumental Music I', in Stephen Banfield (ed.), *The Blackwell History of Music in Britain Vol. 6: The Twentieth Century* (Oxford: Blackwell, 1995), p. 186.

2 DMPR, p. 191.

3 DMPR, p. 364, and HCBB, p. 51 (the latter quoted from an interview Britten gave to *High Fidelity Magazine* in December 1959).

4 William McNaught, 'String Orchestras', *Musical Times* 78 (November 1937), p. 990.

5 William McNaught, 'The Promenade Concerts', *Musical Times* 79 (September 1938), pp. 702–3.

6 See MCPR, pp. 138–40.

7 Stephen Williams, writing in the *Evening News* on 3 December 1951.

8 For Mitchell's riposte to the early critical reaction to *Billy Budd*, see his 'More Off Than On *Billy Budd*', *Music Survey* 4/2 (February 1952), pp. 386–408, repr. in DMCN, pp. 365–92.

9 Unpublished letter from Britten to Donald Mitchell and Hans Keller, 21 January 1953.

10 Peter Tranchell, 'Britten and Brittenites', *Music & Letters* 34/2 (1953), pp. 124–32.

11 Peter Schaffer, review in *Time and Tide*, 7 June 1962. For a full account of the critical reception of the *War Requiem*, see MCWR, pp. 78–91.

12 Review of Stephen Banfield, *Sensibility and English Song*, and Ian Kemp, *Tippett: The Composer and His Music*, in *Music Analysis* 4/3 (1985), p. 308.

13 Patricia Howard, *The Operas of Benjamin Britten* (London: Barrie & Rockliff, 1969); Eric Walter White, *Benjamin Britten: His Life and Operas* (London: Faber & Faber, 1970). The latter was expanded from White's *Benjamin Britten: A Sketch of His Life and Works* (London: Boosey & Hawkes, 1948), which had appeared in a German translation in its year of publication and was updated in 1954. White's 1970 text was revised by John Evans for publication by Faber in 1983 (EWWB).

14 HCBB, p. 290.

15 HCBB, pp. 213 and 512.

16 Robin Holloway, 'Benjamin Britten: Tributes and Memories', *Tempo* 120 (1977), pp. 5–6.

1 Juvenilia (1922–1932)

1 The *Sinfonietta* was Britten's second publication: the first was a set of three songs for two-part women's voices to poems by Walter de la Mare: see HCBB, pp. 41–2.

2 See MSBC, p. 114, and Benjamin Britten, 'Early Influences: A Tribute to Frank Bridge', *Composer* 19 (1966), pp. 2–3.

3 In saying this, I do not intend to suggest that Britten was trying to give the impression he was a better composer as a child than in fact he was – though it is noticeable that the published scores of the *Five Walztes* and the 1931 Quartet give no indication of any revision having taken place.

4 Chief among these were the *Quatre chansons françaises* (1928; first broadcast on 30 March 1980, and first performed in concert on 10 June of that year; published and commercially recorded in 1982) and the *Quartettino* (1930; first performed on 23 May 1983; published in 1983; commercially recorded in 1986).

5 See CMEB, p. ix, and PEMB, p. 548.

6 The following works are investigated in more detail in CMEB: *Humoreske*, *Quatre chansons françaises*, *Quartettino*, the originals of the songs published under the title *Tit for Tat*, *A Hymn to the Virgin*, the String Quartet in D major of 1931, and the Phantasy Quintet.

7 Beth Britten, *My Brother Benjamin* (Bourne End: The Kensal Press, 1986), p. 49. For a biographical note on Audrey Alston, see DMPR, p. 162.

8 CMEB, p. 7.

9 See CMEB, p. 10; extracts from the beginning and the end of the first movement, and from the beginning of the slow movement, are transcribed on pp. 291–3.

10 See CMEB, p. 8; the Waltz is reproduced in facsimile on pp. 273–6.

11 Britten may have played Schumann's Etudes Symphoniques by this time, but he did not apparently own a score: what seems to be a shopping list on the back of the viola part for the viola and piano piece 'First Loss' dated 6 April 1926 itemizes the following works (see Britten–Pears Library Microfilm A70, Frame 166):

    1 Etudes Symphoniques Schumann Op. 13 No. 8430 price 2/4

    2 Liszt Campanella 26 No. 5912 2/6

3 (Pianoforte) Duet Beethoven Septet Op. 20 price 2/6 No. 8518
4 Piano solo Beethoven Concertos (1–4) price 3/- each No. 7998 a–d
5 Brahms Sonata in F minor price 3/- [? indecipherable] 5105 Op. 5.
12 HC*BB*, p. 27.
13 Britten started collecting miniature scores in 1925, numbering them in acquisition order. A list of those extant in the Britten–Pears Library can found in CM*EB*, Appendix II, pp. 335–41.
14 Reproduced in facsimile in CM*EB*, pp. 281–2.
15 'Beware!' is reproduced in Imogen Holst, *Britten* (London: Faber & Faber, 1966), p. 15. See also MK*B*, pp. 2 and 3.
16 DMPR, p. 88.
17 The score was submitted with an accompanying letter written by Britten's father: see DMPR, pp. 86–7, which gives a facsimile of the opening to the overture.
18 Reproduced in facsimile in CM*EB*, pp. 278–9.
19 See DMPR, p. 13.
20 The term 'dissolving ending' was coined by Arnold Whittall to describe the ending of the Phantasy Quartet: see AW*BT*, p. 23.
21 HC*BB*, p. 16.
22 See, for example, Britten, 'Early Influences'.
23 See CM*EB*, p. 11.
24 Prefatory note to the collection *Tit for Tat* (London: Faber Music, 1969).
25 Britten's source for his texts was *The Oxford Book of French Verse: XIIIth Century – XIXth Century*, selected by St John Lucas (Oxford: Clarendon Press, 1924): see DMPR, p. 92.
26 Identified as the folksong 'Biquette' in DMPR, p. 92.
27 These lines are translated in the vocal score (London: Faber Music, 1982) as 'The poor sweet creature sang all day, and the mother coughed all night.'
28 See PE*MB*, p. 550, and CM*EB*, pp. 18–19.
29 See DMPR, pp. 8–9 and 96–7.
30 HC*BB*, p. 30.
31 DMPR, pp. 127–8.
32 See CM*EB*, p. 30.
33 DMPR, p. 418. Layton was also the dedicatee of the first movement ('P.T.') of the quartet entitled *Go Play, Boy, Play* (1933): see DMPR, p. 420.
34 See Britten's diary entries in DMPR, pp. 147, 150, 153, and 154.
35 Preface to the score of the 1931 String Quartet in D major (London: Faber Music, 1975).
36 See CM*EB*, pp. 37–8.
37 DMPR, p. 141.

38 Reproduced in facsimile in CM*EB*, pp. 310–14; the work is discussed on pp. 31–2.
39 'Christ's Nativity' (dated 2 March 1931, though it was rewritten from Friday 13 March: see Britten's diary entry for that date in DMPR, p. 166), 'Sweet was the Song' (13 January), 'Preparations' (11 March), 'New Prince, New Pomp' (25 February), and 'Carol of King Cnut' (16 February).
40 DMPR, p. 171.
41 The first page of the scenario in Violet Alford's hand is reproduced in facsimile in DMPR, p. 189. For a biographical note on Alford, see *ibid.*, p. 188.
42 See the facsimile in DMPR, p. 193.
43 He acquired the piano score of the Viola Concerto on 9 September 1931 before hearing the work, which he very much admired, on the next day: see DMPR, pp. 201 and 204. He heard *Belshazzar's Feast* on 25 November 1931: see DMPR, p. 217.
44 See CM*EB*, pp. 42–4.
45 See DMPR, pp. 243–4 and 190 respectively.
46 See DMPR, p. 245.
47 See CM*EB*, pp. 50–8.

2 Britten, Auden and 'otherness'

1 'Poets and the Crisis', *The Times*, 26 September 1938, p. 13. The leader writer is possibly quoting 'The Poet' by W. H. Davies (1871–1940): 'A human pack, ten thousand strong, / All in full cry to bring me down; / All greedy for my magic robe / All crazy for my burning crown'. Davies is partly referring to Shakespeare's *The Tempest* when, in Act V scene 1, Prospero enters in his magic robe.
2 Quoted in Humphrey Carpenter, *W. H. Auden: A Biography* (Oxford University Press, 1992), p. 291.
3 Britten himself described the genesis of *Peter Grimes* in these terms: 'A central feeling for us was that of the individual against the crowd, with ironic overtones for our own situation [as conscientious objectors]' (MS*BC*, p. 116).
4 W. H. Auden, 'The Prolific and the Devourer', in Edward Mendelson (ed.), *The English Auden* (London: Faber & Faber, 1986), p. 397.
5 *Ibid.*
6 *Ibid.*
7 Auden, 'The Liberal Fascist', in Mendelson, *The English Auden*, p. 322.
8 Benjamin Britten, 'How to Become a Composer', *Listener*, 7 November 1946, p. 624.
9 Based on the catalogue of Britten's juvenilia, Britten–Pears Library.
10 Britten's *Quatre chansons françaises* were also composed in this year.
11 Arnold Whittall, 'The Signs of Genre:

Britten's Version of Pastoral', in Chris Banks, Arthur Searle and Malcolm Turner (eds.), *Sundry Sorts of Music Books: Essays on The British Library Collections Presented to O. W. Neighbour on his 70th Birthday* (London: The British Library, 1993), p. 363.

12 Auden, 'The Prolific and the Devourer', in Mendelson, *The English Auden*, p. 397.

13 The contrast to the period 1940–79 – from the advent of the wartime coalition government to the formation of Margaret Thatcher's Conservative government – could not be more complete: the Conservatives were in power for only 17 years, as was Labour, and they both formed the wartime coalition.

14 A. H. Halsey, *British Social Trends Since 1900* (London: Macmillan, 1988), pp. 304–5. Support for the Conservatives was 55% in 1931, 54% four years later. If figures are calculated on a 'two party preferred' basis, support for the Conservatives was 67% in 1931 and 59% in 1935.

15 Halsey, *British Social Trends*, p. 318. In 1931 the figures were 77% and 55%. By contrast, in 1938 only 1.7% of the pertinent British age group attended university.

16 Ross McKibbin, *The Ideologies of Class: Social Relations in Britain 1880–1950* (Oxford: Clarendon Press, 1994), pp. 266–7; my italics.

17 *Ibid.*, p. 275.

18 Auden, 'The Liberal Fascist', in Mendelson, *The English Auden*, p. 325.

19 Auden, 'The Prolific and the Devourer', in Mendelson, *The English Auden*, p. 400.

20 Carpenter, *W. H. Auden: A Biography*, p. 52.

21 Mark Simpson, *It's a Queer World* (London: Vintage, 1996), p. 26.

22 The Earl of Arran, speaking in the House of Lords on 21 July 1967, quoted in Patrick Higgins, *A Queer Reader* (London: Fourth Estate, 1993), p. 196; my italics.

23 Bernard Macfadden developed theories on kinesiology – the study of the mechanics of body movements – and espoused them in his own journal and in his *Encyclopaedia of Physical Culture* (1920). Percy Grainger was a devotee.

24 Samuel Hynes, *The Auden Generation* (London: Pimlico, 1976), p. 122.

25 Auden, 'Underneath the abject willow', in Mendelson, *The English Auden*, p. 160. This poem is dedicated to Britten.

26 Britten's diary, 28 July 1937 (Britten–Pears Library).

27 See Donald Mitchell, 'Schoolroom and Cabaret', in DM*BA*, pp. 103–31. See also his introduction in DMPR, pp. 17–23.

28 Valentine Cunningham, *British Writers of the Thirties* (Oxford University Press, 1993), p. 142. But then, joked John Strachey, the real

world is a schoolboy world, where you join the Communist Party in a huff at not getting into the Eton Cricket XI (*ibid.*, p. 131.)

29 Even the near-mythical and masculine T. E. Lawrence, according to Isherwood, had a 'giggling laugh, played practical jokes and interspersed his conversation with schoolboy slang' (Cunningham, *British Writers*, p. 143).

30 Whilst still at school, Esmond and Giles Romilly – whom Britten met in 1936 – published an infamous magazine *Out of Bounds*, 'against Reaction, Militarism and Fascism in the Public Schools'. Gresham's response to the first two issues was significant: 'At a recent debate a motion that "In the opinion of this House a Fascist Dictatorship is preferable to Socialism" was carried by ninety-nine votes to fifty-four' (DMPR, p. 403).

31 Cunningham, *British Writers*, pp. 150–1.

32 Britten to Mrs Britten, 28 July 1936 (DMPR, p. 436). Four days earlier Britten had written in his diary: 'A long walk after dinner, after which I sketch a bit of a funeral march to those youthful Spanish martyrs.'

33 Nevill Coghill, 'Sweeney Agonistes', in Richard March and James Meary Tambimuttu (eds.), *T. S. Eliot: A Symposium* (London: Editions Poetry London, 1948), p. 82.

34 Auden, 'I have a handsome profile', in Mendelson, *The English Auden*, p. 123.

35 Britten in discussion with the Earl of Harewood, BBC 'People Today', [May/June] 1960; my italics.

36 Hynes, *The Auden Generation*, p. 166. *The Poet's Tongue* dates from the year in which Auden and Britten first met. Eliot had also experimented with such popular forms.

37 Auden, 'Here on the cropped grass of the narrow ridge I stand', in Mendelsohn, *The English Auden*, p. 142.

38 Cunningham, *British Writers*, pp. 280 and 285.

39 D. L. LeMahieu, *A Culture for Democracy* (Oxford: Clarendon Press, 1988), p. 310.

40 John Carey, *The Intellectuals and the Masses* (London: Faber & Faber, 1992), p. 38.

41 It did not help that the majority of those working in the GPO Film Unit were graduates of either Oxford or Cambridge. See Stuart Hood's essay 'John Grierson and the Documentary Film Movement', in James Curran and Vincent Porter (eds.), *British Cinema History* (London: Weidenfeld & Nicolson, 1983), pp. 99–112.

42 Auden, 'Coal Face', in Mendelsohn, *The English Auden*, p. 290.

43 Cf. 'And kiss me, Kate, we will be married o' Sunday' (*The Taming of the Shrew*, Act II scene 1, line 317).

44 Stephen Spender, *Forward From Liberalism* (London: Victor Gollancz, 1937), pp. 192–3; my italics.

45 Christopher Isherwood, *Mr Norris Changes Trains* (London: Hogarth Press, 1935), p. 77; my italics.

46 J. M. Hay, 'Writers' International', *Left Review* 1/6 (1935), p. 221, quoted in LeMahieu, *A Culture for Democracy*, p. 313.

47 Cunningham, *British Writers*, p. 274. Britten set Swingler's *Advance Democracy* in 1938.

48 DM*BA*, pp. 86–9.

49 *Ibid.*, p. 67.

50 The *Pacifist March* is reproduced in DM*BA*, pp. 68–9. The chorus begins with this imploration: 'March, stride to resist, strong with force not with fist.'

51 See Donald Mitchell's essay accompanying W. H. Auden, *Paul Bunyan: The Libretto of the Operetta by Benjamin Britten* (London: Faber & Faber, 1988), pp. 87–148.

52 The destructive nature of this eclecticism is underlined by the independent popularity of 'Inkslinger's Song': it is the most 'authentic' Britten piece in the opera.

53 Mitchell, essay accompanying Auden, *Paul Bunyan*, pp. 147–8.

54 Olin Downes in the *New York Times*, 6 May 1941 (quoted in DMPR, p. 915).

55 Britten described Downes as the 'snarkiest and most coveted' of the New York critics in a letter to Kit Welford, 4 April 1940 (quoted in DMPR, p. 792).

56 Mitchell, essay accompanying Auden, *Paul Bunyan*, pp. 94–8.

57 Auden, 'August for the people and their favourite islands', in Mendelsohn, *The English Auden*, p. 157.

58 This was first published by Little, Brown and Company in 1942.

59 DM*BA*, p. 38.

60 Randall Swingler, 'You who stand at your doors', set by Britten in *Ballad of Heroes*.

61 Carpenter, *W. H. Auden: A Biography*, p. 245.

62 *Ibid.*, p. 246.

63 It should be noted that certain key statements in Britten's interview with the Earl of Harewood are incorrect.

64 Auden, 'September 1939', in Mendelsohn, *The English Auden*, p. 246.

3 Britten in the cinema: *Coal Face*

1 For a discussion of the music for *The King's Stamp*, see Philip Reed, 'The Incidental Music of Benjamin Britten: A Study and Catalogue Raisonné of His Music for Film, Theatre and Radio', Ph.D. dissertation (University of East Anglia, 1987), pp. 48–69.

2 *Weather Forecast* (New Era for GPO/New Era, 1934), first shown in 1934. Producer: John Grierson; director: Evelyn Spice; sound supervision: Alberto Cavalcanti. Rachael Low describes the film as possessing 'some beautifully chosen shots further embellished by a soundtrack showing the influence of Cavalcanti. Music, commentary, and the sound of the sea, the winds, gulls screaming, dance music on the radio, a soft background of women's voices as they relay storm warnings complement the visuals . . . this modest but satisfying little film, though neglected later, was a pioneer of free cutting of the soundtrack and made with considerable style' (Rachael Low, *Documentary and Educational Films of the 1930s* (London: Allen & Unwin, 1979), p. 77).

3 *Spring on the Farm* (New Era for EMB/New Era, 1933), first shown 1934. Producer: John Grierson; director: Evelyn Spice; music direction: J. E. N. Cooper.

4 Quoted in Elizabeth Sussex, *The Rise and Fall of British Documentary – The Story of the Film Movement Founded by John Grierson* (Berkeley: University of California Press, 1975), p. 29. Ms Sussex does not commit herself to any interpretation of this evidence; the surviving documents relating to the script for *Coal Face*, notably the three draft typescripts at the Britten–Pears Library, Aldeburgh (see p. 57), probably invalidate Legg's recollection (which was made forty years after the event). The typescripts were surely the matrix on which any library footage was assembled.

5 See Paul Rotha, *Documentary Diary* (London: Secker & Warburg, 1973), p. 232.

6 See Reed, 'The Incidental Music', pp. 222–38, and DMPR, pp. 414–17.

7 The winning entry was Montagu Slater's *Easter 1916*, first performed in December 1935 with incidental music by Britten. See Reed, 'The Incidental Music', pp. 205–21.

8 Of these three projects, only *The Tocher* – a 'silhouette' film by the pioneer of the technique, Lotte Reiniger – could be considered experimental. This delightful film was accompanied by a charming set of Rossini arrangements by Britten, some of which later found their way, in altogether grander orchestrations, into the concert suites *Soirées musicales* and *Matinées musicales*.

9 *Coal Face* is thus named by Grierson in one of his notebooks including a list of 'films to be done' held in the collection of the John Grierson Archive, University of Stirling (G3N10: 16/17).

10 See Charles Osborne, *W. H. Auden: The Life of a Poet* (London: Eyre Methuen, 1980), p. 109.

11 Walt Whitman, *Leaves of Grass (1) and Democratic Vistas*, with an introduction by Horace Traubel (London: Dent, 1912; 1935 imprint), p. 183.

12 Whitman, *Leaves of Grass*, pp. 160–1.

13 See Sussex, *The Rise and Fall of British Documentary*, p. 65.

14 See John Grierson, 'The G.P.O. Gets Sound', *Cinema Quarterly* 2/4 (Summer 1934), p. 221.

15 Humphrey Carpenter, *W. H. Auden: A Biography* (London: Allen & Unwin, 1981), p. 178.

16 Osborne, *Life of a Poet*, p. 109.

17 From Auden's unpublished contribution to Anthony Gishford (ed.), *A Tribute to Benjamin Britten on His Fiftieth Birthday* (London: Faber & Faber, 1963). This memoir first appeared in Osborne, *Life of a Poet*, p. 111. Although Auden's contribution arrived too late for inclusion in the Britten *Festschrift*, the poet made a characteristic appearance in a televised tribute to the composer broadcast by the BBC in 1963.

18 See Donald Mitchell's annotated interview with Enid Slater in PB*PG*, pp. 23, 27–8. Enid Slater recalled: 'Montagu got to know quite a few miners in Millom [his home town, in Cumbria] – to his family's horror, because that wasn't the sort of thing that was done. So he knew quite a lot about mining.' Edward Mendelson, in the first volume of his magisterial complete Auden edition, states categorically that Slater was the author of the 'prose narration about coal mining' (but *not* the chants), although he, like Rachael Low, gives no source for this important piece of information. See W. H. Auden and Christopher Isherwood, *Plays and Other Dramatic Writings by W. H. Auden, 1928–1938*, edited by Edward Mendelson (London: Faber & Faber, 1989), p. 665.

19 *Stay Down Miner (Reportage 1)* (London: Martin Lawrence, 1936). It was the publisher Martin Lawrence who initiated a series of reportage accounts of contemporary industrial conditions. Slater subsequently made a dramatized account of the Welsh miners' protests under the same title, first performed by the Left Theatre in May 1936 with incidental music by Britten. See Reed, 'The Incidental Music', pp. 222–38, and DMPR, pp. 415–17.

20 See Walter Leigh, 'The Musician and the Film', *Cinema Quarterly* 3/2 (Winter 1935), pp. 70–74, and Reed, 'The Incidental Music', pp. 41–6.

21 Donald Mitchell recalls: 'Britten himself had some interesting memories of what was involved technically in securing the right sonority for a particular passage. I remember, for instance, his recalling the realization of the characteristic "swish" of a train passing through a tunnel ... in *Coal Face*. This was achieved by striking a light jazz cymbal with a hard beater and then reversing the recorded sound at high speed' (DM*BA*, p. 85).

22 A telling example of both techniques from the composer's last years can be found in *Canticle IV: Journey of the Magi* (1971), a setting of Eliot's famous poem for countertenor, tenor, baritone and piano. As Donald Mitchell has observed: 'Britten seizes on Eliot's own unforgettable art of significant repetition (very much part of Eliot's "music", this) and builds on it, so that it becomes as it were an Eliot-like feature of the Canticle's compositional technique' (Sleeve-note to Decca SXL 6608).

23 Grierson, 'The G.P.O. Gets Sound', pp. 215–21.

24 Britten was later memorably to employ whistling in 'The driving boy' from the *Spring Symphony* (1949): see the passage between Figs. 16 and 18.

25 For further information about the GPO Film Unit's earlier experiments with the sound-film, see Reed, 'The Incidental Music', pp. 33–46. Leigh himself acknowledged the influence of Satie's 'ballet réalistique', *Parade* (1917), on the scoring of *Six-Thirty Collection*, and further comparisons might be drawn with the work of Russolo and the Italian Futurists.

4 'He descended into Hell': Peter Grimes, Ellen Orford and salvation denied

1 PB*PG*, pp. 148–9.

2 Quoted in Alan Blyth, *Remembering Britten* (London: Hutchinson, 1981), p. 20.

3 See Britten's handwritten annotations to his copy of the miniature score of the *Four Sea Interludes*, quoted in BB*PG*, p. 205.

4 For example, Peter Porter has written that 'almost everything in *Peter Grimes* is superbly realized by the music, except the character of Peter himself. Yet the miracle of Britten's score is that this does not injure the effect of the whole work. Our noses are simply pointed in other directions.' ('Benjamin Britten's Librettos', in Nicholas John (ed.), *Peter Grimes/Gloriana*, ENO Opera Guides No. 24 (London: John Calder, 1983), p. 13.)

5 DMHK, pp. 111–31 (repr. in PB*PG*, pp. 105–20).

6 Philip Hope-Wallace, 'Peter Grimes', *Time and Tide*, 14 June 1945, p. 496.

7 DMPR, p. 1189.

8 BB*PG*, p. 67.

9 *The Life of George Crabbe by his Son* – another Rev. George Crabbe – with a foreword by E. M. Forster (London: Oxford University Press,

1932) is still highly recommended as an introduction to the poet. Kenneth Green's early costume design for the operatic character of Rector Horace Adams had his face drawn to look like Crabbe's (who was himself an Anglican clergyman of Aldeburgh) as depicted in the painting by Thomas Philips. This lends a note of implied criticism of Crabbe when Boles upbraids the Rector in Act II scene 1 with the lines: '[Is it] Your business to ignore Growing at your door Evils, like your fancy flowers?' and his constant references to watering his roses in Act III scene 1 (Crabbe was a noted collector and analyst of plant life).

10 *The Poetical Works of the Rev. George Crabbe* (London: John Murray, 1851). See BB*PG*, p. 172, for further information on this source.

11 Crabbe, *The Borough*, lines 26–54.

12 Montagu Slater, 'The Story of the Opera', in Eric Crozier (ed.), *Benjamin Britten: Peter Grimes* (London: John Lane/The Bodley Head, Sadler's Wells Opera Books No. 3, 1945), p. 26. Slater's more misogynistic and sinister view of Ellen Orford, unlike the positive views held by Britten and Pears, is also expressed in this essay.

13 The operatic Ellen performs a spiritual role equivalent to that of Peter Grimes's father in Crabbe's poem. Britten removed Grimes senior from his earlier operatic sketches, originally paralleling the poem with a cathartic deathbed confrontation between him (being waited on by Ellen) and Grimes junior. It is possible that the spirituality embodied in the father was transferred to the operatic Ellen. The significance of this is also noted by Eric Walter White, who quotes the same four lines of Crabbe's poem as Slater (lines 26–54): see EWW*B*, pp. 122–3.

14 MK*B*, p. 170.

15 Stephen Walsh, 'A Commentary on the Music', in John (ed.), *Peter Grimes/Gloriana*, p. 20.

16 Peter Pears, 'On Playing Peter Grimes', in CP*BC*, p. 105. Joan Cross commented (in conversation with Pears and John Evans) that she 'always regarded Ellen's attitude towards Grimes as one of sympathy and understanding and a desire to help him out of his difficulties. She has a deep regard for him and a feeling that here is a poet, a man that nobody understands . . . I remember I used to take great pleasure in performing in the Prologue . . . I never took my eyes off Peter during this scene, willed him to do this, that and the other, and was saddened and grieved and distressed by the fact that everybody turned against him at the end' (John (ed.), *Peter Grimes/Gloriana*, pp. 64–5). In the original production, Pears was aged thirty-five and Cross forty-five, and part of Britten's desire

to use Cross in the role was her maturity. This, in combination with Britten's purging of certain aspects of the relationship between Grimes and the boy in the libretto sources, suggests that the kind of love Britten envisaged between Ellen and Grimes was more like a mother's for her son.

17 Letter to Pears dated 19 January 1944 (DMPR, p. 1181).

18 Philip Reed has observed that in neither sketch of the duet does Britten use key signatures to notate the bitonality (BB*PG*, p. 99).

19 Cf. Hans Keller's remark that 'every second Interlude in the opera . . . is a Grimes Interlude' (DMHK, p. 122).

20 The same may be said of their cry (not to God) at the end of the storm chorus: 'O Tide that waits for no man spare our coasts!', a reference to 'Time that waits for no man.'

21 Christopher Palmer commented of this moment (when the Borough questions Ellen with 'What! And be Grimes' messenger?'): 'the sound of the chorus, as it intones the line to the major seventh chord [of Interlude I] is curiously angelic, almost implying that Ellen as Grimes' messenger is heaven-sent, sea-delivered, joined with Grimes in elemental unity' (CP*BC*, p. 116).

22 CP*BC*, p. 106.

23 PE*MB*, p. 106.

24 Where Ellen is not physically present, Balstrode invariably is. The fact that Balstrode to a lesser extent also stands outside the Borough, and that after initiating Grimes's suicide he leaves the stage with Ellen, would strongly suggest his supportive perspective. Hans Keller implied Freudian Mother, Father and sibling resonances in these two characters in his *Three Psychoanalytic Notes on 'Peter Grimes'*, edited by Christopher Wintle (London: Institute of Advanced Musical Studies, King's College London, 1995). In the final analysis, whatever the degree of mother–father love in any relationship, it is whether true and sincere love exists that is the proving criterion.

25 Sackville-West, 'The Musical and Dramatic Structure', in Crozier (ed.), *Benjamin Britten: Peter Grimes*, p. 33. Joan Cross also commented: 'a most extraordinary effect emotionally is Ellen's exit after she agrees to go and collect the new apprentice for Grimes. The succession of downward phrases in the orchestra is so moving. Time after time I used to land up off the stage in tears. I cannot tell you why. It had such incredible dignity and power, and it was something that made these villagers, these people who were being so tiresome, give way to her as she walked through them, and it's in the music' (John (ed.), *Peter Grimes/Gloriana*, pp. 64–5).

26 For an early and perceptive discussion of the function of these tonal centres in the opera, see Anthony Payne, 'Dramatic Use of Tonality in *Peter Grimes*', *Tempo* 66/67 (1963), pp. 22–6.

27 CP*BC*, p. 106.

28 Deryck Cooke regarded Ellen's phrase 'Glitter of waves, and glitter of sunlight' as an example of a melodic shape 'almost always employed to express the innocence and purity of angels and children, or some natural phenomenon which possesses the same qualities in the eyes of men'. See Deryck Cooke, *The Language of Music* (Oxford University Press, 1959; repr. 1989), pp. 151–5 and Ex. 64j.

29 Mervyn Cooke, 'Britten's Prophetic Song: Tonal Symbolism in *Billy Budd*', in MCPR, p. 89.

30 PB*PG*, p. 130.

31 CP*BC*, p. 106.

32 John (ed.), *Peter Grimes/Gloriana*, p. 27.

33 *Ibid.*, p. 14. Porter does not appear to be aware of the connection he is making between the nature of Grimes and that of the overtly evil John Claggart in *Billy Budd*.

34 Joan Cross and John Evans linked the quartet with the trio at the end of Richard Strauss's *Der Rosenkavalier*, the score of which Britten requested from Ralph Hawkes to study while in hospital with measles during the writing of *Grimes* (John (ed.), *Peter Grimes/Gloriana*, p. 66). The effect of Strauss's trio for Sophie, the Marschallin and Octavian (the last sung by a woman) in Act III, bars 285–93, is preserved by the three-part textures of Britten's quartet – in which both Nieces sing a single line – and by the yearningly high tessitura of the vocal writing. According to Pears, the quartet was included at Britten's insistence to provide 'some softening, some change, some relaxation after the intensity of the march to the hut' (*ibid.*, p. 66).

35 Arnold Whittall, *Music Since the First World War* (Oxford University Press, 1995), p. 112.

36 Wilfrid Mellers, 'Through *Noye's Fludde*', in CP*BC*, p. 158.

37 PE*MB*, pp. 119–20. Wozzeck's 'Wir arme Leut!' ('What it is to be poor!') is linked to his relationship with his young son who – as he explains to the Captain in Act I (bar 136), where the motif first occurs – was born outside of wedlock as a result of his poverty. It recurs in Act II (bar 114) in exchanges with Marie, the boy's mother, as Wozzeck gives her money. Tellingly, it is next heard in the mouth of the Drum-Major, with whom Marie is conducting a sexual relationship, in Act II scene 5 (bar 778) as he humiliates Wozzeck. Finally (Evans's point) it emerges orchestrally in the interlude preceding the final scene in which Wozzeck's

and Marie's young boy is informed by his playmates that his murdered mother's body has been discovered. Wozzeck has killed her and then, like Grimes (though perhaps in more 'accidental circumstances'), drowns himself.

38 As in the case of the handwritten programmatic designations in Britten's earlier sketches and miniature score of the *Four Sea Interludes*, his annotations to his miniature score of the *Passacaglia* (BB*PG*, p. 205) are perhaps to be understood in the concert rather than operatic context.

39 Again Berg's *Wozzeck* is possibly an influence, particularly the dance scene in Act II scene 4 (extended scherzo and trio movement) and the recapitulation of dance music in Act III scene 4 (invention on a six-note chord, bars 240ff.) as Wozzeck stumbles across the body of Marie, whom he has previously murdered.

40 PE*MB*, p. 115.

41 I am indebted to Bram Gay, formerly administrator at the Royal Opera House, for this insight. Joan Cross, remembering Britten's attendance at all of her and Pears's performances of Verdi's *La Traviata* and Mozart's *Così fan tutte* at Sadler's Wells from 1943 onwards, said: 'I've often wondered whether *Come scoglio* gave him ideas. All those wide leaps and difficult intervals in the Mozart could have influenced his writing of the "Embroidery" Aria' (John (ed.), *Peter Grimes/Gloriana*, p. 65).

42 AW*BT*, p. 100.

43 Christopher Wintle has observed that 'for his part, Grimes describes "her breast" as a "harbour" that "shelters peace", to music that transforms the kiss motif from *Otello*: here understanding resides in not neglecting Verdi, the overt sexuality of whose music is transformed by Britten into a regressive cry for the protection of the good mother' ('The Living Conflict', *Times Literary Supplement*, 26 April 1991, p. 20).

5 The chamber operas

1 Letter to Ralph Hawkes, 30 June 1946, cited in HC*BB*, p. 225.

2 HC*BB*, p. 225.

3 See EWW*B*, p. 147.

4 For a full discussion of the opera's genesis, see Margaret S. Mertz, 'History, Criticism and the Sources of Benjamin Britten's Opera *The Rape of Lucretia*' (Ph.D. dissertation, Harvard University, 1990).

5 Peter Porter, 'Benjamin Britten's Librettos', in Nicholas John (ed.), *Peter Grimes/Gloriana*, ENO Opera Guides No. 24 (London: John Calder, 1983), p. 11.

6 EWW*B*, p. 145.
7 For Duncan's own account, see RD*WB*, especially pp. 75–7. See also HC*BB*, pp. 235–6.
8 Philip Brett, 'Grimes and Lucretia', in Nigel Fortune (ed.), *Music and Theatre: Essays in Honour of Winton Dean* (Cambridge University Press, 1987), p. 360.
9 *Ibid.*, p. 360.
10 Donald Mitchell, 'The Serious Comedy of *Albert Herring*', Glyndebourne Festival Programme Book, 1986; repr. in DM*CN*, pp. 352–64.
11 Philip Brett, 'Character and Caricature in *Albert Herring*', *Musical Times* 127 (1986), p. 545.
12 *Ibid.*, p. 547.
13 *Ibid.*, p. 547.
14 Guy de Maupassant, 'Le Rosier de Madame Husson' (1887). For an accessible English version, see 'Madame Husson's May King' in Guy de Maupassant, *Mademoiselle Fifi and Other Stories*, trans. David Coward (Oxford University Press, 1993), pp. 167–84.
15 Erwin Stein, 'Form in Opera: *Albert Herring* Examined', *Tempo* 5 (Autumn 1947), pp. 4–5.
16 Norman Del Mar, 'Albert Herring', in DMHK, p. 154.
17 *Ibid.*, p. 149.
18 See Antonia Malloy, 'Britten's Major Setback? Aspects of the First Critical Response to *Gloriana*', in PB*BG*, pp. 49–65, and pp. 113–28 of the present volume.
19 See HC*BB*, pp. 332–3.
20 *Ibid.*, p. 331. For a full discussion of issues concerning the libretto, see PH*TS*, pp. 23–62.
21 See Arnold Schoenberg, *Theory of Harmony*, trans. Roy E. Carter (London: Faber & Faber, 1978), p. 323.
22 See PH*TS*, pp. 64–5.
23 Although the published score of the opera numbers the scenes of Act II from 1 to 8, I will preserve the parallel numbering with the variations in this commentary.
24 See Donald Mitchell, 'Britten's Revisionary Practice: Practical and Creative', *Tempo* 66–7 (Autumn–Winter 1963), pp. 15–22; repr. in DM*CN*, pp. 393–406.

6 *Gloriana*: Britten's 'slighted child'

1 *The Tongs and the Bones: The Memoirs of Lord Harewood* (London: Weidenfeld & Nicolson, 1981), pp. 134–5.
2 London: Chatto & Windus, 1928, repr. Harmondsworth: Penguin, 1971.
3 Material survives from the early stages of work on two such operas, both of which were later abandoned: *The Tale of Mr Tod* (which was to have been based on the story by Beatrix Potter) and *Tyco the Vegan* (with an original space-travel scenario, unusual amongst Britten's operatic projects in not deriving from a literary original).
4 The Festival of Britain operas were Arthur Benjamin's *A Tale of Two Cities*, Alan Bush's *Wat Tyler*, Berthold Goldschmidt's *Beatrice Cenci* and Karl Rankl's *Deidre of the Sorrows*. At the same time, Tippett's *The Midsummer Marriage*, Walton's *Troilus and Cressida* and Lennox Berkeley's *Nelson* were being completed. Of the seven, only *Nelson* achieved its première ahead of *Gloriana*.
5 Stanley Bayliss, headline in *Daily Mail*, 9 June 1953.
6 Marie Stopes, letter to *The Times*, 20 June 1953, p. 7.
7 D. Watkins, letter to *Music and Musicians* 1/12 (August 1953), p. 23.
8 Anon., '*Gloriana*', *Times Educational Supplement*, 19 June 1953, p. 561.
9 Martin Cooper, '*Gloriana* and Benjamin Britten', *The Score* 8 (1953), p. 61.
10 Anon., 'Royal Opera House *Gloriana*', *The Times*, 1 July 1953, p. 5.
11 Martin Cooper, 'Britten at Bay', *Spectator*, 19 June 1953, p. 783.
12 For a more detailed discussion of the critical reaction to the première, and other aspects of *Gloriana*'s early history, see PB*BG*, pp. 49–65.
13 Work on the libretto began in summer 1942, and the orchestration was completed in early 1945.
14 Britten first mentioned *Sumidagawa*, the Japanese Nō play on which the first Church Parable is based, in a letter to Plomer dated 13 May 1956, but *Curlew River* was not premièred until 14 June 1964: see pp. 179–81. Similarly, Britten's strong interest in the Henry James story that formed the basis for *Owen Wingrave* (1970) dated from some sixteen years before the opera came to be composed, originating when he was preoccupied with *The Turn of the Screw*.
15 RD*WB*, p. 61.
16 For a detailed description of the evolution of *Billy Budd*, see Eric Crozier, 'Staging First Productions', in DH*OB*, pp. 31–3.
17 *Ibid.*, p. 33.
18 *Billy Budd* was reduced from four acts to two some eight years after its première (see MCPR, pp. 74–84), and *Paul Bunyan*, Britten's first operatic venture, underwent major revision at the end of his life.
19 Eric Crozier, 'Staging First Productions', p. 33.
20 Towards the end of 1952 it became obvious that this commission would have to wait, and La Fenice eventually agreed to postpone the première of the opera – which was to have taken

place in September 1953 – for a further year. *The Turn of the Screw* was finally premièred on 14 September 1954 as part of their festival of contemporary music.

21 While he was working on the libretto he continued to act as a reader for the publisher Jonathan Cape, produced several poems and also saw a new book, *Museum Pieces*, through the press.

22 Quoted in Peter F. Alexander, *William Plomer: A Biography* (Oxford University Press, 1989), p. 239.

23 These problems notwithstanding, Plomer clearly proved to be a highly sympathetic colleague, since Britten returned to him for the libretti of the three Church Parables (*Curlew River, The Burning Fiery Furnace* and *The Prodigal Son*) in the 1960s.

24 Edmund Tracey, 'Benjamin Britten talks to Edmund Tracey', *Sadler's Wells Magazine* 4 (Autumn 1966), pp. 5–7.

25 Quoted in anonymous article, 'Mr Britten Discusses *Gloriana*', *Lowestoft Journal*, 17 April 1953.

26 Quoted in Robert Muller, '*Gloriana* is Born', *Picture Post* 59/11, p. 67.

27 J. E. Neale, *Queen Elizabeth I* (London: Jonathan Cape, 1934, repr. Harmondsworth: Pelican, 1971).

28 See, for example, the opening of *The Murder on the Downs*:

Past a cow and past a cottage,
Past the sties and byres,
Past the equidistant poles
Holding taut the humming wires ...

29 William Plomer, 'Notes on the Libretto of *Gloriana*', *Tempo* 28 (Summer 1953), p. 6.

30 Quoted in Tracey, 'Benjamin Britten talks to Edmund Tracey'.

31 In fact, as early as January 1954 an experimental version of the ending – from which the ghostly visitors were removed – had been performed. Britten's comment (in a letter to Plomer dated 31 January) that it 'worked well' obviously paved the way for the formal rewriting that took place before the 1966 production. Interestingly, the same performance also cut Act II scene 1 in its entirety; according to Britten, 'Everyone missed "Norwich", but many agreed the work gained in dramatic intensity, if it lost in open-airness or splendour.' Presumably these reductions were originally made with the needs of a touring company in mind; the opera visited the provinces (and then Bulawayo) at this time.

32 Fortunately, Britten anticipated Plomer's material remarkably accurately and made little alteration to his 'setting' when he received the words. On 23 November he wrote to Plomer thanking him for them and commented: 'the lovely Essex speech fits what I'd planned (and even sketched in!) like a glove. A lovely case of thought transference!'

33 Unpublished letter to Basil Coleman (who produced the opera's première), 6 October 1952.

34 Britten's original suggestion, Frederick Ashton, had been refused because he might be needed for a possible separate ballet on the same gala evening. Then John Cranko's name was put forward and seemingly agreed upon. Once it became clear that there was to be no ballet other than that required within the opera, however, Ninette de Valois wrote to Britten telling him that Ashton would, after all, be available, and was preferable to Cranko. In the end, Britten prevailed and Cranko was reinstated, thus beginning a creative association that was to result in Britten's only full-length ballet, *The Prince of the Pagodas* (see p. 171).

35 Quoted by Donald Mitchell in *CPBC*, p. 91.

36 Quoted in 'Mr Britten Discusses *Gloriana*' (see note 25 above).

37 From the *Second Set of Madrigals* (1609).

38 Throughout his life, Britten retained a liking for this literal kind of quotation: see, for example, his use of the hymn tune 'Mount Ephraim' in his setting of Thomas Hardy's 'The Choirmaster's Burial' (in *Winter Words*), a poem which deals with a church musician's dying wish to have 'Mount Ephraim' played at his graveside.

39 Imogen Holst recalled in her diary that Pears was not in favour of this ending to the act, but Britten refused to change it, because he felt that 'the orchestra during the slow curtain would be absolutely terrifying, and was necessary to the drama'.

40 Her contribution to Britten scholarship is also considerable: the diary she kept during work on *Gloriana* contains fascinating personal reminiscences of day-to-day work on the opera and is an important source of firsthand documentation of Britten's working methods. A copy of her diaries is deposited at the Britten–Pears Library, Aldeburgh.

41 Other alterations made at this time included the shortening of the Queen's soliloquy and prayer at the end of Act I scene 2 and the entrance of Cecil in Act III scene 1.

42 Quoted in Tracey, 'Benjamin Britten talks to Edmund Tracey', p. 6.

43 It is perhaps fitting that the music he provided for two of the pageant scenes (the Norwich masque and the courtly dances) has found itself a place outside the opera house, in

the form of the *Choral Dances* and the
Symphonic Suite, both of which are popular
additions to the repertory of amateur groups
the like of which he sought to encourage. A
version of the *Courtly Dances* for school
orchestra was prepared for Boosey & Hawkes by
David Stone in 1963: see PB*BG*, pp. 143–4.
44 Quoted in MS*BC*, p. 118.
45 This economy also extended to the opera's
motivic structure, which is far simpler than that
of its predecessor, *Billy Budd*.
46 The conflict of Britten's public and private
responsibilities, and its reflection in the
material of the opera, is sensitively and
perceptively discussed by Donald Mitchell in
his essay 'Public and Private in *Gloriana*' in
CP*BC*, pp. 170–6.
47 Robert Henderson, '*Budd* and *Gloriana*
Reconsidered', *Tempo* 68 (Spring 1964), p. 31.

7 Britten and Shakespeare: *A Midsummer Night's Dream*

1 Benjamin Britten, 'A New Britten Opera',
Observer Weekend Review, 5 June 1960, p. 9.
2 Line references correspond to the Arden text
of Shakespeare's play, ed. Harold Brooks
(London: Methuen, 1979).
3 In Shakespeare's play, the nuptials follow a
single night of woodland scenes in spite of the
implications of Theseus's opening lines 'four
happy days' (quoted on p. 134): the larger
interval of time is necessary to justify the duke's
impatience, and the effect is nullified by
Britten's drastic relocation of the speech to Act
III of the opera. Shakespeare's double-time
device is also to be seen in *Othello*, where
(presumably deliberate) inconsistencies allow
for two interpretations, one of which sees the
plot taking several months to develop and the
other only a few days, thus capturing both the
protracted nature of inexorable fate and the
bewildering speed of the eventual dénouement.
4 Britten, 'A New Britten Opera'. The
composer's facsimile of the First Quarto was a
present from Imogen Holst inscribed in March
1960, by which time most of the opera's music
had been composed.
5 William Shakespeare, *A Midsummer Night's
Dream*, ed. G. B. Harrison (Harmondsworth:
Penguin, 1953).
6 Cuenod was apparently offered the part, but
turned it down because of prior commitments:
see HC*BB*, p. 395.
7 PE*MB*, p. 238. It should be noted that an
optional cut Britten sanctioned between Figs.
17 and 19a in Act III unfortunately weakens the
effect of the gradual approach of Theseus's horn

calls. This cut is observed in Britten's own
recording of the work (Decca 425663-2).
8 Brooks (ed.), *A Midsummer Night's Dream*,
p. xcv. This function of the wood corresponds
to that of the forests in *The Two Gentlemen of
Verona* and *As You Like It*, the tomb in *Much
Ado About Nothing*, the cave in *Cymbeline* and
the island in *The Tempest*.
9 On 14 December Britten declared in a letter
to Pears that he was 'well into the 2nd Act'. The
composer thanked Mrs Piper for her Prologue
in a letter dated 29 December ('I am
considering it'), and on 9 January he wrote
again to Pears to say 'I struggle on with Act 2,
sometimes good, sometimes not so.'
10 For the complete text of Mrs Piper's
Prologue, see Mervyn Cooke, 'Britten and
Shakespeare: Dramatic and Musical Cohesion
in *A Midsummer Night's Dream*', *Music &
Letters* 74/2 (1993), pp. 255–6. See also William
H. L. Godsalve, *Britten's 'A Midsummer Night's
Dream': Making an Opera from Shakespeare's
Comedy* (London and Toronto: Associated
University Presses, 1995), pp. 72–3, where the
author expands on observations first made by
the present writer in an undergraduate
dissertation in 1984.
11 The sketch is reproduced in Cooke, 'Britten
and Shakespeare', p. 256.
12 For a concise summary, see EWW*B*,
p. 224.
13 It is intriguing to note the similar intervallic
construction of the lovers' distinctive theme
and Mrs Grose's equally pregnant melody of
foreboding at Fig. 39 in Act I of *The Turn of the
Screw*.
14 Personal communication from the librettist
of *Cantata Misericordium*, the late Patrick
Wilkinson. A classicist and onetime Senior
Tutor of King's College Cambridge, Wilkinson
had been suggested by E. M. Forster (also a
Fellow of King's) as a librettist capable of
producing the Latin text required by Britten for
this international commission. Wilkinson later
compiled an anthology of Latin love poetry in
the hope that it might be set to music by
Walton, but this projected song-cycle came to
naught.
15 For further instances of Britten's
characteristic delight in musical puns of this
nature, see MC*WR*, p. 71 and p. 106, n. 24.
16 Compare the directly analogous tonal
tension between B minor and B♭ major in *Billy
Budd* (1951), and between E♭ minor and D
major in *The Burning Fiery Furnace* (1966).
17 See Mervyn Cooke, 'Britten's Prophetic
Song: Tonal Symbolism in *Billy Budd*', in
MC*PR*, pp. 85–110.

18 For a listing of comparable instances of Britten's symbolic use of A major, see MCPR, p. 165, n. 5. See also p. 84 above.
19 Noël Goodwin, 'The Aldeburgh Festival', *Musical Times* 101 (1960), p. 503.
20 John Russell Brown and Bernard Harris (eds.), *Early Shakespeare* (Stratford-upon-Avon Studies, 3; London, 1961), p. 183.

8 Eros in life and death: *Billy Budd* and *Death in Venice*

1 See Clifford Hindley, 'Britten's Parable Art: A Gay Reading', *History Workshop Journal* 40 (1995), pp. 63–90.
2 F. Barron Freeman, *Melville's Billy Budd* (Cambridge, Mass.: Harvard University Press, 1948), p. 64. E. M. Forster acquired this volume during the writing of the libretto.
3 E. M. Forster, *Aspects of the Novel* (London: Edward Arnold, 1927; Harmondsworth: Penguin, 1976 repr. 1987), pp. 129–30. Attention was drawn to the passage (including the extracts quoted in the text) in a radio discussion between Britten, Crozier and Forster, broadcast by the BBC on 12 November 1960 (BBC transcript, pp. 3–4).
4 See Philip Brett's chapter 'Salvation at Sea: *Billy Budd*', in CP*BC*, pp. 133–43.
5 The development of the friendship is well portrayed by Philip Reed in MCPR, pp. 42–5.
6 Crozier's own account of the collaboration was published in 'The Writing of *Billy Budd*', *Opera Quarterly* 4/3 (1986), pp. 11–27.
7 The four-act version was revived at Covent Garden in 1995. Act and scene numbers given in this chapter refer to the two-act version, published by Boosey & Hawkes in 1961.
8 Billy's remarkable influence on the sailors' morale in his former ship, *The Rights o' Man*, is stressed in Melville's narrative. It may be reflected in Britten's derivation of the theme for the sailors' fervour for battle from Billy's arpeggio motif: see Brett, 'Salvation at Sea', p. 140.
9 On the preoccupation with mutiny and its links with the key of B minor, see Mervyn Cooke in MCPR, pp. 18, 31 and 91ff.
10 For a fuller account of the music associated with fate see Clifford Hindley, 'Britten's *Billy Budd*: The "Interview Chords" Again', *Musical Quarterly* 78/1 (1994), pp. 99–126.
11 Herman Melville, *Billy Budd, Foretopman*, introduction by William Plomer (London: John Lehmann, 1946), p. 8. Crozier specifies this edition in his account of 'The Writing of *Billy Budd*', p. 12.
12 Letter from Forster to Lionel Trilling, 16

April 1949: see Mary Lago and P. N. Furbank (eds.), *Selected Letters of E. M. Forster* (London: Collins, 1985), No. 389. Melville had described Billy lying in chains between two guns as 'nipped in the vice of fate'. (Herman Melville, *Billy Budd, Sailor and Other Stories* ed. Harold Beaver (Harmondsworth: Penguin, 1967, repr. 1981), p. 396.)
13 Forster's sympathy with this kind of Stoicism is seen in the lengthy quotation from Father Mapple's sermon in *Moby Dick* which he transcribes in *Aspects of the Novel*, p. 127.
14 For a description of these papers and the full text of Forster's note, see Clifford Hindley, 'Love and Salvation in Britten's "Billy Budd"', *Music & Letters* 70/3 (1989), pp. 363–81.
15 A more detailed analysis of the libretto drafts from this point of view is given in Hindley, 'Love and Salvation'. See also the subtle manipulation of the reference to Billy's 'flower of masculine beauty and strength' as a source of sexual attraction for Vere (*ibid.*, p. 376).
16 For this view of these operas, see Clifford Hindley, 'Homosexual Self-affirmation and Self-oppression in Two Britten Operas', *Musical Quarterly* 76/2 (1992), pp. 143–68, and 'Not the Marrying Kind: Britten's *Albert Herring*', *Cambridge Opera Journal* 6/2 (1994), pp. 159–74.
17 Lago and Furbank (eds.), *Selected Letters of E. M. Forster*, No. 394.
18 One of the most remarkable (though tiniest) modifications recorded in the libretto drafts is the change of 'God has blessed me' into 'He [i.e., Billy] has saved me and blessed me.' This reflects Forster's deep humanist convictions, and confirms our inferring a human rather than divine significance for the phrase 'the love that passes understanding'. (See Hindley, 'Love and Salvation', pp. 371ff.)
19 Britten's recognition of this tradition at a more popular level is seen in the central section of his *Canadian Carnival* (1939), where a slow waltz with its melody in consecutive thirds is marked 'Andante amoroso' (Fig. 13) and subsequently 'Andante, più amoroso che prima' (Fig. 16).
20 Of Billy's last cry, Forster wrote (in an unpublished letter) that it was 'insoluble' but expressed 'compassion, comprehension, love. I wish it could have been purely musical' (letter from Forster to Britten, dated 8 August 1951, in the Britten–Pears Library). I cannot help feeling that Britten's ethereal concord wonderfully meets that wish.
21 Barrie Emslie, '*Billy Budd* and the Fear of Words', *Cambridge Opera Journal* 4/1 (1992), pp. 43–59.

22 For Britten's views on communication, see Hindley, 'Britten's Parable Art', pp. 76–7.

23 Relevant passages include 'Antique' (dedicated to Wulff Scherchen) from the song-cycle *Les illuminations*; 'Sokrates und Alkibiades' from the song-cycle *Sechs Hölderlin-Fragmente*; several passages to accompany avowals of love in *A Midsummer Night's Dream* (see pp. 139–43); the brass chords which sound at Aschenbach's first meeting with Tadzio, and the three piano triads which punctuate the older man's declaration of love at the beginning of Act II in *Death in Venice*.

24 Other examples are the Borough's appropriation of Grimes's theme in *Peter Grimes*; the sharing (with variations) of much thematic material between Quint and the Governess in *The Turn of the Screw*; and the use of Tadzio's theme in *Death in Venice* in both Apollonian and Dionysiac contexts. See Clifford Hindley, 'Homosexual Self-affirmation and Self-oppression' and 'Why Does Miles Die: A Study of Britten's "Turn of the Screw"', *Musical Quarterly* 74/1 (1990), pp. 1–17.

25 See PE*MB*, pp. 163–87, and – for much insight in respect of *Billy Budd* – Mervyn Cooke, 'Britten's "Prophetic Song": Tonal Symbolism in *Billy Budd*', in MCPR, pp. 85–110.

26 For different views of the extent to which the opera may function as a parable of redemption, see Arnold Whittall, ' "Twisted Relations": Method and Meaning in Britten's *Billy Budd*', *Cambridge Opera Journal* 2/2 (1990), pp. 145–71, and Hindley, 'Britten's *Billy Budd*: The Interview Chords Again'.

27 In his book *The Enchafèd Flood* (London: Faber & Faber, 1951), W. H. Auden provides a quasi-theological analysis of Melville's Billy Budd as Christ figure. But though often quoted in opera programmes, this work was first published (in New York) only in 1950, at a time when the friendship between Britten and Auden was strained if not already broken, and it seems unlikely to have influenced the creation of the opera. (In Hindley, 'Britten's *Billy Budd*: The Interview Chords Again', n. 11, the publication date is wrongly given as 1949.)

28 'Letter from E. M. Forster', *Griffin* 1 (1951), pp. 4–6. Cf. also Forster's letter to Britten of 20 December 1948 (*Selected Letters*, No. 387), where he writes, 'Billy *is* our Saviour, yet he is Billy, not Christ or Orion.' In *Aspects of the Novel* Forster had spoken more cautiously of Billy's securing 'harmony and *temporary* salvation' (my emphasis). On Orion, see P. N. Furbank, *E. M. Forster, a Life* (Oxford University Press, 1979), vol. I, p. 162.

29 Letter of 20 December 1948 (see preceding note); cf. the quotation from *Aspects of the Novel* on pp. 147–8 above. The idea of universalization was also reflected in the broadcast discussion where, with Britten's agreement, Crozier spoke of the ship as an image of the world, '[floating] on the sea of time and of infinity' (BBC transcript, p. 5). It does not seem to me that the opera's Epilogue implies (as some have suggested) a perpetual repetition of Vere's self-reproach.

30 See T. J. Reed, 'Mann and His Novella: "Death in Venice"' and 'I was Thomas Mann's Tadzio', in DM*DV*, pp. 163–7 and 184–5.

31 For the quotations from Mann and George, see the letter of 4 July 1920 from Mann to Carl Maria Weber in *Letters of Thomas Mann 1889–1955*, selected and translated by Richard and Clara Winston (London: Secker & Warburg, 1970), vol. I, pp. 103 and 105.

32 T. J. Reed, 'Mann and His Novella'.

33 Myfanwy Piper, 'The Libretto', in DM*DV*, p. 45.

34 See Rosamund Strode, 'A *Death in Venice* Chronicle', in DM*DV*, p. 28.

35 HC*BB*, pp. 542–51.

36 Letter from Auden to Britten, 31 January 1942, in DMPR, pp. 1015–16. Britten's comment is in a letter to his brother-in-law Kit Welford, 1 March 1942 (*ibid.*, p. 1021). See the discussion of this issue in DM*DV*, pp. 21–3. For Pears's recollection, see Christopher Headington, *Britten* (London: Eyre Methuen, 1981), p. 139.

37 DM*DV*, p. 207, n. 15.

38 For Mann's subtly ironic deployment of the classical references, see Clifford Hindley, 'Contemplation and Reality: A Study in Britten's "Death in Venice"', *Music & Letters* 71/4 (1990), pp. 512–16.

39 Thomas Mann, *Death in Venice, Tristan, Tonio Kröger*, trans. H. T. Lowe-Porter (Harmondsworth: Penguin, 1955, repr. 1986), p. 190. At the end of the novel Kröger declares, 'For if anything is capable of making a poet of a literary man, it is my bourgeois love of the human, the living and usual. It is the source of all warmth, goodness, and humour . . .' Cf. Myfanwy Piper, in DM*DV*, pp. 45ff.

40 See DMPR, letters No. 201 (to Enid Slater, 29 July 1939) and No. 227 (to Wulff Scherchen, 8 December 1939).

41 For detailed arguments in support of this interpretation, see Hindley, 'Contemplation and Reality', pp. 511–23, and 'Platonic Elements in Britten's "Death in Venice"', *Music & Letters* 73/3 (1992), pp. 407–29.

42 Plato, *Symposium* 210, a passage noted by Mann: see T. J. Reed, *Thomas Mann: Der Tod in Venedig* (Oxford University Press, 1971, repr. 1978), p. 179, n. 210.

43 As published in Archibald T. Davison and Willi Apel, *Historical Anthology of Music* (Cambridge, Mass.: Harvard University Press, 1946), vol. I, no. 7a.

44 I address the published text of the opera. There is, however, evidence in an unpublished section of the composition sketch (in the Britten–Pears Library at Aldeburgh) that Britten considered, only to reject, the idea that Aschenbach's 'moment of reality' would be fully experienced in the physical consummation of his love for Tadzio (see Hindley, 'Platonic Elements', pp. 420–4). This possibility surely leaves its trace in the mounting agitation of the interludes between the clauses of Aschenbach's aesthetic creed.

45 P*EMB*, p. 534.

46 Myfanwy Piper in DM*DV*, p. 50.

47 See T. J. Reed's introduction to *Der Tod in Venedig*, pp. 41–3.

48 Compare the conflict between Claggart (fourths) and Vere/Billy (thirds, and their close allies sixths and tenths) in *Billy Budd* (above, p. 151), and that between false gods, Merodak and Jehovah (fourths) and the purity of the Young Men's obedience to conscience (thirds) in *The Burning Fiery Furnace*, for which see Hindley, 'Homosexual Self-affirmation and Self-oppression' (note 16 above).

49 A reminiscence surely of Plato *Symposium* 183, which speaks of the tolerance afforded by Athenian society to the lover in this predicament.

50 P*EMB*, p. 535.

51 The Elderly Fop and the operation of the Barber in creating Aschenbach in the Fop's image are woven into the plot of musical ambiguity by two interrelated references. First, there is the brief rising sequence of two-note chords comprising all twelve tones which occurs when the Fop first speaks to Aschenbach (Fig. 31): it is reiterated as they part, following the Fop's 'Pray keep us in mind' (Fig. 40^{+4}). This request is ironically fulfilled when the chord sequence is recalled at the beginning of Aschenbach's invocation of Tadzio in his hymn to Apollo (Fig. 176). The recall adds to the elements of ambiguity and warning in Act I the hint that idolization of Tadzio will in the end lead Aschenbach to assume the Fop's image. This in fact happens in Scene 16, where the Fop's reference (in Act I) to the 'pretty little darling' is conflated with Tadzio's chord, implying that Tadzio has now, for Aschenbach, taken over the role of 'the pretty little darling'. (In this note I am indebted to various insights by Mervyn Cooke, John Evans and Donald Mitchell in DM*DV*, pp. 111, 126 and 213, n. 7.)

52 The words are attributed to Plato's Socrates in conversation with Phaedrus, but in fact neither the form nor the sentiments have much to do with the Platonic dialogues. Peter Evans speaks of 'a terrible access of clear-eyed vision' (P*EMB*, p. 533).

53 *Death in Venice*, Fig. 3: *Billy Budd*, Act II, lead up to Fig. 100. The Aschenbach theme recurs briefly to confirm Aschenbach's self-esteem (Fig. 62, trumpets only, Fig. 103^{+7-8}, Fig. 234, and, at the end with bitter irony, Fig. 307^{+2}).

54 Contrast Plato, who envisages the development of a positive relationship between lover and beloved (*Symposium* 208–9).

55 Donald Mitchell, 'A *Billy Budd* Notebook', in MCPR, p. 116.

56 'The pearl of great price', Matthew 13:46. E. M. Forster said that in creating Billy he was concerned to make goodness interesting: see the radio discussion (note 3, above), BBC transcript, p. 6. 'Goodness' of course includes intolerance of evil – in Forster's description, a 'goodness of the glowing aggressive sort which cannot exist until it has evil to consume' (*Aspects of the Novel*, p. 128).

57 Mitchell, 'A *Billy Budd* Notebook', in MCPR, pp. 129ff., and references there given, especially to Christopher Palmer (following Hans Keller) in Nicholas John (ed.), *Peter Grimes/Gloriana*, ENO Opera Guides No. 24 (London: John Calder, 1983).

58 As the drafts show, the librettists found a good deal of difficulty in deciding upon the stance to be taken by Vere at the trial: see Hindley, 'Love and Salvation', pp. 372–5. There seems to be no ground in the opera for suggesting that Vere was motivated by the need to repudiate his 'sexual self', and nothing in his utterance comparable to Queen Elizabeth's 'From my other self I turn.' Indeed it is improbable that either Forster or Britten, having gone so far to develop a relationship between Vere and Billy, would have wished to draw back in this way.

59 One cannot help feeling that this is what Forster meant when, in writing to Britten after the first performance, he said, 'You and I have both put into it something which lies deeper than artistic creation, and which we both understand . . . this opera is my *Nunc dimittis*, in that it dismisses me peacefully and convinces me I have achieved' (*Selected Letters of E. M. Forster*, No. 398).

60 BB*AA*, especially pp. 10–12.

61 Compare Humphrey Carpenter's suggestion that the opera was intended as an *apologia pro vita sua* (HC*BB*, p. 553).

9 Distant horizons: from Pagodaland to the Church Parables

1 Quoted in Donald Mitchell, 'What Do We Know About Britten Now?', in CP*BC*, p. 40, n. 23.

2 See Noel Stock, *The Life of Ezra Pound* (London: Routledge & Kegan Paul, 1970), p. 356.

3 78rpm set 513/4. These recordings were first issued on CD in 1995 (Pearl GEMM CD 9177), transferred from a copy of the 78s in the International Piano Archives at the University of Maryland: the production team appears not to have been aware of the existence of Britten's set. Britten's copies of the recordings were transferred to CD to accompany the publication of MC*BE* in 1998.

4 See DMJE, Plate 174.

5 *Ibid.*, Plate 176.

6 See David Matthews, 'Act II Scene 1: An Examination of the Music', in PB*PG*, pp. 122–4, where the discovery of this connection is credited to Bayan Northcott. See also p. 89 of the present volume.

7 See Somsak Ketukaenchan, 'A (Far Eastern) Note on *Paul Bunyan*', in PR*MB*, pp. 275–9.

8 The itinerary of Britten's world tour may be reconstructed in some detail, since he wrote many substantial letters home during the tour and Pears kept an informative but somewhat erratic diary during its latter stages (PR*PP*, pp. 16–72). From January 1956 these accounts are augmented by a travel diary compiled by Britten's travelling companion, Prince Ludwig of Hesse, which relates their movements in the Far East and in the Indian subcontinent on the journey home (Prince Ludwig of Hesse, *Ausflug Ost* (Darmstadt: privately printed, 1956); brief extracts in English translation were included in Anthony Gishford's *Tribute to Benjamin Britten on His Fiftieth Birthday* (London: Faber and Faber, 1963), pp. 56–65). For a full account of Britten's activities in Bali and Japan, see MC*BE*, pp. 50–85 and 112–29.

9 Prince Ludwig of Hesse, *Ausflug Ost*, pp. 30–1.

10 *Ibid.*, pp. 34–5.

11 For Pears's evocative description of the island, see PR*PP*, pp. 43–7.

12 Their story is recounted in John Coast's memoirs, *Dancing out of Bali* (London: Faber and Faber, 1954). For the extraordinary trail of coincidences linking this gamelan with Britten's *Young Person's Guide to the Orchestra*, see Donald Mitchell, 'An Afterword on Britten's *Pagodas*: The Balinese Sources', *Tempo* 152 (March 1985), pp. 7–11.

13 Letter from Britten to Imogen Holst, written from Ubud on 17 January 1956.

14 Jaap Kunst, *Music in Java*, trans. Emile van Loo (The Hague: Martinus Nijhoff, 1949; 3rd edn, 1973), vol. I, p. 362.

15 Personal communication.

16 Hans Keller, 'Introduction: Operatic Music and Britten', in DH*OB*, pp. xxix–xxx.

17 Prince Ludwig of Hesse, *Ausflug Ost*, p. 65.

18 Although carrying the same title (in a variant spelling), this piece is not the same as the 'Taboeh Teloe' transcribed by McPhee in his *Balinese Ceremonial Music*.

19 *The Prince of the Pagodas* was finally performed on New Year's Day 1957, and revived at Covent Garden in 1958, 1959 and 1960 before being dropped from the repertory in spite of a triumphant production under Britten's baton at La Scala, Milan (May 1957) and a favourable reception in New York (October 1957). Cranko went on to stage the ballet in Stuttgart in November 1960; in their 1971–2 season, the Kirov Ballet mounted a new production in Leningrad. British public interest in *Pagodas* notably revived following a concert performance of large sections from the score at the 1988 Aldeburgh Festival by the London Sinfonietta under Oliver Knussen, and the ballet returned to the Covent Garden stage in December 1989 (with choreography by Kenneth Macmillan). Knussen recorded the complete ballet for Virgin Classics in 1990, reinstating the four dances which Britten had completely excised in the shortened version of the work he had recorded for Decca in 1957. An extended concert suite from the ballet (which, unlike that prepared by Norman Del Mar under the title *Prelude and Dances*, includes the Balinese sections) has been compiled by Mervyn Cooke and Donald Mitchell, and was first performed at the Concertgebouw, Amsterdam, on 4 June 1997 by the Deutsches Symphonie-Orchester Berlin under Vladimir Ashkenazy.

20 See Mitchell, 'An Afterword on Britten's *Pagodas*'. A detailed analysis of Britten's Balinese sketches is to be found in MC*BE*, pp. 75–85.

21 For further on the Poulenc Concerto, and on Western composers' gamelan borrowings in general, see Mervyn Cooke, 'The East in the West: Evocations of the Gamelan in Western Music', in Jonathan Bellman (ed.), *The Exotic in Western Music* (Boston: Northeastern University Press, 1998), pp. 258–80.

22 Personal communication from the late Mrs Piper. Her telling remark calls to mind Debussy's cultivation of a gamelan sound-world in open rejection of outmoded Austro-German musical procedures.

23 For further on the Balinese dimension in

Death in Venice, see Mervyn Cooke, 'Britten and the Gamelan', in DM*DV*, pp. 115–28, and M*CBE*, pp. 220–44.

24 William Plomer, programme note on Britten's Church Parables, *Edinburgh Festival Programme Book* (1968), p. 28.

25 Originally published in two volumes as *Certain Noble Plays of Japan* (Dublin: Dundrum Cuala Press, 1916) and *'Noh' or Accomplishment* (London: Macmillan, 1916), the latter title referring to the literal meaning of the word *nō*. Britten's copy was a first edition of *The Translations of Ezra Pound* (London: Faber & Faber, 1953).

26 Prince Ludwig of Hesse, *Ausflug Ost*, p. 90. English translations of Prince Ludwig's description of this seminal encounter with Nō are to be found in Gishford, *Tribute to Benjamin Britten*, and M*CBE*, pp. 118–19.

27 For the circumstances in which this tape recording was procured, see PR*PP*, pp. 64. A representative extract from the tape is included on the CD accompanying M*CBE*.

28 The full text of the address is to be found in *Aldeburgh Festival Programme Book* (1991), pp. 18–19.

29 D. J. Enright, *Memoirs of a Mendicant Professor* (London: Chatto & Windus, 1969), p. 45.

30 Sukehiro Shiba, *Gagaku – Japanese Classical Court Music*, vol. I (Tokyo Ryugin-Sha, 1955).

31 For an examination of specific elements borrowed from Western mediaeval religious drama, see M*CBE*, pp. 160–65. Further research in this area has been carried out by Stephen Arthur Allen, who has investigated Britten's creative reaction to the Beauvais *Play of Daniel* (which the composer saw in a performance by the New York Pro Musica at King's Lynn in 1960), and made a detailed assessment of the composer's debt to Karl Young's two-volume study *The Drama of the Medieval Church* (Oxford: Oxford University Press, 1933).

32 Japanese Classics Translation Committee, *Japanese Noh Drama* (Tokyo: Nippon Gakujutsu Shinkokai, 1955).

33 Letter to the present author, 24 January 1986. Graham subsequently studied Nō in greater depth, prior to working on *The Burning Fiery Furnace*. See also Colin Graham, 'Staging First Productions 3', in DH*OB*, p. 49.

34 Kunio Komparu, *The Noh Theater: Principles and Perspectives* (New York and Tokyo: Weatherhill/Tankosha, 1983), p. 190.

35 See Shigeo Kishibe's description of what he describes as 'chaophony' in his book *The Traditional Music of Japan* (Tokyo: Japan Foundation, 1984), p. 27. The same type of canonic ensemble, which is used for the

dancers' entrances and exits, is described in Robert Garfias, *Music of a Thousand Autumns: The Tōgaku Style of Japanese Court Music* (Berkeley: University of California Press, 1975), p. 76.

36 See M*CWR*, p. 70.

37 For further on Britten's knowledge of shō technique, see Mervyn Cooke, 'Britten and the Shō', *Musical Times* 129 (1988), pp. 231–3, and M*CBE*, pp. 124, 129 and 181–4.

38 For the work's continuing debt to Japanese models, see Mervyn Cooke, 'From Nō to Nebuchadnezzar', in PR*MB*, pp. 135–45, and M*CBE*, pp. 190–205.

39 For a penetrating critical reaction to all three parables, see Robin Holloway, 'The Church Parables II: Limits and Renewals', in CP*BC*, pp. 215–26.

40 The event took place on 14 June 1958. I am grateful to Jenny Doctor for providing me with details both of this performance, and of the Indian event mounted at the Aldeburgh Festival in 1965 (see following note).

41 The performance, which took place on 21 June in the Jubilee Hall, featured the Indian dancer Balasaraswati in a recital of Bharatanatyam (classical dance from South India).

42 PR*PP*, pp. 94–5.

43 Alain Daniélou, *The Râga-s of Northern Indian Music* (London: Barrie & Cresset, 1968), p. 269. Britten and Pears met Daniélou in person in Madras on 11 March 1956, on which occasion they had lunch together: see PR*PP*, p. 71. For further on *The Prodigal Son*, see Mervyn Cooke, 'Eastern Influences in Britten's *The Prodigal Son*', *Melos* 19/20 (Stockholm, 1997), pp. 37–45, and M*CBE*, pp. 205–19.

44 Kunst, *Music in Java*, vol. I, p. 326.

45 Neil Sorrell, *A Guide to the Gamelan* (London: Faber & Faber, 1990), p. 3.

46 Philip Brett, 'Eros and Orientalism in Britten's Operas', in Philip Brett, Elizabeth Wood and Gary C. Thomas (eds.), *Queering the Pitch: The New Gay and Lesbian Musicology* (New York and London: Routledge & Kegan Paul, 1994), pp. 235–56.

10 Violent climates

1 Britten wrote in his diary on 8 April 1936: 'The fuss caused by the Censor not passing that little Rotha Peace film is colossal. ½ centre pages of [Daily] Herald & News Chron'cle, & Manchester Guardian – BBC. News twice. Never has a film had such good publicity!'

2 *Advance Democracy*, a film directed by Bond and released in October 1938, the end-title music of which, according to Philip Reed, took

the shape of a 'medley of various left-wing songs including *The Internationale* and *The Red Flag.*' (See Philip Reed and John Evans, 'The Incidental Music: A Catalogue Raisonné' in *BSB*, p. 143.) Another work of the same title as the film, though without musical connections with its predecessor, was to follow in 1938, taking the shape of an unaccompanied chorus for mixed voices to words by Randall Swingler. This was the time of the Munich crisis, but even that political and moral mess scarcely justifies the awful *agitprop* banalities of Swingler's text, e.g.

> There's a roar of war in the factories,
> And idle hands on the street
> And Europe held in nightmare
> By the thud of marching feet.
> Now sinks the sun of surety,
> The shadows growing tall
> Of the big bosses plotting
> Their biggest coup of all.

3 Interestingly enough, a scrutiny of *Voices for Today* and the early item of choral propaganda, *Advance Democracy* (see also note 2 above), reveals a hitherto unobserved communality of musical treatment. I am not thinking of a shared transparency of texture but, more importantly, of at least one stroke of invention that foreshadows the future. The most striking idea in *Advance Democracy* is the very opening of the chorus – 'Across the darkened city / The frosty searchlights creep' – where the nervy, disjointed chant of the tenors and basses is accompanied by a wordless *legatissimo* obbligato for the sopranos – on 'Ah'. This device was to be precisely replicated in 1965 in *Voices*, the opening of the setting of Virgil. The boys' voices have an obbligato on 'Ah', while the chorus chant the Eclogue. The wheel has turned full circle, from the threatening days of Munich in 1938 to a plea for peace in 1965, first heard at the United Nations. Despite their contrasts in political and historical context, it is fascinating to discover that these two works share a similar realization of their musical ideas. The consistency of imagery should not go unremarked, while recognizing that Virgil in this instance was a better bet for Britten than Swingler.

4 *New Statesman*, 21 May 1971, p. 713.

5 In *The Times* ('Saturday Review' section), 15 May 1971.

6 The 'Peace' chord with which Owen's aria concludes (at Fig. 260) calls for special attention, introducing as it does A♭ – the twelfth – into the sequence of triads. We note that the triad incorporates F, endowing the A♭ triad with the status of an added sixth (all other eleven preceding chords are straight triads). This type of chord plays a special role as the opera comes

to an end – see for example the overwhelming eruption of C major at Fig. 279 as Owen enters the haunted room – and elsewhere in Britten's music, for example in the finale – 'Requiem aeternam' – of *Sinfonia da Requiem* (1940) and, as Mervyn Cooke has pointed out, in the great orchestral interlude between Scenes 1 and 2 of Act III of the full-length ballet, *The Prince of the Pagodas* (1956; see the climax leading up to Fig. 25). Two very different works from very different periods; but the added sixth (again in C in *Pagodas*) which, undoubtedly, was permanently impressed on Britten's consciousness by Mahler's use of it in the final bars of the 'Abschied' of *Das Lied von der Erde*, might be said to play a common role, i.e. in both cases it represents a kind of conciliation, a kind of spiritual victory: the *Sinfonia*'s 'Requiem aeternam' restores and heals what has been violently disrupted and dismembered in the preceding 'Dies irae', while in *Pagodas* – a speculation, this – the chord celebrates the transformation of the exiled Prince from reptile to radiant manhood by the compassion of the Princess. Likewise the 'Peace' chord at the end of Owen's aria. It is certainly possible to read this (hear it, that is) as Owen's triumph over the ancestors who are his foes. On the other hand, because of the particular composition of the chord it is no less possible to read it as a defeat. I have gone into this more fully in a short text in *DMCN*, pp. 335–7, n. 8.

7 Closely allied to the image of the hunt, specifically so in *Grimes*, was that of the 'trial', again a recurring feature in Britten's dramatic works. I have myself pursued this topic in '*Peter Grimes*: Fifty Years On', in *BBPG*, pp. 125–66.

8 For example, on 5 November 1936 Britten wrote in his diary: 'Madrid bombed by air for umpteenth time. No. of children not specified. 70 were killed in one go the other day. What price Fascism?'

9 See for example Britten's letter to Ursula Nettleship, 31 October 1944, in *DMPR*, pp. 1228–9. There are in fact numerous references in volume II of *DMPR* to air-raids on London during the period 1942–5.

10 The sixth song, 'Slaughter', provides us in its accompaniment with a further brilliant example of heterophony, the type of polyphony that increasingly invaded Britten's contrapuntal techniques towards the end of his life. Its closest and similarly agitated parallel is with the accompaniment of Vere's aria, 'Scylla and Charybdis', in *Billy Budd*, Act II, which belongs to 1951 and thus dates from well before Britten's world tour. This only goes to show that the heterophonic principle was already in fertilizing place at an earlier stage, probably as a

result of Britten's encounter with Colin McPhee and South-East Asian techniques in the early 1940s. For further on Britten's heterophonic techniques, see pp. 169ff.

11 See, for example, DMPR, pp. 485–6, n. 3.

12 To begin with, I have no doubt, Britten was seized by this concept under the potent influence of Auden who, in 1933, had written a play entitled *The Dance of Death* for the Group Theatre. It was dedicated to Robert Medley and Rupert Doone. Britten was to be closely associated with the Group Theatre and its leading members during the 1930s: see DM*BA*, and W. H. Auden and Christopher Isherwood, *Plays and other Dramatic Writings by W. H. Auden, 1928–1938*, ed. Edward Mendelson (London: Faber & Faber, 1989). A crucial and specifically relevant collaboration was of course on *Our Hunting Fathers*. Thereafter the shape the concept assumed was dilated, developed, and finally dictated by Britten's imagination. He had made it his own.

13 Incidentally, the relationship of animals and men was to show up again in the 'operetta', *Paul Bunyan*, that Britten and Auden were to write in New York in 1940–1. Indeed, 'Animals and Men' are among the very last words we hear as the work concludes. Interesting, too, that in the 1990s *Bunyan* leaves one thinking deeply about Conservation.

14 One notes, though, a certain intellectual confusion in the *Ballad*, which honours the dead but falls short of outright condemnation of the acts of violence that inevitably entail the sacrifice of young lives. In this respect the work is perhaps peculiarly representative of its period. The Spanish War had iconic status, even among pacifists for whom – perhaps – it was a 'just' war even if they were themselves unwilling to participate in the violence. There was an apparent schism here that is apparent in the *Ballad* and makes it peculiarly part of the history of its time.

15 See, for example, DMPR, p. 761.

16 In 1946, Ronald Duncan, the librettist of *The Rape of Lucretia* and himself a pacifist, 'attempted to interest Britten in a post-Hiroshima oratorio to be entitled *Mea Culpa*' (see Mervyn Cooke, 'Owen, Britten and Pacifism' in MC*WR*, p. 17). In 1948 there was also some discussion, again with Duncan, of a requiem in honour of Gandhi, who had been assassinated that year. This project, like *Mea Culpa* before it, came to nothing; on the other hand *War Requiem* might be thought of as a fulfilment, in part at least, of those earlier ideas. (See also Philip Reed, 'The *War Requiem* in Progress', in MC*WR*, p. 20.)

17 In BB*PG*, pp. 135–51.

18 The concerto has been recorded with the original slow version in place as an option by Joanna MacGregor on Collins Classics 1022, with the English Chamber Orchestra conducted by Steuart Bedford.

19 Perhaps it is worth mentioning here that this invasion of poison has its equally graphic counterpart in one of Britten's last works, *Phaedra*, though in the cantata of 1975 it is by means of harmony that the poison spreads through Phaedra's veins, not counterpoint.

20 See Michael Tippett, *Those Twentieth Century Blues: An Autobiography* (London: Pimlico, 1991), and in particular 'The World's Stage' and 'The Heart's Assurance'.

21 Ian Kemp, *Tippett: The Composer and his Music* (London: Eulenburg Books, 1984), p. 152.

22 Tippett, *Those Twentieth Century Blues*, p. 187.

23 It is my own view that another basic distinction may be made that is possibly not altogether irrelevant to my consideration of the two composers' philosophies: Tippett, I believe, was basically an optimist, Britten a pessimist.

24 See MC*WR*, p. 19 and p. 103, n. 51.

25 In this context one should not forget *Owen Wingrave*, the commission of which for television provided Britten with a ready-made 'mass' – in this case, global – audience to see and hear the case against militarism and for Peace. It was an opportunity, typically, that he seized. However, it is hard to believe that a television opera espousing anti-militarism and Peace was precisely what the BBC would have been looking for when the idea was first floated.

26 See 'Mapreading: Benjamin Britten in conversation with Donald Mitchell', in CP*BC*, pp. 95–6.

27 See Philip Reed, 'The *War Requiem* in Progress', in MC*WR*, p. 36.

28 The relevant files may be consulted at the Britten–Pears Library at Aldeburgh.

29 Copland too was a victim. On 22 May 1953 he received a telegram from Senator Joseph McCarthy

'directing him to appear before the State Permanent Subcommittee on Investigations. The hearing into his alleged communist affiliations took only two hours, and Copland acquitted himself well. But the mere fact that he had been called to testify was to reverberate in many unpleasant ways, including anonymous, cancelled performances and passport problems [*sic*].

Copland tried to treat the hearing humorously sometime mimicking the way committee counsel Roy Cohn pronounced "communist" with a bovine moo. But the toll on time and money was exceeded only by the terrible emotional drain – something recalled decades later in 1980 when Copland was celebrating his eightieth birthday and a glowing tribute to him was read into the *Congressional Record*. Learning of this, Copland quipped, "Has anyone told Roy Cohn?" ' (Patricia Edwards Clyne, 'Fanfare for an Uncommon Man', *Hudson Valley*, March 1997, pp. 67–8.)

11 Britten as symphonist

1 See his telegram to Boosey & Hawkes, 2 April 1940 (DMPR, p. 791). At this same time Britten also described his Piano Concerto as 'No. 1', and had actually sent it to his publisher with that title towards the end of 1939.

2 Several statements and criticisms will illuminate Britten's urgent need for self-redefinition and the genre transgressions that attended this. Britten said the following in 1969: 'Almost any situation *could* be made into an opera. I do hope, as I'm sometimes told, that my operas *are* all different, each with a style appropriate to itself, but I hope that comes from absorption with each subject while it is at hand' ('No Ivory Tower: Benjamin Britten Talks to Opera News', *Opera News* 63, 5 April 1969, p. 10). Critic Tom Sutcliffe ridiculed the Church Parables purely for their transgressions of genre, calling them 'a new brain-wave recipe mixing plainchant and monks and Japanese Noh theatre and percussive Balinese timbres' (Documentary television series *J'accuse*, 1991; cited by Philip Brett, 'Eros and Orientalism in Britten's Operas', in *Queering the Pitch: The New Gay and Lesbian Musicology* (New York and London: Routledge, 1994), p. 254, n. 15). Such reactions to Britten's handling of genre were common even at the outset of his career, and were not necessarily negative responses; for example, in 1940 Olin Downes greeted the Violin Concerto as 'something that has a flavor of genuine novelty in the violin concerto form' (cited in DMPR, p. 789).

3 Instead of evasion, it might be more appropriate to speak of generic 'uncertainty' in the sense that Philip Rupprecht has applied that word to Britten's tonality: see Rupprecht, 'Tonal Stratification and Uncertainty in Britten's Music', *Journal of Music Theory* 40 (1996), pp. 311–46. Whether seen from the perspective of harmony or texture, Rupprecht says, there is an 'inbuilt ambivalence of Britten's idiom' that lies in a characteristic and 'precarious balance between dichotomy and unity'. Britten's 'uncertainties' of genre should encourage us to expand upon and develop the connections that

Rupprecht draws between Britten's 'uncertain' manipulations of tonality and more general aspects of his style.

4 For some of Britten's views on Beethoven and Brahms, see Charles Stuart, 'Britten "The Eclectic" ', *Tempo* II/4 (Spring 1950), p. 247; MSBC, p. 119; and Alan Blyth, *Remembering Britten* (London: Hutchinson, 1981), p. 20. In the second of these sources, Britten complains particularly bitterly of the last movement of Beethoven's Piano Sonata in C minor, Op. 111: 'The sound of the variations was so grotesque I just couldn't see what they were all about.' More to the point, Murray Perahia's discussions of Beethoven with Britten left him with the understanding that 'Britten found Beethoven too intellectual, in the sense that his melodies had often been worked out in great detail and did not flow as naturally as Schubert's, for example. They were not vocal tunes. He was also chary of the insistence in Beethoven's musical make-up' (Perahia paraphrased by Alan Blyth in *Remembering Britten*, p. 170).

5 Carl Dahlhaus, *Between Romanticism and Modernism: Four Studies in the Music of the Later Nineteenth Century*, trans. Mary Whittall (Berkeley, Los Angeles, and London: University of California Press, 1980), p. 50. One of Britten's statements particularly illuminates his working methods: 'Usually I have the music complete in my mind before putting pencil to paper. That doesn't mean that every note has been composed, *perhaps not one has*, but I have worked out questions of form, texture, character, and so forth, in a very precise way so that I know exactly what effects I want and how I am going to achieve them' (MSBC, p. 123; my italics). Compare this with Eric Crozier's account: 'My impression was that he worked from forms towards detail in all the time that I worked with him. It seemed to me that he thought first in terms of shapes, of balancing sections, fast sections against slow sections, rather like an architect planning a building' (Crozier, 'Staging First Productions I', in DHOB, p. 26).

6 There is some truth to Elizabeth Lutyens's disapproving description of Britten as 'a brilliant journalist, able to produce an instant effect at first hearing, understandable to all' (cited in DMPR, p. 264). Likewise, Desmond Shawe-Taylor's description of Britten hardly sounds like the developmental essence attributed to middle-period Beethoven: 'I feel tolerably sure that his ideas never occur to him as anything but sheer sensuous sound, and that it is to this fact that they owe the force and freshness with which they strike the listener's ear' (cited in Keller, 'The Musical Character', in

DMHK, p. 326). See also Christopher Mark's comments on pp. 14–15.

7 Charles Reid, 'Back to Britain with Britten', *High Fidelity* 9 (December 1959), p. 74. See also the present volume, p. 2.

8 From a liner-note written by Schoenberg in 1936 and reprinted in Ursula von Rauchhaupt (ed. and trans.), *Schoenberg, Berg, Webern/Die Streichquartette: Eine Dokumentation* (Hamburg: Deutsche Grammophon, 1987), p. 33.

9 A *Times* reviewer singled out the finale for comment, describing it as 'built out of rhythmic figures rather than purely musical themes [*sic*]. On this occasion Mr. Britten permits himself to indulge effects of barbarism, which at least hold the attention' (cited in DMPR, p. 344).

10 Britten, 'On Behalf of Gustav Mahler', *Tempo* II/2 (February 1942); repr. in *Tempo* 120 (March 1977), p. 14.

11 AW*BT*, pp. 64–5.

12 PE*MB*, p. 19.

13 A B minor reading of this second large bass-interruption does seem plausible, but only in retrospect, and F surfaces constantly if also fleetingly to conflict with B. For a full account of the harmonic implications here, see CM*EB*, pp. 204–6.

14 Keller writes, 'He is probably incapable of those dramatic sonata forms which expose extremely contrasting, yet complementary ideas within a narrow space, and of which the first movement of Beethoven's Fifth is a supreme example' (DMHK, p. 344). See also Keller, 'Introduction: Operatic Music and Britten', in DH*OB*, pp. xiii–xix.

15 From a letter that Auden drafted, with Britten's input, to the Japanese Vice-Consul in New York (DMPR, p. 890).

16 Shostakovich also shared many gestures and points of style with Mahler, and in later Britten it becomes difficult to separate the voices of those two composers from Britten's own. But it is not yet known how much of Shostakovich's work – especially among the symphonies – Britten knew before their meeting and friendship in the 1960s. For an account of the mutual influences over that decade, see Eric Roseberry, 'A Debt Repaid? Some Observations on Shostakovich and His Late-Period Recognition of Britten', in David Fanning (ed.), *Shostakovich Studies* (Cambridge University Press, 1995), pp. 229–53.

17 Thus Donald Mitchell's observation: 'There is no doubt that Britten learned a great deal from Mahler: but . . . the *Sinfonia da Requiem* shows that learning only partially digested' (Mitchell, 'A Note on *St. Nicolas*: Some Points of Britten's Style', *Music Survey* 2 (1950), p. 224).

18 Alfred Einstein, *Mozart: His Character, His Work* (London: Cassell, 1946), p. 250.

19 Britten once even hinted at a possible Shintoist interpretation of the *Sinfonia da Requiem*: 'The *Sinfonia* as I had originally conceived it was in memory of my mother, but in scale and type it was well suited to a festival. Through the British Council I cabled to the Japanese a description of the work, with titles and subtitles, all of which struck me as compatible with a creed that involves ancestor worship' (Reid, 'Back to Britain with Britten', p. 76). For an account of the commission and rejection of this work by the Japanese government as seen through Britten's letters and other primary sources, see DMPR, pp. 880–4.

20 Britten, 'A Note on the Spring Symphony', *Music Survey* 2 (Spring 1950), p. 237.

21 In a description of his Eighth Symphony, Mahler himself drew a distinction between his later use of the voice as an instrument and his earlier use of 'words and the human voice merely to suggest, to sum up, to establish a mood . . . to express something concisely and specifically' (from a 1906 conversation with Richard Specht, cited by Constantin Floros, *Gustav Mahler: The Symphonies*, trans. Vernon and Jutta Wicker (Portland, Oreg.: Amadeus Press, 1993), p. 214).

22 There is no better demonstration of the ' "naive" operatic character' and 'love of human drama' that Keller attributed to Britten in contradistinction to the 'sentimentalic' Mahler – who, had he written operas, might have fallen into Keller's 'sentimentalic' tradition of 'writing oratorios for the stage' (DH*OB*, pp. xvi-xvii). Still, Britten stops short here of dividing vocal styles along the lines of recitative and aria: the *Spring Symphony* is based entirely on measured lyric poetry, and differs from a cantata like *Saint Nicolas* in that it has no recitatives or dramatic scenes.

23 Britten's 'reawakening of the earth and life' narrative for the *Spring Symphony* proves uselessly vague as a tool for understanding the structure of this work – especially when compared with the more concrete narratives of Schubert's *Schöne Müllerin*, or Mahler's 'Resurrection' Symphony, *Das Lied von der Erde*, and *Kindertotenlieder*. Keller described the composer's account of the *Spring Symphony* as 'vapid', with some justification. Britten's description does tell us little about a narrative aspect that is not very significant to an understanding of the *Spring Symphony*, and it has induced various misleading Mahlerian readings of this work. (See Britten, 'A Note on the Spring Symphony', p. 237; and Keller's

contribution to Blyth, *Remembering Britten*, p. 88.)

24 Carl Dahlhaus, 'Mahler: Finale der Zweiten Symphonie', in *Analyse und Werturteil* (Mainz: B. Schott's Söhne, 1970), pp. 89–93. In this light, one can only question the comparisons Anthony Milner has drawn between the *Spring Symphony* and Beethoven's Ninth and Mahler's Second as works that are end-directed (Anthony Milner, 'The Choral Music', in *CPBC*, p. 335). Indeed, an interesting detail of the *Spring Symphony*'s publication would seem to suggest that the constituent songs need not necessarily be performed with all the others, or even in any particular sequence: in the 1950 Boosey & Hawkes edition the copyright information appears anew at the beginning of each song, suggesting independent availability and possibilities for independent performance.

25 As Peter Porter has written, 'Britten's song cycles of mixed origin show a poetic taste which reflects Auden's many popular compilations. The *Nocturne*, for instance, and the *Serenade* are excellent pocket anthologies, much more like Auden's vision of poetry than any other literary person's' (Porter, 'Composer and Poet', in *CPBC*, p. 283). Regarding compositional predecessors, it is interesting that the original *London Times* review of the *Spring Symphony* (23 July 1949) invoked Arthur Bliss's *Pastoral* and *Morning Heroes* as a context for Britten's anthologizing. But the fact that the reviewer mentioned Bliss and not Mahler is perhaps more a sign of Mahler's neglect in England in the 1940s than a delineation of any non-Mahlerian aspects to Britten's composition.

26 Britten, 'A Note on the Spring Symphony', p. 237.

27 *PEMB*, p. 324.

28 Cited by John Evans, 'The Concertos', in *CPBC*, p. 411.

29 Eric Roseberry wrote the following on the works that Britten wrote for Rostropovich in the 1960s, the Cello Symphony among them: 'These works seemed to fulfil at last the hopes of his admirers who had waited for a sequel to his earlier instrumental music . . . It would be absurd to imply that "absolute music" is a higher goal of creative endeavour than vocal music, but we can be grateful to the Russian virtuoso for turning Britten's thoughts once again to these modes of musical discourse and expression' (Roseberry, 'The Solo Chamber Music', in *CPBC*, p. 380).

30 See the 'Voice' chapter in Joseph Kerman, *The Beethoven Quartets* (New York and London: W. W. Norton, 1966), pp. 191–222.

31 *AWBT*, pp. 65–6.

32 Roseberry, 'A Debt Repaid?', p. 236.

12 The concertos and early orchestral scores: aspects of style and aesthetic

1 See DMPR, p. 665 (letter to Ralph Hawkes).

2 Britten's notorious remark 'The rot (if that isn't too strong a word) began with Beethoven' (see Charles Stuart, 'Britten the Eclectic' in *Music Survey* II/4 (Spring 1950), pp. 247–50) was only one of many such pronouncements made in public and private throughout his career. As for Brahms, Britten's own outlook strongly rejected 'the Brahms influence on English music' of the older generation (see DMPR, p. 397), and this prejudice was maintained. See also Arved Ashby's remarks on p. 218.

3 DMPR, p. 502.

4 Prophetically, because in the Piano Concerto of 1938 Britten's original titles ('Toccata', 'Waltz', 'Recitative' and 'Aria' [in the later substitution, 'Impromptu'] and 'March') would seem to correspond to the same suite-like deposition of the 'absolute' genre. In the slow passacaglia finale of the Violin Concerto and the Requiem Mass titles of the three movements of the *Sinfonia da Requiem* a corresponding shift away from the traditional sonata-cycle aesthetic is evident.

5 See, in this connection, Peter Evans's acute perceptions in PEMB, p. 42. It is not generally known that Bridge's theme had already served Britten in an unfinished set of six piano variations dating from 1932 but, beyond the obvious fascination of the theme for Britten, there is nothing in these pianistically devised (and comparatively short) variations to suggest unfinished business that the later work brought to fruition.

6 The programme note is reproduced in full in DMJE, p. 111. Britten was, however, reluctant to see 'meanings' in the concerto. See, for example, DMPR, p. 576.

7 See my article, 'Britten's Piano Concerto: The Original Version', *Tempo* 172 (1990), pp. 10–18.

8 Britten was at pains to deny its apparent pomposity. See DMPR, p. 580.

9 *Listener*, 6 January 1937. See DMPR, p. 579.

10 For this interpretation I am indebted to a conversation with the late Christopher Headington.

11 Even the acutely perceptive Peter Evans refers misleadingly to its 'irritatingly smart vulgarity' (PEMB, p. 47).

12 See, for instance, *The Holy Sonnets of John Donne* and *The Rape of Lucretia*. It seems relevant to point out that even the 'abstract' passacaglia interlude in *Peter Grimes* had, for Britten, quite specific programmatic associations: see PBPG, p. 205.

13 DMHK, p. 288.

14 CP*BC*, p. 403.

15 The idea for such a theme may have been suggested to Britten by the open-string figuration in the first movement of Berg's Violin Concerto.

16 Further parallels with the opera suggest themselves: the variation structure, the cadenza-like allure of its wide conception and the prominent role of solo piano, which in the opera has a whole scene to itself.

17 For further information on the *American Overture* and *Occasional Overture*, see Mervyn Cooke's sleeve notes to 'Rattle Conducts Britten' (EMI CDS 7542702, 1991), p. 11. Simon Rattle was responsible for mounting the posthumous first performance of the *American Overture* in 1983; the *Occasional Overture* received its première under the direction of Adrian Boult in 1946 to celebrate the inauguration of the BBC Third Programme.

13 The chamber music

1 Benjamin Britten, 'Britten looking back', *Sunday Telegraph* (17 November 1963), p. 9. See DMPR, pp. 248–67, for details of Britten's activities as a pianist in chamber-music performances (often *chez* Bridge) during his RCM years.

2 Benjamin Britten, 'On Writing English Opera', *Opera* 12/1 (January 1961), pp. 7–8.

3 DMPR, p. 961. Britten here seems to recognize the predominance of D major in his compositions of the 1930s, from *A Boy was Born* (1933) – a favourite of Mayer's – to the *Michelangelo Sonnets* and *Sinfonia* of 1940. See also Eric Roseberry's comments on the significance of this key in the *Variations on a Theme of Frank Bridge* elsewhere in this volume (p. 235).

4 Peter Evans writes of the sonata form in the *Sinfonietta* (1932), 'Instead of an arch, Britten has drawn a line that continues to rise after the mid-point' (PE*MB*, p. 19).

5 David Matthews (CP*BC*, p. 386) compares the form to the first movement of Mahler's Fourth Symphony (the score of which Britten purchased in 1934); in an article on Mahler published soon after writing the First Quartet, Britten notes especially how 'the form was so cunningly contrived; every development surprised one and yet sounded inevitable' ('On Behalf of Gustav Mahler' [1942]; repr. in *Tempo* 120 (1977), pp. 14–15).

6 Two reviewers of the première likened the opening to that of Wagner's *Lohengrin*: see Stephen Banfield, '"Too Much of Albion?" Mrs. Coolidge and her Contemporaries', *American Music* 4/1 (1986), pp. 59–88.

7 Britten's sketches for the third movement suggest an earlier, more cyclic, conception of the quartet. Its canopy textures recall a similar polarization of registers – diatonic clusters above a melodic line – in the 'Lacrymosa' of the recent *Sinfonia da Requiem*, also in D major.

8 For an analytical account of Britten's stratified approach to tonal dualism, see Philip Rupprecht, 'Tonal Stratification and Uncertainty in Britten's music', *Journal of Music Theory* 40/2 (1996), pp. 311–46.

9 CM*EB*, p. 5.

10 See his letter to Mary Behrend, 3 December 1945 (DMPR, p. 1285).

11 Hans Keller, 'Benjamin Britten's Second Quartet', *Tempo* [old series] 18 (March 1947), p. 6.

12 Compare the quartet's development, juxtaposing pedal-based textures and trilling stretto entries, with Grimes's Act I aria, 'Now the Great Bear'. Musical ideas for both quartet and opera date back to at least 1940; p. 9 of Britten's sketchbook, for example, includes notations for *Grimes*'s 'Old Joe has gone fishing' and a 'Tarantella' that became the quartet's Scherzo (DMPR, p. 1044).

13 One might question Keller's view of sonata form – in Beethoven's Op. 31 No. 3, for example, 'introduction' and 'first-theme' functions coalesce (see Janet Schmalfeldt, 'Form as the Process of Becoming: The Beethoven-Hegelian Tradition and the "Tempest" Sonata', in L. Lockwood and J. Webster (eds.), *Beethoven Forum 4* (Lincoln: University of Nebraska Press, 1995), pp. 37–71). But his ideas were familiar to Britten (see Keller, 'Britten's Last Masterpiece', *Spectator* (2 June 1979), pp. 27–8), and the composer commissioned a 'functional analysis' of the Second Quartet from him.

14 Cited in Schmalfeldt, 'Form as the Process of Becoming', p. 54.

15 Keller, 'Benjamin Britten's Second Quartet', p. 8.

16 DMPR, p. 1248.

17 As Eric Roseberry notes (CP*BC*, p. 376), the March from the *Temporal Variations* (1936) is a precursor for that in the Sonata; bitonal fanfares in the latter prefigure the *War Requiem*.

18 See Britten's Foreword to the score of *Curlew River*, and pp. 177–83 of the present volume.

19 In the fourth movement of Quartet No. 8 (1960), Shostakovich frames two self-quotations with the motto from his Cello Concerto No. 2; in Quartet No. 11 (1966), he links seven short movements. Britten, in his Second Suite, pays musical homage to Shostakovich by a direct allusion at the opening to the Fifth Symphony. On stylistic relations

between the two composers, see Eric Roseberry, 'A Debt Repaid? Some Observations on Shostakovich and his Late-period Recognition of Britten', in David Fanning (ed.), *Shostakovich Studies* (Cambridge University Press, 1995), pp. 229–53.

20 Cited in DM*DV*, p. 26.

21 *Ibid.*, p. 215; the vocal line is scored for viola, Britten's own string instrument.

22 Britten's remark to Colin Matthews came at a play-through of the Third Quartet on 8 December 1975: see Colin Matthews, 'Britten's Indian Summer', *Soundings* 6 (1977), pp. 42–50; p. 48.

23 Cf. the orchestral Variation 8 opening Act II of *The Turn of the Screw*.

24 Peter Pople hears further valedictory echoes of the 'Phaedrus' aria in the Passacaglia's closing paragraph, at bar 104 (sleeve note to the Alberni Quartet recording, CRD 1095, 1981).

25 See David Matthews, '"Death In Venice" and the Third String Quartet', in DM*DV*, pp. 154–61; quotations from pp. 157, 160.

26 Cf. *Peter Grimes*, where Britten builds the passacaglia on a theme first uttered by the protagonist at a dramatic turning-point.

27 Britten's theme was 'inspired by the sound of some actual Venetian bells', David Matthews noted when reviewing the quartet's première ('Britten's Third Quartet', *Tempo* 125 (1978), pp. 21–4).

28 Similarly, in the 'Trio' of the 'Burlesque', conflicting key signatures underline dramatic separation between members of the quartet.

29 For a case-study of Britten's tonal symbolism, see Mervyn Cooke, 'Britten's "Prophetic Song": Tonal Symbolism in *Billy Budd*', in MCPR, pp. 85–110. A third pole of tonal attraction in *Death in Venice* is Tadzio's A major. For an account of the later opera's 'tonal ambiguity', see Eric Roseberry in DM*DV*, pp. 86–98.

30 Though Mitchell comments that Britten did not consider the movement a sonata (CP*BC*, p. 373), Keller hears the necessary contrast articulated by textural opposition between the 'duets' of the title and larger instrumental groupings, most notably in the 'development', bars 40–56 ('Britten's last masterpiece', 1979).

31 Britten's very personal adaptation of certain aspects of serial technique, particularly in the later music, belies his public attitude to its supposed intellectualism (cf. MS*BC*, p. 120).

32 As Colin Matthews notes, the 'C majorishness' of Britten's late music is bound up with motions towards harmonic clarity ('Britten's Indian Summer', p. 45).

33 The discarded opera sketch is reproduced in DM*DV*, p. 108.

34 Colin Matthews, 'Working Notes. String Quartet No. 3: Autumn–Winter 1975', in Alan Blyth (ed.), *Remembering Britten* (London: Hutchinson, 1981), pp. 176–9; p. 177.

35 The C^6 chords in 'Duets' (Ex. 13.5) resolve – or transfigure – the intervallic tension of the movement's climax (bar 54). In 'Solo', the added-sixth quality inflects the major triad in each of the quasi-birdsong cadenzas, but the non-triadic pitch is most prominent melodically with the final arrival on C major. Britten's fascination with Mahler's 'Der Abschied' dates back at least to his acquisition of the score in 1936. In June 1937, after listening to the newly released recording of a 1936 performance conducted by Bruno Walter, Britten wrote to Henry Boys, 'that final chord is printed on the atmosphere' (DM*PR*, p. 493).

36 As Christopher Palmer points out, Britten overlays the C root at the end of *Phaedra* with an additional dissonance, D, enhancing the chord's pentatonic impression (CP*BC*, p. 410). In the Third Quartet, the fourth chord of 'Ostinato' presents yet a further extension of this Mahlerian enrichment of a C tonic.

14 Music for voices

1 Benjamin Britten, Preface to *Tit for Tat* (London: Faber Music, 1969).

2 MS*BC*, p. 121.

3 See CM*EB*, pp. 31–2.

4 For a full discussion of the creative relationship between Britten and Auden, including a detailed examination of *Our Hunting Fathers*, see DM*BA*, *passim*.

5 PE*MB*, p. 69.

6 CP*BC*, p. 283.

7 Paul Hamburger, 'Mainly about Britten', *Music Survey* 3/2 (December 1950), pp. 98–107.

8 CP*BC*, p. 277.

9 MS*BC*, p. 121.

10 *Opera* 2/3 (February 1951), p. 114.

11 Imogen Holst (ed.), *Henry Purcell: Essays on his Music* (London: Oxford University Press, 1959), pp. 10–11.

12 CP*BC*, p. 314.

13 Eric Roseberry, 'A Note on the Four Chords in Act 2 of *A Midsummer Night's Dream*', *Tempo* 66 (1963), p. 36; see also the present volume, p. 138.

14 Paraphrased in Alan Blyth (ed.), *Remembering Britten* (London: Hutchinson, 1981), p. 90.

15 MS*BC*, p. 121.

16 Eric Crozier (ed.), *Benjamin Britten: Peter Grimes*, Sadler's Wells Opera Books No. 3 (London: John Lane/The Bodley Head, 1945), p. 8.

17 For further on this compositional borrowing, see MCWR, pp. 67–70, and Eric Roseberry, '"Abraham and Isaac" Revisited: Some Reflections on a Theme and its Inversion', in PRMB, pp. 253–66.

18 CPBC, p. 337.

19 For the relationship between the Missa Brevis and the War Requiem, which was composed soon afterwards, see MCWR, pp. 54 and 56.

20 For the close musical connection between a song Britten excluded from the Serenade ('Now Sleeps the Crimson Petal') and the later Nocturne, see Donald Mitchell, '"Now Sleeps the Crimson Petal": Britten's Other Serenade', Tempo 169 (June 1989), pp. 22–7, repr. in DMCN, pp. 345–51.

21 David Herbert (ed.), The Operas of Benjamin Britten (London: Hamish Hamilton, 1979), pp. xxvii–xxviii.

22 Pears described how Britten's first playing of this song in Pushkin's house was eerily accompanied by the chiming of the Russian poet's own clock: 'It was the most natural thing to have happened, and yet unique, astonishing, wonderful' (Peter Pears, Armenian Holiday (Colchester: Benham & Co., 1965), p. 36; repr. in PRPP, p.133).

15 Britten and the world of the child

1 CPBC, p. 216.

2 For a concise introduction to this Platonic concept, see 'The Archetypal Forms', in Richard Tarnas, The Passion of the Western Mind (London: Pimlico, 1996), pp. 6–12. For further on its relevance to Britten's work, see Clifford Hindley's remarks in Chapter 8 of the present volume.

3 Evelyn Fox Keller, 'Love and Sex in Plato's Epistemology', in Reflections on Gender and Science (New Haven: Yale University Press, 1985), pp. 21–32, and Gregory Vlastos, 'The Individual as an Object of Love in Plato', in Platonic Studies (Princeton University Press, 1973), pp. 3–42.

4 See Clifford Hindley, 'Platonic Elements in Britten's Death in Venice', Music & Letters 73/3 (1992), pp. 407–29.

5 Humphrey Carpenter, 'Overtures of Violence', Sunday Times, 13 November 1996.

6 There are numerous examples of a symbolic use of A major in Britten's music, one being Young Apollo (1939) – a work, significantly, about Wulff Scherchen (see DMPR, p. 742).

7 Philip Brett, 'Britten's Dream', in Ruth A. Solie (ed.), Musicology and Difference (Berkeley: University of California Press, 1993), pp. 259–80.

8 See MCWR, pp. 56–9.

9 See Philip Reed's notes on the work in the new edition of the score published by Boosey & Hawkes in 1994.

10 For perceptive observations on the difference between 'child-like' and 'childish' in Britten's psychology, see Donald Mitchell in DMCN, pp. 367–8.

11 DMHK, p. 346.

12 See PEMB, pp. 271–2; MKB, p. 194; and AWBT, p. 124.

13 PEMB, p. 281; HCBB, pp. 383–4.

14 AWBT, p. 232.

15 Plato's exaltation of the universal Form of Beauty in personal relations tends to deprecate the beloved person as an object (i.e. idol) rather than an individual to be loved for his or her own sake. In political theory, this applies when the ideal republic depreciates individual citizens as mere statistics. See Vlastos, 'The Individual as an Object of Love'.

16 This opinion is shared by Peter Evans: see PEMB, p. 284.

17 Quoted in HCBB, p. 488. For further on the violence in the work, see Donald Mitchell's remarks on pp. 204–5.

16 Old songs in new contexts: Britten as arranger

1 For Britten's hostility to Brahms's influence on English music see, for example, DMPR, p. 397.

2 See Britten's letter to Alfred Goldberg, 7 October 1941: 'I have arranged a few British folksongs which have been a "wow" whenever performed so far' (DMPR, p. 983).

3 See Donald Mitchell, 'The Musical Atmosphere', DMHK, p. 47; Graham Johnson, 'Voice and Piano' in CPBC, p. 303; and Arnold Whittall, 'Along the Knife-Edge: the Topic of Transcendence in Britten's Musical Aesthetic', PRMB, p. 292.

4 On 17 March 1948, Britten wrote to Pears on the subject of The Beggar's Opera: 'I must stop myself too much "canonizing" of the music, which is probably more entertaining to write than to listen to!' (Donald Mitchell and Philip Reed, sleeve notes to The Beggar's Opera, Argo 436850-2, 1993, p. 22.)

5 Whittall, 'Along the Knife-Edge', p. 292.

6 Quoted in DMPR, p. 347.

7 For a remarkable interpretation of this arrangement in the context of the man-hunt chorus in Act III of Peter Grimes, see Donald Mitchell, 'The Composer as Arranger', in the sleeve note accompanying the Collins recording of the complete folksongs (CD 70392, 1993), p. 10, and 'Peter Grimes: Fifty Years On', in BBPG, pp. 125–66.

8 See Lennox Berkeley, 'The Light Music', in DMHK, p. 288.

9 DMPR, p. 347.

10 For a fuller coverage of the work as a whole than space permits here, the reader is referred to Norman Del Mar's account in DMHK, pp. 163–85, and to Hans Keller's key-orientated programme note in CP*BC*, p. 346.

11 See vocal score of the Austin edition (Boosey & Co. Ltd, 1920), pp. 11–12.

12 See BBC report by Julian Herbage, 23 April 1942, in DMPR, p. 653.

13 See Philip Reed's sleeve note to Collins CD 70392 (1993), p. 25.

17 Aldeburgh

1 BB*AA*, p. 21.

2 *Ibid.*, p. 22.

3 Eric Crozier, 'The Origin of the Aldeburgh Festival', in *Aldeburgh Festival Programme Book* 1 (1948), p. 6; repr. in Ronald Blythe (ed.), *Aldeburgh Anthology* (Aldeburgh and London: Snape Maltings Foundation Ltd in association with Faber Music Ltd, 1972), p. 8.

4 Although Eric Crozier wrote in 1948 that 'we could not hope to repeat the experiment another year', the English Opera Group was later to make several tours of Europe.

5 Britten had met Elizabeth Sweeting at Glyndebourne, where she was working as Front of House Manager during the 1947 season at which the EOG performed *Albert Herring* and *The Rape of Lucretia*. When asked to join the EOG at the end of the season, Sweeting knew nothing of plans for a festival; by the following year she found herself in the new post of Festival Manager.

6 Elizabeth Sweeting, 'A History of the Early Aldeburgh Festivals', lecture given to the Aldeburgh Festival Club, 13 October 1988 (cassette recording at the Britten–Pears Library, Aldeburgh).

7 Crozier, 'The Origin of the Aldeburgh Festival', p. 6.

8 E. M. Forster, 'Looking Back on the First Aldeburgh Festival', broadcast talk (BBC Third Programme, 20 June 1948); published in the *Listener*, 24 June 1948, pp. 1011–13 and repr. in *Aldeburgh Festival Programme Book* 2 (1949), p. 7, and Blythe (ed.), *Aldeburgh Anthology*, p. 11.

9 *Saint Nicolas* was written for first performance at the centenary celebrations of Lancing College in July 1948. The Lancing Centenary Committee generously allowed the work to be performed twice at the Aldeburgh Festival before its official first performance in Lancing College Chapel.

10 E. M. Forster, 'Looking Back'.

11 Imogen Holst, *Britten*, The Great Composers (London: Faber & Faber, 1966), p. 47.

12 Peter Pears, interviewed by Donald Mitchell in September 1979 (unpublished cassette at the Britten–Pears Library, Aldeburgh).

13 Crozier, 'The Origin of the Aldeburgh Festival', pp. 6–7.

14 The dedication read 'Affectionately dedicated to the real Gay, Juliet, Sophie, Tina, Hughie, Jonny and Sammy – the Gathorne-Hardys of Great Glemham, Suffolk.' These children included the sons and daughters of the Aldeburgh Festival's Chair, Fidelity Cranbrook. The first performance of the work is described in HC*BB*, p. 276.

15 Stephen Reiss, 'How the Festival Developed', in Blythe (ed.), *Aldeburgh Anthology*, p. 16.

16 The programme book for 1958 does not credit the support of the BBC Transcription Service for the late-night series.

17 Imogen Holst, 'Working for Benjamin Britten (I)' in CP*BC*, p. 49.

18 The 1958 programme book contained an article by John Steuart-Gratton about St Bartholomew's Church, Orford.

19 The success of *A Midsummer Night's Dream* was such that even four performances were not enough to satisfy public demand for tickets.

20 The final cost of the Snape Maltings Concert Hall was £175,000: see Stephen Reiss, 'A Festival in the Making', in Blythe (ed.), *Aldeburgh Anthology*, p. 19.

21 Osian Ellis became Pears's principal accompanist after Britten's stroke in 1973. For further on the folksong arrangements with harp accompaniment, see pp. 304–5.

22 Peter Diamand, interviewed by John Drummond (BBC Radio 3, 18 August 1992).

23 In 1963 Rostropovich described Britten's involvement with the festival as follows: 'Britten's energy and capacity for work during the Festival were phenomenal. He was the heart and brain of the Festival. He took part in it as an organizer and composer, as pianist and conductor. He was at all the rehearsals and concerts, he looked into literally every trifle' (Mstislav Rostropovich, 'Dear Ben . . .', in Anthony Gishford (ed.), *Tribute to Benjamin Britten on his Fiftieth Birthday* (London: Faber & Faber, 1963), p. 18).

24 Holst, 'Working for Benjamin Britten (I)', pp. 49–50.

25 As Rostropovich wrote, 'Britten-the-conductor makes any music he is conducting penetrate the soul of the listener. The music is purified and revealed in its initial beauty, unspoiled by any "interpretation" '

(Rostropovich, 'Dear Ben . . .', p. 17).

26 The Fiftieth Aldeburgh Festival included the première of a major 'new' orchestral work: Britten's Double Concerto for violin and viola (1932), performed on 15 June 1997 by Katherine Hunka and Philip Dukes with the Britten–Pears Orchestra at the Snape Maltings.

27 Recent concerts have featured Julian Anderson and Thomas Adès.

28 The Britten Award for Composition and the Benjamin Britten International Competition for Composers.

29 BB*AA*, p. 20.

Index of Britten's works

General index